# industrialized builders handbook

WITHDRAWN

# industrialized builders handbook

R. J. LYTLE, EDITOR & AUTHOR

*With chapters by:*

W. D. Page, American Wood Systems
John A. Reidelbach, Housing Consultant
Robert C. Reschke, Professional Builder Magazine
Steve Sabo, Slayter Associations, Inc.

STRUCTURES PUBLISHING COMPANY
Farmington, Michigan 48024
USA

66592

**Industrialized Builders Handbook**

Copyright © 1971 by R. J. Lytle, Farmington, Michigan. First Edition. All rights reserved, including those of translation. This book, or parts thereof, may not be reproduced in any form without permission of the copyright owner. Neither the authors nor the publisher, by publication of data in this book, ensure to anyone the use of such data against liability of any kind, including infringement of any patent. Publication of any data in this book does not constitute a recommendation of any patent or proprietary right that may be involved.

*Manufactured in the United States of America*

International Standard Book Number: 0-912336-01-3

Library of Congress Catalog Card Number: 70-147978

Structures Publishing Company
32580 Grand River Avenue
Farmington, Mich. 48024

ARCH
Q
TH 1000
L9

# Foreword

American housing is in the throes of its second industrial revolution. The first began in the 1830's when the products of new industrial production techniques—the wire nail and power sawed lightwood framing members—were used to develop a completely new system of building. It was called variously Chicago, Western and Balloon framing. While it was considered a radical idea, it effectively reduced the cost of housing by 25% over the next score of years and made it possible to supply housing for a growing nation.

Until recently, we have used essentially the same type of building and scores of books were written on its methodology.

Now, a second revolution is underway—building is moving from site to the plant—and a new methodology is evolving. Numerous books have been written on the concepts, design and theory of industrialized building. However, to the best of my knowledge this is the first book written on the fundamentals and techniques used in factory production of housing. As such, it fills a void and should make a strong contribution to even greater efficiency in producing better housing for all America.

*Richard L. Bullock*
Executive Vice President
National Association of Building Manufacurers

January 15, 1971

# Preface

Twenty-five years ago, in December, 1945, the work on this book was really started. I was on a Victory ship returning from World War II in Europe. The seventeen days that the trip required were shortened by reading and contemplation of a book called *American Housing* by Miles Colean—Twentieth Century Fund, 1944.

Having been a carpenter contractor prior to the war, I determined then that industrialization of building was a challenge I could not ignore.

There followed 15 years of seven long days a week of mistakes made; of progress; of setbacks in the business of manufacturing "prefabricated" homes as they were then known. The last 10 years have been from the vantage point of a supplier to the industry which had then become known as "Manufactured Homes" and which was just recently become "Industrialized Building."

There has long been a proliferation of beautiful books describing "System Building," etc., but nothing on the "nuts and bolts" of how it is really done. I say "really done" because in a broad way there have been established normal methods of manufacturing buildings off-site. Always newsworthy to the periodicals are the revolutionary ways of prebuilding—plastic foam domes, panels made of steel, building blocks made of garbage, etc., etc. For some reason they never seem to get off the ground. Meanwhile, unheralded, the real progress is made in dingy little plants in the back of lumberyards or in large modern plants that are too busy producing homes and other buildings to publicize their progress.

This is the way progress has been made over these 25 years—a nailing machine here, a roof truss there, a building code changed, a union restriction loosened, a little more public acceptance, recognition by financial markets, and on into the future. Having been born and brought up in the automobile town of Detroit, I would liken the progress of Industrialized Building to that of the automobile. Constant improvement; always a better way to make it; a faster way; a lower cost way with no development more startling than the "turret top" that some of you may remember replaced the wood and fabric car roof with steel. This, then is the future. Hopefully, an accelerating rate of change propelled by outside factors of housing shortage, on-site wage rates, and by the competitive ingenuity and individual determination within the industry.

This book will provide a source of techniques for those companies within the industry and for new firms coming on the scene. Hopefully, progress will outdate this edition within a few years and it can be followed by a complete revision.

Two years ago I began to assemble the material for this handbook, and the summer of 1970 was spent visiting many industry plants. The owners and managers of most of these firms willingly and proudly displayed their new methods as a contribution to industry progress. At only two plants was I turned away.

No attempt here has been made to cover the technique of mobile home production, but this is no reflection on this part of the industry's growth. Indeed today's modular homes increasingly use mobile home building techniques.

I am deeply indebted to my able co-authors for their expert work in their several fields. They have assisted me greatly in the task of bringing this book to completion.

If, by doing this work, I accelerate the rate of change, the industrialization of this industry, I will be well rewarded.

R. J. Lytle

*February 1, 1971*
*Farmington, Michigan*

# Contents

# Introduction

By way of introduction, we should consider certain important factors involved in the industry so that the material that follows can be viewed in the proper perspective.

## WHY PREFABRICATION?

The obvious answer, of course, is to save money. Quite often, however, money saving is not the prime reason. Even with today's ever increasing wage rates there are many site builders who can compete very well with industrialized building.

The component or modular package offers much more than dollar saving. It replaces the need for skilled craftsmen who may not exist in many areas; provides architectural quality not available in many markets; provides a single source for all of the related materials which may not be available locally; and lowers the completion time drastically, reducing interest costs and improving the turnover of the builder's capital.

For example, a builder may be able to build by conventional methods thirty homes per year with a gross profit of $2,000 each for a total of $60,000 gross profit before overhead expense. If his operation is changed to packaged housing, his gross profit per unit can drop to $1,600 per unit but unit volume can double to 60 units per year with a total gross profit of $96,000. The builder's overhead may actually decline since he doesn't need to supervise and control as many operations; many of his previous operations are included in the package. His building operations probably require no increase in capital investment, hence he may invest more time and money in land development and sales. The net result can be a substantially higher net profit from the same investment. The home buyer can gain in faster delivery, higher quality, and in the long run a lower cost.

## THE MARKET

Statisticians, economists, demographers and government officials are currently engaged in a numbers game, forecasting how many dwelling units are required in the decade of the seventies. Recognize that these learned folk are not going to sign any purchase orders or write any checks for your plant output. Make your own forecasts!

The market is substantial nationwide. Effective demand varies greatly in individual markets and from year to year. Those plants having a market area diversified in types of employment offer the best chance of continuing success.

## HOW COMPLETE THE PACKAGE?

Industrialized buildings vary in completeness from such items as simple wall panels without windows, roof trusses, and gable ends to complete modular units with all appliances installed and ready to be connected to utilities.

As a manufacturer, where should your particular operation fit into this spectrum? This depends on many factors, including the efficiency of present methods in the local market; differential between factory labor and on-site labor; delivery costs; building codes; union restrictions; your capital; availability of competent management, and the sales outlook in the area.

Remember, that the more complete the package, the greater the opportunity to cut costs. However, the simple package of bare wall panels and trusses may be most attactive in markets with an efficient building industry. On the other hand, the complete package, including appliances, may be the most desirable in rural areas.

As time goes on the change to a more complete package in all markets will accelerate. But you are dealing with the here and now, so make your decisions based on existing conditions and then change—always change.

## BUILDING CODES

Your company will be operating under at least one, probably two of the three regional codes: International Conference of Building Officials (ICBO); Building Officials and Code Administrators (BOCA); and the Southern Building Code Congress (SBCC). In addition, you will have FHA, one or more of the state codes, and innumerable local codes or local variations of the regional codes.

You have probably already made up your mind that certain codes (and their administrators) are impossible and you had best forget that municipality. No use tilting at windmills.

There is a movement on foot currently for states to pass state codes with provisions for factory built housing. We need more than this. Needed is a National Housing Code with provision for factory inspection and mandatory acceptance in all parts of the country. I fear that the present trend will not simplify the code problem but proliferate it.

The National Commission on Urban Problems made a detailed study of building codes affecting home manufacturers. In the case of one manufacturer, if he met the requirements of all 75 codes in his market area, he would incur excessive costs of nearly $2,500 per unit (and this without the last two years of inflation) on a typical 1,000 square foot house. These unjust costs would cost the homeowner over $16.00 a month in payments for a total $4,833 in the life of a 25 year mortage!

## UNIONS

Restrictive practices by unions (sometimes, in conjunction with code officials) continue to represent one of the obstacles to industrialized building. Progress is being made. As an example I remember having to knock all the glass out of windows on homes shipped into the Chicago area so local glazers could replace them. This is no longer true.

In establishing a new factory, it may be desirable to arrive at an understanding with the union covering plant personnel before operations are started. The carpenter's union has developed procedures for this.

If at all possible, there should be only one union (or none) in the factory, doing all operations from carpentry to plumbing and electrical. Jurisdictional disputes are bad enough on-site, completely insufferable in plant operations.

## THE ARCHITECT

The architect is trained to work out solutions to problems that occur only once. He must realize that he cannot effectively employ the advantages of industrialized building without understanding the methods and limitations of the factory production process.

In many cases in which architects have set out to design a project to be factory built, the result has been a higher cost than conventional. This is because their design required the manufacturer to completely revise his production process to make something foreign to his everyday production.

One of the most effective ways for an architect to use manufactured housing is to complete the site plan and call for bids based on the number of square feet, number of bedrooms, etc. Manufacturers may then bid products based on their normal production and having the advantage of some years of experience.

Like the automobile industry, technique and styling are a continuing development of the interaction between the production men, sales force, and the "in-house" stylist (designer or architect). These stylists are the little known untitled heroes of the industry. They know or soon develop a feeling for the practicalities of production, site assembly, and sales. It is the play between these factors that is responsible for progress and improvement in design.

The outside architect, on a consulting basis, can make an invaluable contribution to the architectural quality of the production. He can make a periodic restudy of architecture of the buildings produced, providing a refreshing "new look."

## TYPE OF CONSTRUCTION

In recent years the trend has been toward the higher priced home and the apartment. It is apparent now that it is swinging back to economy construction.

The use of "single construction" instead of double construction-sheathing plus siding or brick will begin to come back. This completely sound construction will result in substantial cost savings. The use of studding 24" O.C.; single top plates; single framing around openings and 2 × 3 studs all will become increasingly interesting as the industry searches for ways to hold down costs.

## NONRESIDENTIAL

There are some fabricators who specialize in this type of construction. Temporary classrooms, churches, office buildings, special purpose buildings for franchise chains, and farm buildings all represent opportunities for the aggressive manufacturer.

## INVESTMENT CONSIDERATIONS

How should you weigh the purchase of newer, more efficient equipment? Consider all factors. Under cost, consider total cost, down payment, monthly payment, and companion equipment required, together with its costs and terms. What is the deductibility for Federal Income Tax purposes of interest, lease payments (if leased) depreciation, etc.?

What labor savings will result? How many men can be eliminated; what do they cost? Per month? Per year? What fringe costs are saved? What new skills will be required? What material savings will result? Exactly how and how much? Offsetting, will the new equipment require higher priced nails or other materials? Will it result in higher waste factors? Will additional plant space be required? How much? Heated? What will it cost?

Will the new equipment increase your capacity? Can you sell this increased production? Profitably?

Like any other manufacturer, building manufacturers must evaluate all of the above and many more factors to make a decision to purchase new capital equipment. Many plants are overequipped. Few are underequipped.

## NOW YOU ARE A MANUFACTURER

Building manufacturers generally come from the ranks of builders and as trained builders they have difficulty thinking in the new (to them) terms that apply to their new status. They must become familiar with terms such as "standard cost" "inventory control," "industrial engineering," "quality control," and "plant engineering." This book is not intended to cover these areas in any detail. Many publications are available on these subjects and executives will find their study rewarding.

## DEFINITIONS:

Here are some of the more important definitions:

*Modular:* An adjective applying to all types of construction of a three-dimensional nature. Thus a dwelling unit, several story town house, garden apartment, high rise apartment, or single-family home made of *Modules* is modular construction. Modules are sometimes called *building blocks* or *stack boxes.* Modules can be used to construct schools, office buildings, and other structures as well as homes. This term and its definition has developed from popular usage without reference to previous meanings of the term. The term "Sectional" as applied to some of this construction appears to be disappearing.

*Component:* Any unit of the structure made off-site. Thus a component could be a roof truss, a prehung door unit, a wall panel, a gable end overhang, etc.

*Component Package Manufacturer:* A manufacturer who makes a set of components for his standard plans, to varying degrees of completion, but less than modular for sale to builders and/or individuals.

*Custom Component Package Manufacturer:* A manufacturer making a package to the plans and specifications of the customer.

*Component Manufacturer:* A manufacturer of one or more components. This book is intended for personnel in all of the above classifications.

# industrialized builders handbook

# CHAPTER I

## Material Cutting: Equipment & Methods

100 **General.** The cutting, notching, and other work done to material, mainly wood, is a sizable part of any building manufacturing operation. The related material handling operations also represent substantial cost factors.

In plant layout, careful consideration should be given to these two factors: *cutting* and *material handling.* At the same time, investment in equipment exceeding the requirements of the operation can be wasteful from the investment, maintenance, and plant space standpoint.

Much material can today be purchased cut to length. The standard stud length of 7′ 8 5/8″ is almost a stock item. Other stud lengths are available from "stud mills" when purchased in carload quantities. Other mills specialize in precutting for truss manufacturers. Fabricators in high labor cost areas should give serious consideration to purchasing much of their material precut. In addition to the labor cost saving, there is some reduction in freight costs since the weight of the scrap is not included. A disadvantage is that with the exception of standard studs which have become a commodity, a substantial inventory may have to be maintained due to the distance from the source. Further, stand-by cutting equipment might have to be maintained for emergencies.

101 **Cutting Lists.** The office preparation of detailed lists of materials to be cut, angles, and in many cases, specifications as to the material it is to be cut from can save shop labor and reduce material costs.

101.1 **Walls and Partitions.** Cutting lists for wall and partition panels can be a part of a numerical schedule furnished to the plant, or a schedule like that shown in Fig. 101.1 can be used. If only a limited number of window sizes are used, the window framing (cripples, sills, headers, and jamb studs) can be standardized and cut in considerable quantity in advance of need.

101.2 **Trusses.** Cutting lists for trusses are usually furnished by the truss plate manufacturer. With unusual trusses it is sometimes faster to make up the cutting list from the first truss made rather than spend hours computing the lengths. Fig. 101.2 *A* and *B* shows a typical cutting list.

102 **Cutting, Framing.** This includes floor, wall, partition, and roof framing (except trusses). Cutting for these purposes is usually simple square cut-off work, and all types of equipment may be used depending on the volume. Where the number of pieces of each length is under 30, equipment such as swing saws, radial arm saws, chop saws, etc., may be used. The actual cutting time is minor compared to handling and set-up time.

103 **Cutting, Trusses.** This work is characterized by long lengths, long cuts, and multiple cuts on web members. For the strength of the truss, considerable accuracy is required.

Large automatic cutting machines have been developed primarily for this purpose. Smaller operations may use a radial arm saw of the type that pivots the arm over the work, thus permitting longer cuts. Electric handsaws are not recommended for this operation.

104 **Cutting, Sheets.** Cutting roof and floor plywood sheathing, hardboard paneling, and gypsum and other drywall materials constitutes the bulk of this operation.

Wall sheathing, both fibre and plywood, is usually cut on the wall itself.

Panel saws, table saws, and electric handsaws in appropriate jigs are used.

105 **Using Up the Shorts.** Although material costs have increased, labor costs have

2 - 2x4 ____________________

2 - 2x4 ____________________

2 - 2x4 ____________________

2 - 2x4 ____________________

2 - 2x4 ____________________

2 - 2x4 ____________________

2 - 2x4 ____________________

2 - 2x4 ____________________

2 - 2x4 ____________________

2 - 2x4 ____________________

2 - 2x4 ____________________

2 - 2x4 ____________________

2 - 2x4 ____________________

2 - 2x4 ____________________

2 - 2x4 ____________________

---

________ 2x4 ____________________

________ 2x4 ____________________

________ 2x4 ____________________

________ 2x4 ____________________

________ 2x4 ____________________

________ 2x4 ____________________

________ 2x4 ____________________

________ 2x4 ____________________

________ 2x4 ____________________

________ 2x4 ____________________

---

________ 2x6 ____________________
________ 2x6 ____________________
________ 2x6 ____________________

________ 2x8 ____________________
________ 2x8 ____________________
________ 2x8 ____________________

________ 2x12 ____________________
________ 2x12 ____________________
________ 2x12 ____________________

---

2 - 2x12 ____________________
1 - 2x4 ____________________

2 - 2x12 ____________________
1 - 2x4 ____________________

2 - 2x12 ____________________
1 - 2x4 ____________________

2 - 2x12 ____________________
1 - 2x4 ____________________

2 - 2x12 ____________________
1 - 2x4 ____________________

2 - 2x12 ____________________
1 - 2x4 ____________________

2 - 2x12 ____________________
1 - 2x4 ____________________

2 - 2x12 ____________________
1 - 2x4 ____________________

2 - 2x12 ____________________
1 - 2x4 ____________________

2 - 2x12 ____________________
1 - 2x4 ____________________

---

________ 2x4 ____________L

________ 2x4 ____________L

________ 2x4 ____________L

________ 2x4 ____________L

---

________ 2x4 ____________Studs

________ 2x4 ____________Studs

________ 2x4 ____________Studs

---

________ 2x10 ____________________

________ 2x10 ____________________

________ 2x10 ____________________

________ 2x10 ____________________

---

**JOB #**__________

**Fig. 101.1.**
Typical cutting schedule.

*(Truswal)*

## Cutting Data
## 4/12 Fink

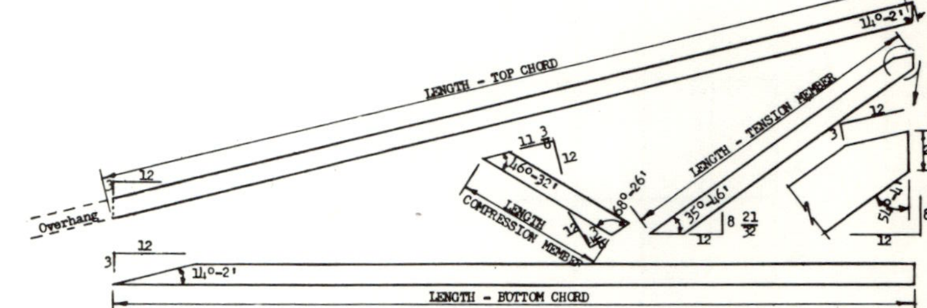


| SPAN | TOP CHORD | BOTTOM CHORD | TENSION MEMBER | COMPRESSION MEMBER |
|---|---|---|---|---|
| 16'-0" | 8'-5 3/16" | 8'-0" + 8'-0" | 43 1/4" | 18 5/8" |
| 17'-0" | 8'-11 1/2" | 8'-0" + 9'-0" | 46 3/16" | 20 1/16" |
| 18'-0" | 9'-5 13/16" | 8'-0" + 10'-0" | 49 1/8" | 21 1/2" |
| 19'-0" | 10'-0 1/8" | 9'-0" + 10'-0" | 52 1/8" | 22 7/8" |
| 20'-0" | 10'-6 1/2" | 8'-0" + 12'-0" | 54 15/16" | 24 5/16" |
| 21'-0" | 11'-0 13/16" | 10'-0" + 11'-0" | 57 7/8" | 25 3/4" |
| 22'-0" | 11'-7 1/8" | 10'-0" + 12'-0" | 60 3/4" | 27 3/16" |
| 23'-0" | 12'-1 7/16" | 11'-0" + 12'-0" | 63 11/16" | 28 9/16" |
| 24'-0" | 12'-7 3/4" | 10'-0" + 14'-0" | 66 9/16" | 30" |
| 25'-0" | 13'-2 1/16" | 12'-0" + 13'-0" | 69 1/2" | 31 7/16" |
| 26'-0" | 13'-8 7/16" | 12'-0" + 14'-0" | 72 7/16" | 32 13/16" |
| 27'-0" | 14'-2 3/4" | 13'-0" + 14'-0" | 75 5/16" | 34 1/4" |
| 28'-0" | 14'-9 1/16" | 12'-0" + 16'-0" | 78 1/4" | 35 11/16" |
| 29'-0" | 15'3 3/8" | 14'-0" + 15'-0" | 81 3/16" | 37 1/8" |
| 30'-0" | 15'-9 3/4" | 14'-0" + 16'-0" | 84 1/8" | 38 9/16" |
| 31'-0" | 16'-4 1/16" | 15'-0" + 16'-0" | 87" | 40" |
| 32'-0" | 16'-10 3/8" | 14'-0" + 18'-0" | 89 15/16" | 41 3/8" |
| 33'-0" | 17'-4 11/16" | 16'-0" + 17'-0" | 92 13/16" | 42 3/4" |
| 34'-0" | 17'-11" | 16'-0" + 18'-0" | 95 3/4" | 44 3/16" |
| 35'-0" | 18'-5 5/16" | 17'-0" + 18'-0" | 98 11/16" | 45 5/8" |
| 36'-0" | 18'-11 11/16" | 16'-0" + 20'-0" | 101 9/16" | 47 1/16" |
| 37'-0" | 19'-6" | 18'-0" + 19'-0" | 104 1/2" | 48 7/16" |
| 38'-0" | 20'-0 5/16" | 18'-0" + 20'-0" | 107 7/16" | 49 7/8" |
| 39'-0" | 20'-6 5/8" | 19'-0" + 20'-0" | 110 5/16" | 51 5/16" |
| 40'-0" | 21'-0 5/16" | 18'-0" + 22'-0" | 113 1/4" | 52 3/4" |

INTERPOLATIONS

| | | | | |
|---|---|---|---|---|
| 0'-2" | 1 1/16" | | 31/64" | 15/64" |
| 0'-4" | 2 1/16" | | 31/32" | 15/32" |
| 0'-6" | 3 1/8" | | 1 7/16" | 11/16" |
| 0'-8" | 4 3/16" | | 1 29/32" | 29/32" |
| 0'-10" | 5 1/4" | | 2 13/32" | 1 9/64" |

NOTE: All dimensions based on camber of 1/60 inch per foot of span (1/2" @ 30') See Approved Truss Designs for 2 X 4 or 2 X 6 top chords and allowable spans for specie and grade of lumber.

## Cutting Data
## 3/12 Fink

| SPAN | TOP CHORD | BOTTOM CHORD | TENSION MEMBER | COMPRESSION MEMBER |
|---|---|---|---|---|
| 16'-0" | 8'-2 15/16" | 8'-0" + 8'-0" | 36 3/4" | 16 7/8" |
| 17'-0" | 8'-9 1/8" | 8'-0" + 9'-0" | 39 19/64" | 18 5/32" |
| 18'-0" | 9'-3 5/16" | 8'-0" + 10'-0" | 41 27/32" | 19 7/16" |
| 19'-0" | 9'-9 1/2" | 9'-0" + 10'-0" | 44 25/64" | 20 23/32" |
| 20'-0" | 10'-3 11/16" | 8'-0" + 12'-0" | 46 15/16" | 22" |
| 21'-0" | 10'-9 7/8" | 10'-0" + 11'-0" | 49 31/64" | 23 9/32" |
| 22'-0" | 11'-4 1/16" | 10'-0" + 12'-0" | 52 1/32" | 24 9/16" |
| 23'-0" | 11'-10 1/4" | 11'-0" + 12'-0" | 54 37/64" | 25 27/32" |
| 24'-0" | 12'-4 7/16" | 10'-0" + 14'-0" | 57 1/8" | 27 1/8" |
| 25'-0" | 12'-10 5/8" | 12'-0" + 13'-0" | 59 43/64" | 28 13/32" |
| 26'-0" | 13'-4 13/16" | 12'-0" + 14'-0" | 62 7/32" | 29 11/16" |
| 27'-0" | 13'-11" | 13'-0" + 14'-0" | 64 49/64" | 30 31/32" |
| 28'-0" | 14'-5 1/8" | 12'-0" + 16'-0" | 67 5/16" | 32 1/4" |
| 29'-0" | 14'-11 5/16" | 14'-0" + 15'-0" | 69 55/64" | 33 17/32" |
| 30'-0" | 15'-5 1/2" | 14'-0" + 16'-0" | 72 13/32" | 34 13/16" |
| 31'-0" | 15'-11 11/16" | 15'-0" + 16'-0" | 74 61/64" | 36 3/32" |
| 32'-0" | 16'-5 7/8" | 14'-0" + 18'-0" | 77 1/2" | 37 3/8" |
| 33'-0" | 17'-0 1/16" | 16'-0" + 17'-0" | 80 3/64" | 38 21/32" |
| 34'-0" | 17'-6 1/4" | 16'-0" + 18'-0" | 82 19/32" | 39 15/16" |
| 35'-0" | 18'-0 7/16" | 17'-0" + 18'-0" | 85 9/64" | 41 7/32" |
| 36'-0" | 18'-6 5/8" | 16'-0" + 20'-0" | 87 11/16" | 42 1/2" |
| 37'-0" | 19'-0 13/16" | 18'-0" + 19'-0" | 90 15/64" | 43 25/32" |
| 38'-0" | 19'-7" | 18'-0" + 20'-0" | 92 25/32" | 45 1/16" |
| 39'-0" | 20'-1 3/16" | 19'-0" + 20'-0" | 95 21/64" | 46 11/32" |
| 40'-0" | 20'-7 3/8" | 18'-0" + 22'-0" | 97 7/8" | 47 5/8" |

INTERPOLATIONS:

| | | | | |
|---|---|---|---|---|
| 0'-2" | 1" | | 27/64" | 7/32" |
| 0'-4" | 2 1/16" | | 27/32" | 27/64" |
| 0'-6" | 3 1/16" | | 1 9/32" | 41/64" |
| 0'-8" | 4 1/8" | | 1 11/16" | 55/64" |
| 0'-10" | 5 1/8" | | 2 1/8" | 1 1/16" |

NOTE: All dimensions based on camber of 1/60 inch per foot of span (1/2" @ 30'). See Approved Truss Designs for 2 x 4 or 2 x 6 top chords and allowable spans for specie and grade of lumber.

**Fig. 101.2*A*.**
Cutting list for trusses.

*(Panel-Clip Co.)*

INVOICE # ____________

NAME ____________ PLAN # ____________ DATE ________ SHOP # ____________

LOCATION ____________ DUE ________ SHEET # ________ of ____

TYPE ________ AMOUNT ________ SPAN ________ PITCH ______ OVERHANGS

GABLES ________

NOTES: ____________

| t. | F | R | g. |
|---|---|---|---|
| | | | |
| | | | |
| | | | |
| | | | |

| | amount | length | | #1 | #2 | #3 | #4 | | size | length | |
|---|---|---|---|---|---|---|---|---|---|---|---|
| BOTTOM CHORD | | | | | | | | | | | OUT |
| | | | | | | | | | | | |
| | | | | | | | | | | | |
| | | | | | | | | | | | |
| | | | oh | | | | | | | | SET UP |
| RAFTER | | | | | | | | | | | |
| | | | | | | | | | | | |
| | | | | | | | | | | | |
| | | | | | | | | | | | TABLE LEADER |
| DIAG. | | | | | | | | | | | |
| | | | | | | | | | | | |
| | | | | | | | | | | | |
| | | | | | | | | | | | TABLE LEADER |
| K.P. | | | | | | | | | | | |
| | | | | | | | | | | | |
| GABLES | SETS | | P | LESS | " | EACH | BLK. | | | | |

**DESCRIPTION:**

LUMBER LIST

| amount | size | length |
|---|---|---|
| | | |
| | | |
| | | |
| | | |
| | | |
| | | |
| | | |
| | | |

INVOICE # ________

**Fig. 101.2*B*.**
Cutting list prepared in office for shop use.

*(Truswal)*

increased more. The use of pieces of "scrap" framing lumber under 24" in length or scrap plywood must be carefully weighed against the cost to retrieve the material and set it up for cutting. For instance, the cutting of 14 1/4" ladder blocks may be more economically done from long lengths rather than from scrap. Each case sould be analyzed if volume is involved.

106 **Equipment.** The following photos show some of the types of equipment frequently used in manufactured building plants.

**Fig. 106.1.**
Clary Craftmaster for cutting all types of components but particularly roof trusses. Will cut top and bottom chords and webs.
*(Clary)*

**Fig. 106.2.**
Detail on the Clary.

*(Clary)*

**Fig. 106.3.**
Idaco Compon-A-Matic. These larger saws have conveyorized waste disposal systems.

**Fig. 106.4.**
Clary Webmaster. Designed primarily for cutting web members.

*(Clary)*

**Fig. 106.5.**
Idaco—"Economatic" lower cost all-purpose component saw. Cuts to 24 feet in length. Optional waste disposal system.

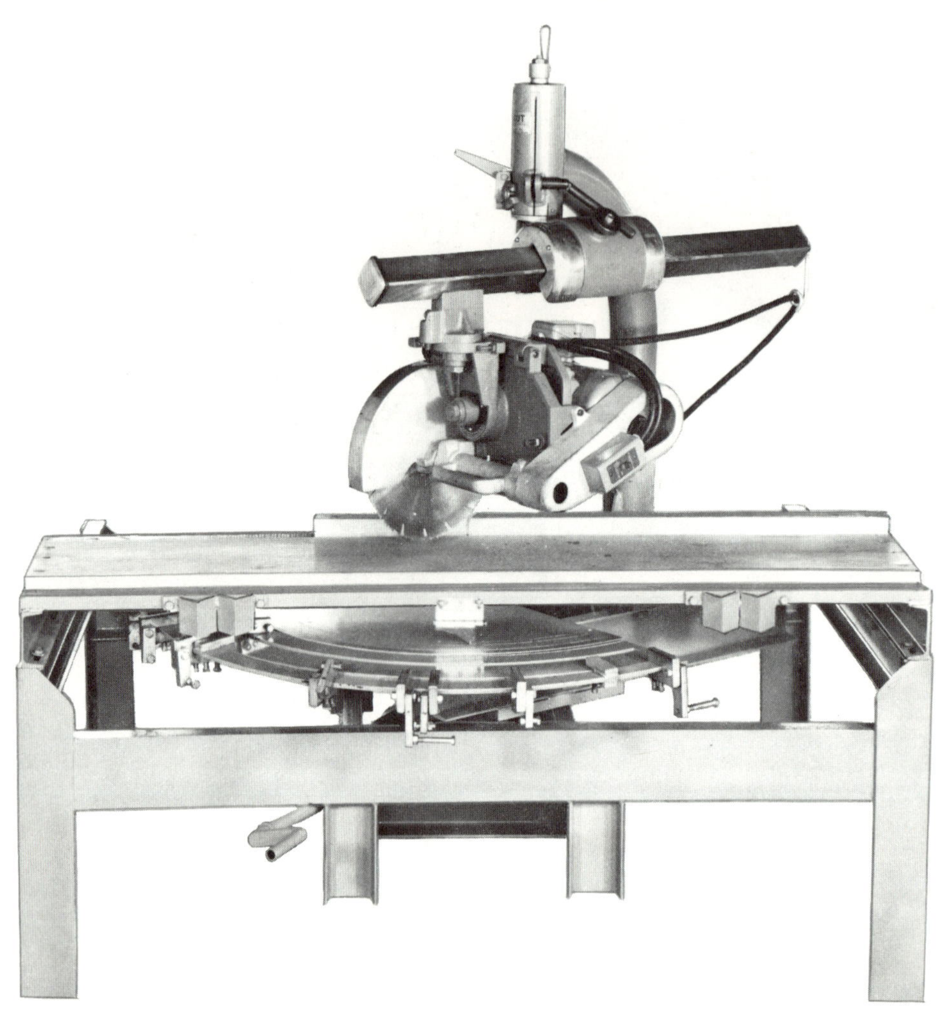

**Fig. 106.6.**

Speed Cut's equipment for general purpose component cutting. Turntable–protractor dial permits rapid change from one angle to another, as when cutting web members.

*(Speed Cut)*

**Fig. 106.7.**
Companion roller table—measuring device for Speed Cut system.
*(Speed Cut)*

**Fig. 106.8.**
Heavy Duty Panel Saw.

*(Parks)*

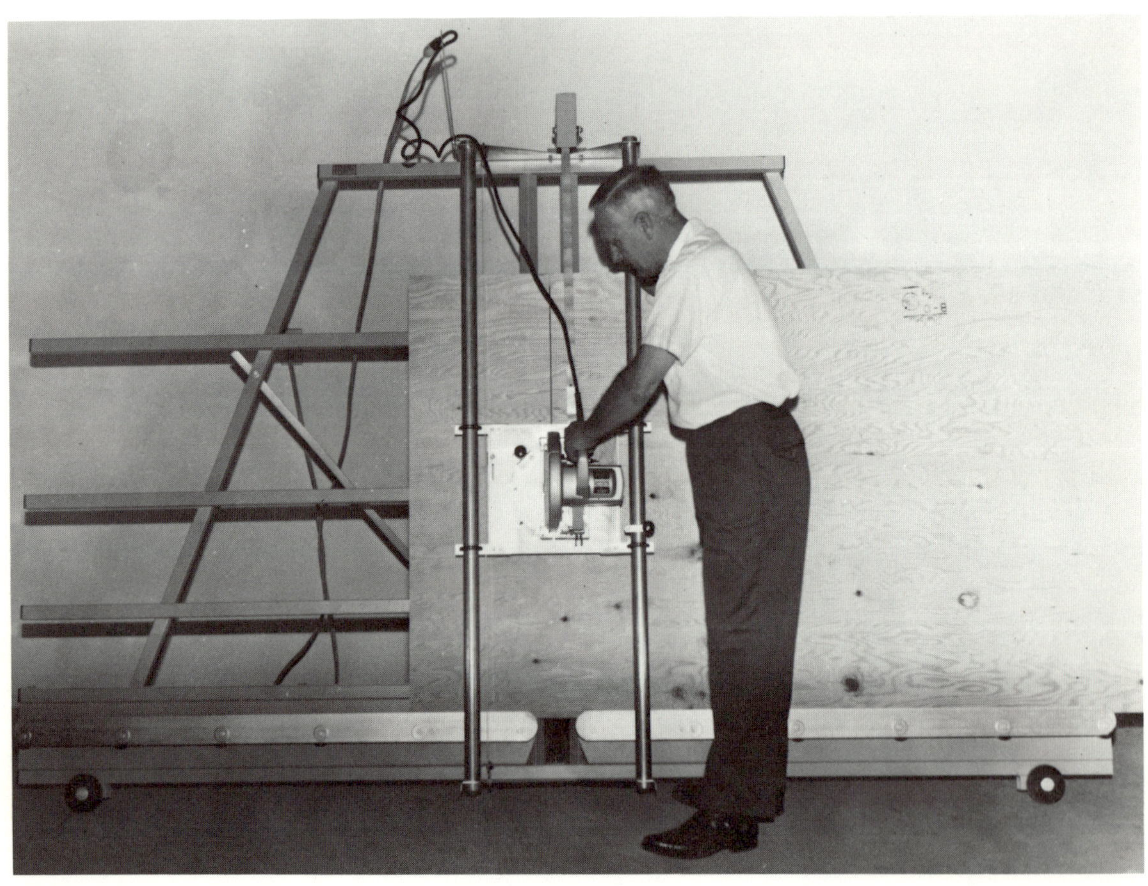

**Fig. 106.9.**
Light Panel Saw.

*(Safety Speed Cut)*

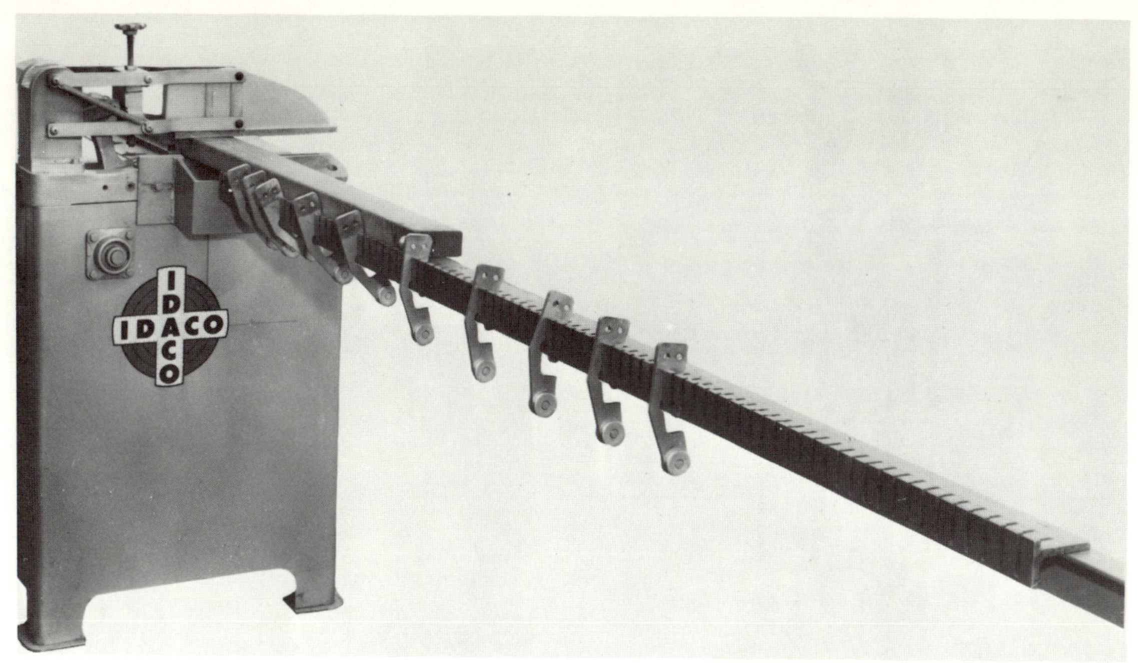


**Fig. 106.10.**
Under-Cutoff Saw with Leaver precision gauges. Foot operated. Safe.

*(Idaco)*

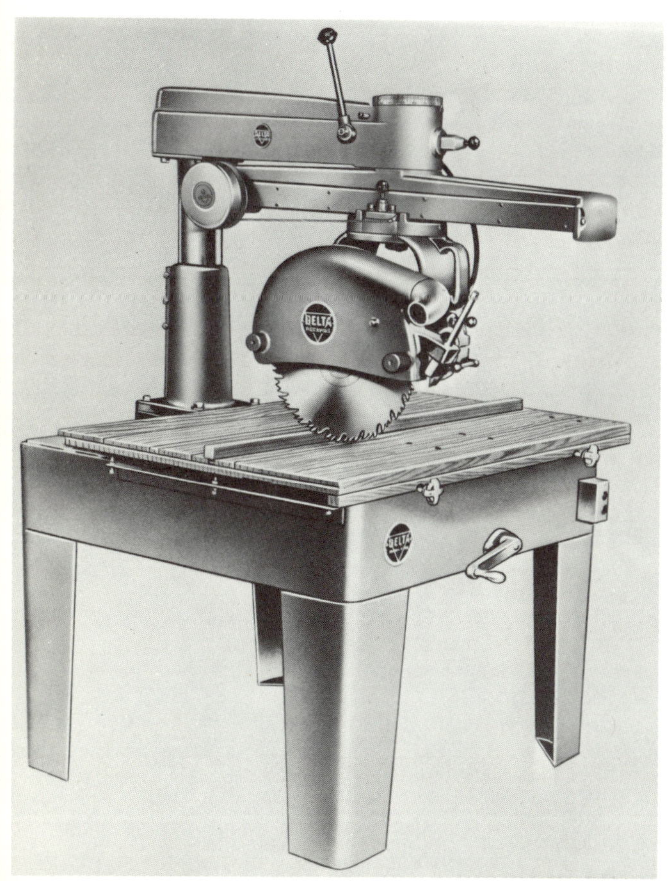


**Fig. 106.11.**
Radial arm saw with automatic safety return attachment. After cut, cutterhead automatically returns behind fence. This feature reduces operator fatigue and increases safety.

*(Delta Rockwell)*

**Fig. 106.12.**
Uni-Point Radial Arm Saw.

*(Northfield)*

**Fig. 106.13.**
Swing saw for fast, simple cut-off work.
*(Fairfield)*

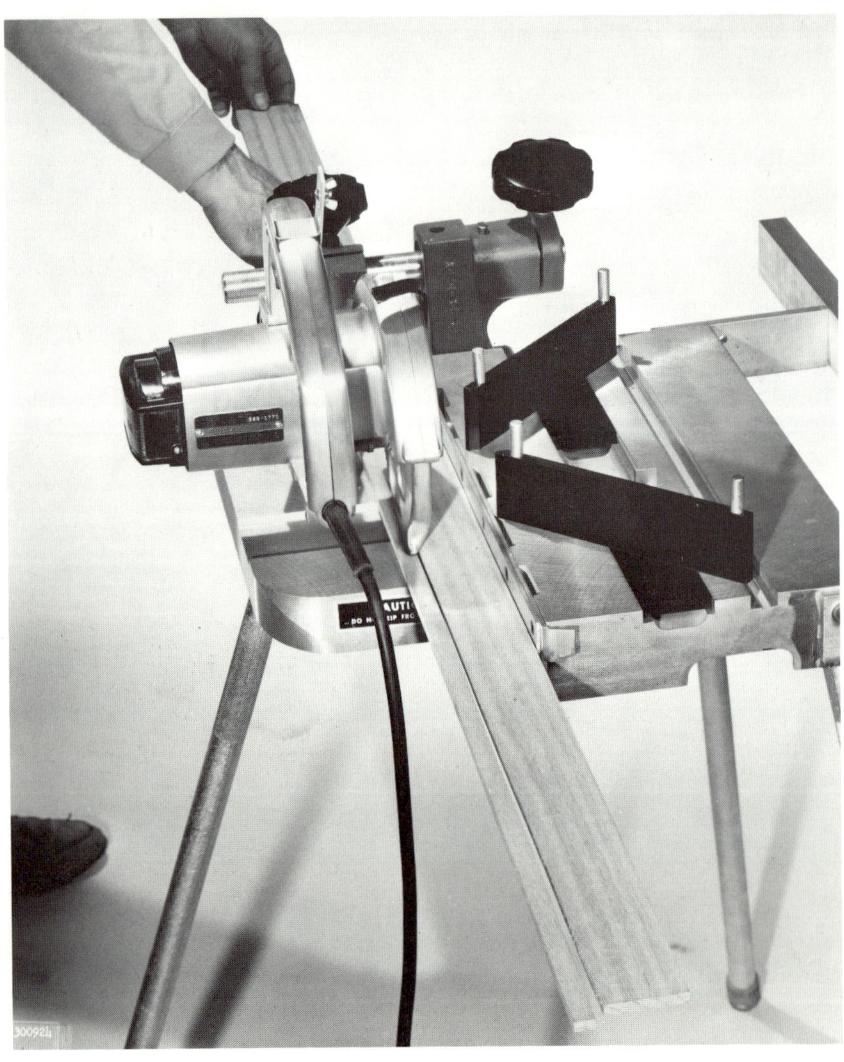

**Fig. 106.14.**
Handy saw for mitering, ripping, and cross cutting trim around modular operations.
*(Milwaukee)*

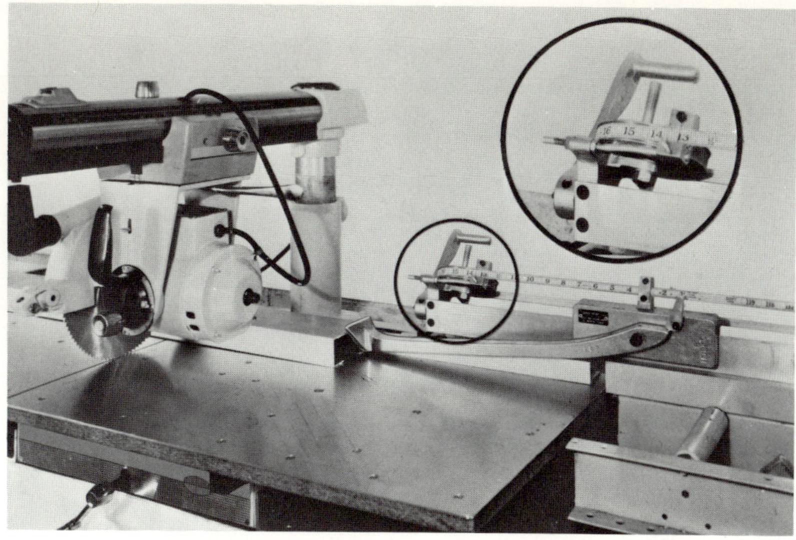

**Fig. 106.15.**
Stop that can be set without the operator leaving the saw.
*(Quick-Stop, Inc.)*

107 **Remote, Air-Actuated Saw.** Pease has a user-built accessory for one of their cutoff saws that permits the saw to be cycled from any point on the feed table. Thus, the operator may bring the end of the stock to the desired length, push a button as much as 20 feet from the saw. The saw cuts and returns without the operator moving.

This equipment consists of an air cylinder with 18″ or 24″ stroke and a solenoid switch. Momentary contact switches are located about 36″ O.C. along the back of the fence.

108 **Feed Tables.** Sections of conveyor of the various types are most commonly used for feed tables. Often these do not provide sufficient stability for accurate cutting. On some cutoff saws it may be desirable to use hardwood planks for this purpose. These planks quickly develop a slick surface but they remain stable. A variation on this is a series of pieces of oak threshold about 16″ O.C. See Fig. 108.

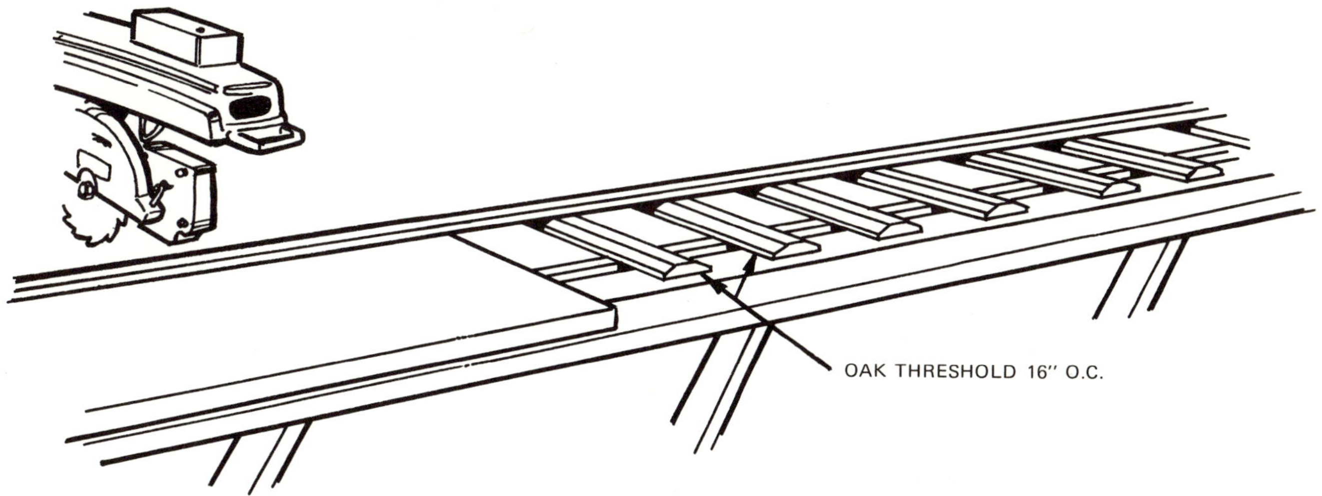


**Fig. 108.**
Oak threshold used for feed table.

*(After Pease)*

# CHAPTER II

## Floor Construction

200 **General.** For Stressed Skin Floors see Chapter VI, "Plywood Components." For modular floor construction, see Chapter XI, "Modular Units." In component and packaged buildings, floors are only occasionally panelized because of the high shipping bulk and small labor increment. However, as on-site costs increase, the use of panelized floor sections is increasing, particularly in labor-short areas.

Fabricators generally provide preassembled girders, spliced joists, partition ladder systems, and precut floor plywood when they furnish a floor system. In many areas, no attempt is made to furnish a floor system other than raw materials, or the building may be erected on a concrete slab.

201 **Spliced Joists.** Joists are spliced on center over beam or girder eliminating "lap" at this point. Advantages are increased flexibility in ductwork; maximum building size with stock joist sizes; and "straight-thru" nailing of subfloor. For splicing joists, a lumber splicer (Fig. 201) is frequently used.

**Fig. 201.**
Lumber splicer for splicing floor joists, etc.
*(Truswal)*

202 **Girders.** These are generally used with crawl space buildings built on piers. Two or three 2 × 8's or 2 × 10's are spiked together with or without a 2 × 2 ledger to support the joists. (Fig. 202*A*.) Girders are typically spiked together with an automatic nailing machine. (Fig. 202*B*.)

203 **Subassemblies.** The two most common subassemblies to be shipped with precut floor systems are "ladders" for under plumbing walls (also for heating ducts) and cantilevers where the joists run parallel to the cantilevers. (See Fig. 203.)

204 **Plywood, Precut.** Precut floor systems frequently include precut and code-marked plywood floor sheathing to eliminate all job-site cutting. Fig. 204 shows a typical schedule.

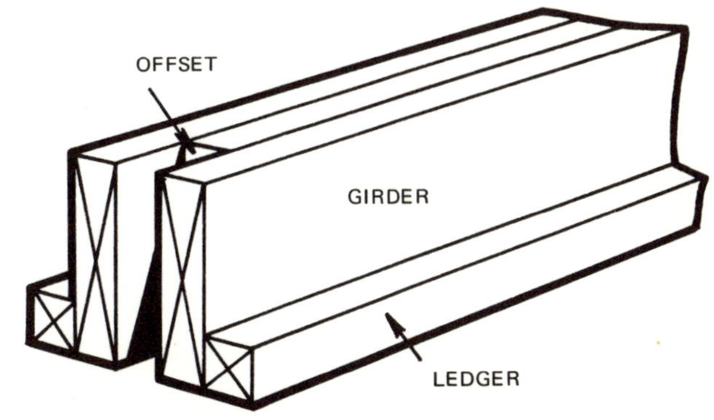


**Fig. 202*A*.**
Typical girder detail.

**Fig. 202*B*.**
Automatic nailing machine spiking girders together.
*(Auto Nailer)*

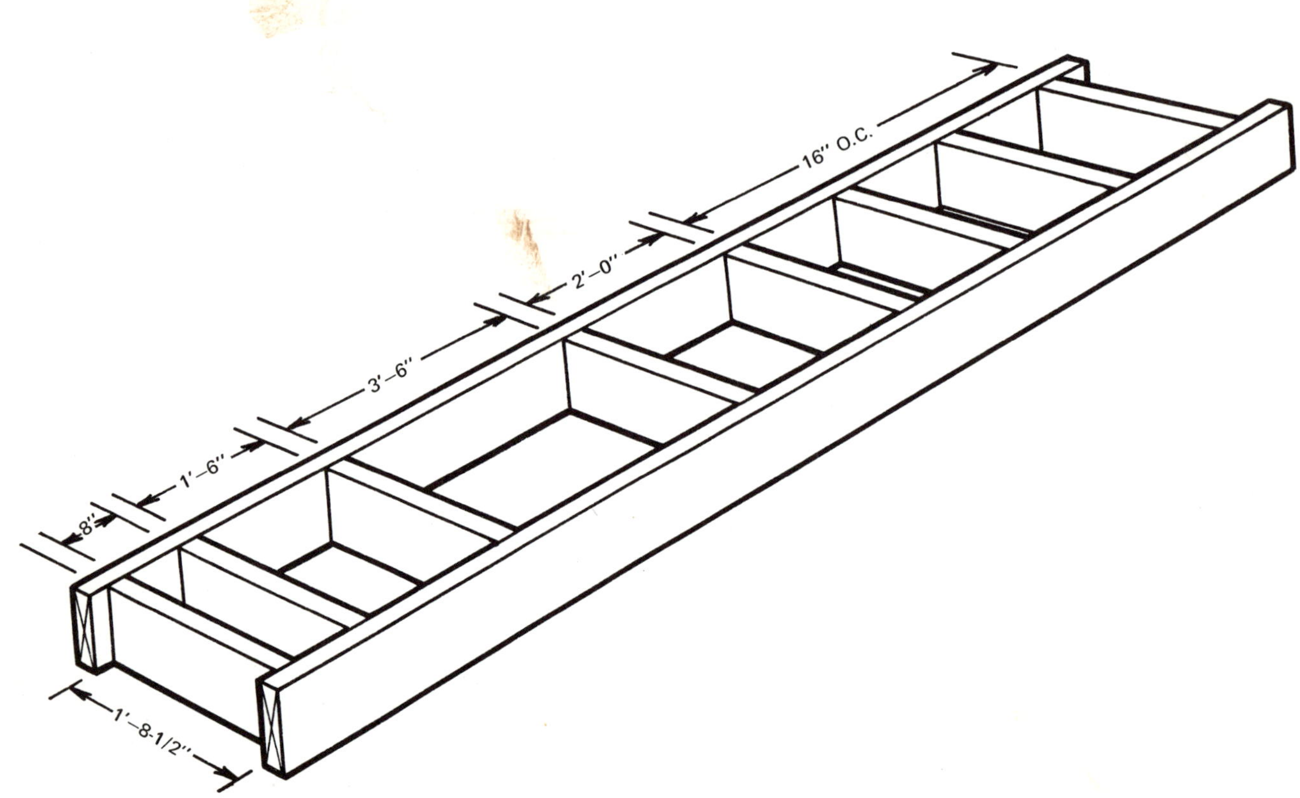


**Fig. 203.**
"Ladders" for plumbing walls and cantilevers.

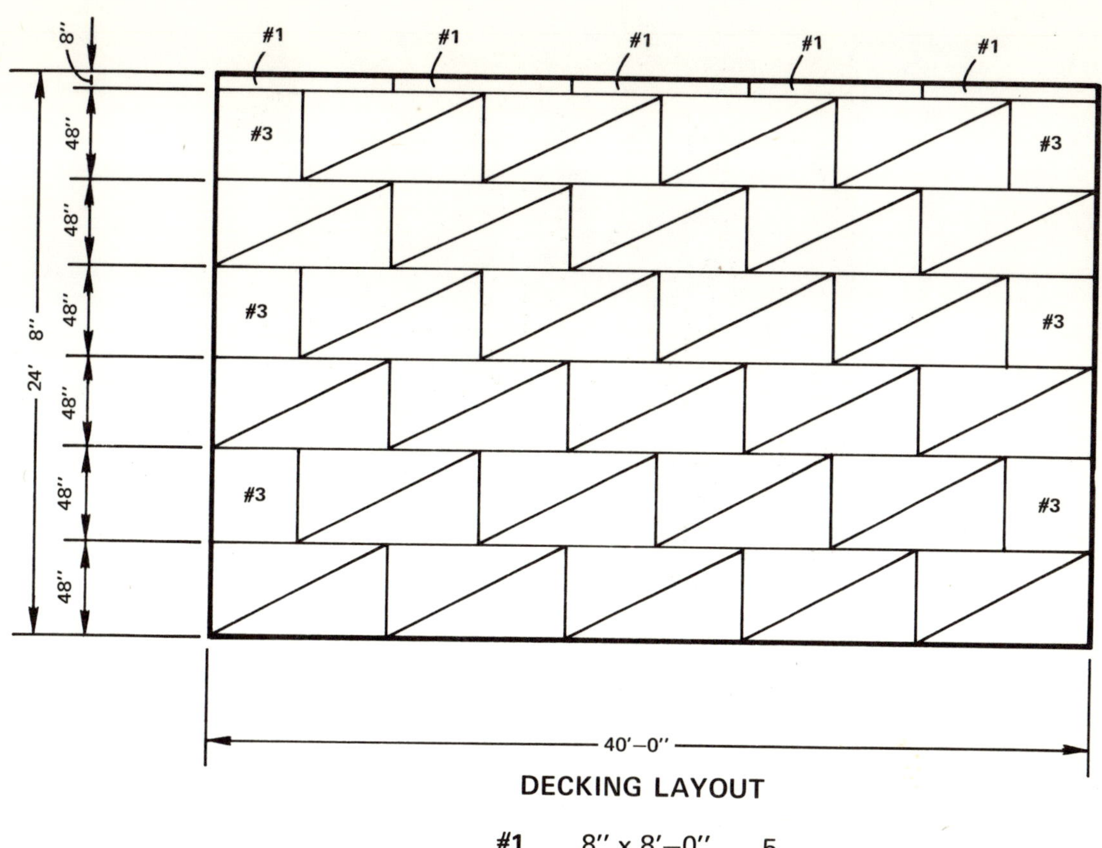


| | | |
|---|---|---|
| #1 | 8" x 8'–0" | 5 |
| #2 | 4'–0" x 2'–0" | |
| #3 | 4'–0" x 4'–0" | 6 |
| #4 | 4'–0" x 6'–0" | |
| FULL | 4'–0" x 8'–0" | 27 |

**Fig. 204.**
Plywood sheathing layout and schedule

*(After Hallmark Homes)*

205 **Floor Panels.** Floor panels are frequently fabricated in panels 8′ wide (for shipping) by the depth of the building. They usually incorporate bridging and blocking as required in the completed structure and may have outlets cut for heating. (See Fig. 205.)

206 **Floor Trusses.** Floor trusses are used to provide clear span between supports. See Chapter V for details.

207 **Stairs.** Shop fabricated stairs are increasingly included in component packages. Plywood router templates are used for standard stair layouts. Basement stairs can be cut with a dado head on the saw and shipped assembled or knock-down. Stairs are often covered with heavy kraft paper to protect them during shipment and construction. (See Fig. 207.)

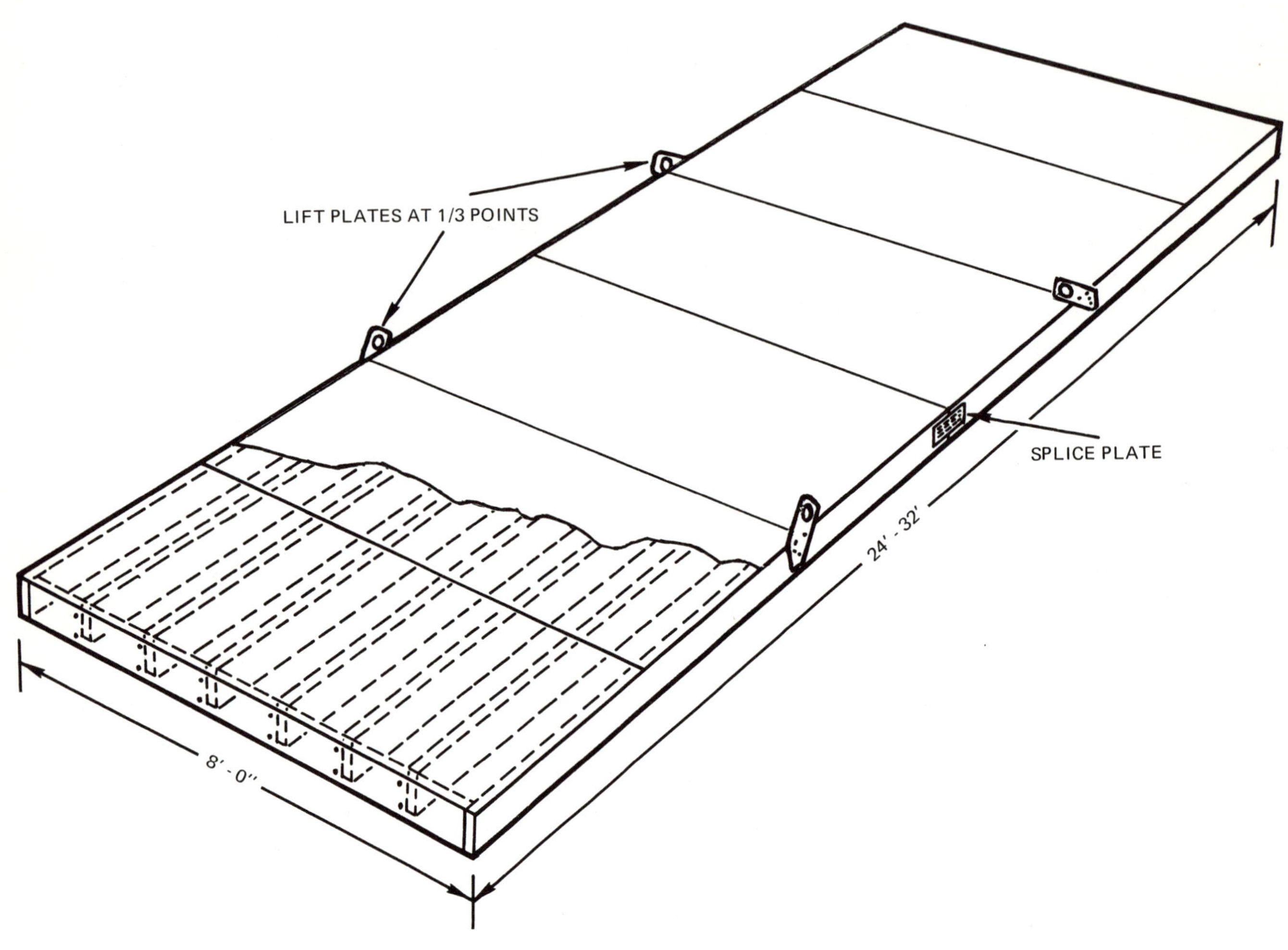


**Fig. 205.**
Typical floor panel, showing lifting hooks.

*(After Components, Inc.)*

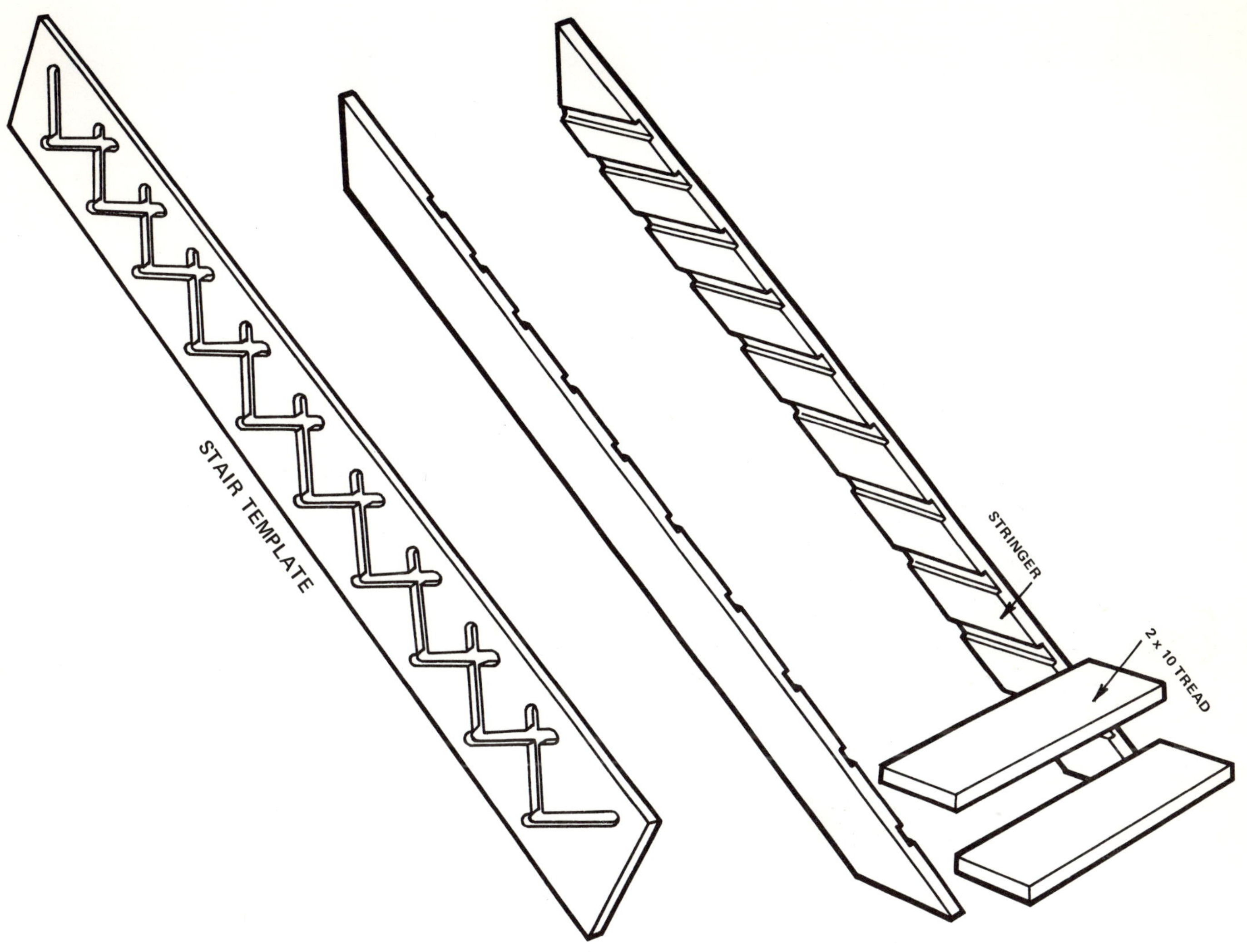


**Fig. 207.**
Stair details.

# CHAPTER III

## Walls and Partitions

300 **General.** The addition of walls and partitions to a manufacturer's output of roof trusses and/or prehung door units usually changes him into a component package manufacturer or a custom component manufacturer. Walls and partitions may be bearing or nonbearing. They can be in varying degrees of completeness, with sheathing, siding, insulation, wiring, and interior finish installed. Marketing objectives, building codes, relative site and factory labor efficiency, and technical proficiency of the fabricator are among the factors affecting the characteristics of the finished product.

The techniques covered in this chapter are also used by modular manufacturers in varying degrees before the panels are installed on the modular unit's floor section.

Of all building components, short of modular units, wall and partition panels present the greatest opportunity for transferring site labor to the factory.

Since few wall and partition panels are manufactured and sold commercially with foam or other core techniques, this chapter will be confined to the typical wood frame construction. There is increasing interest in steel frame construction, both for partitions and walls. However, steel frame construction is basically the same as wood frame and will be so considered herein.

301 **Steps.** The steps in wall and partition fabrication are very much the same, except that partition fabricators can usually eliminate most of the steps outlined below. Much partition fabrication is done on one jig, without moving through any step process. At least one manufacturer (custom components) fabricates partitions directly on the pile of complete partition sections.

301.1 **Office Engineering.** The purpose of office engineering is to minimize the amount of "forehead" work required by production personnel. The size and location of doors and windows, the location of panel points and intersections, details, and exterior and interior finish and mechanicals can be specified in the office before a job is released to the plant. A cutting schedule is frequently prepared at this time. (See 303).

301.2 **Layout.** Location of doors and windows is indicated on top and bottom plates. Individual stud locations are marked out although sometimes this is determined by an assembly jig or by templates.

301.3 **Cutting.** Material is cut for use in both the assembly and subcomponent operations. If not cut by the layout man, top and bottom plates are cut here. Chapter I covers cutting operations in detail.

301.4 **Subcomponent Fabrication.** Window and door headers are manufactured and incorporated into subassemblies.

301.5 **Assembly.** At this point the wall frame is assembled by spiking studs to plates and installing subcomponents. Here the panel need not be exactly square.

301.6 **Insulation.** If included, blanket type insulation is installed at this time, either before or after the wiring. However, if interior wallboard is applied, insulation is sometimes best installed just prior to that operation.

301.7 **Wiring.** Wiring can be installed at this point or, if wall panels are to be installed in modular units, it is frequently installed from the outside of the walls after installation on the modular floor but before sheathing and/or siding is applied. See Chapter XI.

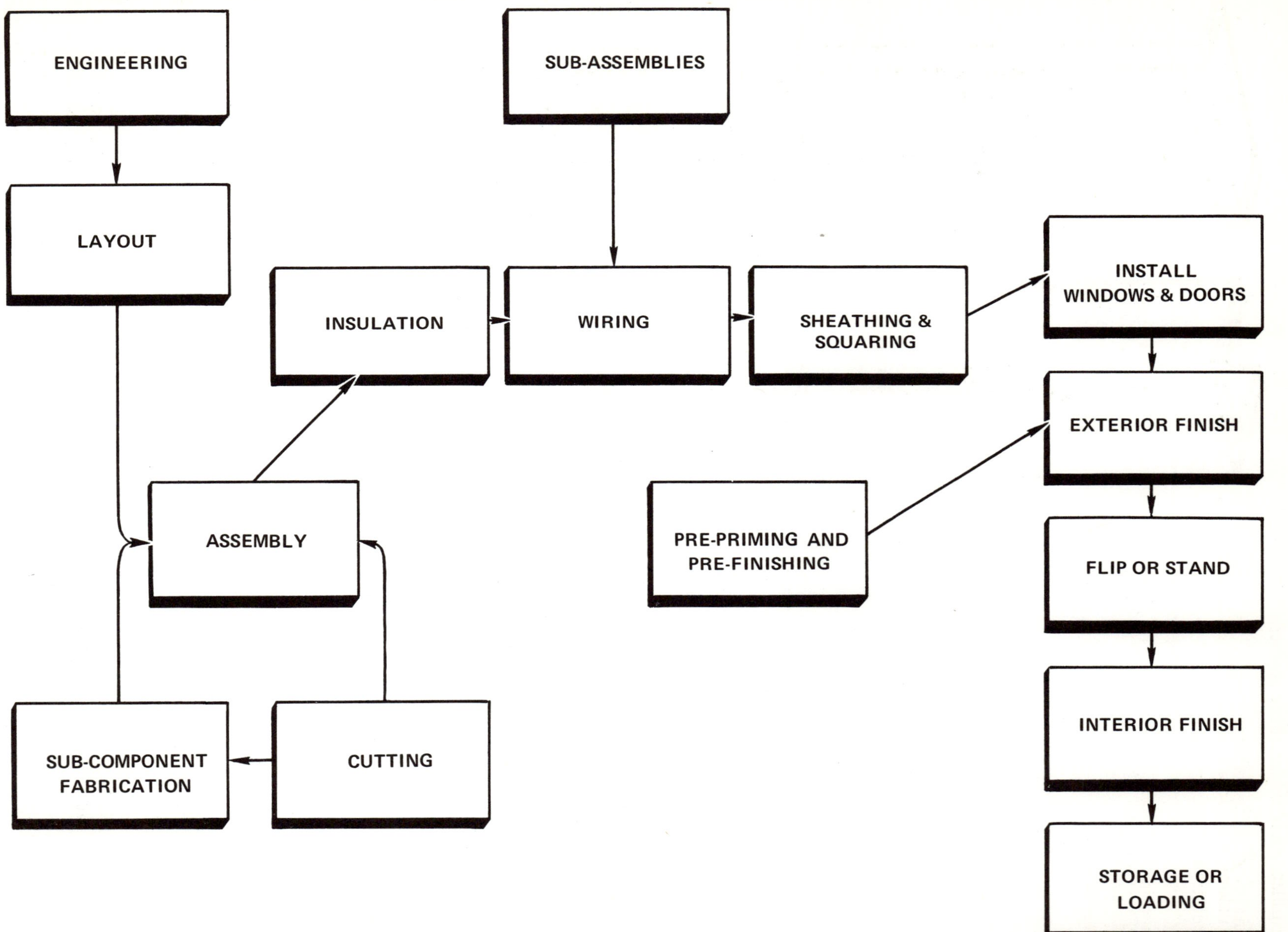


**Fig. 301.**
Schematic view of the steps involved in manufacturing wall and partition panels.

301.8 **Sheathing or Squaring.** Wall sections at this point must be squared, corner braces installed, and/or sheathing applied.

301.9 **Windows and Doors** are installed in many operations at this point.

301.10 **Exterior Finish.** Horizontal or vertical siding, shakes, or other exterior finishes are applied here.

301.11 **Flip or Stand.** If the operation includes interior work, panels must be stood up or flipped over to permit work on the inside.

301.12 **Interior Finish.** Applied here are wallboard, window and door trim, and painting.

301.13 **Storage or Loading.** The last step in the production process is stacking completed panels, horizontally or vertically, or placing on conveyors, ready for shipment.

302 **Variances from Conventional Framing.** A few differences from conventional, on site, construction have been developed which help make the fabrication process more economical.

302.1 **Ladder in Lieu of Partition Junction Post.** (Fig. 302.1) This usually results in a saving of one or two studs over the conventional system. It is assumed that the 14 1/4″ ladder blocks are from scrap.

302.2 **Headers.** Many fabricators use 4 × 4's, 4 × 6's, 4 × 8's, 4 × 10's or 4 × 12's for headers in lieu of doubled 2 × 4's, 2 × 6's, etc. This saves a cutting and nailing operation and eliminates (with 4 × 12's) the need for cripples over the openings.

A variation of this is a combination header made of 2 × 10's and 2 × 4's, glued and nailed. This has been accepted by FHA in some areas. (Fig. 302.2)

302.3 **Top Plates.** The notching, flyby, and holdback of top plates at wall corners and partition intersections is a time consuming item, requiring accuracy not usually possessed by assembly line workers. Some manufacturers minimize this problem by eliminating all notching and flyby. Truss clips are then furnished to effect this connection on site. (Fig. 302.3)

**Fig. 302.1.**
Ladder in lieu of wall junction post.

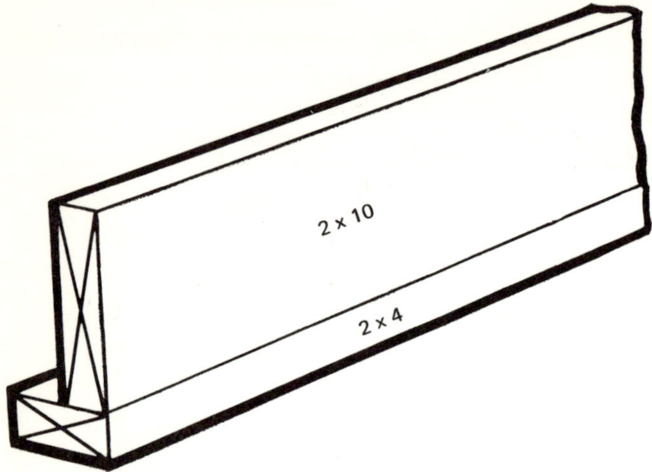


**Fig. 302.2.**
Combination header.

*(After Pease)*

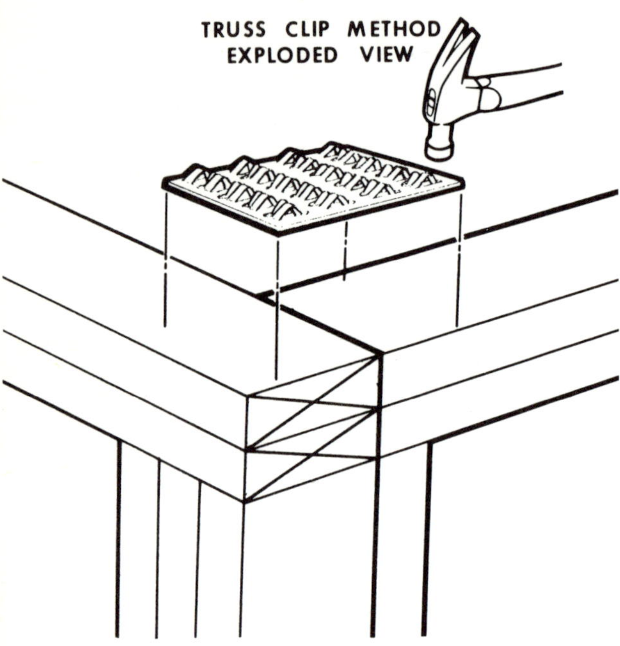


**Fig. 302.3.**
Top plate tie.

*(Panel-Clip)*

303 **Office Engineering.** This includes the preparation of all written or drawn material to be sent into the plant for the actual fabrication operations. It may consist of cutting schedules, numerical panel layouts, individual panel drawings or, in some operations, of nothing more than the builder's plan. It is advantageous, in most operations, to do some of the planning and "figuring" in an office situation.

303.1 **Floor Plan.** A keyed floor plan prepared in the office will locate wall and partition panel points and various other information to simplify the work of the shop layout man. This plan will also number the panels and a copy is sent to the field erection crew to tell them which panel goes where.

303.2 **Individual Panel Drawings.** These are usually required when exterior finish is applied to show details of siding application but they may be used on other panels as insurance against errors. Fig. 303.2 shows a typical panel drawing and its accompanying keyed floor plan.

303.3 **Numerical Panel-Layouts.** These can be sent to the plant and will indicate the number of the panel, length, location and size of openings, partition intersections, etc.

An excellent example of this type of system is provided in Hydro-Air's "Panel Rite System for Shop Manufactured Exterior Wall Panels and Interior Partitions." The section on "The Panel Schedule" is presented herewith:

(Note: Studs are shown as 94 1/4" whereas a more standard length is 92 5/8")

***The Panel Schedule.*** *The first step in componentizing a house is to divide the house plan into exterior wall panels and interior partitions. Length of exterior wall panels is the first consideration. If the exterior walls are to be framed and sheathed only and are to be manhandled at the job site, the preferable length is 12'-0" with no panel to exceed 16'-0". When windows and exterior siding are shop applied, panels to be manhandled on the job site should never exceed 12'-0", and 8'-0" to 10'-0" panels are more desirable. For machine erection at the job site, exterior walls panels up to 40'-0" long can be shop fabricated. Exterior wall panel schedule is shown in Figure 303.3b.*

*Interior partitions up to 16'-0" long can be fabricated in the shop and easily manhandled at the job site. Interior partition schedule is shown in Fig. 303.3B.*

*Another consideration in laying out exterior wall panels is the most economical use of sheathing material and lumber for plates. Multiples of 4'-0" are desirable for sheathing and increments of 2'-0" in even feet for lumber.*

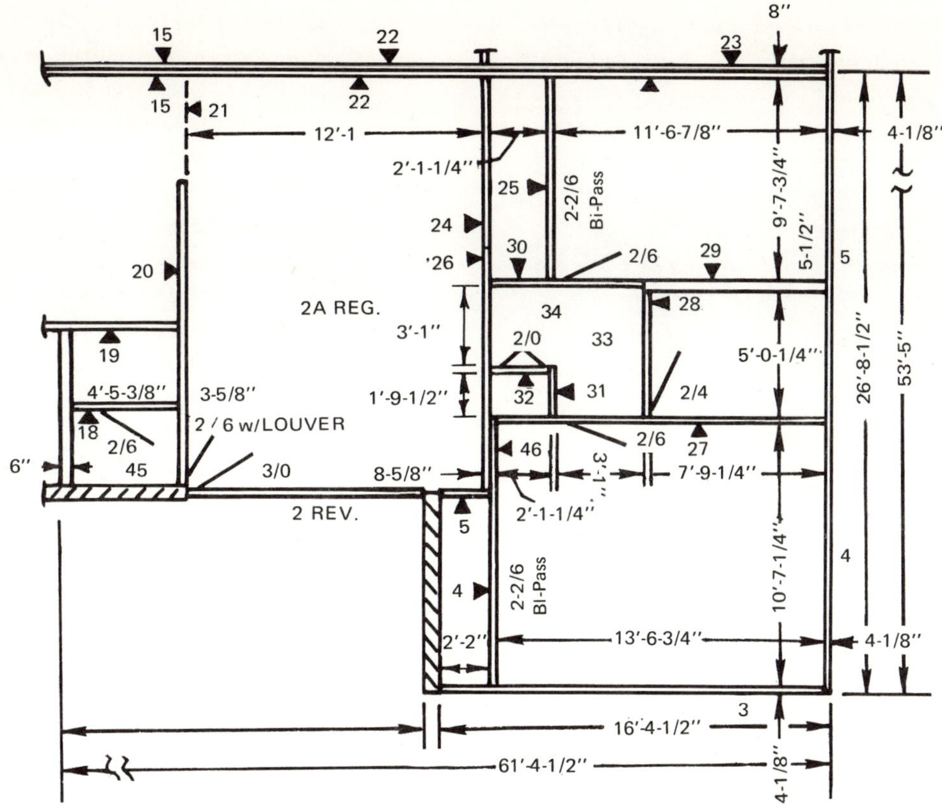


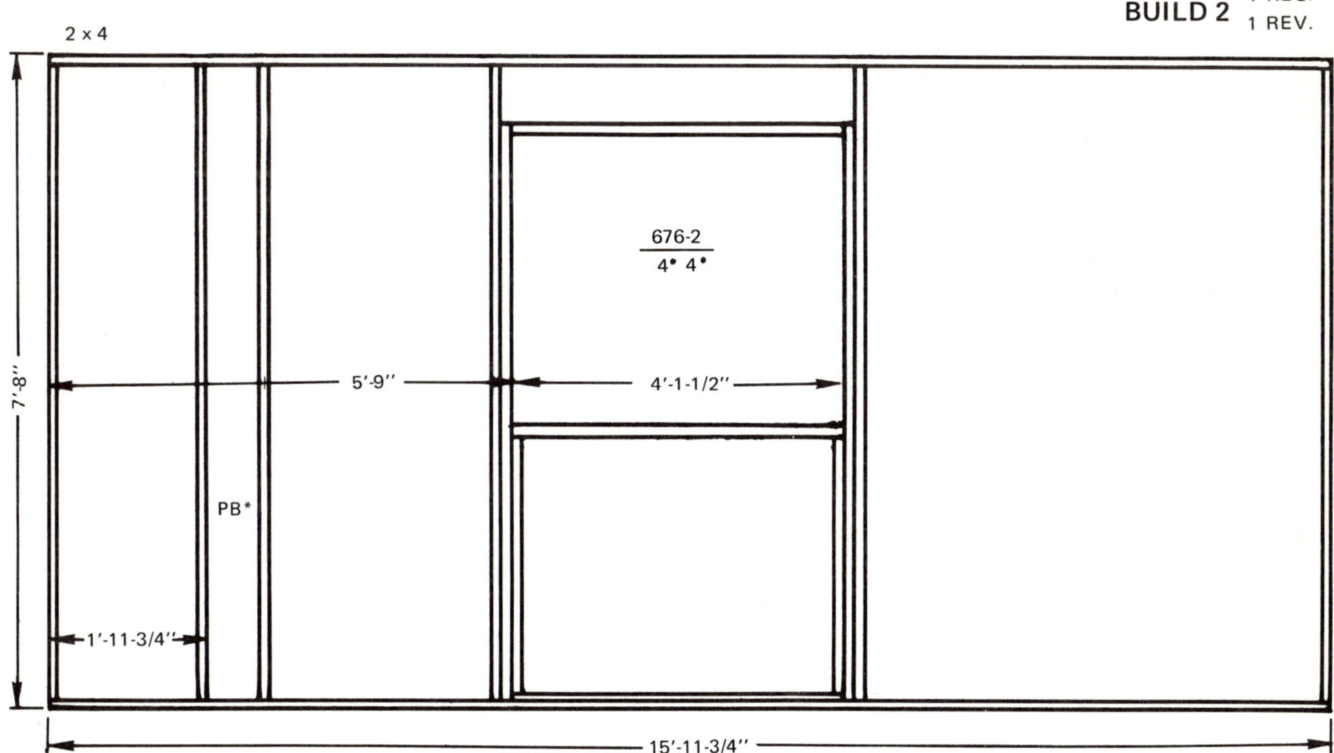


**Fig. 303.2.**

Keyed floor plan and typical panel drawing. Regular, (16" O.C.), studding not indicated as their location is fixed by a jig or a framing machine.

*(Cardinal Industries)*

***Example:*** *A 10'-6" panel requires two full sheets of sheathing plus a piece 2'-6" wide and two plates 10'-6" long cut from 12'-0" long lumber. This panel requires an extra cut on the sheathing and 1'-6" lumber waste on each plate, in addition to a left-over piece of sheathing 1'-6" wide that may or may not be usable.*

*Correct panel layout can save both time and material. When odd sized panels are required, and they will be on most home designs, keep track of odd-sized pieces of sheathing so that they can be used to advantage on another panel.*

*Although many home fabricators lay out the exterior wall panels without regard to the floor joist spacing, it is our feeling that for ease in locating heating ducts and bringing up plumbing and wiring from the basement, location of wall studs over floor joist is important. This eliminates cutting of wall studs in order to bring in any of the utilities. The exterior wall panels should then be laid out so that the majority of wall studs are directly over the floor joists. This may result in more odd-length panels, but will eliminate call backs to repair damage by other crafts to wall sections.*

*The final consideration in laying out exterior walls is the means of access to the foundation. Generally speaking, the first exterior wall panels to be erected will be the front right corner of the house. This allows the erection crew to go counter-clockwise around the house and place the last panel in the opening near the unloading area. If the best means of access is from another direction, start the first panels on the front right hand corner from the unloading area and work counter-clockwise around the house. Method of loading the truck and unloading at the job site will be taken up in detail later.*

*Fig. 303.3*C *and 303.3*D *show a house plan with exterior wall panels and interior partitions laid out for fabrication on the Panel-Rite Machines. Fig. 303.3*A *is the exterior wall panel schedule for the house, and Fig. 303.3*B *is the interior Partition Schedule for the house*

*Exterior wall panels are laid out from the left end of the panel when you stand outside the house looking into the house. The Panel-Rite Framing Machine is designed to locate all dimension from the left end of the panel. All figures are in inches and eighth of inches. For example: 87-2 is 87-1/4" and 92-5 is 92-5/8".*

*Details of all rough openings such as windows and doors are required to lay out the panels correctly. These same details can be used for shop fabrication of the subcomponents. Generally speaking, most home fabricators carry only two lines of windows, and the details for each line will be standard regardless of the house in which the windows are used. The same will hold true for door opening details. A detail for a 2'-0", 2'-2", 2'-4" 2'-6", 2'-8", 2'-10' 3'-0" and double 2'-6" doors will cover most conditions. With the Panel-Rite System of home fabrication, the centerline dimension of the door or window to the left edge of the rough opening on the details is important since most windows and doors are located in the house plan according to their centerlines. By referring to the window or door detail you can easily determine the locations of the rough opening from the left end of the panel.*

***Exterior Wall Panels*** *We are now ready to go through the layout of a few panels. It will be assumed that there is easy access from the front of the house. Panel 1 will be the right front corner of the house with Panel 2, 3, 4, etc., proceeding counterclockwise around the house. The garage panels will be laid out last since they are longer than the house panels and will require a new adjustment in width on the framing and sheathing machines. A general rule is to fabricate all non-standard panels first or last.*

*Working with Fig. 303.3*D, *we find that the joist layout is 16" O.C. from the left front corner of the house. A check of Fig. 303.3*C *shows that we can start with three 12'-0" long exterior wall panels from the left front corner. It is important that no panel start or end in a window or door opening or at a partition lead. Three 12'-0" panels can be fabricated without interference from partition leads or window or door openings. This leaves 9'-8-3/4" for Panel 1.*

*On Fig. 303.3*A *under plate length for Panel 1 we insert 116-6. There are no partition leads in Panel 1, but there is a 3060-1*

HYDRO-AIR ENGINEERING, INC

1210 SOUTH VANDEVENTER
ST. LOUIS, MISSOURI 63110

House Model CAPRI

EXTERIOR WALL PANELS SCHEDULE

Job No. 84036

ALL COMMON STUDS 92-5/8"

| PANEL NO. | PLATE LENGTH | PANEL ENDS | | | INSERT - LOCATION | | | INSERT - LOCATION | | | INSERT - LOCATION | | | PARTITION BLOCK | |
|---|---|---|---|---|---|---|---|---|---|---|---|---|---|---|---|
| | | CORNER POST | SHEATH OVER LAP | SHEATH HOLD | WINDOW OR DOOR | PIN NO. LEFT SIDE | INCHES TO LEFT EDGE | WINDOW OR DOOR | PIN NO. LEFT SIDE | INCHES TO LEFT EDGE | WINDOW OR DOOR | PIN NO. LEFT SIDE | INCHES TO LEFT EDGE | TYPE | INCHES TO THE LEFT |
| 1 | 116-6 | | | RE -4 | 3060-1 | | 35-4 | | | | | | | | |
| 2 | 96-0 | LEFT END | | | | | | NO SHEATHING | | | | | | | |
| 3 | 108-5 | RIGHT END | | | 2'-8" | | 53-0 | NO SHEATHING | | | | | | | |
| 4 | 135-5 | SPACER LE 7-1 | | | | | | NO SHEATHING | | | | | | 2 x 4 | 51-2 114-7 |
| 5 | 84-7 | | | | | | | NO SHEATHING | | | | | | | |
| 6 | 158-4 | BOTH ENDS | | | 4030 | | 25-2 | | | | | | | 2 x 8 | 86-0 |
| 7 | 118-1 | SPACER LE10-5 | LE 4-1 | | 2020 | | 16-6 | 2'-6" | | 65-4 | | | | 2 x 4 | 58-5 104-0 |
| 8 | 112-0 | | | | 5030 | | 15-1 | | | | | | | | |
| 9 | 192-0 | | | | 5036 | | 14-2 | PATIO DOOR | | 116-2 | | | | 2 x 4 | 84-5 |
| 10 | 114-7 | RIGHT END | | RE 4-1 | FIRE PLACE | | 0-0 | | | | | | | 2 x 4 | 99-5 |
| 11 | 148-7 | | RE 4-1 | | | | | | | | | | | 2 x 4 | 46-3 |
| 12 | 96-0 | LEFT END | | | | | | | | | | | | 2 x 4 | 74-1 |
| 13 | 140-3 | | RE 4-1 | | 5036-1 | | 28-2 | | | | | | | | |
| 14 | 192-0 | LEFT END | | | | | | | | | | | | | |
| 15 | 144-0 | | | | 4036 | | 64-6 | | | | | | | 2 x 4 | 14-7 |
| 16 | 172-3 | | RE 4-1 | | | | | | | | | | | 2 x 4 | 18-2 47-1 |
| 17 | 144-0 | LEFT END | | | 3060 | | 47-2 | | | | | | | | |
| 18 | 144-0 | | | | DOUBLE DOOR | | 17-4 | | | | | | | 2 x 4 | 13-1 83-3 |
| 19 | 144-0 | | | | 3060 TWIN | | 1-5 | | | | | | | 2 x 4 | 136-0 |
| 20 | 48-0 | RIGHT END | | | | | | | | | COMMON STUDS - 96-0 | | | | |
| 21 | 12-1 | | LE 4-1 | DOUBLE JACK STUDS RIGHT END - 81-6 | | | | | | | COMMON STUDS - 96-0 | | | | |
| 22 | 14-3 | | RE 4-1 | DOUBLE JACK STUDS RIGHT END - 81-6 | | | | | | | COMMON STUDS - 96-0 | | | | |
| 23 | 144-0 | LEFT END | | | | | | | | | COMMON STUDS - 96-0 | | | | |
| 24 | 105-0 | | | | | | | | | | COMMON STUDS - 96-0 | | | | |
| 25 | | | | | | | | | | | | | | | |
| 26 | | | | | | | | | | | | | | | |
| 27 | | | | | | | | | | | | | | | |
| 28 | | | | | | | | | | | | | | | |
| 29 | | | | | | | | | | | | | | | |
| 30 | | | | | | | | | | | | | | | |
| 31 | | | | | | | | | | | | | | | |
| 32 | | | | | | | | | | | | | | | |
| 33 | | | | | | | | | | | | | | | |
| 34 | | | | | | | | | | | | | | | |
| 35 | | | | | | | | | | | | | | | |
| 36 | | | | | | | | | | | | | | | |
| 37 | | | | | | | | | | | | | | | |
| 38 | | | | | | | | | | | | | | | |
| 39 | | | | | | | | | | | | | | | |
| 40 | | | | | | | | | | | | | | | |
| 41 | | | | | | | | | | | | | | | |
| 42 | | | | | | | | | | | | | | | |
| 43 | | | | | | | | | | | | | | | |

Form No. HA-195 5/68

Fig. 303.3*A*.

HYDRO-AIR ENGINEERING, INC

1210 SOUTH VANDEVENTER
ST. LOUIS, MISSOURI 63110

INTERIOR PARTITIONS SCHEDULE

House Model CAPRI

Job No. 84036

ALL COMMON STUDS 94-1/4"

| PARTITION NO. | PLATE LENGTH | PARTITION ENDS | | INSERT-LOCATION | | PARTITION LEADS | | PARTITION LEADS | | REMARKS |
|---|---|---|---|---|---|---|---|---|---|---|
| | | CORNER POST | TYPE | DOOR | INCHES TO LEFT EDGE | TYPE | INCHES TO LEFT EDGE | TYPE | INCHES TO LEFT EDGE | |
| 101 | 25-0 | | | | | | | | | 2 x 2's |
| 102 | 179-7 | BOTH ENDS | | 2'-6" | 111-0 | 2 x 6 FLAT | 27-5 DN | 2 x 6 FLAT | 146-6DN | |
| 103 | 159-6 | LEFT END | | | | 2 x 6 FLAT | 6-4 UP | 2 x 6 FLAT | 75-1DN | |
| 104 | 158-5 | BOTH ENDS | | 2'-6" | 67-7 | 2 x 6 FLAT | 83-1 UP<br>126-3 DN | 2 x 6 | 59-3DN | |
| 105 | 101-3 | RIGHT END | | | | | | | | |
| 106 | 79-6 | BOTH ENDS | | DOUBLE 2'-6"SL | 8-2 | | | | | |
| 107 | 24-0 | | | | | | | | | 2 x 2's |
| 108 | 155-0 | RIGHT END | | | | 2 x 4 FLAT | 35-0 UP<br>50-4 UP | 2 x 6 FLAT | 122-6UP | |
| 109 | 8-4 | | | | | | | | | 2 x 2's |
| 110 | 144-0 | | | ARCH 7'-0" | 27-7 | | | | | |
| 111 | 2 @ 24-0 | | | | | | | | | |
| 112 | 81-2 | LEFT END | | | | 2 x 6 FLAT | 39-5 DN | | | |
| 113 | 86-7 | | | | | | | | | |
| 114 | 37-0 | | | | | | | | | |
| 115 | 84-7 | | | 2'-6"<br>2'-8" | 4-4<br>44-1 | 2 x 6 FLAT | 39-5 UP | | | |
| 116 | 2 @ 24-0 | LEFT END | | | | | | | | |
| 117 | 86-7 | | | | | | | | | |
| 118 | 67-0 | | | 2'-6" | 3-0 | 2 x 8 FLAT | 57-7 DN | | | |
| 119 | 60-0 | | | DOUBLE 2'-6"SL | 1-5 | | | | | |
| 201 | 114-4 | | | DOUBLE 2'-4"SL | 60-4 | | | | | |
| 202 | 114-4 | | | DOUBLE 2'-0"SL | 66-0 | 2 x 4 FLAT | 55-0 UP | | | |
| 203 | 114-4 | | | | | | | | | |
| 205 | 2 @ 37-0 | | | 2'-6" | 0-6 | | | | | FASTEN 1x4 TO OUTSIDE-BOTH SIDES OF ROUGH DOOR OPENING |
| 207 | 25-0 | | | | | | | | | |
| 208 | 25-0 | | | | | | | | | |
| 209 | 84-0 | | | DOUBLE 3'-0"SL | 6-0 | | | | | |
| 210 | 84-0 | | | | | 2 x 4 FLAT | 49-3 UP | | | |
| 211 | 84-0 | | | | | | | | | 2 x 2's |
| 212 | 54-0 | LEFT END | | | | | | | | 2 x 2's |
| 213 | 31-5 | RIGHT END | | | | | | | | 2 x 2's |
| 214 | 72-1 | | | 2'-6" | 3-0 | | | | | |
| 215 | 72-1 | | | DOUBLE 1'-3" | 18-3 | | | | | |
| 216 | 192-0 | LEFT END | | | | 2 x 6 FLAT | 182-5 | | | |
| 217 | 87-5 | | | | | | | | | |
| 218 | 92-3 | | | | | 2 x 6 FLAT | 62-3 DN | | | |
| 219 | 92-3 | | | | | 2 x 6 FLAT | 62-3 UP | | | |
| 220 | 2 @ 57-0 | | | | | | | | | 2 x 2's |

Form #HA-196 6-68

**Fig. 303.3*B*.**

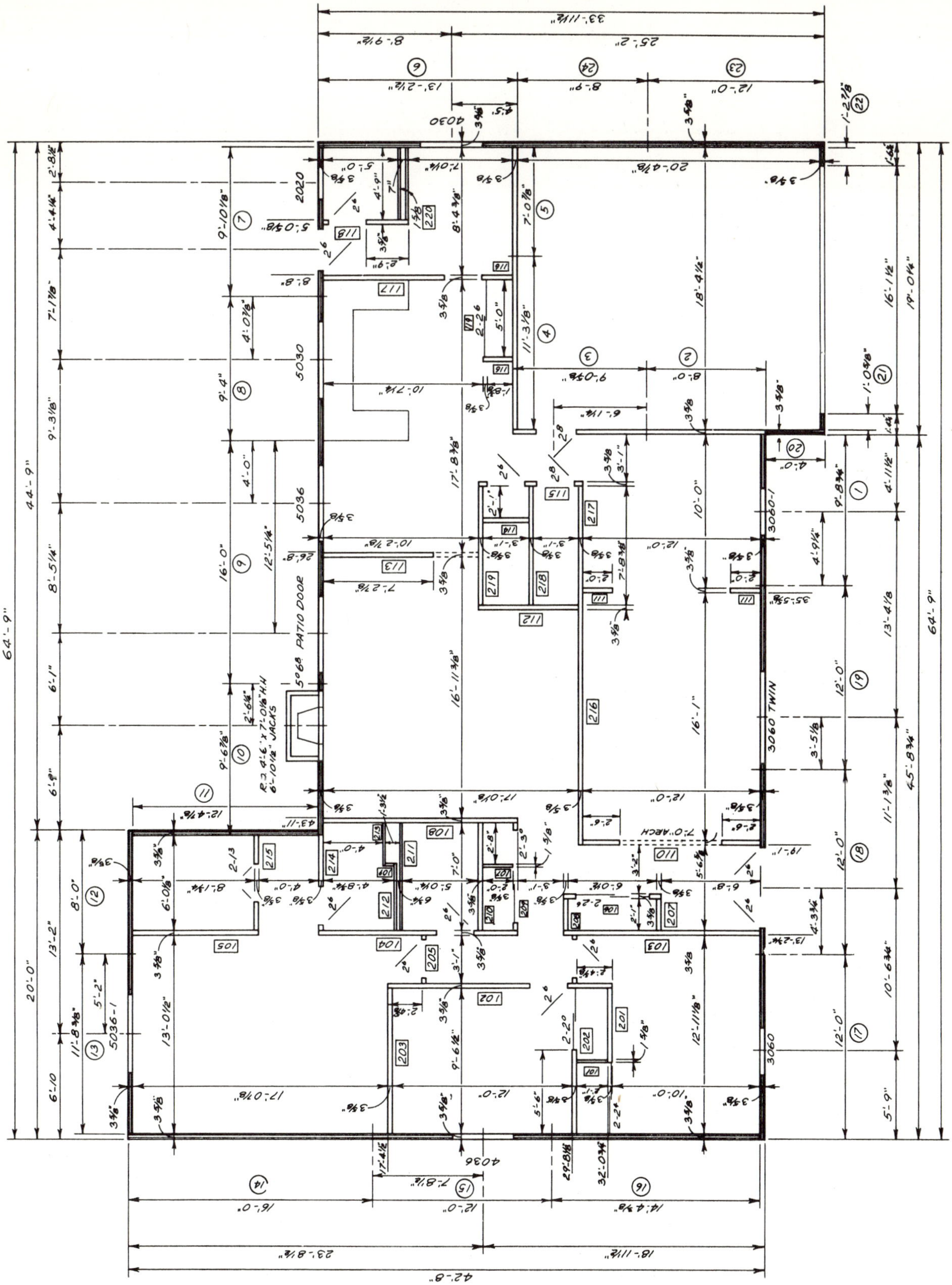
64'-9"
44'-9"
20'-0"
42'-8"
33'-11½"
25'-2"
PATIO DOOR
3060 TWIN
5030
5036
4030
4036
3060

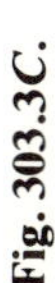

Fig. 303.3C.

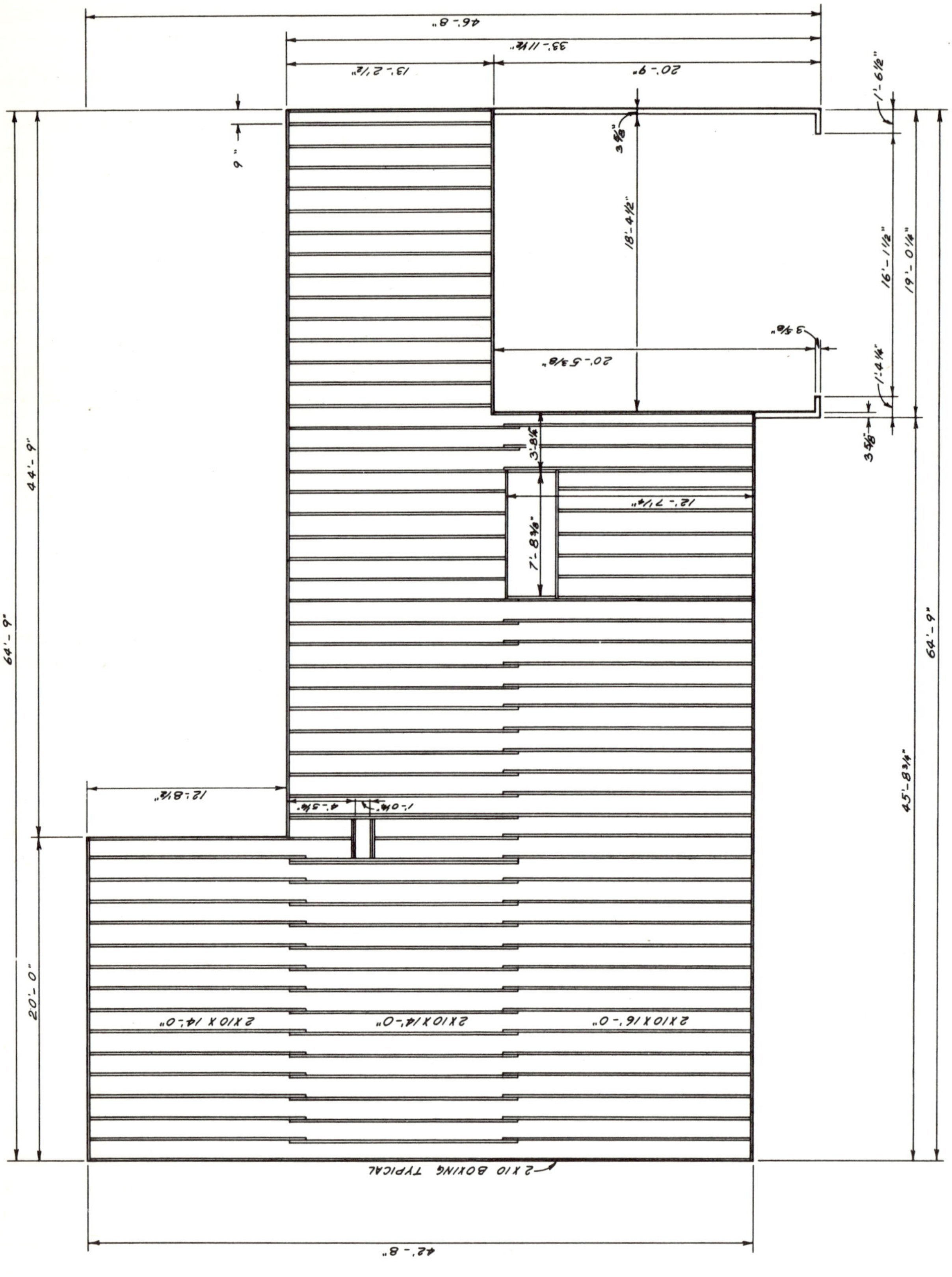

Fig. 303.3*D*.

*window. The dimension from the centerline of the window to the left end of Panel 1 is 4'-9-1/4". Referring to the detail of window 3060, the dimension from the centerline to the left edge of the rough framed opening is 1'-9 3/4". Subtracting 1'-9-3/4" from 4'-9 1/4" leaves 2'-11 1/2" (35-4). The designation 35-4 is entered in the column "Inches to Left Edge." It will be necessary to hold the sheathing 1/2" (0–4) at the right end of the panel so that Panel 20 can fit tightly against the corner. This is noted in the "Sheathing Hold" column.*

*Panel 2 is 8'-0" (96-0) long and will have a corner post at the left end. The corner post is noted in the column "Corner Post."* RE *is right end,* LE *is left end, and* BE *is both ends. Since this wall will have no sheathing, this is noted on the schedule.*

*Panel 3 is 9'-0 5/8" (108-5) long and will have a corner post at the right end. The centerline of the 2'-8" door is 6'-1 1/4" from the left end of the panel. Referring to the exterior door details, the dimension from the centerline to the left edge of a 2'-8" door is 1'-8 1/4. Subtracting 1'-8 1/4" from 6'-1 1/4" leaves 4'-5" (53-0). The figure 53-0 is entered on the column "Inches to the Left Edge," and the 2'-8" door is entered in the column "Window or Door." Since the panel is not sheathed, this is noted on the schedule.*

*Panel 4, because of the odd spacing of the floor joists (Fig. 303.3*D*) is 11'-3 5/8" (135-5) long and requires a 7" spacer at the left end. There are no window or door openings in the panel but it does require two partition leads. One partition lead is determined by the following method:*

| | | |
|---|---|---|
| *Inside width of garage* ............. | *18'-4 1/2"* | |
| *Less width of right upper corner room* ........... | *8'-4 3/8"* | |
| *Net* | *10'-0 1/8"* | |
| *From partition lead detail subtract (3 5/8" + 1 5/8"* ............ | *5' 1/4"* | |
| *Distance from partition lead to left end Panel 4 =* ............... | *9'-6 7/8"* | *(114-7)* |

*From the remaining partition lead is 5'-3 5/8" from the above partition lead or 4'-4 1/4" (51-2) from the left end of Panel 4. Enter 51-2 and 114-7 in column "Inches to Left Edge" under "Partition Block" heading. A line sketch under column marked "Type" indicates whether the center backer is 2 × 4, 2 × 6, or 2 × 8. Panel 4 has no sheathing, and this is noted on the schedule.*

*Panel 5 is 7'-0 7/8" long (84-7). There are no openings or partition leads. Panel 5 does not have sheathing, so this is noted on the schedule. Panel 6 is 13'-2 1/2" (158-4) long, has corner post at each end in addition to a 4030 window and one partition lead. The centerline of the 4030 window is 4'-5" from the left end of the panel. Referring to the detail of window 4030, the dimension from the centerline of the window to the left edge of the rough opening frame is 2'-3 3/4", therefore, the distance from the left end of the panel to the left edge of the rough opening frame is 2'-1 1/4" (25-2). The window number, 4030 is placed in the "Window or Door" column and the dimension 25-2 is placed in the "Inches to the Left Edge" column.*

*The centerline of the two partitions forming the pipe chase for the plumbing is 7' -0 1/4" plus 3 5/8" plus 3 1/2" or 7'-7 3/8" from the left edge of the panel. In this case the partition lead should be fabricated with a 2 × 8 backer instead of 2 × 4. This is noted in the "Type" column, under the "Partition Block" heading. Referring to the partition lead detail the dimension from the centerline to the left edge is 5 3/8", therefore the distance from the left end of the panel to the left edge of the partition lead is 7'-2" (86-0). The 2 × 8 backer will allow the partition lead to pick up both plumbing chase walls.*

*Panel 7 has a few features that have not been considered up to this point. The left end of the panel connects to the corner post of Panel 6. This means that the left end of Panel 7 must have a sheathing overlap of 4 1/8" from the width of the 2 × 4 wall plus the 1/2" sheathing. In order to maintain the 16" O.C. spacing of the studs in subsequent Panels 8, 9, and 10 it will be necessary to place 7 1/8" spacer against the stop to match the studs with the floor joist spacing. All dimensions for Panel 7 are to the stop and not the left edge. Panel 7 is 9'-10 1/8" (118-1) long, has a window 2020, a 2'-6" door and two partition leads. Window 2020 is 2'-8 1/2" from the left stop to the centerline. Referring to the detail of window 2020 the dimension from the centerline to the left edge of the rough opening frame is 1'-3 3/4", therefore, the distance from the left stop to the left side of the rough opening frame is 1'-4 3/4" (16-6).*

*The centerline of the 2'-6" door is 2'-8 1/2" plus 4'-4 1/4" or 7'-0 3/4" from the left stop. Referring to the detail of the 2'-6" door, the dimension to the left edge of the rough opening is 1'-7 1/4", therefore the distance from the left stop to the left edge of the door rough opening is 5'-5 1/2" (65-4). The partition leads must be nailed directly to each side of the door rough opening. This makes the dimension to the left end of the first partition lead 4'-10 5/8" (58-5) and the second 8'-8" (104-0). The partition leads will not centerline on the partition, but there will be backing for the sheet rock in each interior corner.*

*The balance of the exterior wall panels are laid out for fabrication in a similar manner. It is suggested that you continue on and lay out two or three more panels and check them against the panel schedule. Remember all dimensions are in feet and inches to the nearest eighth, and all dimensions given are from the left end of the panel or stop. Work all openings and partition leads with the location in the panel and the detail of the item.*

***Interior Partitions** There are many ways to divide the interior of the house into interior partition panels. The one we prefer is to number all partitions across the width of the house with one hundred numbers, such as 101, 102, 103, etc., and those running the length of the house with two hundred numbers such as 201, 202, 203, etc. The numbers are placed on the side of the partition that the layout man is standing facing the partition. This immediately orients the left end of the partition for the layout schedule, production, and erection. The crew that erects the components must also be familiar with how the panel is laid out and fabricated.*

*Looking at the house plan (Fig. 303.3C) and also the interior partition schedule (Fig. 303.3B), let's lay out a few partitions. Since the houses will use trussed rafters, the interior partitions are non-load bearing and therefore will have only a single top plate. This will increase the length of the common studs to 7'-10 1/4" which is noted at the top of the schedule.*

*Partition 101 is very simple. The length is 2'-1" (25-0) and is fabricated from 2 × 2's which shows up in the "Remark" column.*

*Partition 102 has one 2'-6" interior door, corner posts at both ends and two partition leads. Corner posts will be fabricated the same for the exterior wall panels. Although some fabricators may use other types of corner posts for interior partition leads, we prefer a single 2 × 6 flat for 2 × 4 walls and a 2 × 4 flat where 2 × 2 wall intersects. In some cases, it is advantageous to use the "U" partition block, especially in an area where a plumbing chase occurs. The corner posts are noted in the column "Corner Posts."*

*Two partition leads are required. Both will be 2 × 6 flat and both will be "down" when fabricated in the panel. Down means that the lead is flush with the down side of the top and bottom plates when fabricating the partition, and "up" means that lead is flush with the top side of the plates. Since a 2 × 6 is 5 1/2" wide and a 2 × 4 is 3 5/8" wide, there is a difference of 1 7/8" and 2" in width, respectively of intersecting partitions and the partition lead. This means that the partition lead will have one inch extending on one side and the balance on the other side of the intersecting partition. The first partition lead will be 2'-4 5/8" minus one inch or 2'-3 5/8" (27-5) from the left end of the panel, and the second partition lead will be the plate length 179-7 minus (2'-4 5/8" + 4 1/2") or 179-7 minus 33-1 which will be 146-6. Both dimensions are placed in the "Inches to Left Edge" column under "Partition Leads" heading.*

*Interior doors are located on the plan only if the location is critical. Generally speaking, the inside of the finished opening is four inches from the nearest rough wall. This will allow the finish trim to be placed around the door without having to cut or fit. The dimension from the rough opening to the nearest rough wall will be three inches. Using this criteria, the 2'-6" door will be located in Partition 102 as follows: From the plate length of 179-7 subtract (2'-4 5/8" + 3 5/8" + 2'-9 5/8") or 179-7 minus 68-7 which will result in 111-0. Place the 111-0 in the "Inches to Left Edge" column and 2'-6" in the "Door" column under the "Insert Location" heading. The list of dimensions subtracted above are obtained as follows: 2'-4 5/8" from plan, 3 5/8" thickness of intersecting wall, 3" is the distance from intersecting wall to rough door opening, 2'-9 5/8" is the rough door opening of 2'-8" plus the thickness of the 2 × 4 rough opening framing member. (See detail of interior door rough openings.)*

*Partition 103 is 159-6 long. This is obtained by adding (6'-8" + 3 5/8" + 6'-0 1/2" − 3 5/8") which equals 13'-3 3/4" (159-6). The partition has a corner post on the left end and two partition leads. Both partition leads are 2 × 6 flat. One is 159-6 minus (10'-0" + 2'-4 5/8" + 3 5/8" + 1" = 12'-9 1/4") or 6-1/2" (6-4) from the left end and is up. The other partition lead is (3 5/8" + 6'-0 1/2" − 1") or 6'-3 1/8" (75-1) from the left end and is down. This is noted under the "Partition Leads" heading.*

*Partition 104 is 158-5 long. This obtained by adding (3 5/8" + 2'-0" + 3 5/8" + 5'-0 1/4" + 6 3/4" + 3 5/8" = 13'-2 5/8"). The partition has a corner post at each end, three partition leads, and one 2'-6" door.*

*The 2'-6" door is (3 5/8" + 2'-0" + 3 5/8" + 3" + 2'-9 5/8" = 5'-7 7/8") from the right end or 158-5 minus 67-7 = 90-6 from the left end of the partition. The list of dimensions above are obtained as follows: 3 5/8", 2'-0" and 3 5/8" from the plan. 3" is the distance from intersecting wall to rough door opening, and 2'-9 5/8" is the rough door opening of 2'-8" plus the thickness of the 2 × 4 rough opening framing member.*

*A U-shaped partition lead with a 2 × 6 member will be used for the plumbing chase wall. Distance from the left end of the partition is (3 5/8" + 4'-8 3/4" + 3 3/8" − 4 3/8" = 4'-11 3/8") or 59-3. Dimensions 3 5/8" and 4'-8 3/4" are obtained from the plan; 3 3/8" is the distance to the center of the plumbing chase wall, and 4 3/8" is the distance from the center line to the left edge of the partition lead as obtained from the detail. The partition is placed down in the frame as is indicated in the "Remarks" column.*

*Location of the partition lead for Partition 205 is obtained as follows: (17'-0 7/8" + 2'-4 5/8" − 1" − 8'-1 3/4" − 3 5/8" − 4'-0" = 6'-11 1/8") or 83-1. The 2 × 6 flat is placed up in the frame. The dimensions are obtained as follows: 17'-0 7/8" and 2'-4 5/8" from the plan, 1" distance to left edge of partition lead, 8'-1 3/4", 3 5/8", and 4'-0" from the plan.*

*The last partition lead in Partition 104 is the one for Partition 210. This is located by adding (2'-9 5/8" + 2'-11 5/8") to the location of the 2'-6" door. The dimension of the partition lead to the left end of the panel is therefore 90-6 + 35-5 = 126-3 and is down in the panel. The 2'-9 5/8" is the dimension previously used to locate the door, and 2" is the distance to the intersecting wall (3") minus 1" to the left edge of the partition lead.*

*After going through the previous examples it is suggested a few more partitions be laid out and checked with the schedule. Partitions are more difficult to lay out than exterior wall panels because there are more dimensions to work with and therefore more chance for errors. Partitions are generally located by a series of room and wall thickness dimensions. Location of partition leads may require using dimensions from another area and then adding or subtracting as was the case for the partition lead in Partition 104 for intersecting Partition 205.*

*When the Interior Partition Schedule and the Exterior Wall Panel Schedule are completed, four copies of each should be made and sent to the shop. One copy will go to the man cutting the plates, one to the man who heads up the framing operation, one to the man who heads up the sheathing operation, and one to the man on the Sub-Assembly Machine. One print of all subassemblies such as windows and doors should go to the man in charge of the Panel-Rite Sub-Assembly Machine, one to the man on the Panel-Rite Component Spike Driver and one to the man on the saw for cutting headers. The number of jack studs, corner posts, and partition leads should be marked on the detail sheet and a copy given to the man on the Panel-Rite Component Spike Driver. It is not necessary to give the shop the exact number of pre-cut studs or number of pieces of sheathing. These items are standard on every house and can be brought to the fabrication area in bunk lots.*

303.4 **Computer Systems.** There are several of these now on the market and it is necessary to prepunch the tape in the office to instruct the framing machine on the location of the studs, etc.

303.5 **Customer Check.** In custom component operations, it is advisable to have a representative of the customer check all shop drawings and instructions for accuracy. This method is useful in reducing later claims and controversy.

304 **Layout.** In this operation a skilled individual lays out (and cuts if not done separately) the top and bottom plates for all panels. In this work the layout man uses whatever information is furnished by office engineering and prepares the plates to be placed in the jig.

Some systems lay out the plates in detail showing the location of each stud, corner post, partition junction post, window, etc. Others rely on the jig or wall machine to locate the common studs.

If plates are laid out and stacked in the order (or reverse order) in which they are to be erected, the panels will be on the truck in the proper order.

Layout tables usually incorporate permanently attached measuring devices and means for displaying plans and schedules. They may also be equipped with cutoff saws. Where a regular floor plan is used, it is advantageous to clip it to the center pivoted piece of plywood so that the layout man is always "looking at the outside of wall." Two layout tables are shown in Fig. 304*A* & *B*.

A device is available for use in adding

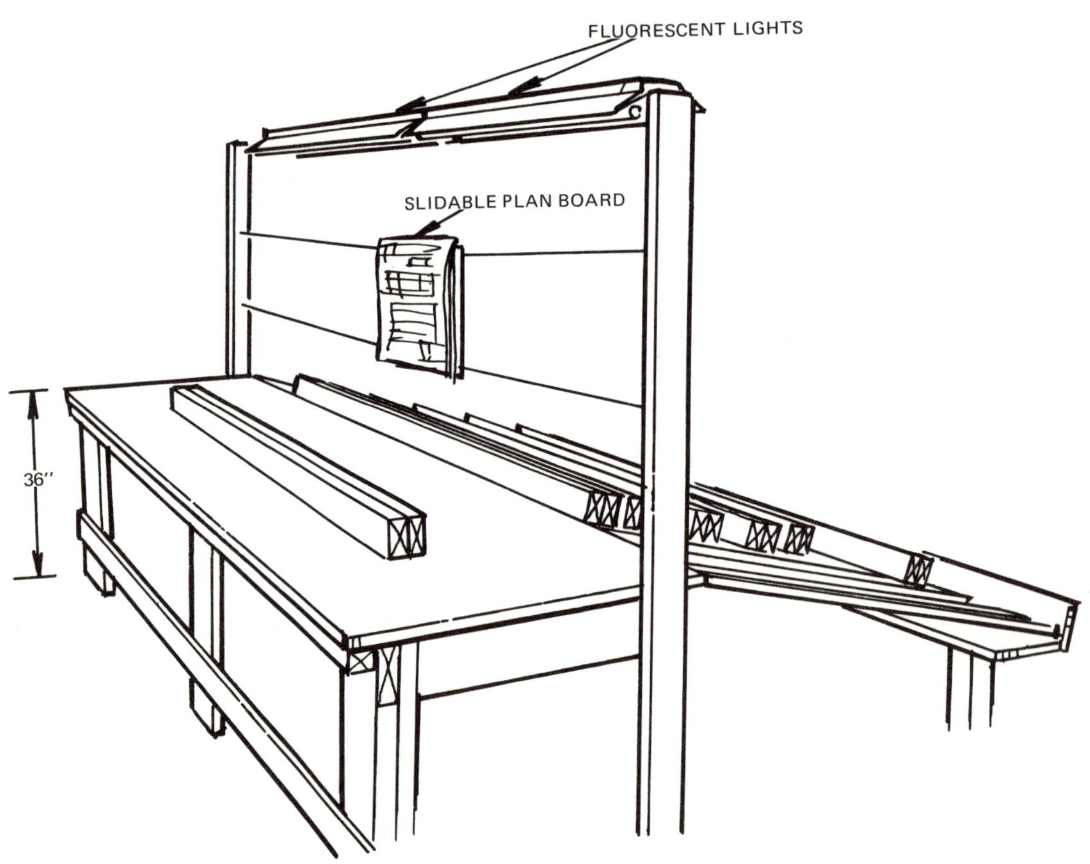


**Fig. 304*A*.**
Layout table incorporating a smooth work surface and rack for storage of plates in the desired order.
*(After Pease)*

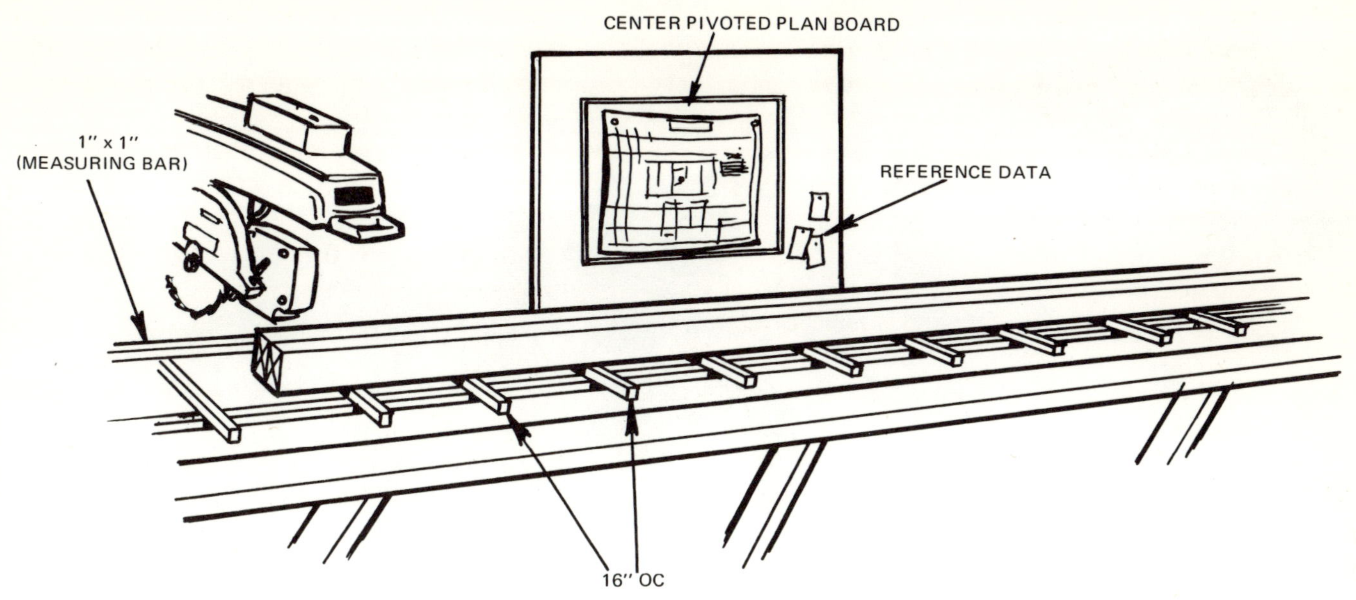


**Fig. 304*B*.**
Layout table incorporating cut off saw, steel tape and 16" O.C. guides.

*(Cardinal Industries)*

and subtracting feet, inches and fractions that has been found desirable in layout work in both plant and office. It is called the Addometer (Appendix). (See Fig. 304*C*.)

304.1 **Repetitive Layouts.** Where buildings are repeated frequently, layouts may be placed on 1" × 2" templates which are placed in the jig. These are either dadoed for each stud or marked. When placed in the jig one way, the building is regular plan; the opposite way, reverse plan. An interesting tape–template is shown in Fig. 304.1

305 **Subcomponent Fabrication.** This includes the fabrication of window and door headers; corner posts; junction posts; jamb posts; partition ladders; and door and window bucks. The area set aside for this operation should be close to or on a line with cutting operations and initial wall and partition assembly operations. Drawings of various subcomponents are shown in Fig. 305.

305.1 **Equipment.** In smaller operations, a simple wooden jig with 16d air nailer may be adequate. Where volume exceeds 3–4 homes per day, consideration should be given to the equipment in Fig. 305.1*A*.

306 **Assembly.** This operation consists of spiking studs to plates and installing subcomponents in a suitable jig. Panels may not be completely squared in this operation. The equipment used to assemble wall panels varies from a simple wooden jig with a 20 oz. carpenter's hammer to completely automated, tape-operated machines.

The method selected should depend on many factors including; the number of units produced per day, the wage rates and labor productivity, cost of equipment, current interest rates, variety of production (wall heights, various materials, standard plans, or custom components), expected growth of the business.

It should be kept in mind that wall panel fabrication is often the most dramatic part of the operation and, therefore, sometimes attracts a disproportionate investment, often leaving important areas like materials handling without adequate cost control.

In the following material we shall present these methods in order of increasing investment.

Almost all of the systems can produce panels full length (up to 40') or the convenient handling size of 12 feet or less. Some manufacturers make full length walls and then cut or disconnect them into easily handled lengths.

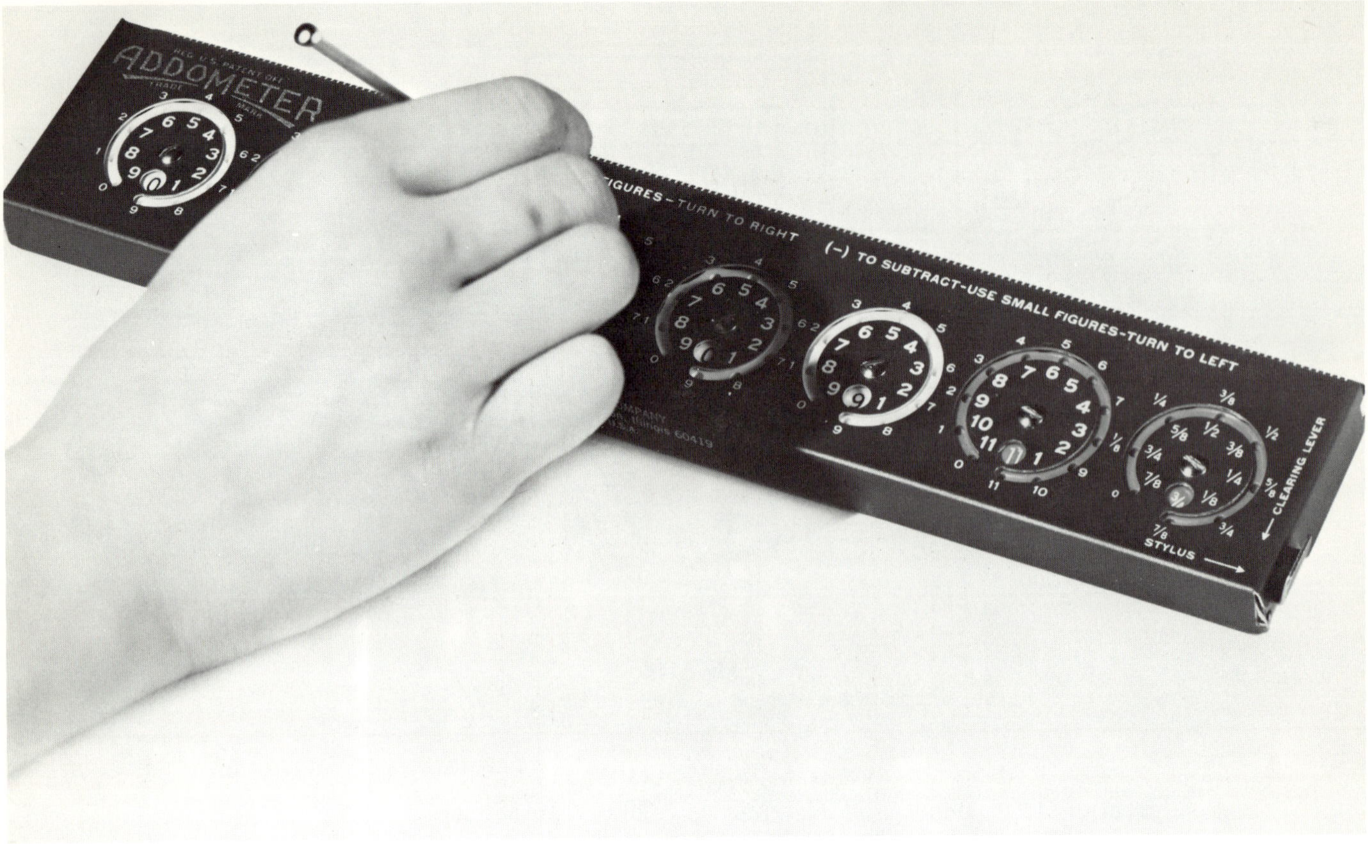

**Fig. 304*C*.**
Device for adding and subtracting feet, inches and fractions.

*(Addometer)*

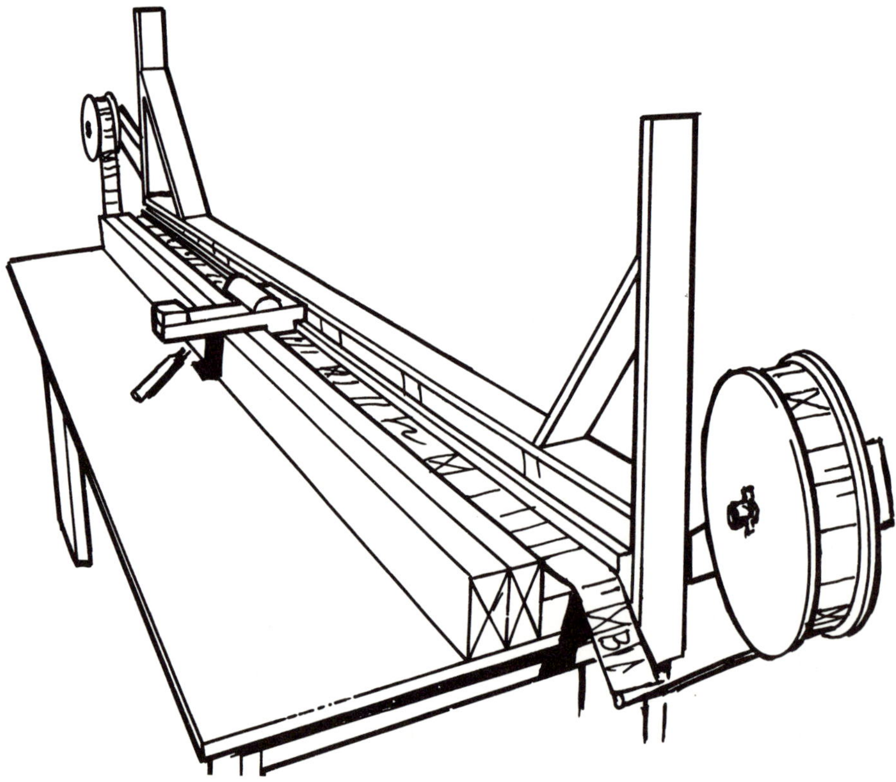

**Fig. 304.1.**
Rolls of lawn chair webbing store layouts in minimum space for a custom component manufacturer. Rollers at each end provide tension and transfer gauge transfers marks to plates.

*(Components, Inc.)*

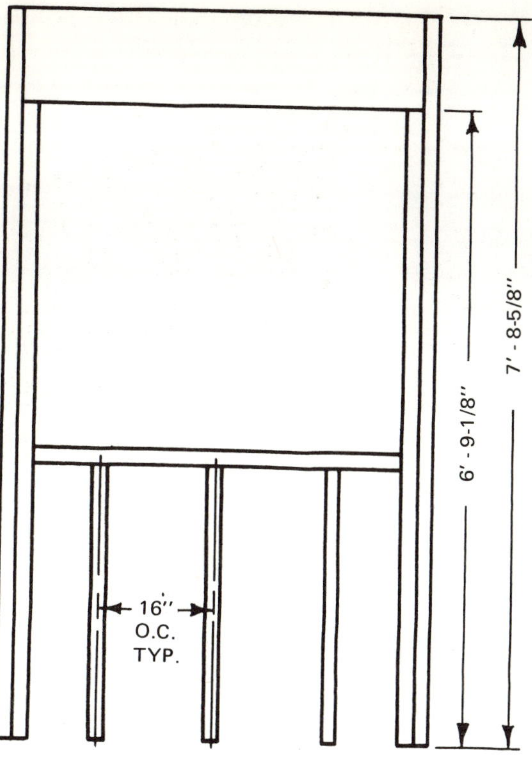


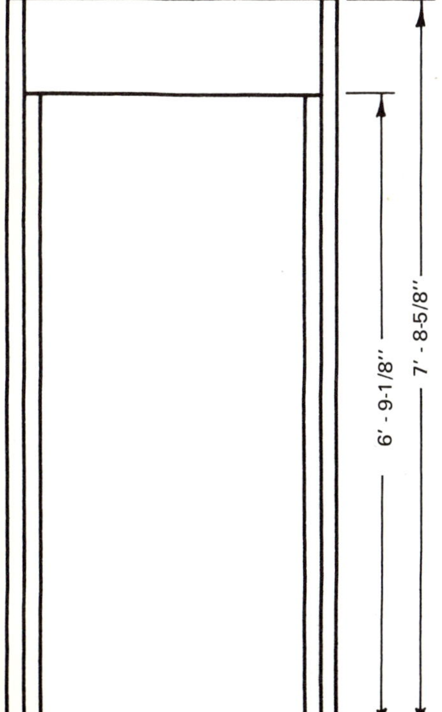


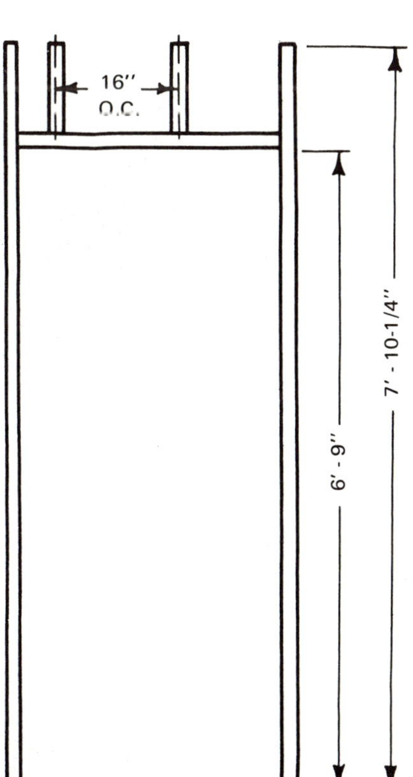


**Fig. 305.**
Various sub-components.

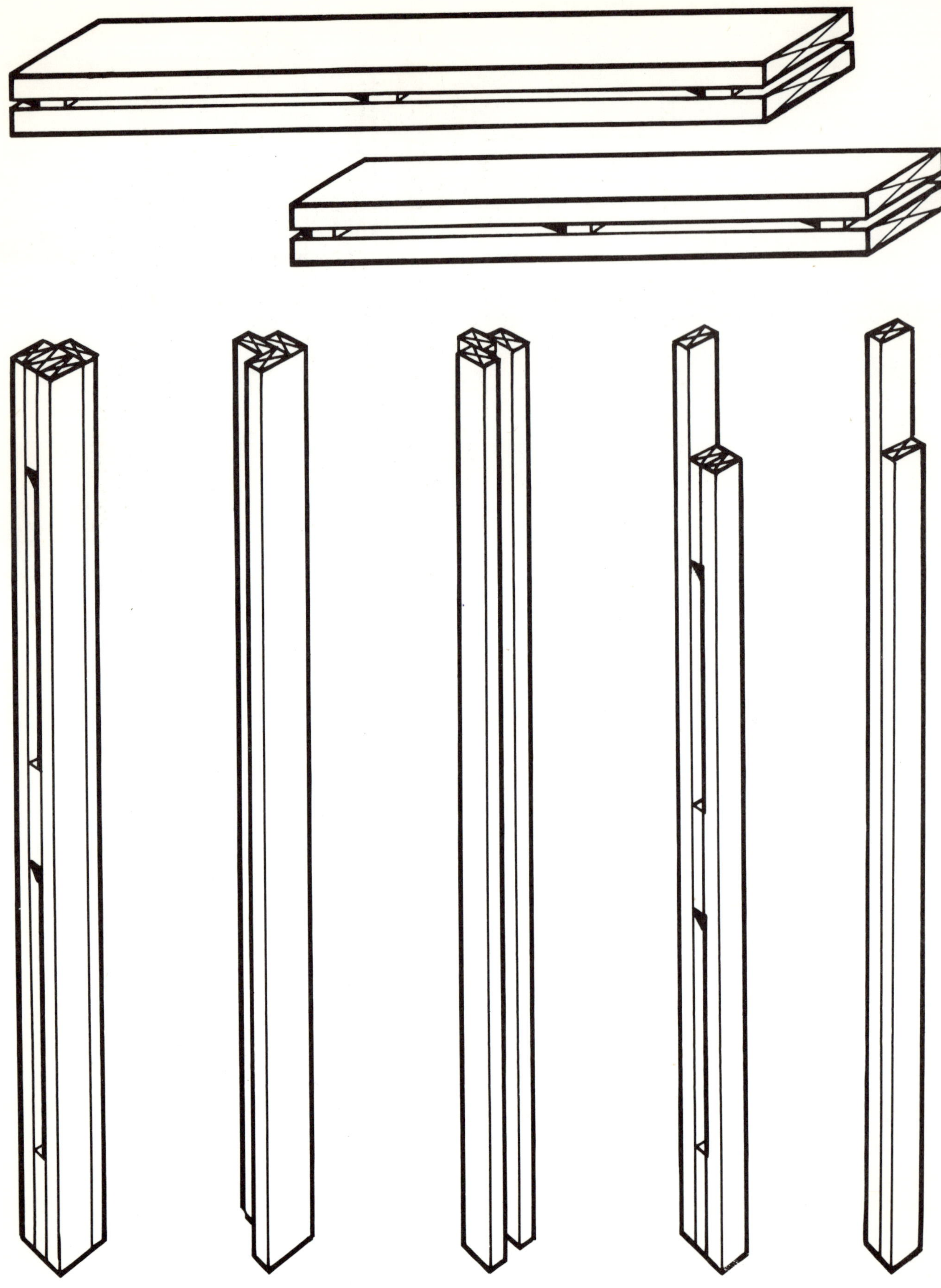

**Fig. 305.**
Various sub-components.

**Fig. 305.1*A*.**
Spike Driver, Model II.

*(Triad)*

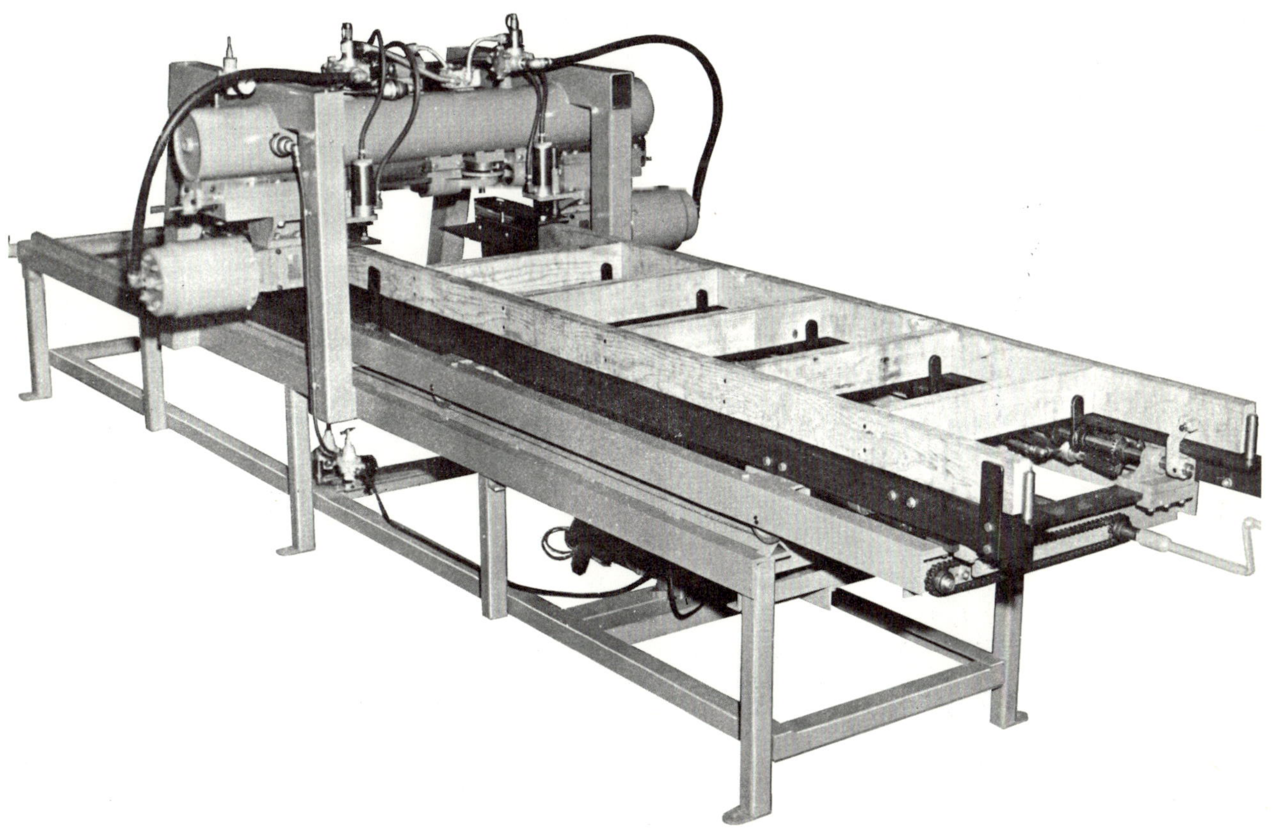

**Fig. 305.1*B*.**
Ladder Machine.

*(Triad)*

**Fig. 305.1*C*.**
Sub-Component Machine.

*(Douglas)*

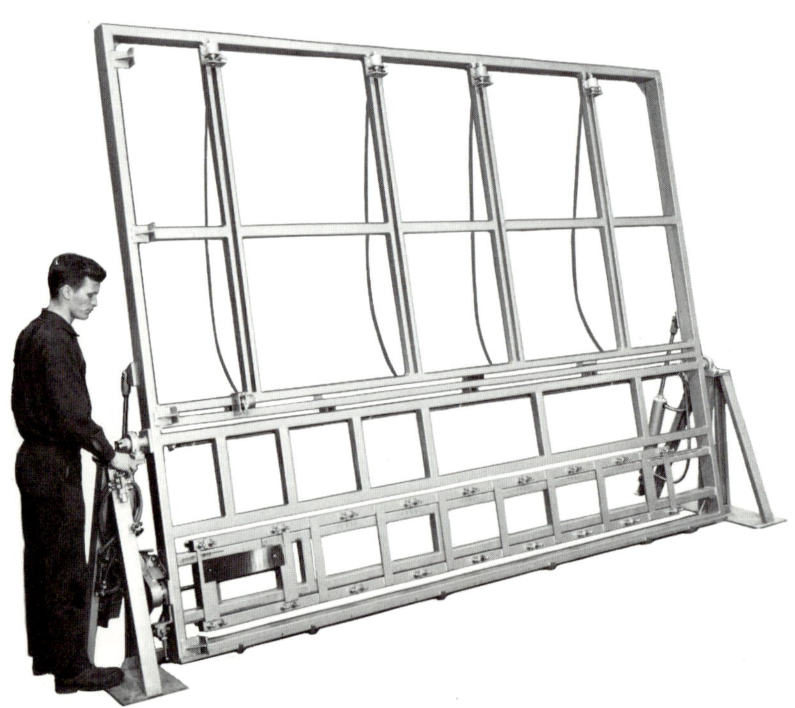

**Fig. 305.1*D*.**
Subcomponent jig rotates horizontal or vertical position, air clamps.

*(Hydro-Air)*

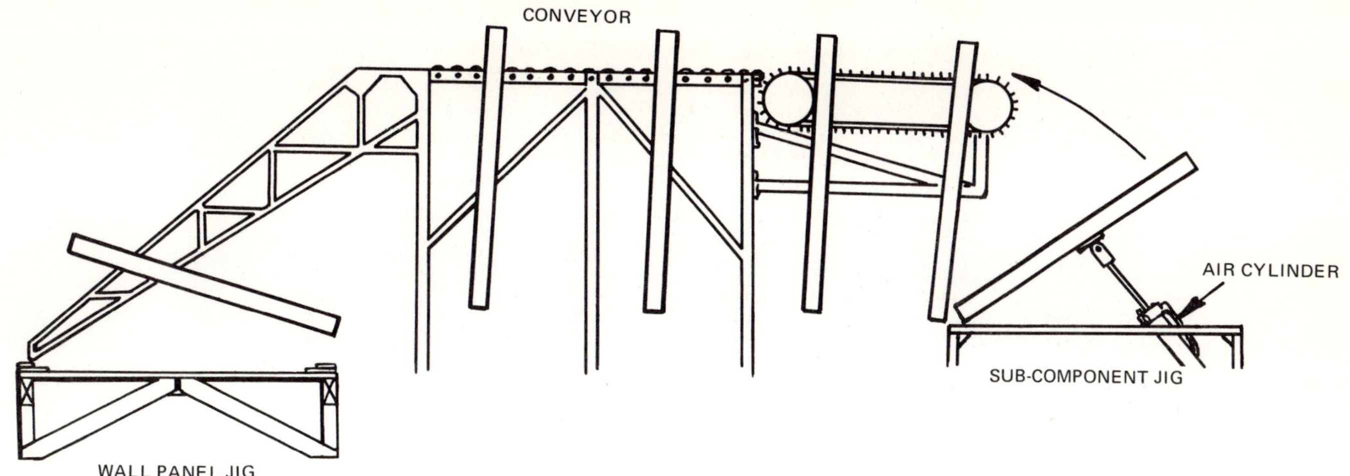


**Fig. 305.1*E*.**
Method of moving and storing subcomponents. Air cylinder stands completed door and window buck where it is engaged by dogs on motorized belt and then to level conveyor surface. As needed, bucks are slid down the incline onto the jig. This is used in a plant with women manning the wall panel jig.

*(Presidential Homes)*

306.1 **Wood Jig.** A simple wood jig, with steel fittings, can be completely adequate for many operations. Equipped with steel, hardwood, or roller bearing surfaces the completed framework can easily be slid onto the next station, although quite often all operations are completed at this one station.

Jigs should be heavily constructed so as not to have any "bounce" when used with hand or power nailer. Some jigs incorporate a slot in the surface to accommodate 1″ × 2″ templates. Clamping or squaring devices are not required at this station unless the panel is to be completed without moving.

Height of jigs from the floor to the underside of the panel varies from 24″ to 30″. The lower jigs are used to facilitate reaching to the center of the panel. However, one manufacturer uses a jig only 16″ high because his work arrangement requires assemblers to step on and off the jig. Fig. 306.1*A* shows two basic designs for low cost wooden jigs.

306.2 **Advanced Steel and Wood Jigs.** Figs. 306.2*A* through 306.2*D* show a number of variations on user built jigs and equipment.

306.7 **Commercially Available Machinery.** Equipment shown in the following photographs is commercially available with many options. Consult manufacturer's literature for details.

307 **Insulation.** The most common insulation system is the use of reverse flange blanket type insulation applied from the outside face of the studs with vapor barrier facing inside before the application of sheathing and/or siding. Flange may be either face stapled or inset stapled to insure that the vapor barrier is close to the warm side of the wall. (See Fig. 307.)

In modular construction, the interior wall board is frequently jig-applied before installation of the panel on the modular platform. In this case, regular (not reverse flange) insulation can be jig-applied before the application of interior wallboard.

Where wallboard incorporates the vapor barrier or where large sheet plastic film vapor barrier is used, plain blanket insulation (not paper encased) may be installed.

308 **Sheathing and Squaring.** In this operation, the panel is squared, corner brace installed (if required), sheathing (or siding if single construction) installed, openings cut out, and sheathing nailed.

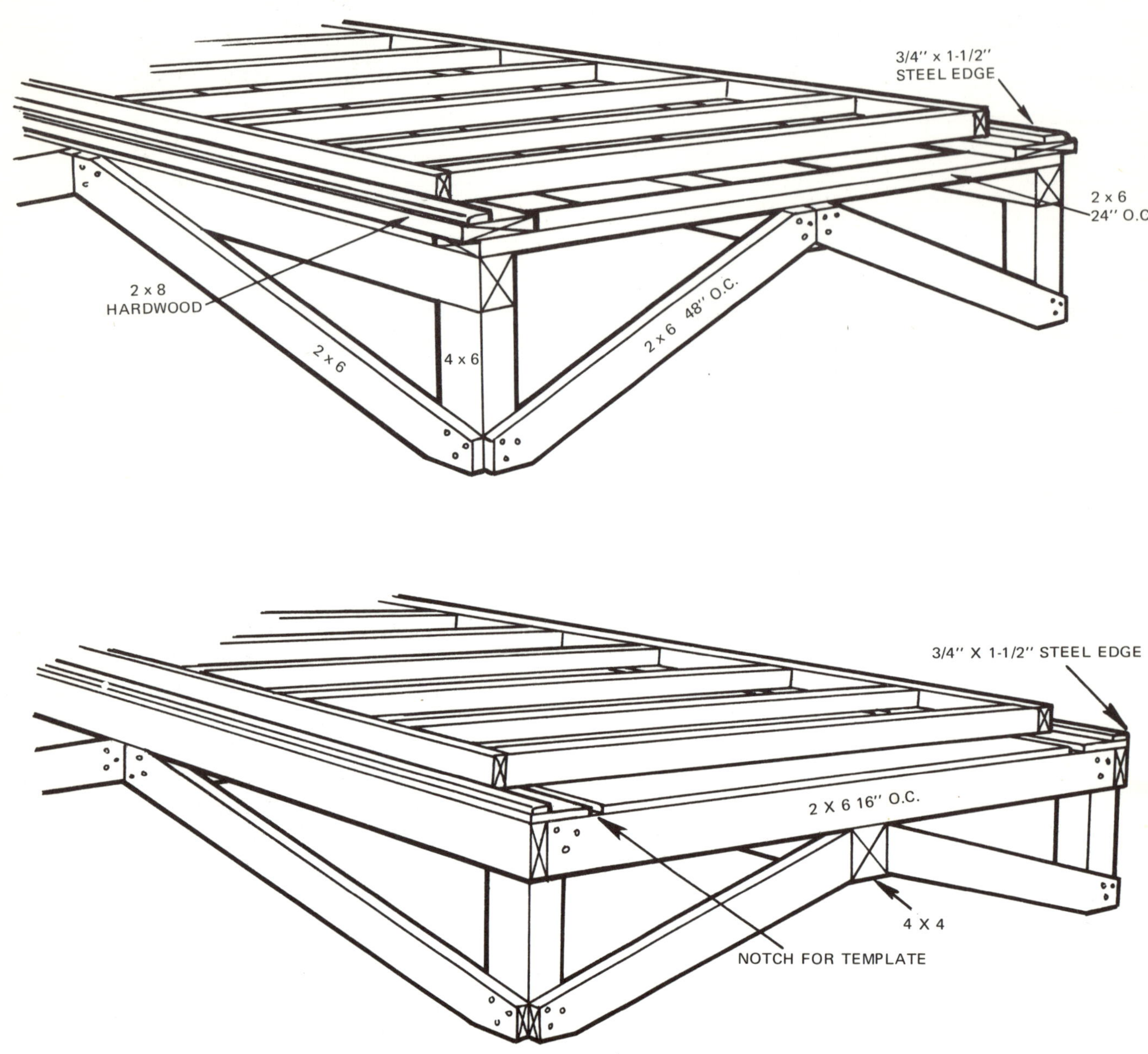


**Fig. 306.1*A*.**

Low cost wooden jigs. Upper drawing shows open work jig which allows chips to fall through to the floor.
Lower drawing shows plywood capped jig which provides solid surface for nailing sheathing or finish materials and groove for template.

**Fig. 306.1*B*.**
A plywood topped jig being used with 16d nailers. Note operators offset for safety.
*(Senco Products, Inc.)*

**Fig. 306.2*A*.**
Note track for air lines.
*(Hodgson Homes; Photo by Fastener Corporation)*

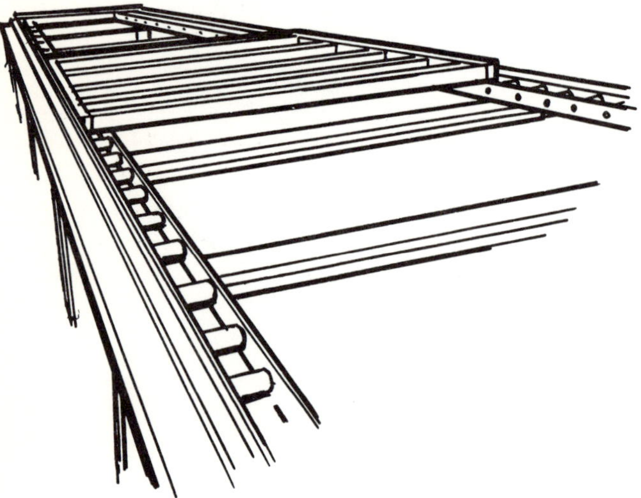

**Fig. 306.2*B***
Steel jig with rollers.
*(Richmond Homes)*

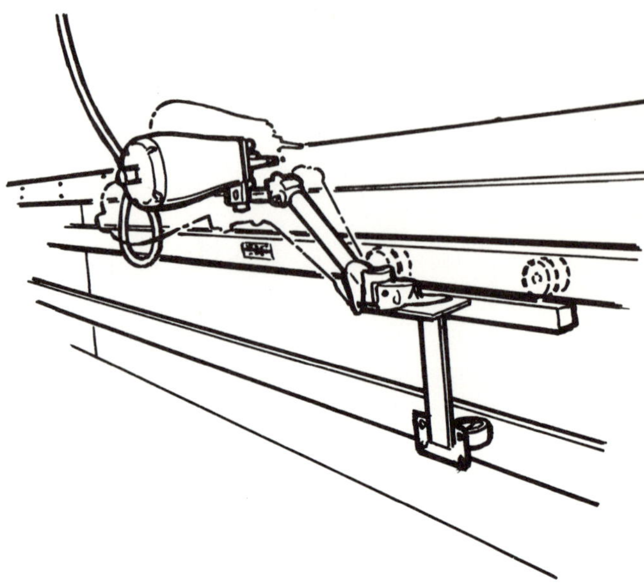

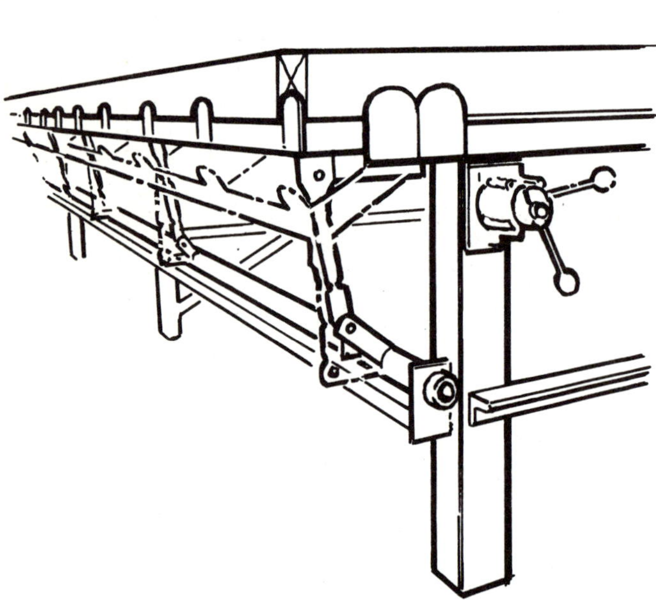

**Fig. 306.2*C*.**
Air operated clamping device.
*(Manufactured Homes)*

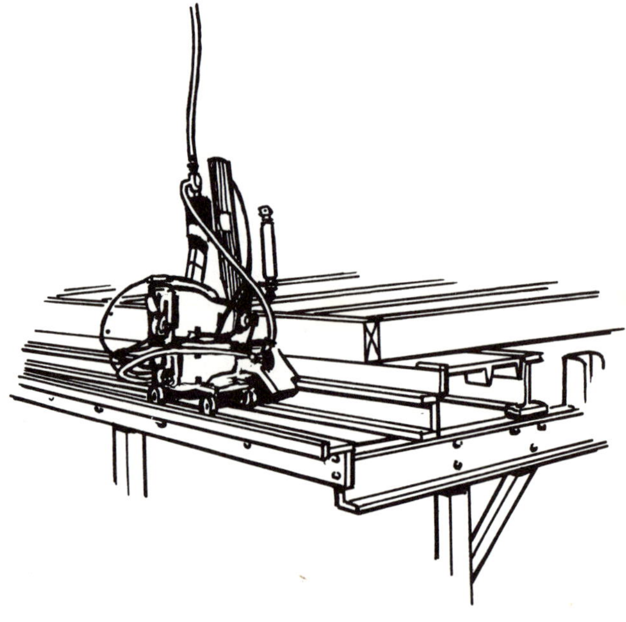

**Fig. 306.2*D*.**
Track mounted nailing machines.
*(Components, Inc. & Presidential Homes)*

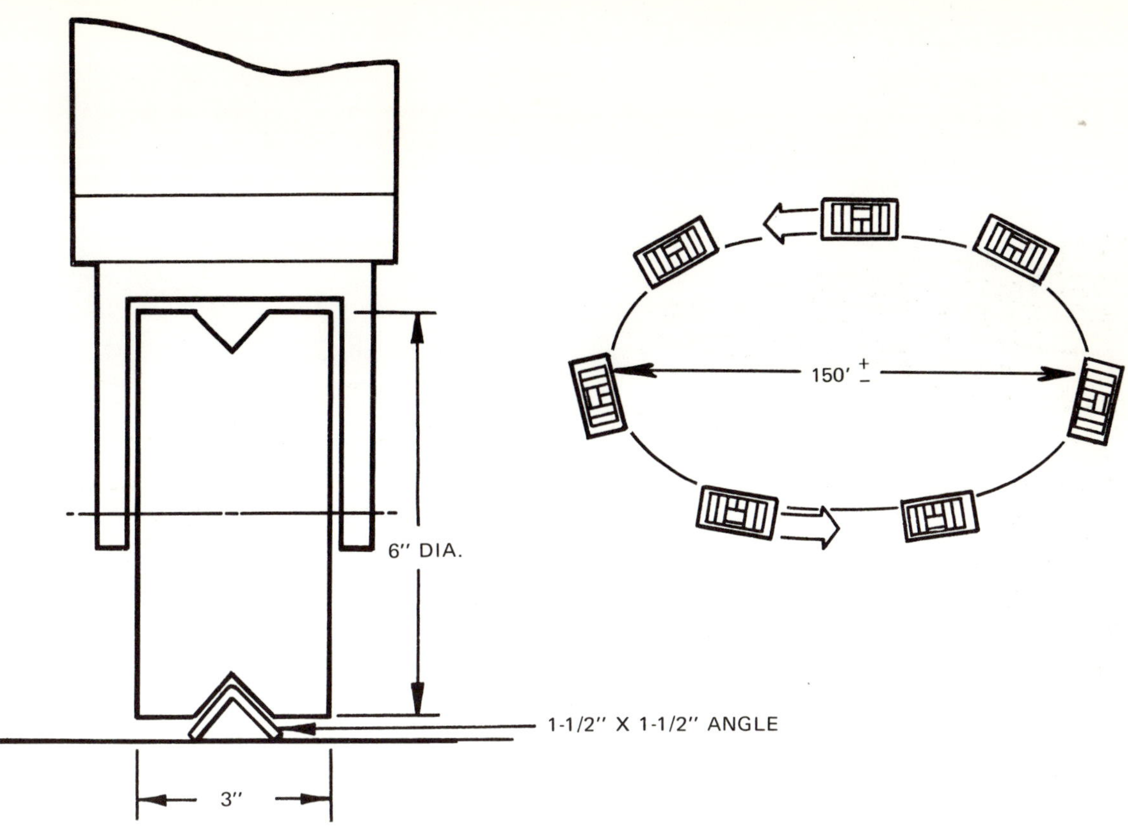


**Fig. 306.3.**
Straight line layout is best for jig stations but shape of buildings may require track mounted jigs moving past stations. Casters move on "V" shaped track.

**Fig. 306.7A.**
Jig with adjustable wall height; air operated "flippers" position studs and when nailing is complete, wall is automatically unloaded by chain drive.

*(Triad)*

**Fig. 306.7*B*.**

Nailing machine can be used with user designed jig or jig shown in 306.7*A*. Adjustable wall height 4′-9″ to 9′-0″. Automatically clamps and nails studs with special "J" nails.

*(Triad)*

**Fig. 306.7*C*.**

Machine features ability to add additional components as firm's growth requires. Three carriages shown nail studs, route out and staple sheathing.

*(Douglas)*

**Fig. 306.7*D*.**
Framing machine. Automatically clamps and nails. Plate rollers provide easy movement on powered chain to next position.

*(Panel-Rite) (Hydro Air)*

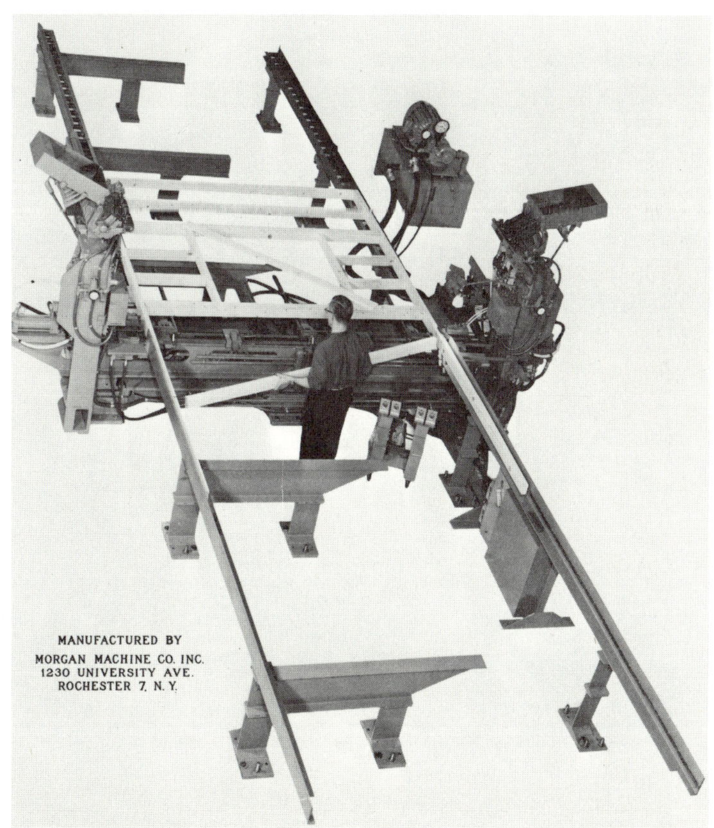


**Fig. 306.7*E*.**
Frame nailer. Automatically positions and nails studs, openings, junction posts, etc. with aid of numercial data provided by office engineering. Any length or width to nine feet.

*(Morgan)*

**Fig. 306.7*F*.**
Tape controlled framing machine automatically locates and nails studs and sub-components. Three feet to fourteen feet wall height, any length.

*(General Construction Automation)*

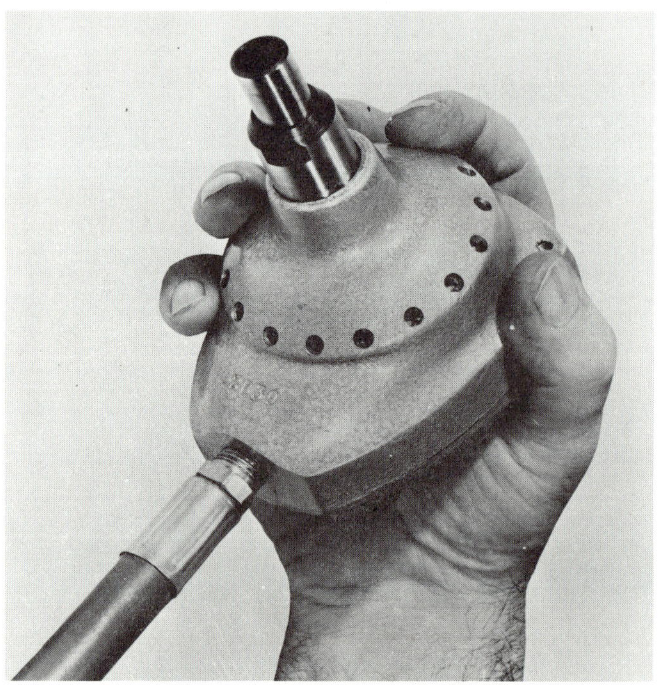

**Fig. 306.7*G*.**
Hand held air operated 16d nailer uses regular nails. Safe. Nails are fed by hand.

*(Aerosmith)*

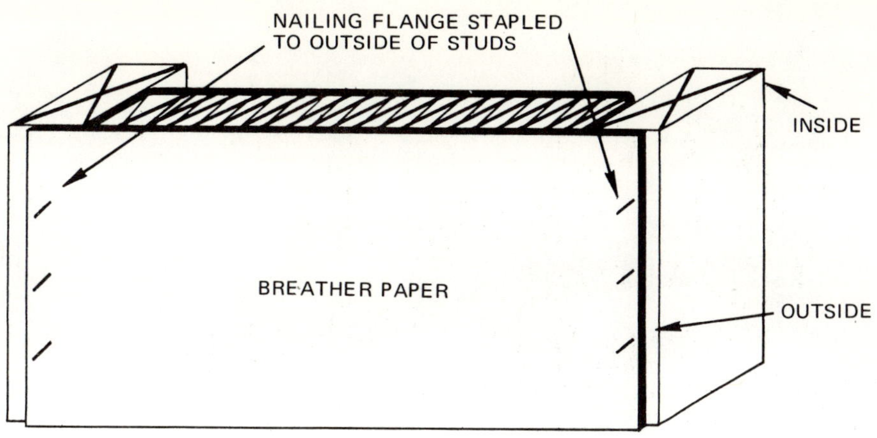


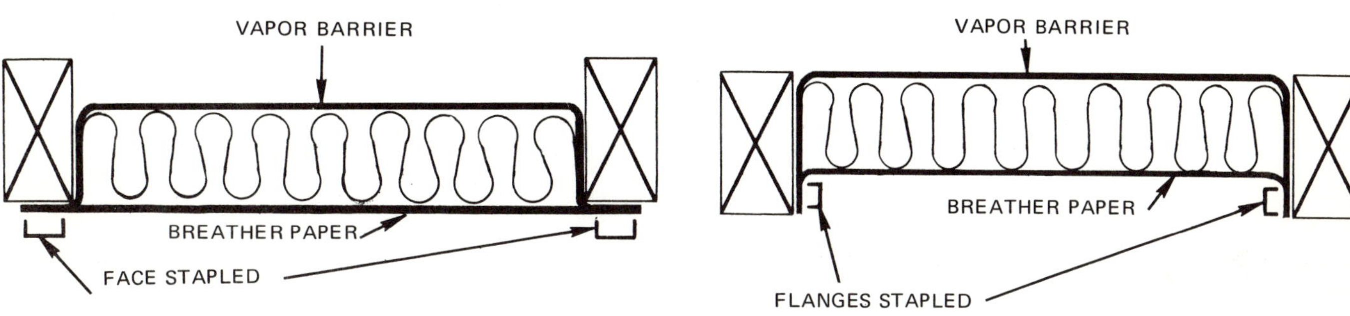


**Fig. 307.**
Reverse flange insulation.

**308.1 Squaring.** This is done in a number of ways.

**a.** Using the first sheet of sheathing as a squaring device. This may not be accurate enough for some operations, particularly modular.

**b.** Using a tape measure to check the diagonals of the panel.

**c.** Clamping and squaring devices built into the jig at this point. This is the most common method.

**308.2 Corner Brace.** The use of heavier weight 1/2″ insulation sheathing has generally made this unnecessary. In those areas where corner braces are still required, sometimes a sheet of 1/2″ plywood installed at the corner in lieu of the fibre sheathing will suffice. When a 1 × 4 brace must be applied a dado head on a hand power saw or router with a template can be used with several passes. Alternatively, the corner brace is marked on the studs and a power saw kerfs the stud four or five times. The operation is completed with the ripping claws on a hammer.

**308.3 Sheathing Application.** Sheathing is laid on the panel, usually covering it completely, disregarding openings. Fibre sheathing saved out of openings is not generally worth the labor to save it. Sometimes the sheathing is only partially cut out around large sliding door openings, so the builder may leave this on to keep the building "weathered in." Prior to cutting openings, the sheathing is only tacked at the edges so as not to interfere with the router.

**308.4 Sheathing Material.** Sheathing is usually purchased in the 4′ × 8′ size, but several manufacturers have it available in the 8′ × 12′ size. This minimizes joint nailing.

**308.5 Sheathing Routing.** Sheathing is cut with a router similar to Fig. 308.2. A user built variation of this has only one handle and requires only one man to operate. The router must be heavier to provide stability.

**308.6 Sheathing Nailing or Stapling.** Once the openings are cut out, the panel moves to an area for nailing or stapling on the

**Fig. 308.5.**
Two man router for cutting openings.
*(Automated Construction Equipment)*

sheathing. This is usually done mechanically either with an individual stapler/nailer or with gang-operated stapling machines of the type shown in Fig. 308.3A and B.

309 **Exterior Finish.** Exterior finishes frequently used are hardboard, plywood, metal and wood horizontal siding; hardboard, and plywood in 4′ wide vertical panels and wood shakes, either individually or in sections. Most exterior materials are either pre-primed or pre-finished.

In low cost construction, the sheathing is eliminated and the exterior panels of hardboard or plywood perform a double function.

309.1 **Exposure Gauges** for horizontal siding may be of the steel or wood. (See Fig. 309.1.)

309.2 **Guidlines for Nailing.** Since most exterior finish is hand nailed (either with a carpenter's hammer or a hand held pneumatic stapler) some guide must be provided for the nailing operation. This can be done with a chalk-line, marking a straightedge or a shadow light as shown in Fig. 309.2. The light shown must be modified for the purpose but the manufacturer plans to soon have a light planned for use by industrialized building manufacturers.

310 **Interior Finish.** Wall and partition panels must be stood vertically or flipped over to permit interior finish work. Fig. 310*A* shows standing wall panels to permit work on both interior and exterior finish. See Chapter VIII for details on interior finish.

311 **Storage.** While awaiting loading, panels can be stored on pallets, in piles on casters, standing in racks or hung on conveyors.

311.1 **Tongs.** To lift individual panels out of jigs various "tongs" have been developed. Two of these are shown in Fig. 311.1*A* and *B*.

**Fig. 308.6*A*.**
Automatic sheathing stapler. Machines of this type are usually set so as not to fire over openings and to offset 3″ to double nail at panel ends and joints.

*(Panel-Rite, Hydro-Air)*

**Fig. 308.6*B*.**
Panel Staper by Triad is companion to stud nailer shown in Fig. 306.7*B* can be used on user's table. Also available with stud-nailing equipment.

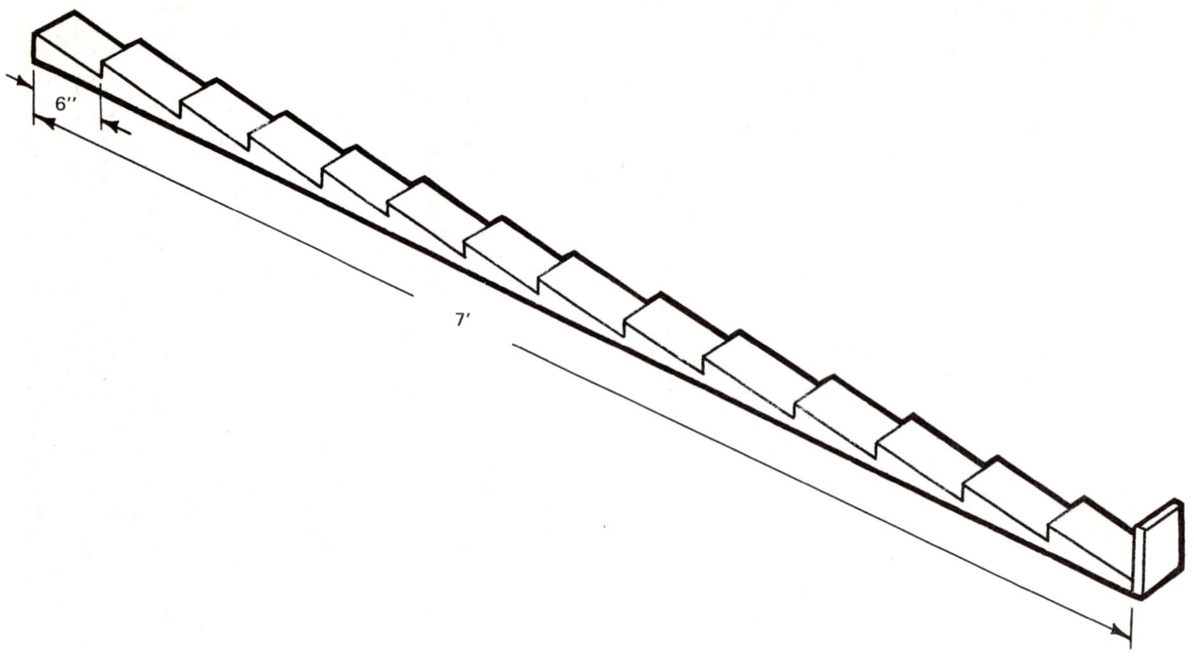


**Fig. 309.1.**
Exposure gauge for horizontal siding may be of metal or wood.

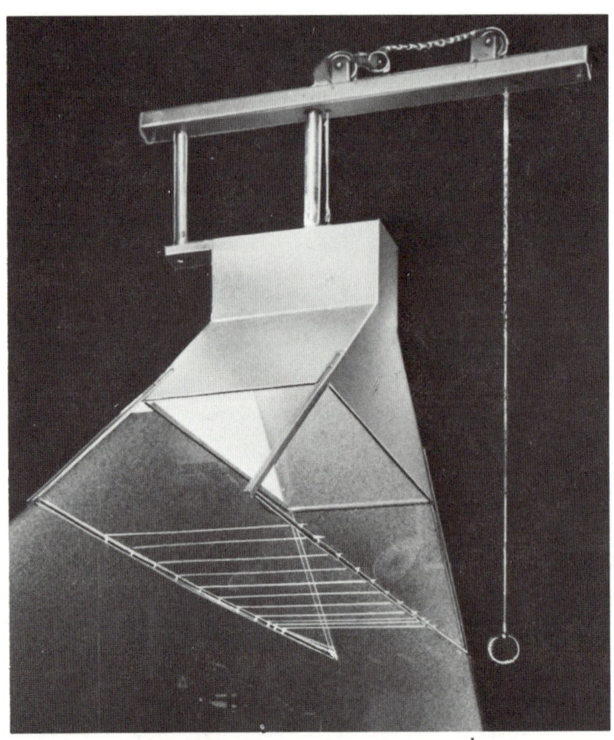

**Fig. 309.2.**
Shadow light for nailing guide lines. Also may be used for siding exposure gauge.

*(Carter Products Co., Inc.)*

**Fig. 310.**
Wall panels in standing position for interior and exterior finish work.

*(Wausau Homes)*

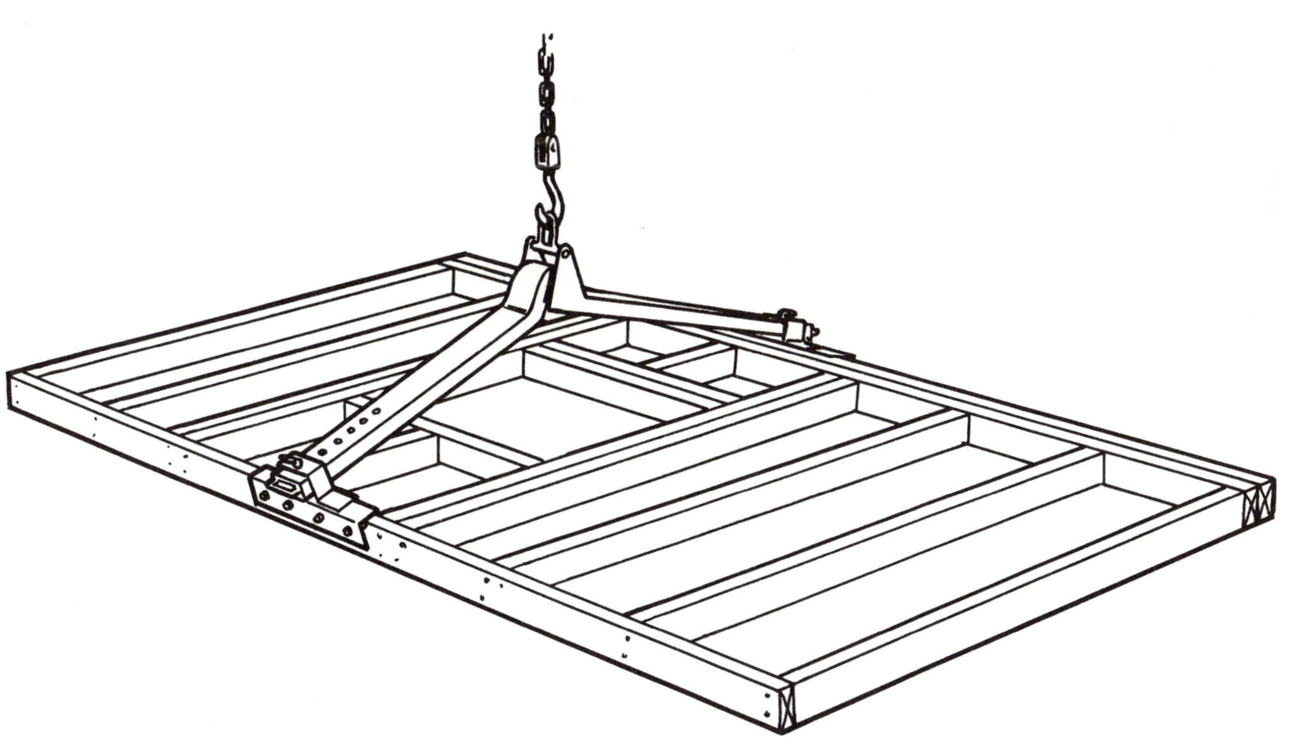

**Fig. 311.1*A*.**
Tongs for lifting wall panels.

*(After Panel-Rite, Hydro-Air)*

**Fig. 311.1*B*.**
User built tongs.

*(Church & Church) (Reschke Photo)*

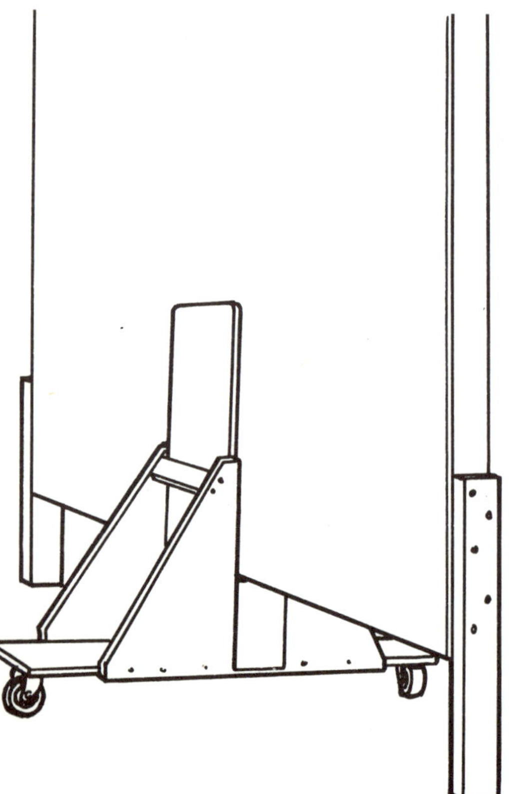

**Fig. 311.2.**
Dolly for wall panels destined for modular installation 2 × 4 "leg" is tacked on end of panel for stability. This panel is elevated to accommodate protruding plumbing stack.

*(After Wausau Homes)*

**311.2 Modular Panels.** For storing wall panels in a vertical position so that they take up a minimum amount of floor space and may be moved readily for eventual installation on modular units, a dolly, Fig. 311.2, has proved useful.

**311.3 Flat Panels.** For storing stacks of flat panels, caster assemblies as shown in Fig. 311.3 are valuable. They permit stacks of panels to be moved about the storage area pending loading.

**311.4 Vertical Storage.** For storing stacks of vertical panels, a rack like that shown in Fig. 311.4 is desirable.

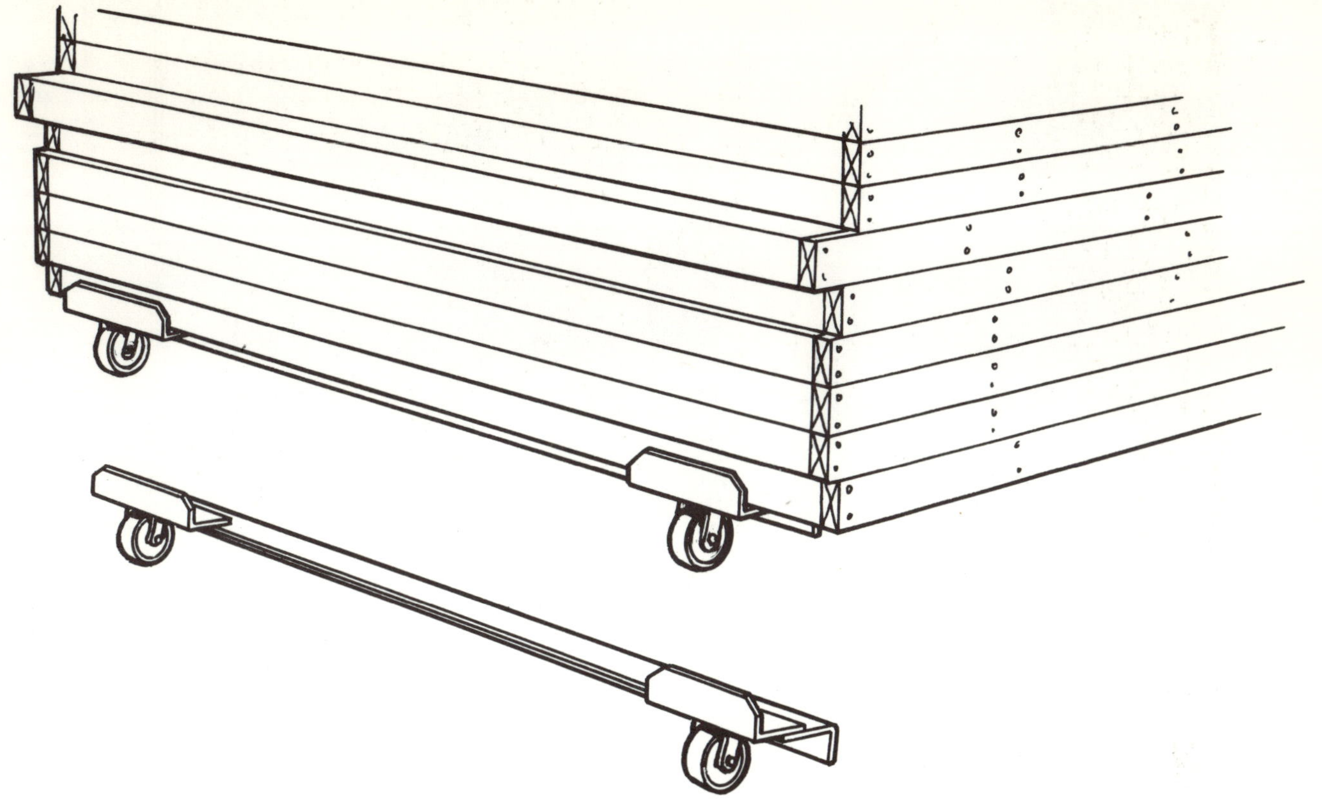

**Fig. 311.3.**
Caster assemblies for storing stacks of flat panels.

*(After Pease)*

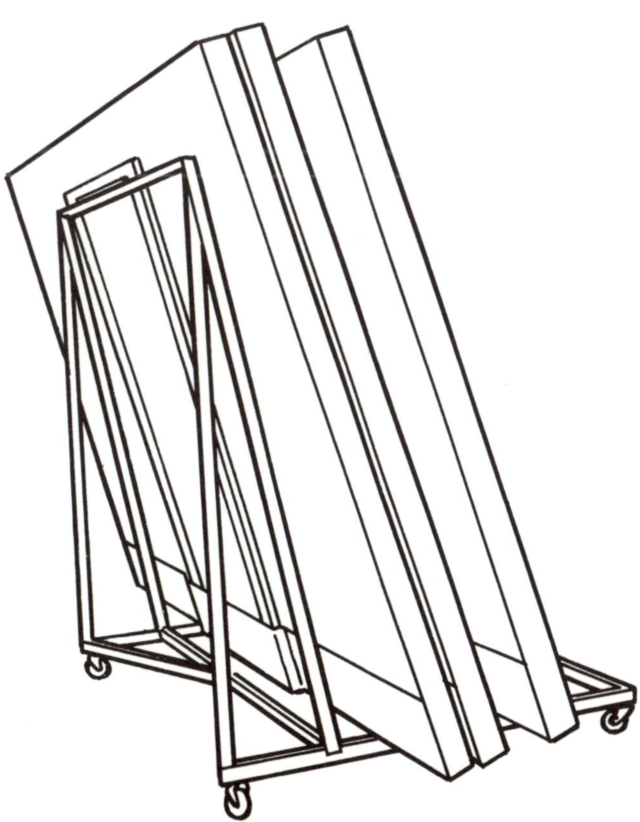

**Fig. 311.4**
Steel rack with casters for storing vertical wall panels.
*(After Imperial Homes)*

# CHAPTER IV

## Trusses: Floor and Roof

400 **General.** Wood trusses are the most popular component manufactured for the light construction industry. The beginning manufacturer often has started in business by manufacturing wood roof trusses before branching into wall panels and other components.

400.1 **Definition.** A wood truss can be defined as a series of triangles, utilizing the strongest qualities of lumber—tension and compression rather than bending and connected together by suitable connectors of adequate strength.

Names of parts of roof trusses are shown in Fig. 400.1.

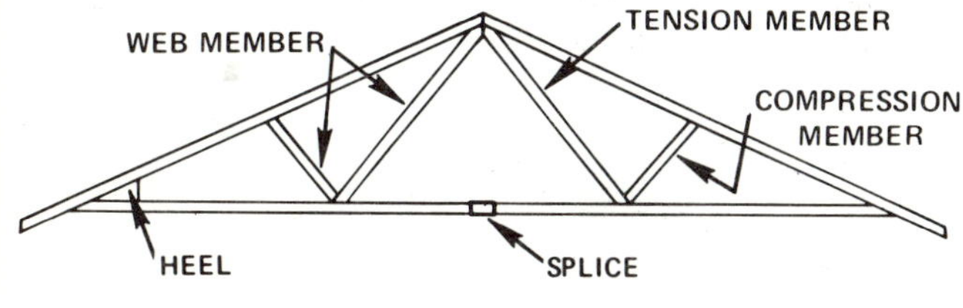


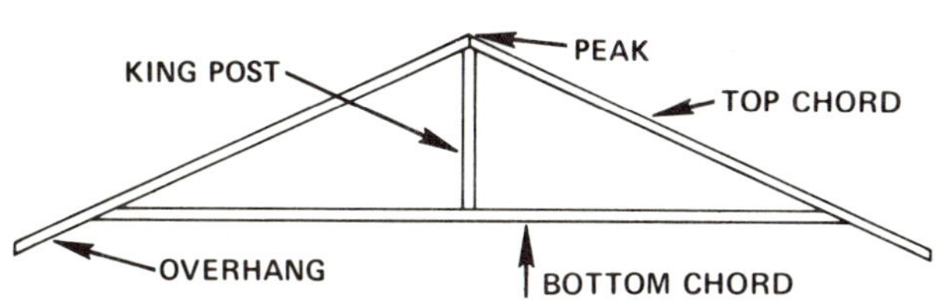


**Fig. 400.1.**
Names of truss members. Heel indicated is with a wedge.

400.2 **Advantages.** Trusses have advantages over conventional rafter or joist construction.

**a.** Material saving. Most wood trusses are spaced 24″ on center as opposed to 16″ on center for conventional construction. Trusses use smaller members (2 × 4 members in most residential roof trusses versus 2 × 6 for rafters).

**b.** The clear span of most trusses permits savings in the underlying structure by concentrating roof and/or floor loads on the exterior walls so that interior foundations and partitions may be framed of 2 × 3 (or lightweight steel studs) with single top plates and single framing around openings.

**c.** Labor installing trusses is substantially less than conventional stick building and the wider spacing reduces man hours in nailing roof sheathing or subfloor.

**d.** Freedom in planning is another advantage of clear/span trusses, permitting partitions to be located where desired without being affected by structural considerations.

**e.** Strength. Trusses are designed to meet safety factors of 3 to 1, whereas most conventional wood construction is only 1 1/2 to 1.

400.3 **Disadvantages.** There are some cases, however, where trusses may not be the most economical solution, particularly in shorter spans and where only a few trusses of complicated configuration are required.

401 **Types of Trusses.** The following illustrations show the types of trusses in general use.

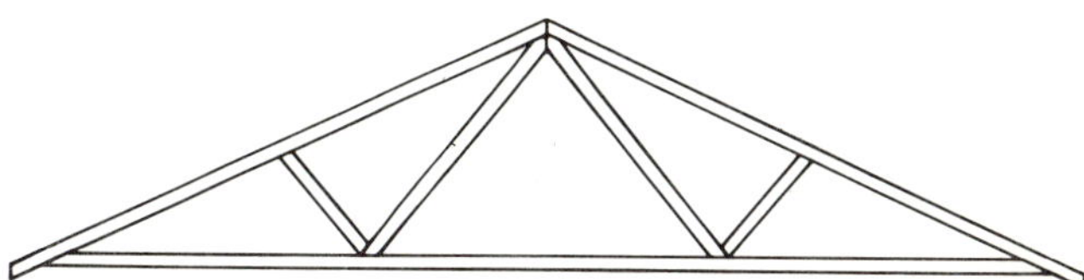

**Fig. 401.1**
The Fink or "W" truss is the most common roof truss for spans under forty feet.

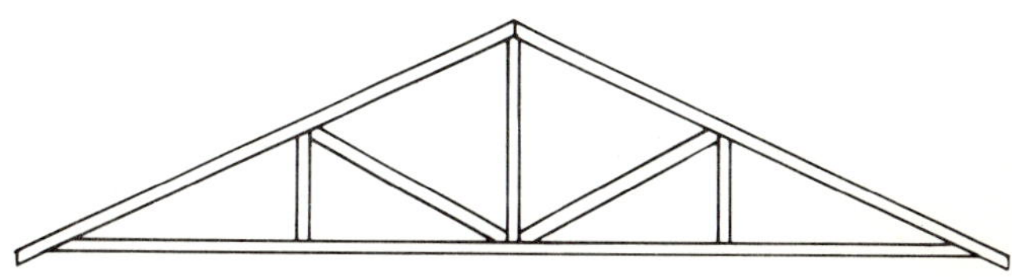

**Fig. 401.2.**
The Howe truss (also known as a "King Post" truss) has the advantage of shorter spans on the bottom chord.

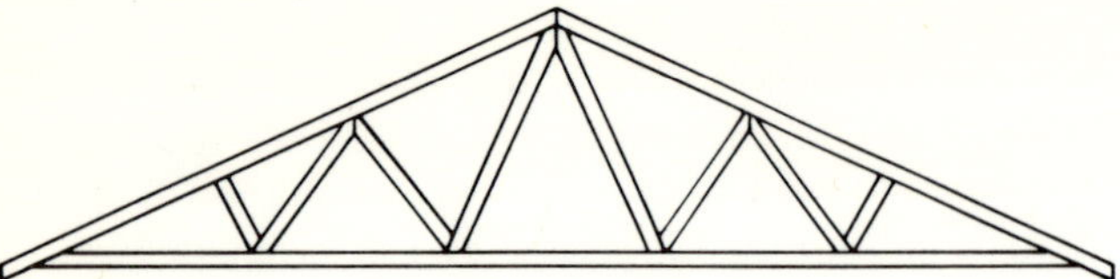

**Fig. 401.3.**
Warren (or double "W") truss widely used for spans over 40 feet.

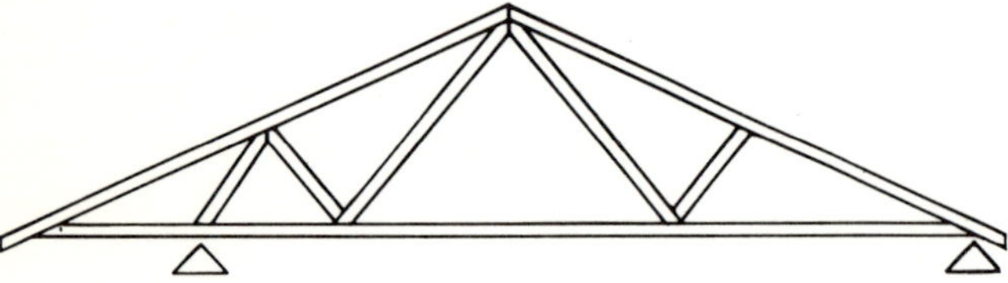

**Fig. 401.4.**
Cantilver truss is used to extend roof line over supporting wall, in addition to overhang.

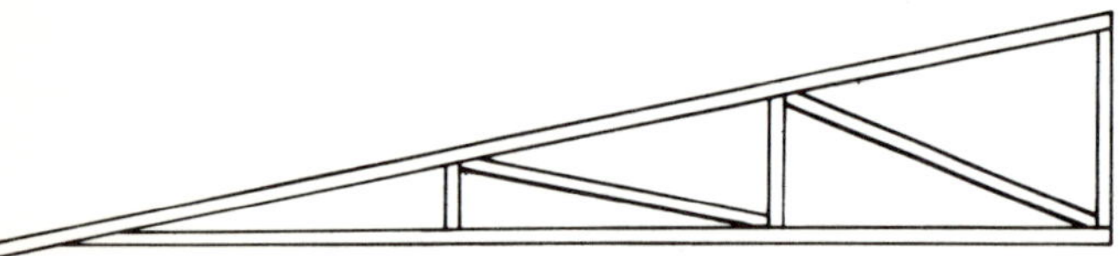

**Fig. 401.5.**
Monopitch or half truss. Variations widely used on modular units.

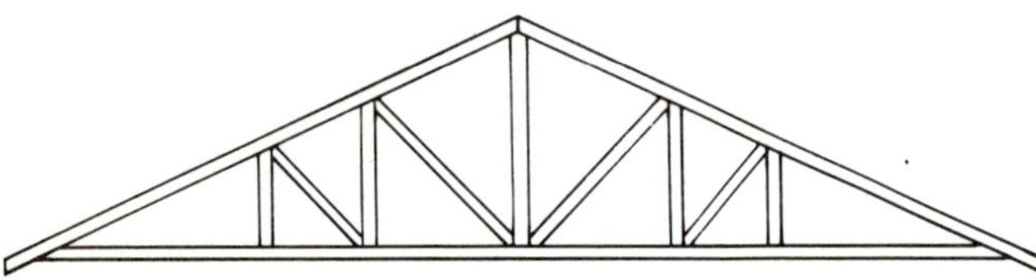

**Fig. 401.6.**
Girder truss. Often used to carry trusses from intersecting roof lines such as on an "L" shaped building.

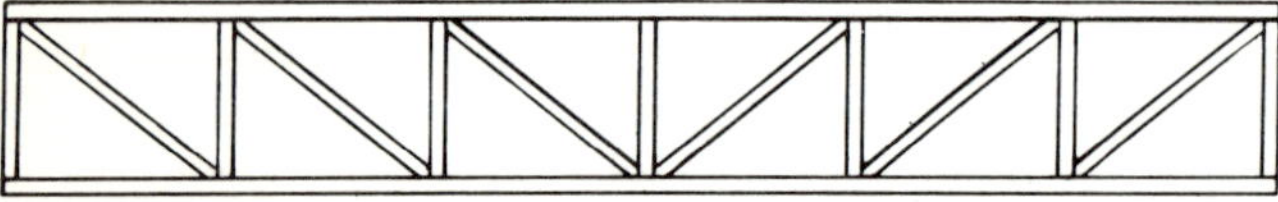

**Fig. 401.7.**
Flat Top. Used for both floor and roof trusses.

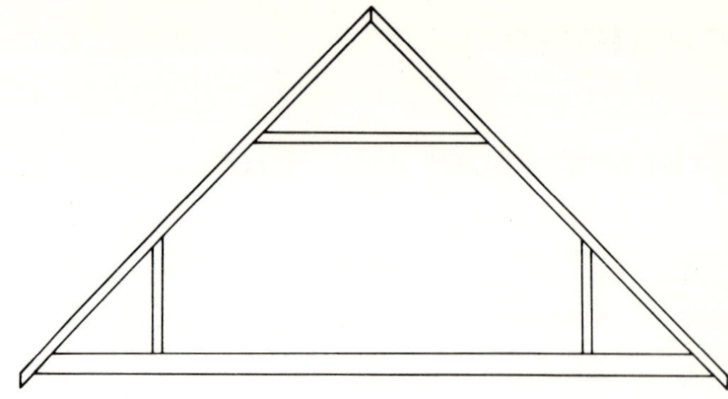

**Fig. 401.8.**
Story and one half. Used for Cape Cod type units. Frequently fabricated on site because of transportation. Truss shown is not a true truss because triangles are not closed.

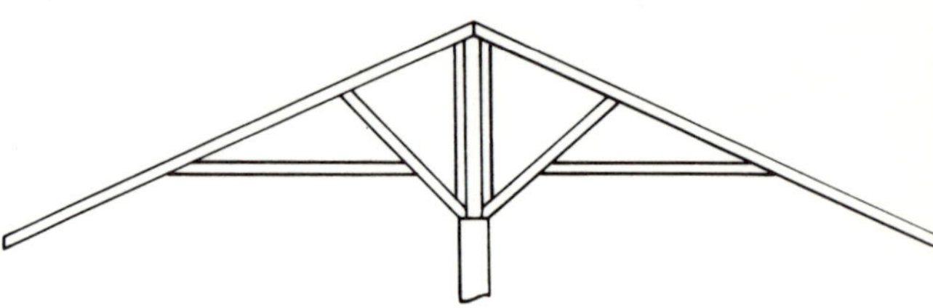

**Fig. 401.9.**
Umbrella truss. Provides easy access to covered storage by materials handling equipment.

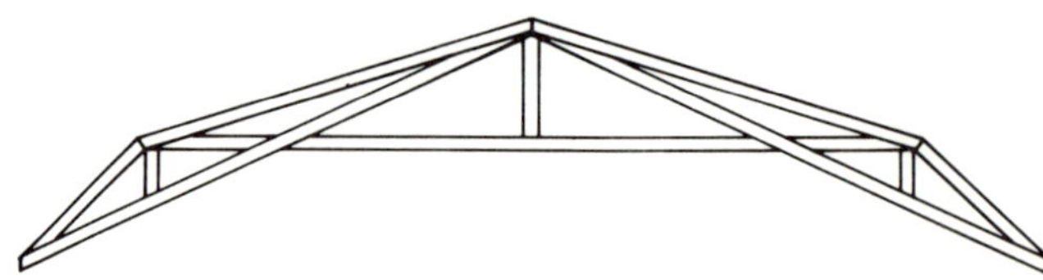

**Fig. 401.10.**
Gambrel truss.

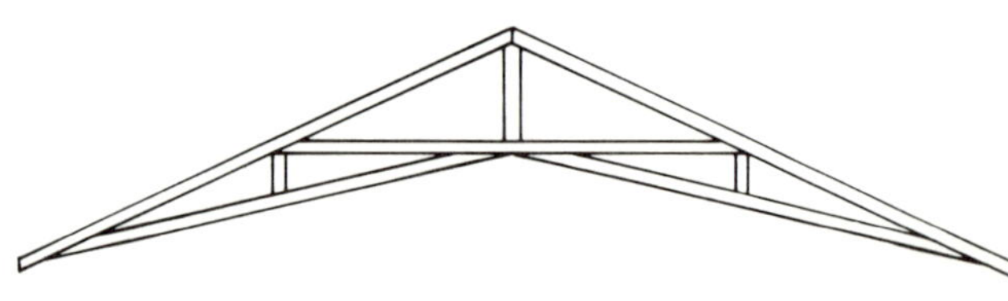

**Fig. 401.11.**
Scissor truss.

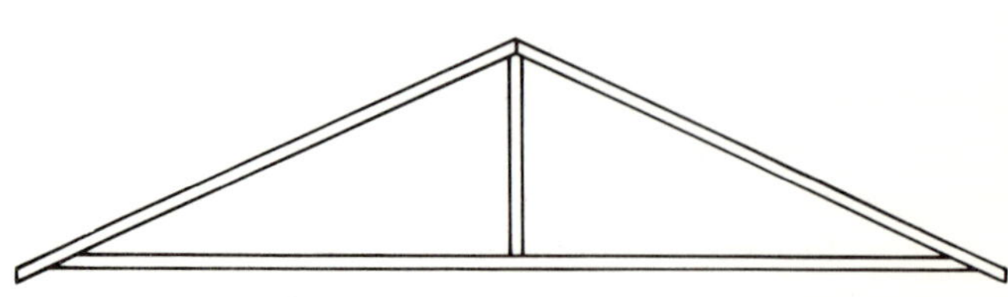

**Fig. 401.12.**
King Post truss.

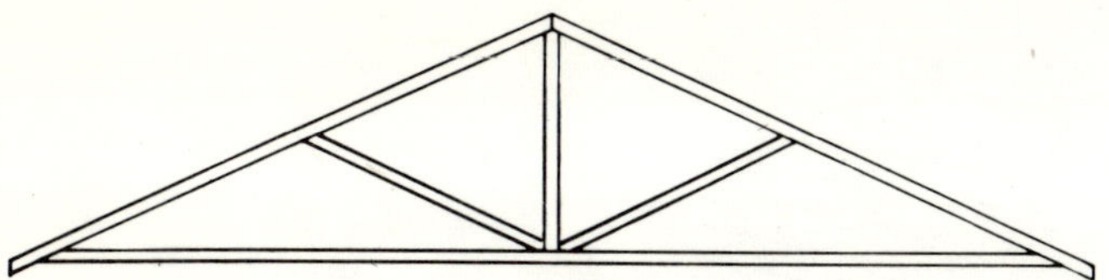

**Fig. 401.13.**
Modified King Post.

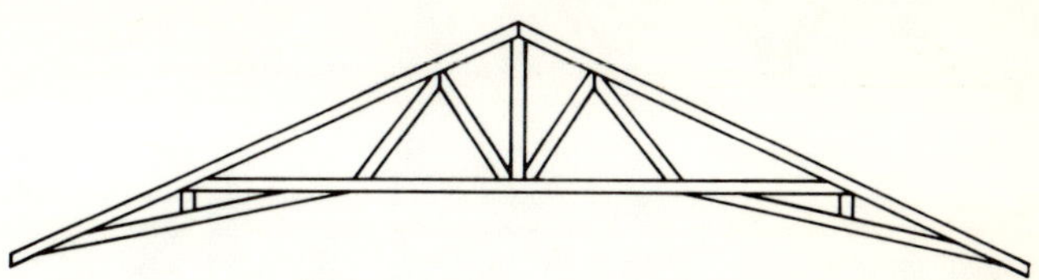

**Fig. 401.14.**
Cambered Fink Truss. Widely used in farm machine storage buildings to achieve high center with low side walls.

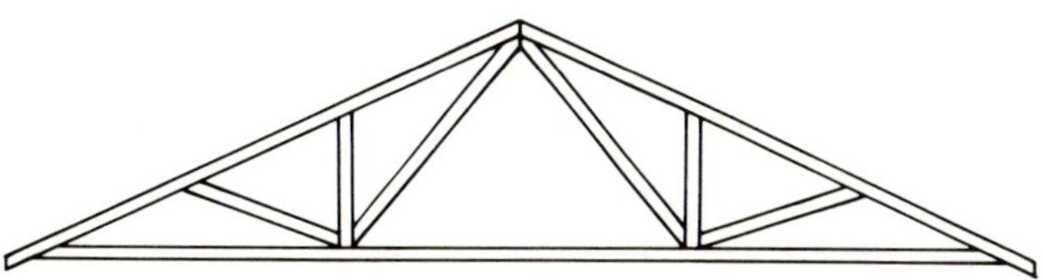

**Fig. 401.15.**
Fan Truss.

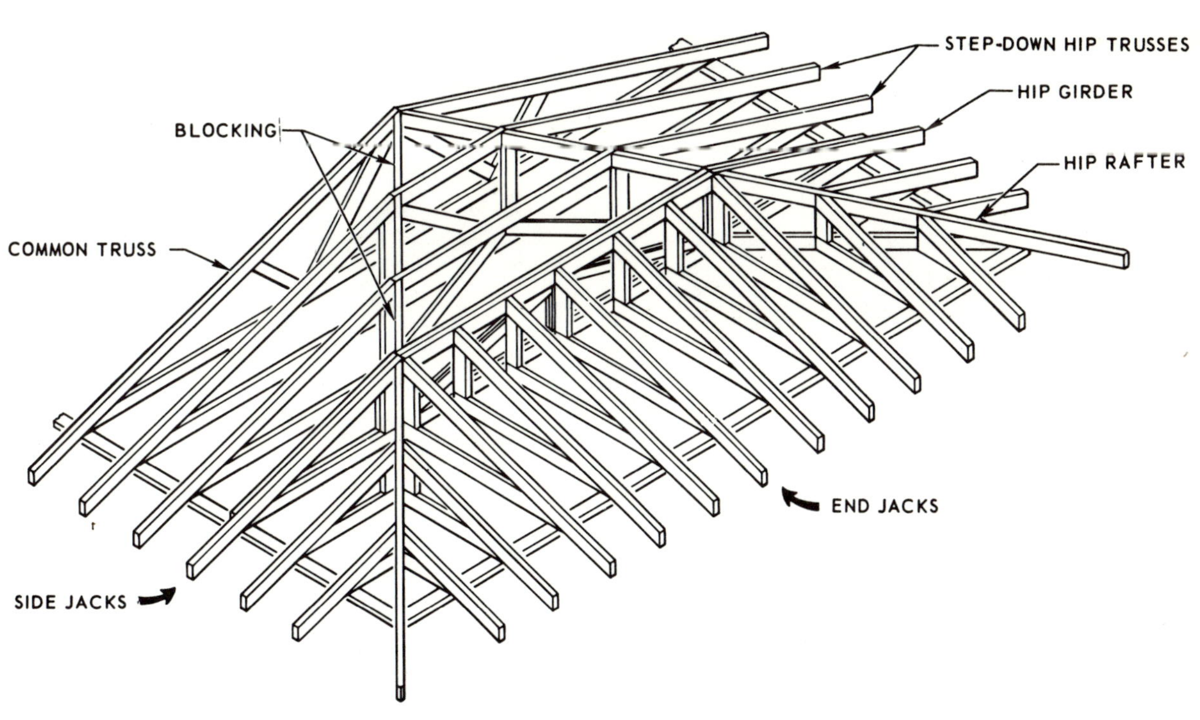


**Fig. 401.16.**
Step-Down Hip System.

*(Hydro-Air Drawing)*

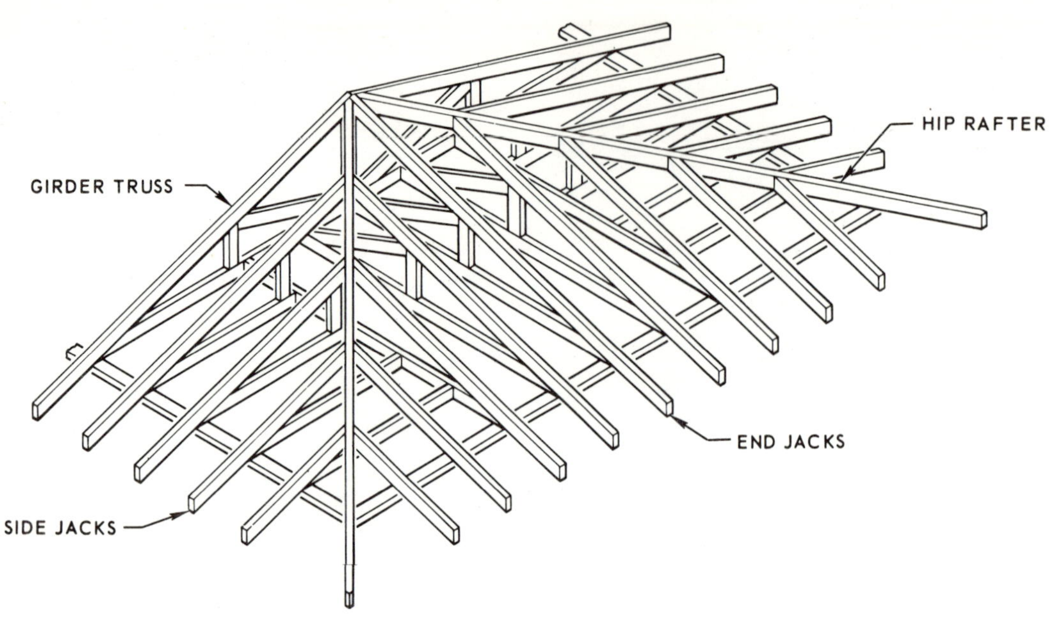


**Fig. 401.17.**
Terminal Hip System.

*(Hydro-Air Drawing)*

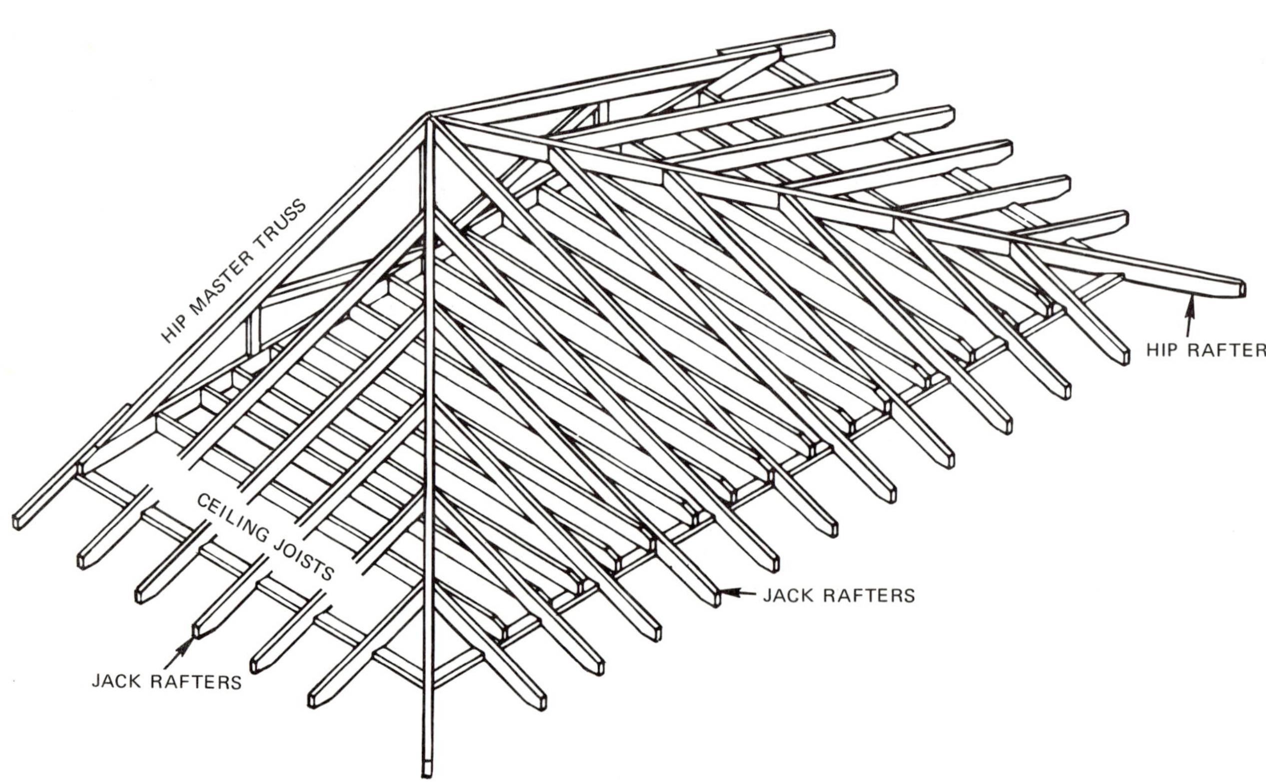


**Fig. 401.18.**
Hip Master System. Essentially a girder truss supporting a conventionally framed hip.

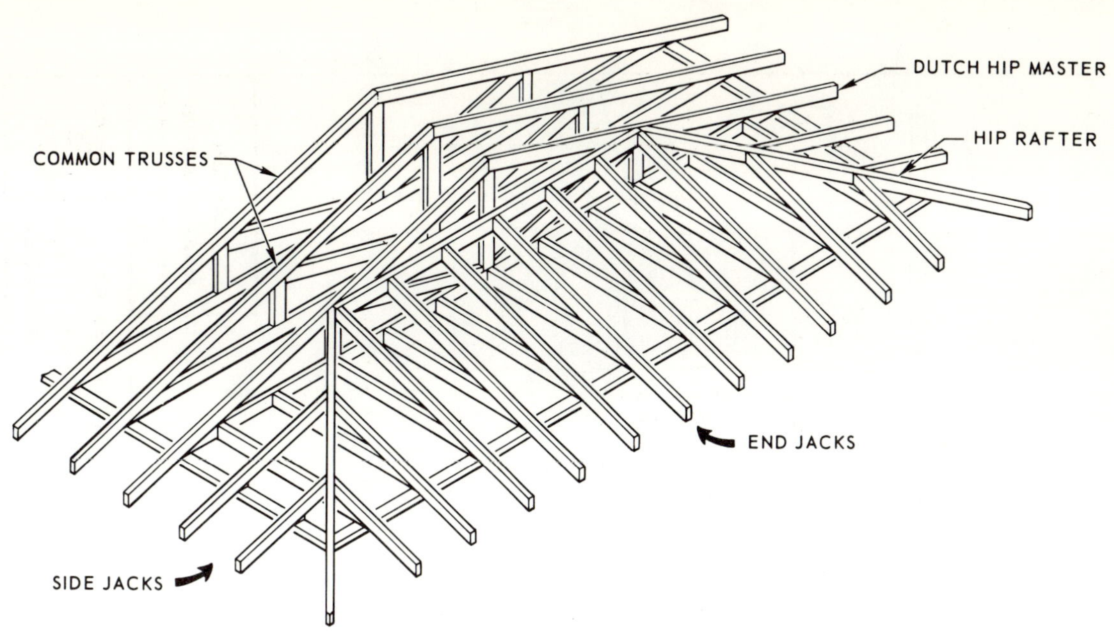


**Fig. 401.19.**
Dutch Hip Truss System.

*(Hydro-Air Drawing)*

402 **Building Codes.** Building code acceptance and requirements on roof trusses, (with a few exceptions) have become fairly uniform in recent years. The Truss Plate Institute has developed design specifications published as "TPI-70." Depending on the manufacturer's market, he must make provision for one or more of the following major codes, in addition to any local requirements.

402.1 **U.S. Dept. of Housing & Urban Development (HUD)**—FHA G-4541.1 similar to TPI-70.

402.2 **International Conference of Building Officials (ICBO)** publishes the Uniform Building Code and requires prior approval of truss plates, issuing a numbered "Research Recommendation" on each type. Prevalent in the western half of the country.

402.3 **Building Officials's Conference of America (BOCA).** Prevalent in the Midwest and East.

402.4 **Southern Building Code Congress.** Prevalent in the Southeast and Texas.

402.5 **State Building Code Council, state of New York.** Code may be adopted by localities in the state. Requires approval of systems. Generally higher loading criteria than other codes.

402.6 **Wisconsin State Industrial Safety & Building Division.** Applies to buildings for public occupancy such as motels, office buildings, etc. Prior approval required for systems.

406 **Engineering Design.**

406.1 **Trusses should be designed** by the staff of the connector manufacturer or by registered architect or engineer experienced in the field.

406.2 **A typical truss design** is shown in Fig. 406.2. The upper left hand corner area has a "Loading" and "Stress Diagram." The "Loading Diagram" indicates loads on the truss based on roof and ceiling areas according to design loads and the resulting reactions at the bearing points. The Stress Diagram graphically translates the loads into member forces for the particular span and slope.

Some truss designs omit these diagrams. Others do not show the location of the truss plates stating that they should be placed symmetrically about the joint. In high wind

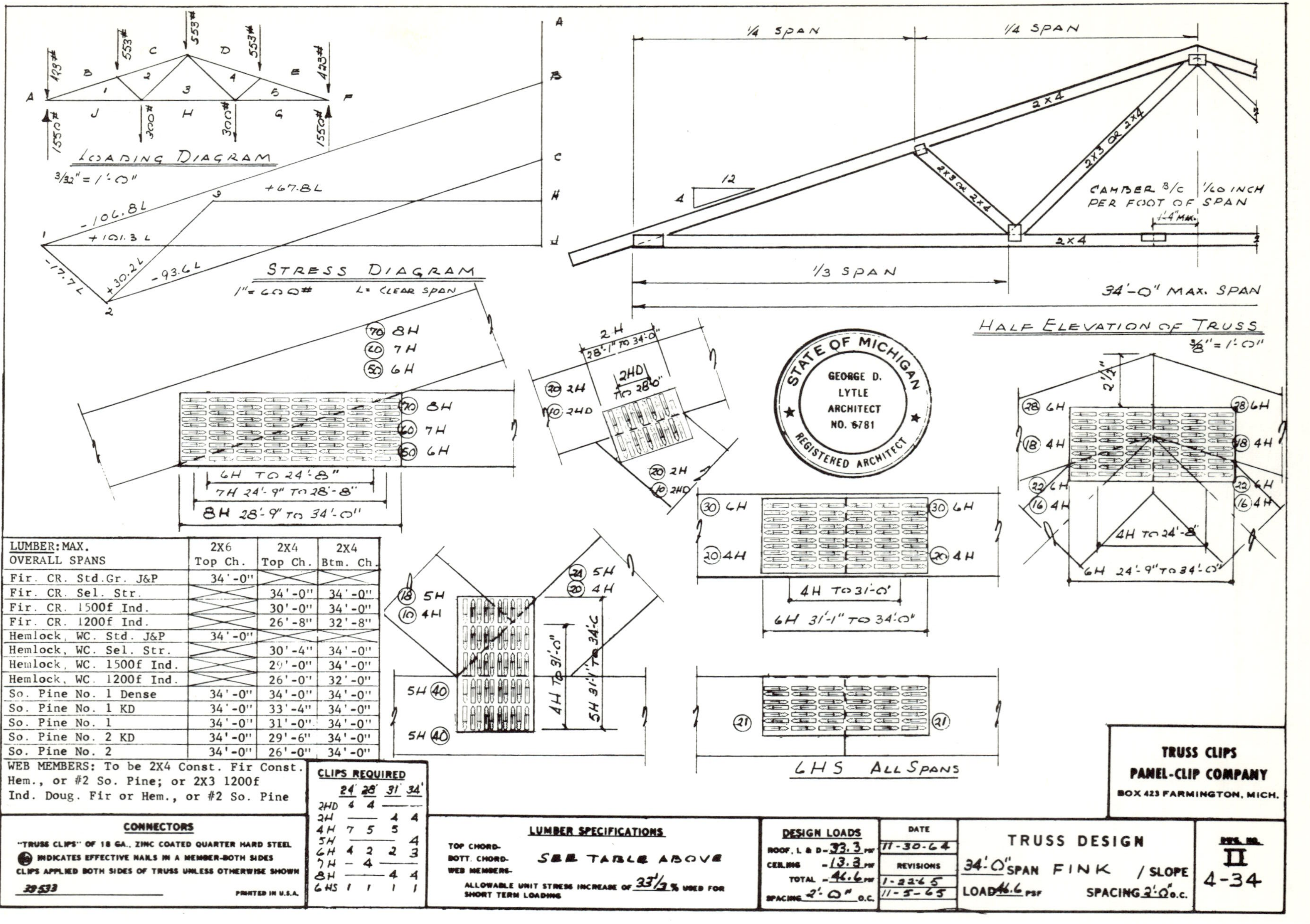


| LUMBER: MAX. OVERALL SPANS | 2X6 Top Ch. | 2X4 Top Ch. | 2X4 Btm. Ch. |
|---|---|---|---|
| Fir. CR. Std. Gr. J&P | 34'-0" | | |
| Fir. CR. Sel. Str. | | 34'-0" | 34'-0" |
| Fir. CR. 1500f Ind. | | 30'-0" | 34'-0" |
| Fir. CR. 1200f Ind. | | 26'-8" | 32'-8" |
| Hemlock, WC. Std. J&P | 34'-0" | | |
| Hemlock, WC. Sel. Str. | | 30'-4" | 34'-0" |
| Hemlock, WC. 1500f Ind. | | 29'-0" | 34'-0" |
| Hemlock, WC. 1200f Ind. | | 26'-0" | 32'-0" |
| So. Pine No. 1 Dense | 34'-0" | 34'-0" | 34'-0" |
| So. Pine No. 1 KD | 34'-0" | 33'-4" | 34'-0" |
| So. Pine No. 1 | 34'-0" | 31'-0" | 34'-0" |
| So. Pine No. 2 KD | 34'-0" | 29'-6" | 34'-0" |
| So. Pine No. 2 | 34'-0" | 26'-0" | 34'-0" |

WEB MEMBERS: To be 2X4 Const. Fir Const. Hem., or #2 So. Pine; or 2X3 1200f Ind. Doug. Fir or Hem., or #2 So. Pine

CLIPS REQUIRED

| | 24' | 28' | 31' | 34' |
|---|---|---|---|---|
| 2HD | 4 | 4 | | |
| 2H | | | 4 | 4 |
| 4H | 7 | 5 | 5 | |
| 5H | | | | 4 |
| 6H | 4 | 2 | 2 | 3 |
| 7H | | 4 | | |
| 8H | | | 4 | 4 |
| 6HS | 1 | 1 | 1 | 1 |

Fig. 406.2.
Typical truss design.

(Panel-Clip Co.)

areas the "uplift" should be computed and adequate anchorage provided.

407 **Lumber.** The several species of lumber are not all of the same structural strength nor do they have the same connector holding power. Some connector manufacturers make separate truss designs for each specie and others like the design in Fig. 406.2 cover the three popular species—Fir, Yellow Pine and Hemlock on one design.

407.1 **Connector Sizes in Various Species.** When one specie of lumber is substituted for another, the substitution should be approved by the engineer or the connector manufacturer who at the same time should designate any change in connector size. As a general guide, using Douglas Fir and Southern Yellow Pine as a standard, connector sizes should be increased for other species as follows:

| | |
|---|---|
| West Coast Hemlock | +25% |
| White Fir | +50% |
| Larch | 0% |
| All Spruces | +50% |

407.2 **1 1/2″ vs 1 5/8″ Lumber.** As we enter this period of change in our lumber standards, many code authorities are permitting the direct substitution of 1 1/2″ lumber for 1 5/8″ lumber. Others are requiring redesign of all trusses. Where a lower net section is recognized for the 1 1/2″ lumber, it may mean an increase in chord sizes in certain critical truss spans. Fabricators should know the position of local code authorities and have trusses designed accordingly.

408 **Office Procedure.** Typical forms are shown in Chapter I, Material Cutting.

409 **Material Cutting.** Accurate cutting of lumber in trusses to insure tight joints is vital to the strength of the truss. The labor cost of this operation can often exceed the cost of fabrication. This is described in detail in Chapter I, Material Cutting.

410 **Manufacturing Methods.** Truss manufacturing methods vary in required level of investment, flexibility, space requirements, productivity, and cost of the connectors. The speed of truss making or number of trusses per day is an overrated factor. Most large truss fabricators find that 120 trusses per 8 hour day with 3 men and 4 to 5 changes, a separate setup man and including time for coffee breaks, washup time, etc. is a practical limit. This is true even though the equipment is rated at 250 trusses per day with two men. Each of the systems described here has its place, and the fabricator must make a decision based on these factors:

410.1 **Expected volume** in roof trusses per week, month, and year.

410.2 **Funds available** for investment and present interest rates.

410.3 **Types of trusses** to be made—Will volume be concentrated on standard house size trusses or spread over the spectrum of types—farm trusses, floor trusses, scissors trusses, etc.? Setup time may govern here.

410.4 **Available space** in present or projected building and value of this space if leased out to others.

410.5 **Quality of the trusses,** speed of operation, installation costs, and connector costs.

411 **Truss Systems Presently in Use.** In order of the investment required, these are the systems commonly used in fabricating trusses:

411.1 **Nailed or Nail-Glued Plywood Gussets.** This system produces a rather rigid truss with good handling characteristics. The truss must usually be turned over and labor costs are high. Designs are available from the American Plywood Association. Minimum jig investment.

The following is quoted from FHA G4541.1, "Design Criteria for Trussed Rafters."

*6. GLUE NAILED TRUSSED RAFTERS.*

*a.* ***General.*** *Nail-glued trussed rafters shall be fabricated in a shop where close supervision and control of moisture content can be maintained. Nail-gluing shall preferably be done in a heated building. It shall* *not be attempted in an unheated building where temperature may fall below 50 degrees F. when protein type glue, such as casein, is used or 70 degrees F. when an exterior type glue, such as resorcinol is used.*

*b.* ***Glue.***

*(1) Exterior type glues such as resorcinol are preferred, especially in areas having high humidity. Only exterior type glue shall be used where the construction is to be exposed to the weather, such as the underside of roof overhangs, porches and carports.*

*(2) Where protein type glues, such as casein, soybean, or blood, are used, they shall have mold resistance equal to that of plain protein glue to which has been added 5 lbs. of pentachlorophenol or its equivalent per 100 lbs. of dry glue base. Trussed rafters using these glues must be protected from the weather at all times.*

*(3) Because they lack durability when subjected to roof temperatures or high humidities, urea-resin glues are not acceptable for nail-glued trussed rafter construction.*

*c.* ***Gusset Installation.*** *Wood or plywood gussets shall be installed on both sides of all joints. The moisture content at the time of gluing gussets and framing members should be between 10 and 15 percent. (See Section 5a for gusset thickness)*

*(1) The value assigned for the design strength of the glue bond is 60 pounds per square inch.*

*(2) The glue shall be applied to those portions of the gussets and truss members which will be in direct contact, at the rate of approximately 100 pounds per 1000 square feet of glue line. When assembled after nailing firmly in the manner herein specified, there should be a slight, continuous "squeeze-out" if sufficient glue has been applied. The nails specified are to assure tight, unbroken contact between the glued surfaces until the glue is set.*

*(3) To provide proper pressure between the freshly glued surfaces, at least two rows of 4d common nails not more than 4" on centers in a row shall be used for truss members of 4" nominal width, and three rows for members 6 or more inches wide. If staples are used, 16 gage, 7/16" crown, 1-1/2" long galvanized staples spaced not more than 3" o.c. in double rows shall be provided for members up to 4" nominal width, and triple rows for 6" and 8" wide members.*

*d.* ***Curing Period.*** *Within one hour from beginning of gluing, nail-glued units shall be completely fabricated and set aside for a curing period of at least 24 hours, to avoid damage to the glue bond because of handling during the glue-setting period.*

**411.2** **Perforated Metal Plates,** with special nails hand or power driven through the holes. This makes a rigid truss but labor cost is high. Cost of plates is low. Minimum jig investment. May be used on or off site.

**411.3** **Hand Nailed Panel-Clip Plates** Fig. 411.3. Labor is somewhat less than the foregoing. Plate cost is high. Minimum jig investment. May be used on or off site.

**411.4** **Klincher System.** Panel-Clip company uses same plates as above with small hand-held hydraulic press. Larger plates require several squeezes. Fig. 411.4. Truss does not have to be turned over. Labor cost low. Minimum equipment investment. Plate cost is high. Set up time low.

**411.5** **Clinch Nail System.** Bostitch Company Air driven special nails are driven through top plate, lumber and bottom plate, clinching within a one quarter inch cardboard against hardened steel plate. See Fig. 411.5. Labor cost low. Truss does not have to be turned over. Minimum equipment investment. Plate cost high. Set up time medium.

**411.6** **Roller Method.** Several manufacturers. Plates are positioned with air or hand driven nails on both sides, and then truss is run through the roller, imbedding plate teeth. Truss must be turned over but a special "flip jig" is available for this purpose. Labor cost low. Medium equipment. Plate cost low. Set up time low. Unless care is taken, sometimes the trailing end of the truss will separate in the roller. Roller should be equipped with safety release. Typical roller plate is shown in Fig. 411.6*A*. Roller press is shown in Fig. 411.6*B*.

**Fig. 411.3.**
Hand nailed plates with integral nail.

*(Panel-Clip Co.)*

**Fig. 411.4.**
Klincher System.

*(Panel-Clip Co.)*

**Fig. 411.5.**
Clinch-Nail System.

*(Bostitch)*

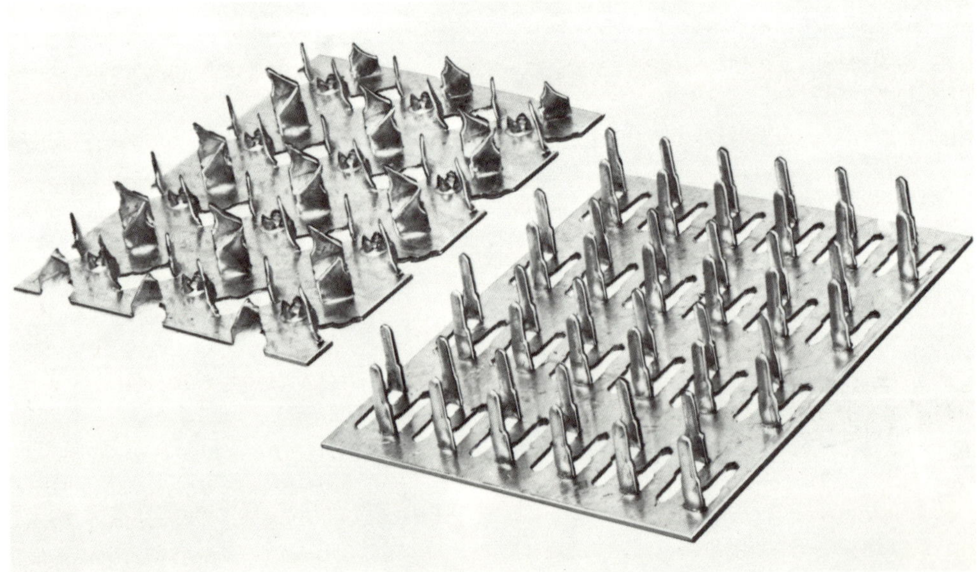

**Fig. 411.6*A*.**
Upper left shows typical roller type truss plate, lower right an 18 gauge press-applied plate.

*(Truswal)*

**Fig. 411.6*B*.**
Typical truss roller with safety bar.

*(Clary)*

411.7 **Single Press Method.** Overhead traveling press squeezes truss plate at each pedestal. Medium to high equipment investment. Labor and plate cost low. Setup time medium to high.

Fig. 411.7 *A*. and *B* show two systems of this type. Fig. 411.7*C* shows typical 20 gauge plates.

411.8 **Transom Press.** Fig. 411.8 shows this system.

411.9 **Multiple Press Method.** Presses are part of each pedestal and all joints are pressed at one time. High equipment investment. Labor and plate cost low. Setup time high. (See Fig. 411.9.)

411.10 **Half Truss Equipment.** As modular units increased, special equipment has been developed for the typical 1/2 truss. (See Fig. 411.10.)

412 **Techniques.**

412.1 **Symmetry.** To insure that trusses are symmetrical, turn the first truss end for end in the jig to make sure it fits both ways.

412.2 **Overhangs.** Typical details are shown in Fig. 412.2.

412.3 **Cantilevers.** Typical details are shown in Fig. 412.3. Cantilevers over three feet should be engineered.

412.4 **Fireplace Framing.** Typical details are shown in Figs. 412.4 *A*, *B*, and *C*.

412.5 **"L" Shaped Roofs and Valley Construction.** Typical details are shown in Figs. 412.5 *A* and *B*.

413. **Storage of Completed Trusses.** Completed trusses should be stored neatly prior to shipment, preferably strapped together in unit loads. Details are suggested in Fig. 413.1 and 2.

**Fig. 411.7*A*.**
Press is counter balanced overhead.

*(Hydro-Air)*

**Fig. 411.7*B*.**
Press travels on a gantry.

*(Truswal)*

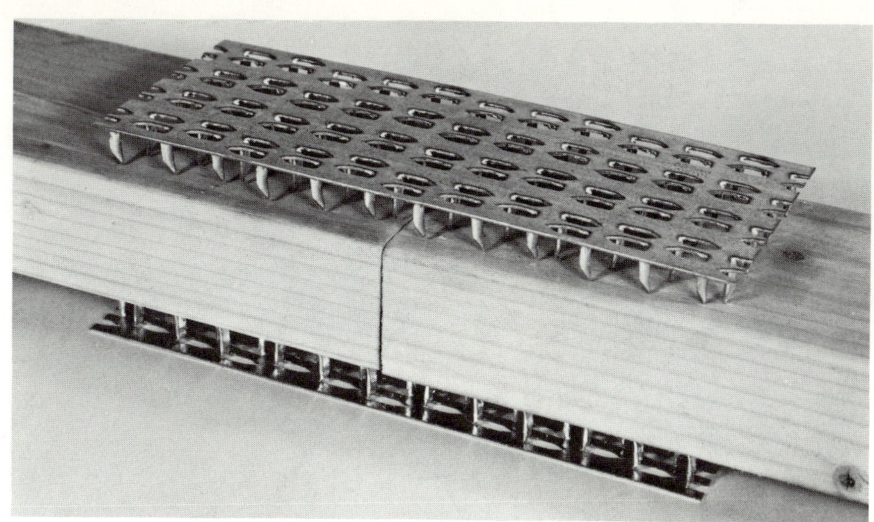

**Fig. 411.7*C*.**
Typical 20 gauge plates.

*(Hydro-Air)*

**Fig. 411.8.**
Moving press squeezes several joints at a time. A variation has a fixed press with moving jigs.

*(Automated Building Components)*

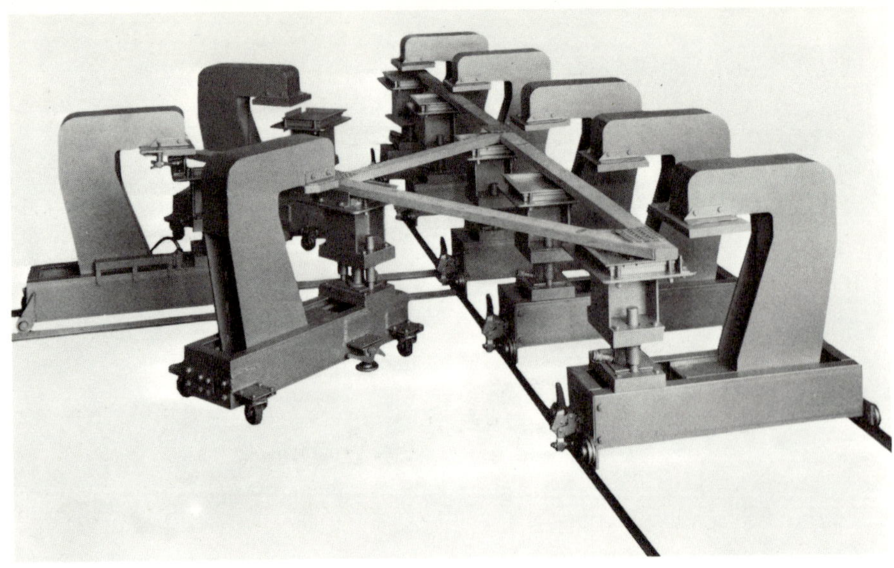

Fig. 411.9.
Multiple Press System.

*(Idaco)*

Fig. 411.10.
Typical half-truss machine.

*(Truswal)*

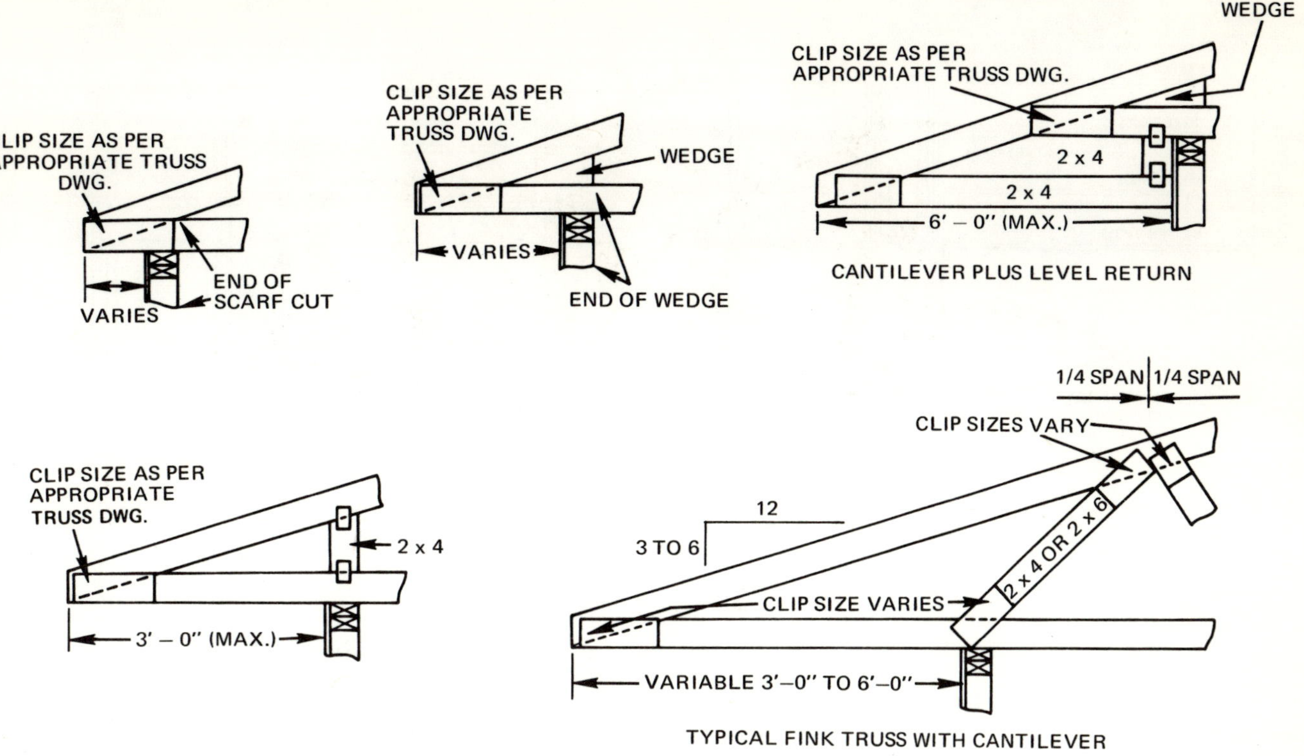


**Fig. 412.2.**
Typical eave overhangs.

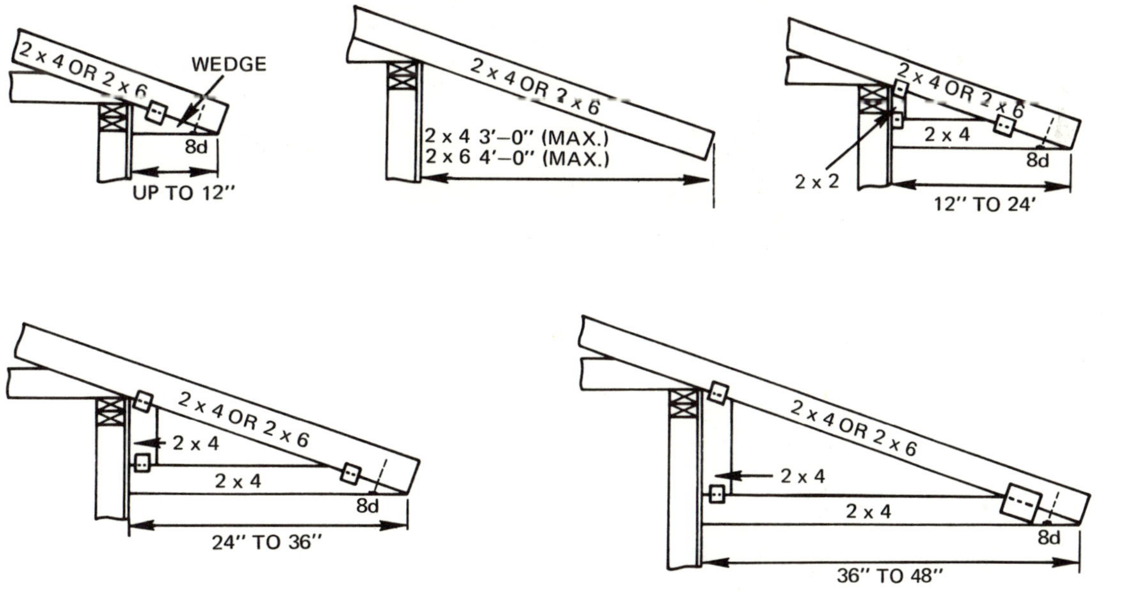


**Fig. 412.3.**
Cantilever details.

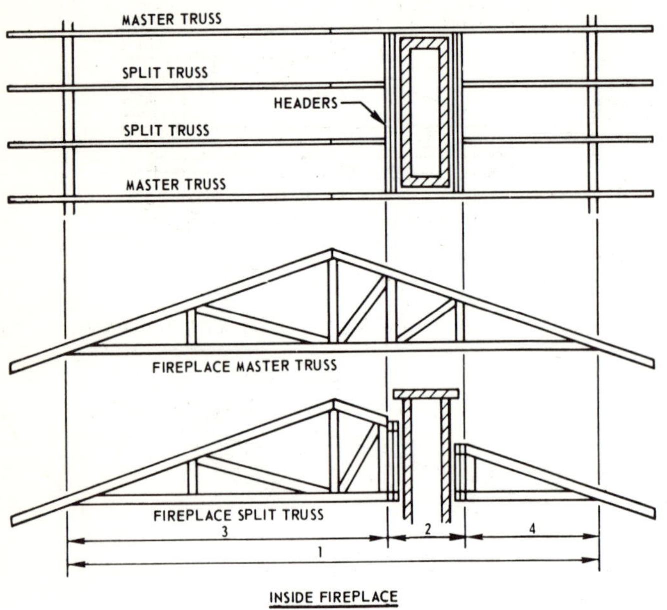


**Fig. 412.4*A*.**
The Inside Fireplace Master and Split Trusses are used where fireplace intersects the truss span in the middle or inside of the house. Fireplace may be placed parallel or perpendicular to the truss.

*(Hydro-Air)*

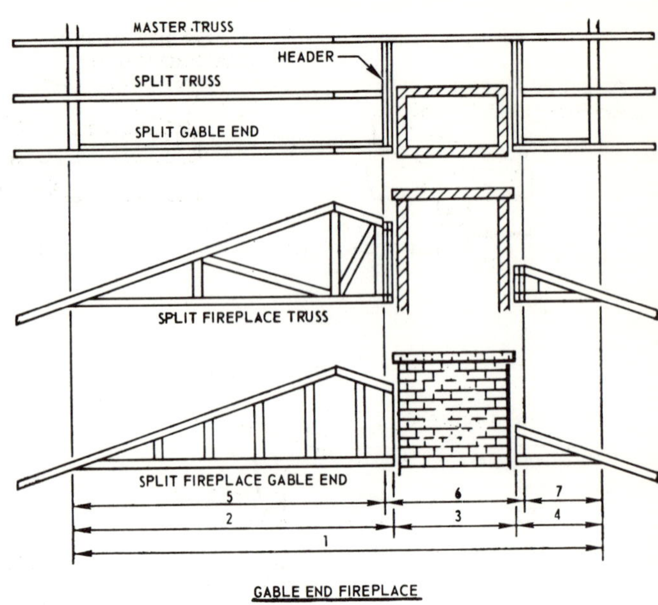


**Fig. 412.4*B*.**
The Gable End Fireplace Master and Split Gable End Trusses are used where fireplace is in the end or gable wall and intersects truss span. Double joist hangers are used to attach headers to master truss. Single joist hangers are used to attach truss section to headers.

*(Hydro-Air)*

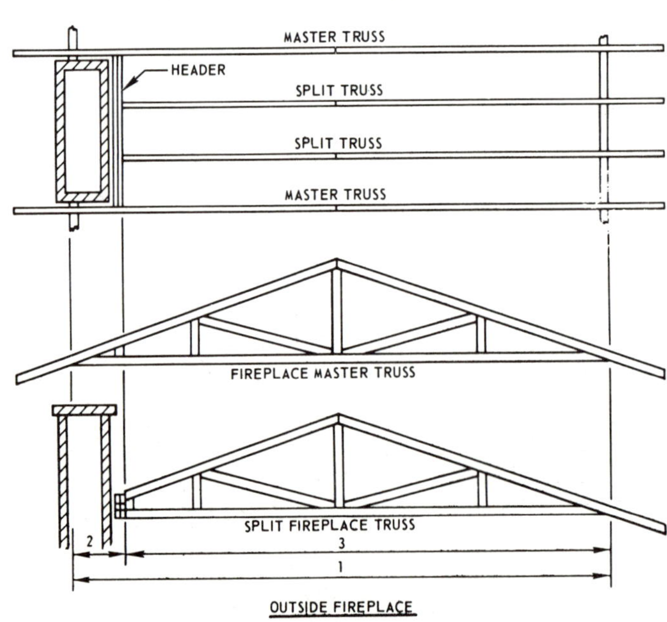


**Fig. 412.4*C*.**
The Outside Fireplace Master and Split Trusses are used where fireplace intersects truss span on the outside wall of house.

*(Hydro-Air)*

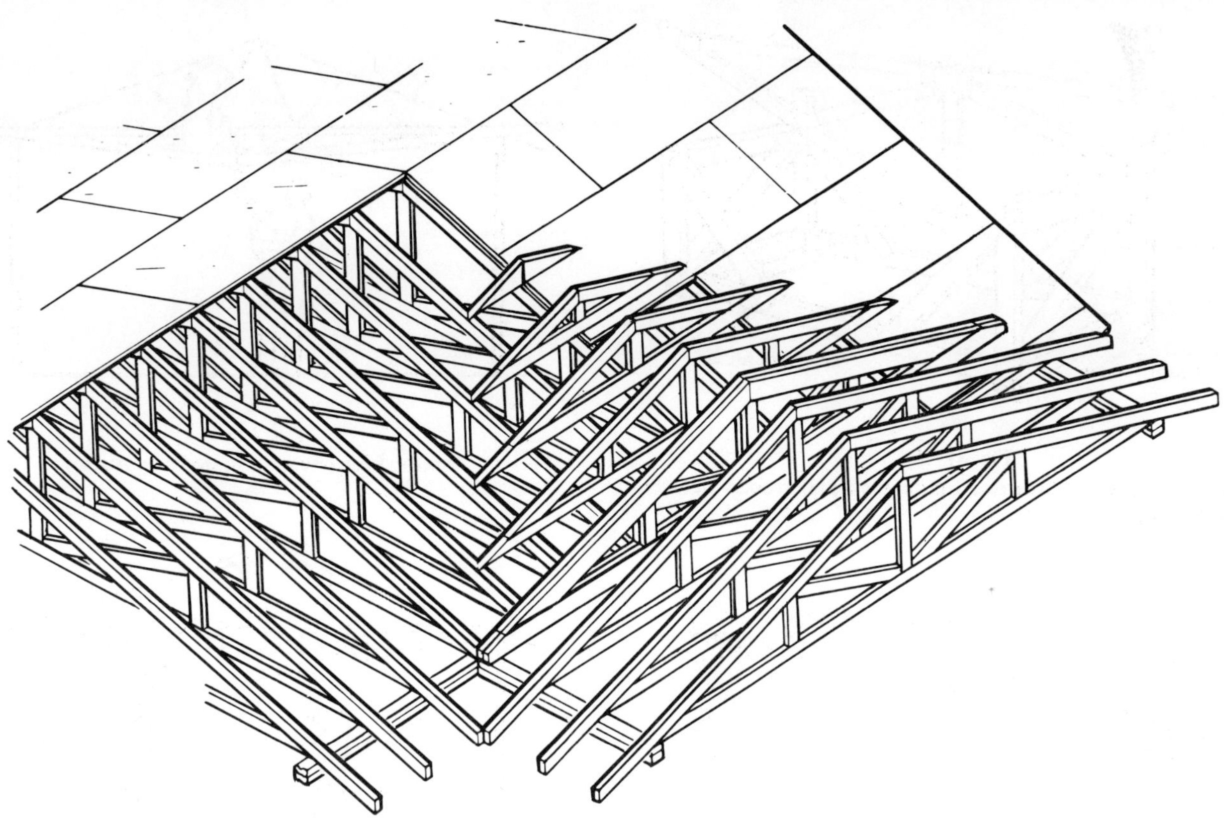

**Fig. 412.5*A*.**
Girder (double) truss is supporting trusses on main roof, while valley trusses rest on top of sheathing. Use joist hangers between supported trusses and girder truss.

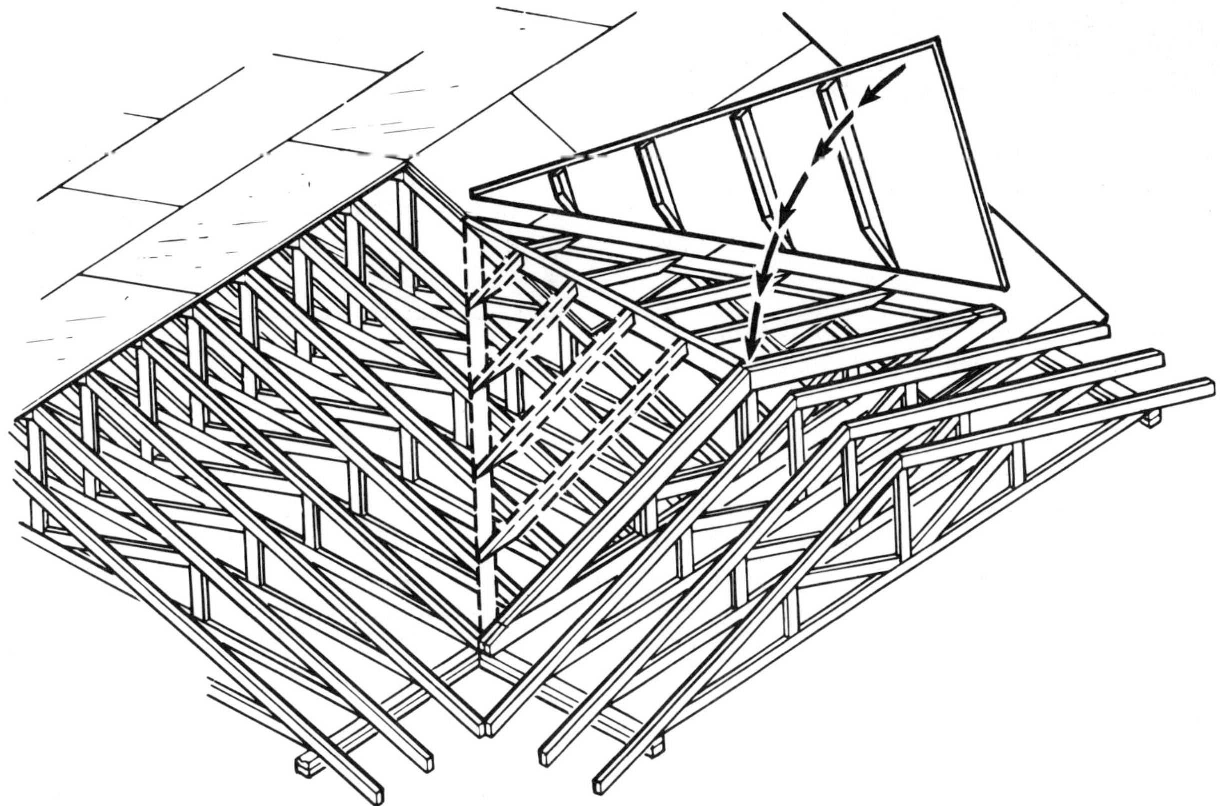

**Fig. 412.5*B*.**
Two variations in valley framing. Ridge with valley jacks resting on a valley ledger on top of sheathing. Inset shows a panelized version.

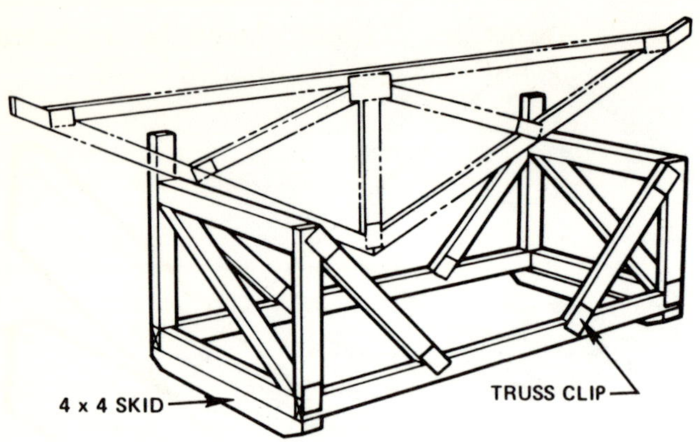


**Fig. 413.1.**
Storage rack for roof trusses. Entire rack and trusses may be handled by lift truck.

**Fig. 413.2.**
Truss Cart for in plant storage. Trusses may also be stored inverted.

*(Speed-Cut)*

**414** **Transportation.** Methods of delivery are covered in Chapter XIII, "Delivery and Installation."

**415** **Truss Handling.** Care should be used to insure against excessive lateral strain when moving trusses in plant or on site. Minimum size truss plates may "pop off" or become weakened by careless handling. The following details are similar to those recommended by the Truss Plate Institute.

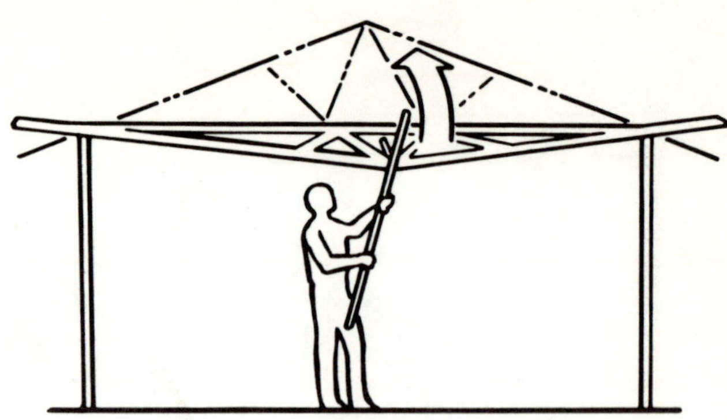

**Fig. 415.1.**
Method for one man to position trusses.

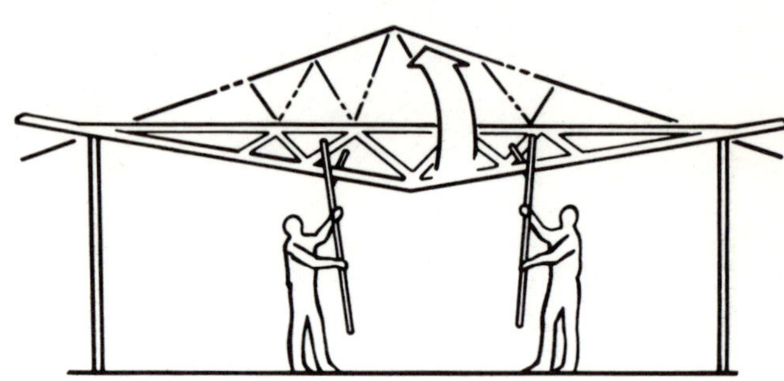

**Fig. 415.2.**
Two men.

**Fig. 415.3.**
Single hook for small trusses.

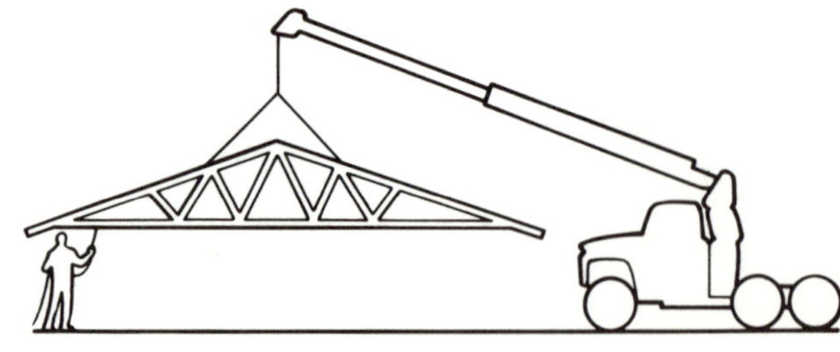

**Fig. 415.4.**
Sling for larger trusses.

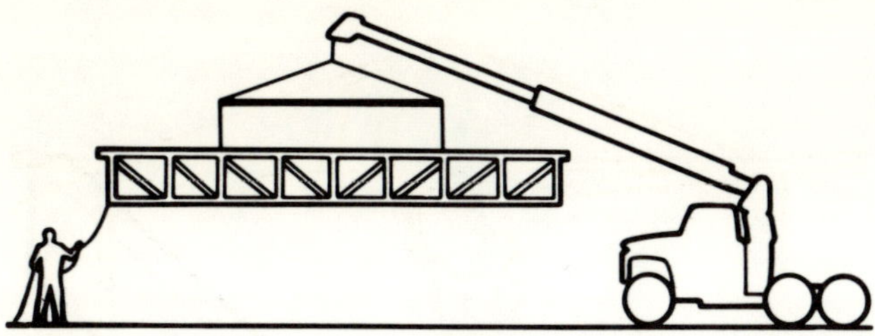

**Fig. 415.5.**
Spreader bar for flat trusses.

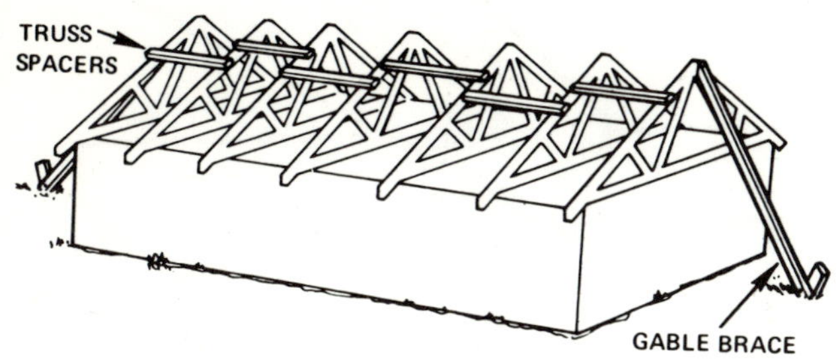


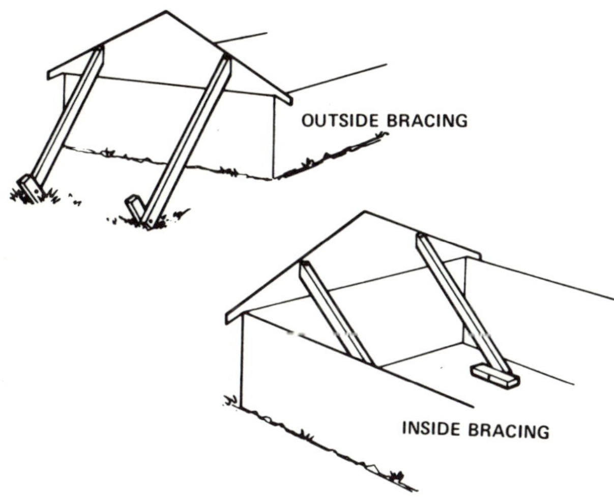


**Fig. 415.6.**
Brace gable ends to provide anchorage for truss braces and spacers.

**Fig. 415.7.**
Diagonal bracing in addition to spacers on longer trusses.

**416** **Anchorage.** Trusses should be anchored against wind uplift as required locally:

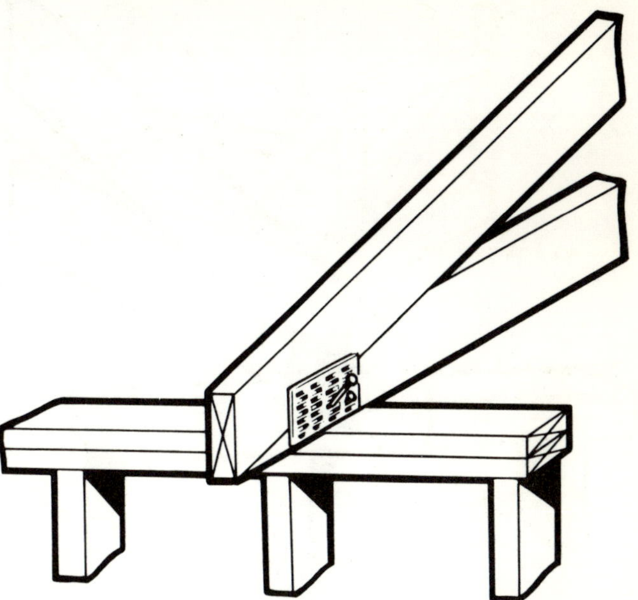

**Fig. 416.1.**
Minimun anchorage, two 16d nails.

**Fig. 416.2.**
Plumber's pipe strap.

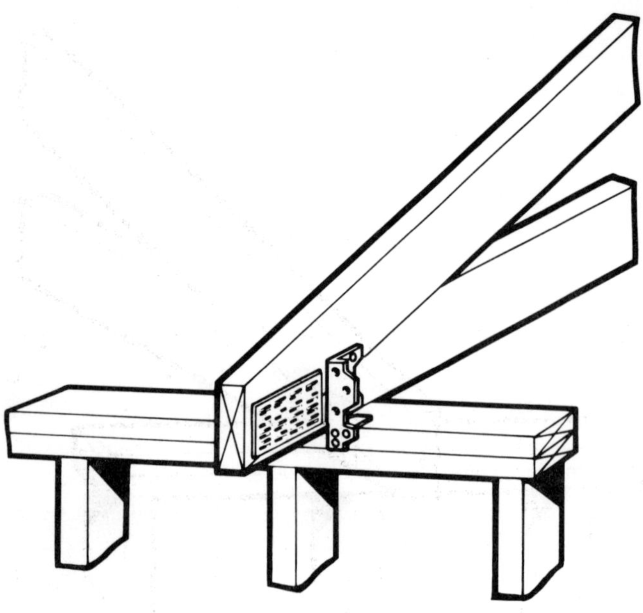

**Fig. 416.3**
Framing Clip.

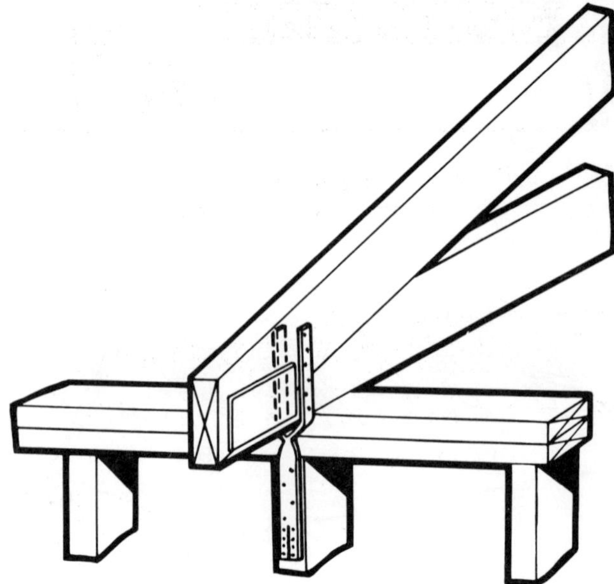

**Fig. 416.4.**
Anchor clip attached to stud for maximum anchorage.

# CHAPTER V

## Roof Construction

500 **Purpose**

The purpose of this chapter is to cover all of the elements of roof construction, other than roof trusses. Trusses are covered in Chapter IV. Roof construction in modular units is covered in Chapter XI.

501 **Rafters.** A number of manufacturers use rafters, at various spacings, either to support plywood sheathing or purlin-panels. Rafters are also a part of post and beam construction, usually with purlins or purlin-panels.

A rafter-type roof has the advantage of requiring less bulk for shipment than roof trusses. Offsetting, of course, is the need for heavier members, bearing walls, foundations, and higher site labor costs.

Where rafters must be precut in quantity, special dado equipment is available for notching the seat cut.

502 **Roof Construction.** Roofs may be completely panelized and then be supported by post and beam construction, by full height walls, center bearing walls, or center girders. Where completely panelized, the roof panels can incorporate insulation and finished ceiling material.

Any material may be used for the finish ceiling including Upson board, Gypsum board, hardboard, etc. Of course, provision must be made for ventilation of the panel to prevent moisture accumulation. A roof panel of this type is shown in Fig. 502*A*.

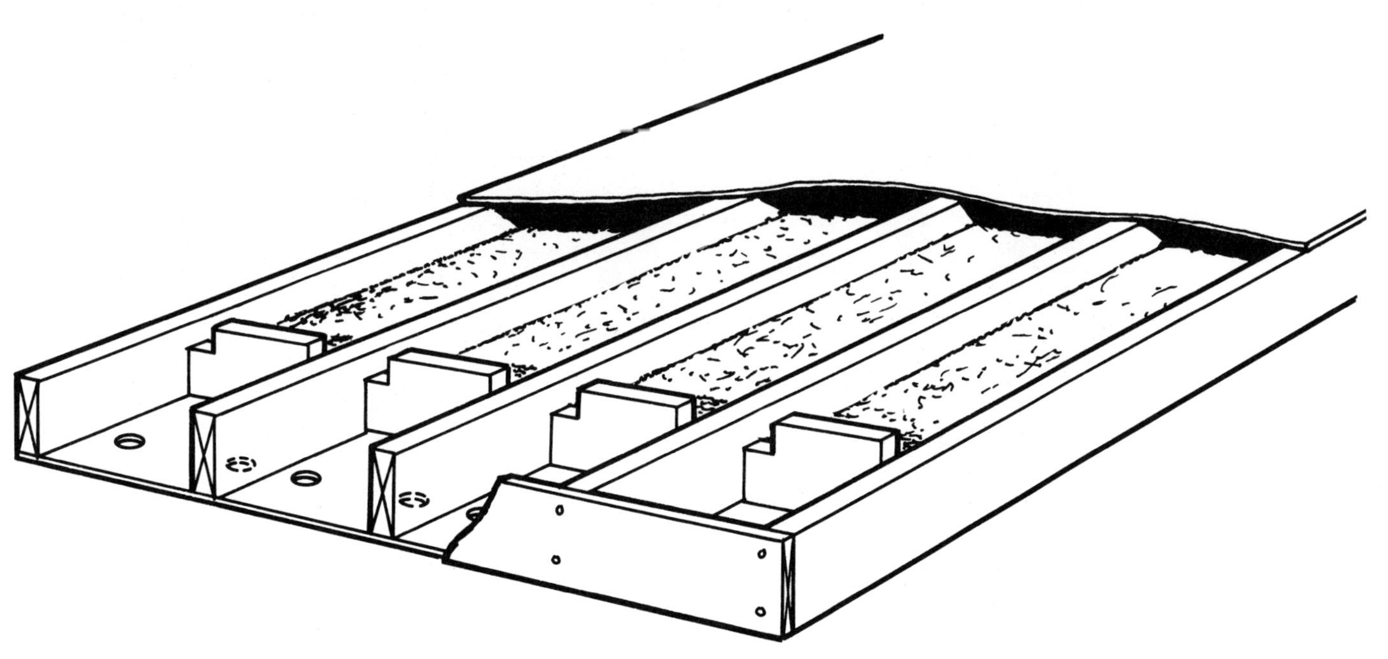

**Fig. 502*A*.**
Typical roof panel.

**Fig. 502*B*.**
Installation of panelized roof.

(*Wausau Homes*)

503 **Gable Ends.** Gable ends are usually overbuilt. Most common is the use of a full size top and bottom truss chord with 2 × 4 studs on the flat. Others turn studs on edge. Where the material sizes are available, 2 × 3 and 2 × 2 members are adequate. Studding should not be closer together than 24" O.C. and sheathing has little value. Types of gables follow:

**Fig. 503.1.**
Standard gable—full studded. Provides framing for gable end finish from plate line to roof line. It is placed flush with the end of the building and is used when rake overhangs are 16" or less.

**Fig. 503.2.**
Drop top chord gable provides for laddering out further than 16". Gable is usually dropped the thickness of ladder material. Lookouts on ends are optional, depending on construction of eave soffit.

**Fig. 503.3*A*.**
Drop bottom chord gable. Usually dropped to provide framing for siding coming down over a frieze at the window heads in brick veneer construction.

**Fig. 503.3*B*.**
A variation on the above for greater projection.
*(After Best Homes)*

**Fig. 503.4.**
Gable for triangular louvre.

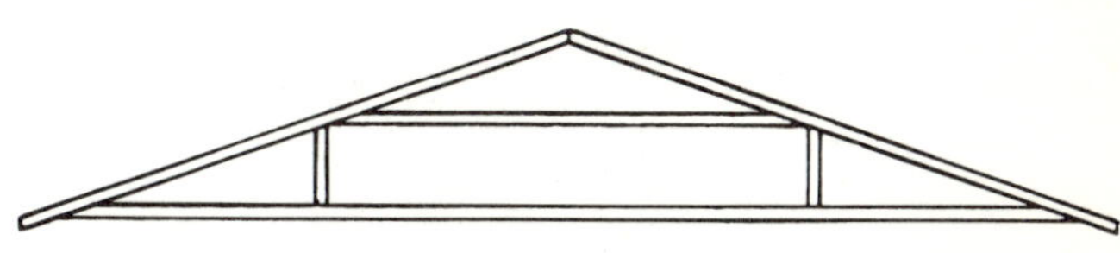

**Fig. 503.5.**
Gable for vertical siding.

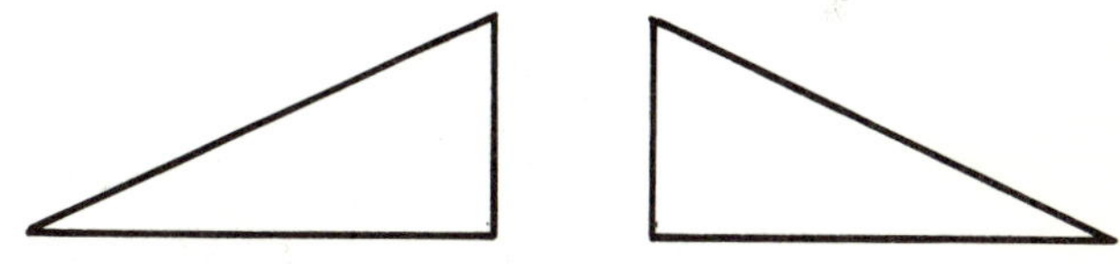

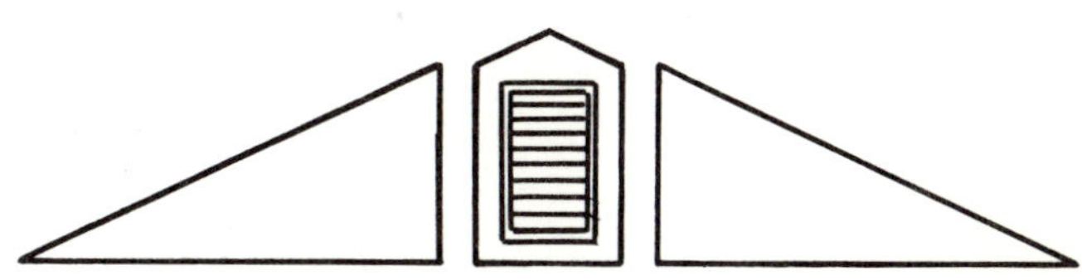

**Fig. 503.6.**
Two- and three-piece gables for handling ease—large gables.

504 **Rake Overhangs.** When under 16", these are simply nailed to the gable end and then reinforced with a steel strap over the top and down the back of the gable. Overhangs 16" to 30" should be laddered back to the first truss, provided it is at least 24" back. Overhangs beyond 30" should be laddered back two or more truss spaces so that the cantilever portion is less than 2/3 of the portion behind the gable. Sheathing can be applied to the cantilever overhang but not

to the nail on type, as it should be sheathed into the roof for additional support.

Ventilation may be provided by cutting and screening holes in the soffit, which should be shop applied.

Ladders can be of either 2 × 4 or 1 × 4 construction. Details are shown in Fig. 504*A* and *B*.

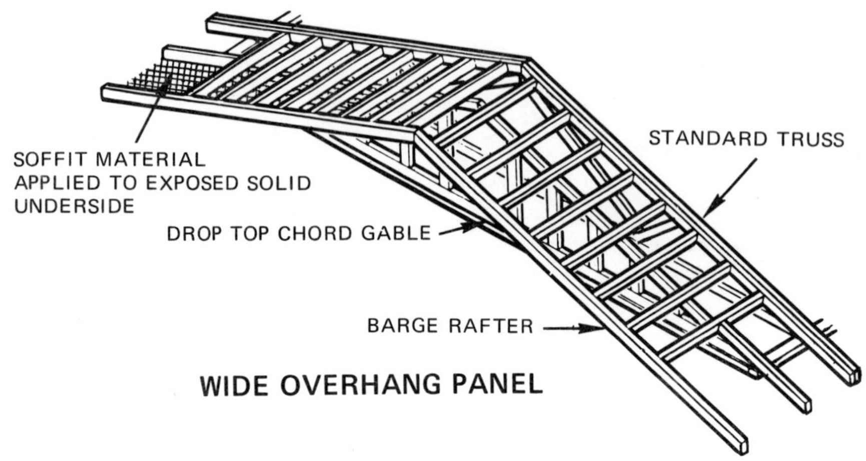


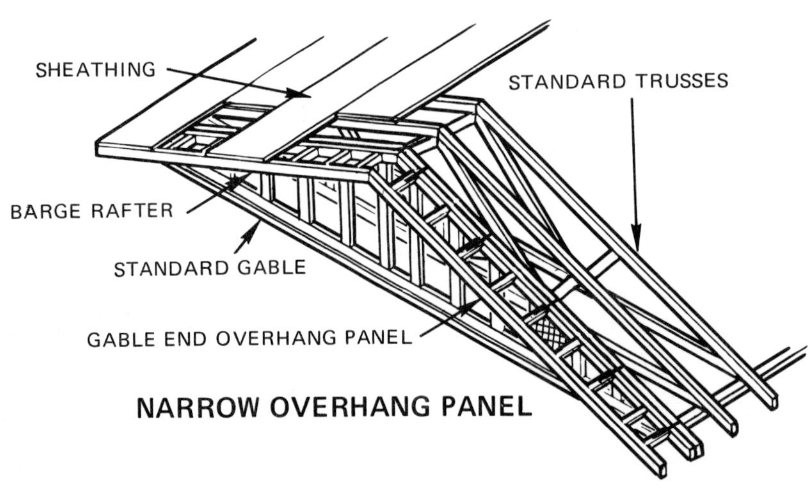


**Fig. 504.**
Typical overhang details.

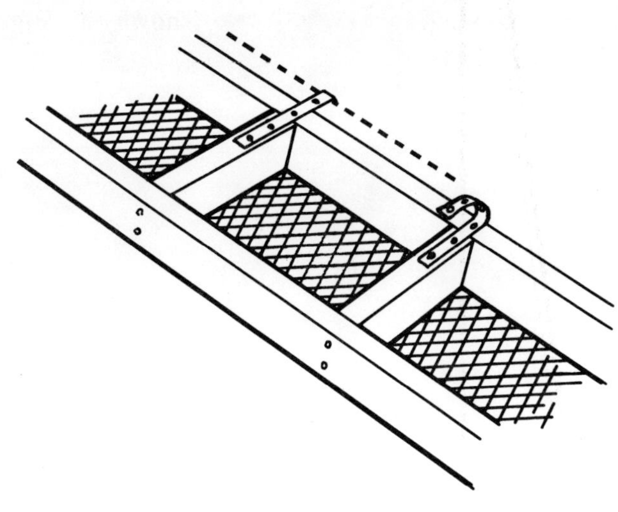

Fig. 504*A*.
Rake ladder for overhang of 16″ or less.

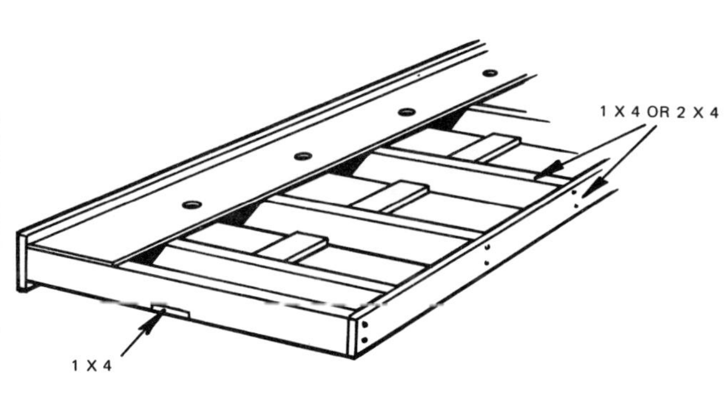


Fig. 504*B*.
Ladder for rake overhang over 16″.

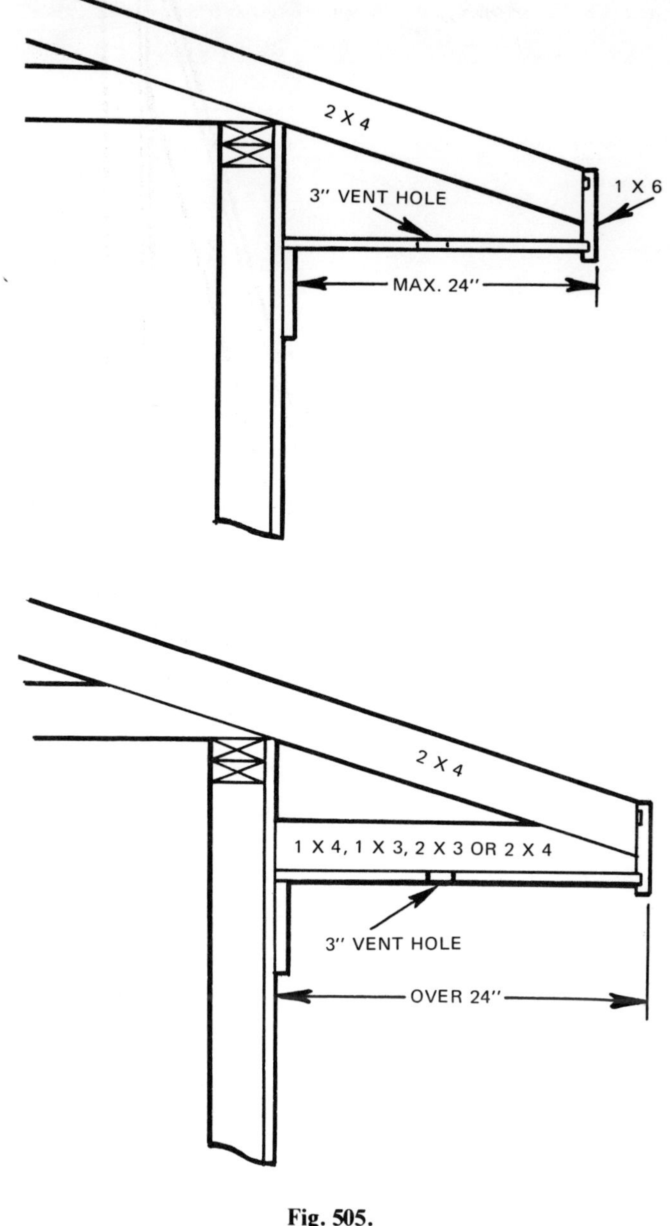


Fig. 505.
Eave cornice.

505 **Eave Cornice.** Structurally, eave overhangs are supported by truss or rafter construction. Where level overhang does not exceed 24″ the soffit may be self-supporting, material permitting. Grooved fascia material of this type shown is Fig. 505 is commercially available and is usually grooved top and bottom so the board may be turned either way. Beyond 24″ the level soffit should be supported by level returns as a part of the trusses or by panelizing the soffit.

506 **Mansard Construction.**

506.1 **Full Wall Type.** These can be of two types, where the wall itself provides the mansard effect and where an overlay is required. Fig. 506.1 shows variations.

506.2 **Cornice Type.** Fig. 506.2 shows several ways mansard lookouts may be fabricated.

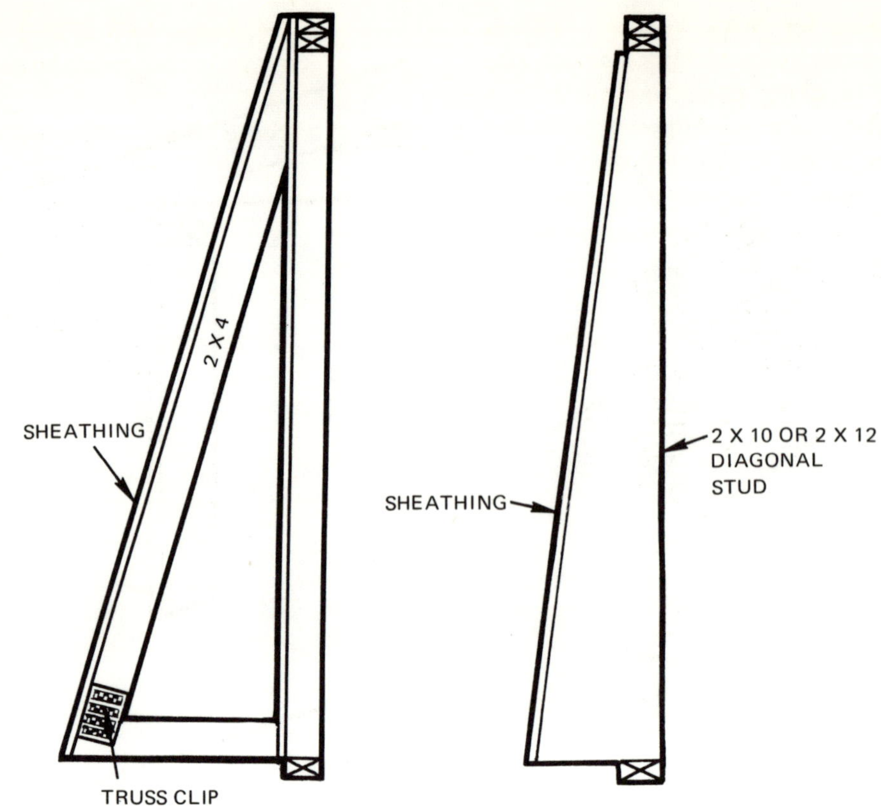


**Fig. 506.1.**
Two types of full wall mansard framing.

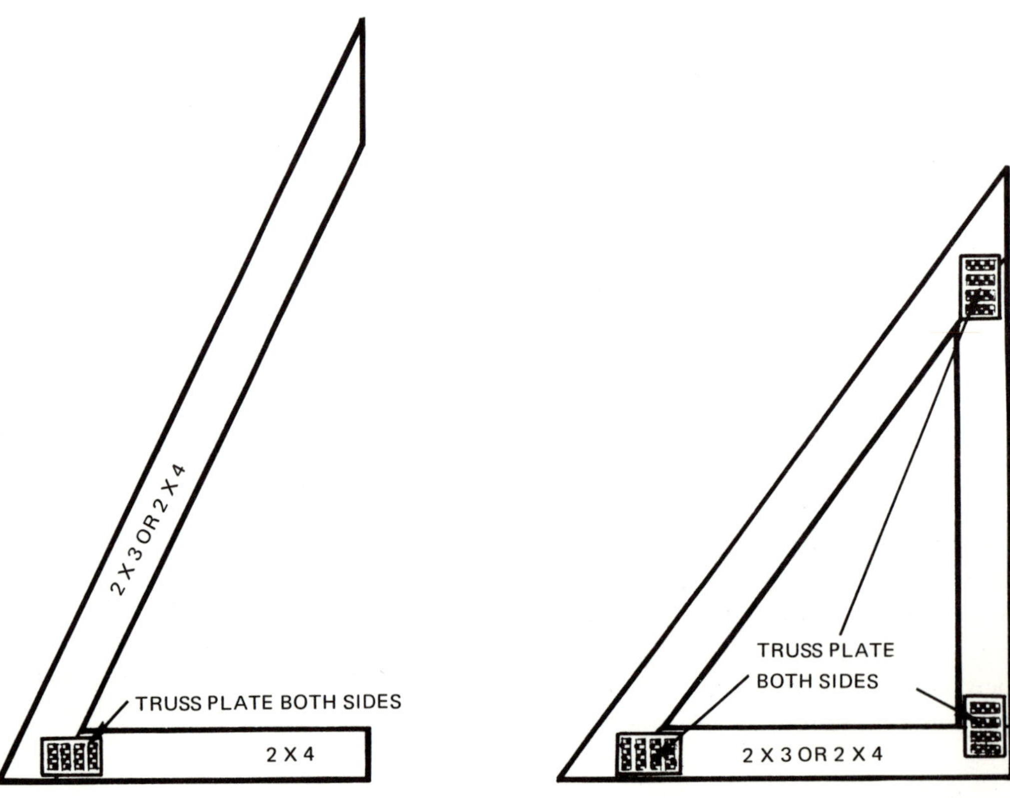


**Fig. 506.2.**
Mansard lookouts.

507 **Frieze Blocking for Brick Veneer.** This is most often done by furnishing, for job site installation, blocking consisting of 2 × 4 blocks about 5″ long nailed to a 1 × 4 or 1 × 6. This produces a projection of 4 3/8″ which is acceptable for brick veneer, although a total of 4 3/4″ is more desirable. The change to 3 1/2″ 2 × 4 may require a change in this procedure. (See Fig. 507.)

508 **Precut Roof Plywood.** Plywood roofing sheathing is precut and marked very similar to that for floors. (See Fig. 204.)

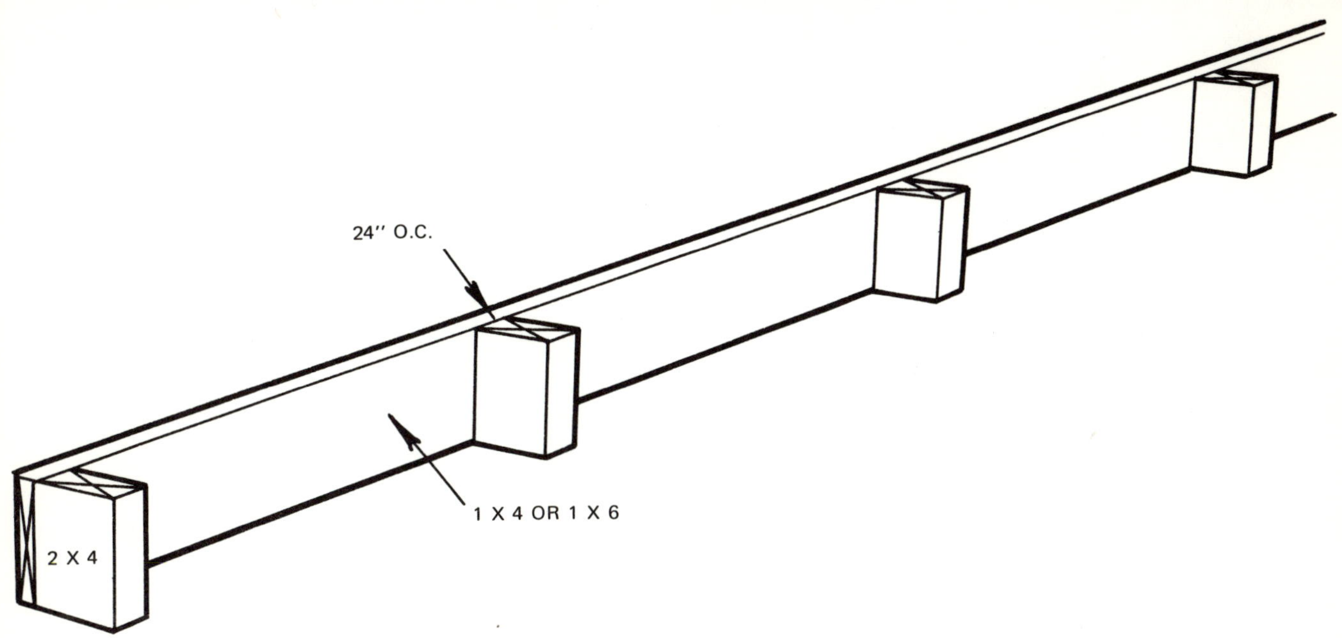


**Fig. 507.**
Blocking frieze for brick veneer construction.

# CHAPTER VI

# Plywood Components

W. D. Page*

## 600 Introduction

Because of its unique structural properties coupled with its large panel size in modular dimensions, plywood has been an integral part of the trend to componentization in construction—a trend which began with prefabrication during World War II. In the late 1930's adhesives were developed which produced strong, permanent bonds with either moisture-resistant or fully waterproof durability. This opened the way for plywood to become a major factor as a durable construction material.

These same adhesives and others which came along, when used imaginatively in conjunction with some sound engineering principles, opened up the possibility of another giant leap forward in the trend to componentization. Through bonding plywood to lumber and other materials with structural adhesives, the Forest Products Laboratory, U.S. Forest Service, developed the principle of stressed skin action. The principle, illustrated in Fig. 600, means simply that when two plywood skins are bonded to a series of lumber stringers, the result is a series of interconnected I-beams. The I-beams and other structural shapes achieved in a similar manner can be designed mathematically just as the same shape created with other materials. As a result, wood fibers can be placed where they are needed and where they will function most efficiently.

The design accomplishment of stressed skin action is only half of the story. The dimensional control possible in sophisticated factory fabrication and the dimensional stability inherent in glued wood assemblies provide a degree of refinement which the wood user expects from cabinetry. From the production line comes large structural elements which when delivered to the job site, go together quickly and accurately thereby reducing expensive and inefficient on-site labor to a bare minimum.

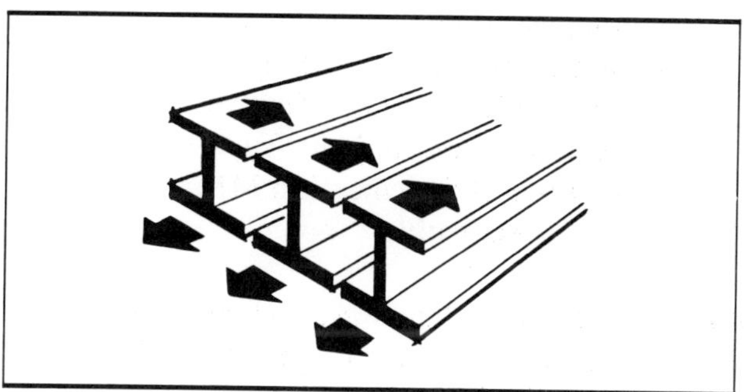

**Fig. 600.**
Stressed skin action is similar to a series of adjoining I-beams.

## 601 Adhesives

To produce stressed skin action requires adhesives with three basic properties. They must be (1) strong, (2) rigid, and (3) durable. This means adhesives of specific types and formulations, properly handled, applied, and cured. The design of the assembly assumes that the bond between the pieces will be under load throughout the life of the building. (See Fig. 803.1*E* for use of adhesives during application of wall finishes.)

601.1 **Interior Adhesives.** The earliest adhesive to appear which met these requirements, was of the casein type. These adhesives are still used today in applications where dura-

*W. D. (Dub) Page heads up American Wood Systems, an affiliate of the American Plywood Association. This represents a new entity to market pre-engineered systems. In 1959, he founded the Plywood Fabricator Service, also a Plywood Association affiliate. Nationally recognized in the components field, Mr. Page holds a master's degree in Forestry and has had 22 years experience in the plywood field.

bility requirements can be satisfied by an adhesive classed as interior or moisture-resistant, but not fully waterproof. The minimum specification states that when the equilibrium moisture content in the wood member does not exceed 18 percent, this type of an adhesive may be used. Such adhesives are covered under Federal Specification MMM-A-125, Type II (Casein type containing a mold inhibitor).

The basic constituent of a casein adhesive is the casein powder, a derivative of milk with alkaline chemicals added. It is sold as a dry, light brown powder which is mixed with water in ratios specified by the manufacturer. Normally, the mix ratio is 1/3 powder and 2/3 water by weight and is subsequently spread at a rate of about 60 pounds per 1000 sq. ft. of glue line.

Casein adhesives cure primarily through the loss of water. Required minimum curing temperature is about 50° F. Unfortified caseins are subject to attack by mold and fungus which means that those used for structural purposes should have a preservative added by the adhesive manufacturer. Adhesives meeting the Type II requirement of Federal Specification MMM-A-125 have this preservative.

601.2 **Exterior Adhesives.** When subjected to outdoor exposure or to extended periods of very high humidity, adhesives producing bonds which are 100 percent waterproof should be used. The only products fully established as producing such bonds are synthetic resins of the phenol, resorcinol, and melamine types.

These adhesives are covered by two specifications—Military Specifications MIL-A-5534A for high temperature setting resin adhesives and Federal Specification MMM-A-181-A for room or intermediate temperature setting resin adhesives.

Phenols, resorcinols, or blends of the two consist of a liquid resin and a powdered or liquid hardener or catalyst. The resin is usually dark brown or deep red in color, and tends to slightly strain the wood adjacent to the glue line.

Melamine adhesives are normally furnished in a powder together with a powdered catalyst. These two parts are mixed with water and tend to produce glue lines that are virtually colorless. Melamines are sometimes blended with urea resin to lower cost and provide better working characteristics. As long as the mix is at least 60 percent melamine these blends are considered to give structural performance.

All of the phenols and resorcinols must be cured at temperatures of 70° F. or above. Curing cyles can be substantially reduced through the application of heat. Melamine adhesives require a minimum of 140° F. in the glue line.

601.3 **Other Adhesives.** Several other adhesive types have appeared in recent years and are promising, but as yet unproved in providing the required strength, durability, and rigidity for structural components. These include epoxies, latex-phenolics, and catalyzed-polyvinyl resins.

Among the most promising are the elastomeric adhesives, whose use in field gluing of plywood floors to wood framing is rapidly growing. They are already recognized for their ability to increase stiffness, but more information is needed on their creep characteristics before recognizing their ability to increase strength.

Still in the experimental stage are adhesives of the polyurethane type which appear to offer some very desirable characteristics.

## 602 Structural Component Types

Plywood structural components which employ the principle of stressed skin action are of four basic types—flat stressed skin panels, curved stressed skin panels, folded plates, and box beams. A description of each follows:

602.1 **Flat Stressed Skin Panels.** In these panels the top and bottom skins are bonded to the longitudinal framing members, called stringers (see Fig. 602.1*A*) with the skin taking the compression and tension stresses and the stringers taking the shear.

Stressed skin panels may also have just a single skin bonded to stringers functioning as a T-beam. Another variation replaces the stringers with a sandwich core material which takes the shear stress in the panel. Core materials commonly used include

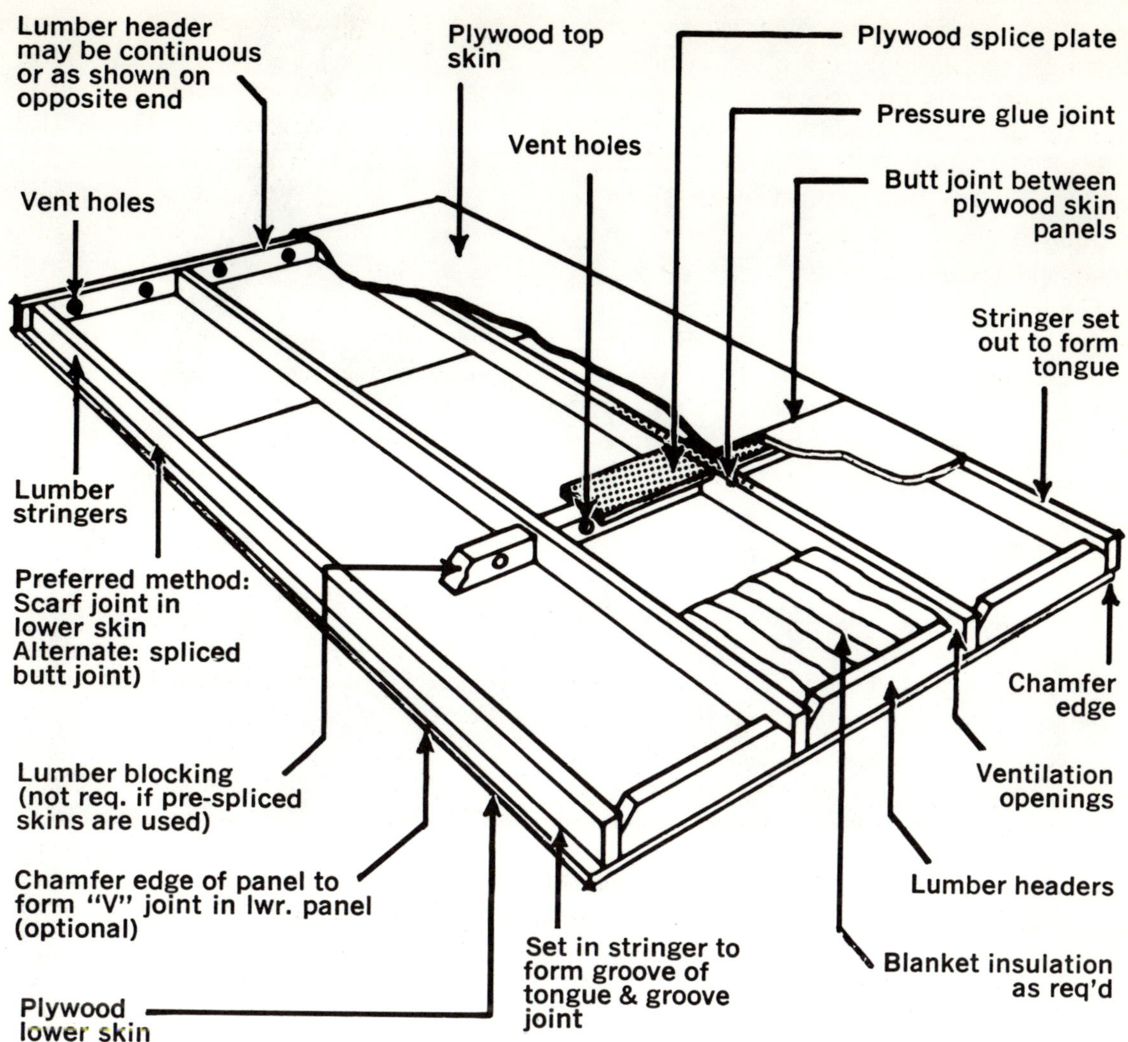


**Fig. 602.1*A*.**
Essential elements of flat stressed skin panels.

paper honeycomb, polystyrene foam, polyurethane foam.

Stressed skin panels are practical wherever traditional flat plane surfaces for walls, floors, and roofs are desired. They are used for spans ranging from 8′ to 40′ although spans from 12′ to 28′ are more common. Fig. 602.1*B* shows a typical application of flat stressed skin roof panels.

602.2 **Curved Stressed Skin Panels.** One of the most popular and dramatic applications of the structural component principle is found in the curved stressed skin panel. It offers the designer an economical solution for obtaining the aesthetic appeal of the arch, and at the same time the arching action permits large spans with relatively thin cross sections.

Three different panel sections are available: the ribbed panel (see Fig. 602.2*A*), the solid core panel, and the sandwich panel. Curved panels can be designed as arches and in this case tie rods are required. They may also be designed as highly cambered flat panels, which eliminates the tie rods, but those designs call for panels that are relatively thicker and, therefore, more expensive. Also with the latter, provision

**Fig. 602.1*B*.**
4′ × 47′ (40′ span) stressed skin panel covers large roof area.

must be made at the bearings for horizontal movement under load. (See Fig. 602.2*B*.)

The supporting beams, normally required, can be eliminated if a complete bay is designed and fabricated as a thin shell vault which functions as a unit and as a larged curved beam.

Chord distances for curved panels normally range from 8′ to 20″ and radii vary from 6′ to 14′. Typical load-span tables are shown in Fig. 602.2*C*; application shown in Fig. 602.2*D*.

602.3 **Folded Plates.** Folded plates are, in essence, large tilted beams which function as diaphragms. Ridge and valley chords, laminated from lumber, together with lumber rafters form the basic frame which has a stressed plywood cover on one or both sides. (See Fig. 602.3*A*.)

A form of shell structure, the folded plate, achieves strength and stiffness through shape rather than mass and is, therefore, particularly economical for the design effect created. Spans up to 100′ and more are quite practical. A typical load-span table is shown in Fig. 602.3*B*.

Design flexibility is considerable with plywood folded plate roofs. By varying the bay spacing, plate slope, number of folds, and overall span, many varied roof forms may be created. (See Fig. 602.3*C*.)

The typical folded plate is characterized by parallel ridge and valley chords. However, the design principle can be varied to produce other configurations including the popular radial folded plate. (See Fig. 602.3*D*.) A compression ring is located at the apex and a tension tie is located over the perimeter supports.

## Roof panels – series PFS-RA

TOP SKIN: ⅜" INT-DFPA • STRUCTURAL I
STRINGERS: E = 1.8 × $10^6$ psi.
BOTTOM SKIN: ⅜" EXT-DFPA • A-C GROUP 1

48"

| PANEL NO. | WEIGHT (psf) / PANEL DEPTH | DESIGN CRITERIA | | ALLOWABLE SPANS TOTAL LOAD (LL + DL) (psf) | | | | | | |
|---|---|---|---|---|---|---|---|---|---|---|
| | | | | 20 | 25 | 30 | 35 | 40 | 45 | 50 |
| RA | 2.85 | STRENGTH | SCARFED | 11'-8" | 11'-2" | 10'-2" | 9'-5" | 8'-10" | 8'-4" | 7'-10" |
| | | | SPLICED | 10'-4" | 9'-2" | 8'-5" | 7'-9" | 7'-3" | 6'-11" | 6'-6" |
| 2 | 2¼" | DEFLECTION | UNPLASTERED | 10'-6" | 9'-9" | 9'-2" | 8'-9" | 8'-4" | 7'-11" | 7'-7" |
| | | | PLASTERED | 9'-7" | 8'-10" | 8'-4" | 7'-9" | 7'-3" | 6'-11" | 6'-7" |
| RA | 3.65 | STRENGTH | SCARFED | 18'-11" | 18'-2" | 16'-7" | 15'-4" | 14'-4" | 13'-6" | 12'-10" |
| | | | SPLICED | 17'-2" | 15'-4" | 14'-0" | 13'-0" | 12'-0" | 11'-5" | 10'-10" |
| 4 | 4¼" | DEFLECTION | UNPLASTERED | 18'-0" | 16'-8" | 15'-8" | 14'-11" | 14'-3" | 13'-7" | 12'-11" |
| | | | PLASTERED | 16'-4" | 15'-2" | 14'-3" | 13'-3" | 12'-5" | 11'-10" | 11'-4" |
| RA | 4.39 | STRENGTH | SCARFED | 25'-1" | 24'-0" | 21'-11" | 20'-4" | 19'-0" | 17'-11" | 17'-0" |
| | | | SPLICED | 23'-8" | 20'-7" | 18'-10" | 17'-5" | 16'-3" | 15'-4" | 14'-7" |
| 6 | 6⅛" | DEFLECTION | UNPLASTERED | 24'-6" | 22'-9" | 21'-5" | 20'-4" | 19'-6" | 18'-6" | 17'-8" |
| | | | PLASTERED | 22'-3" | 20'-8" | 19'-6" | 18'-1" | 17'-0" | 16'-2" | 15'-9" |

## Floor panels – series PFS-FA

TOP SKIN: ⅝" INT-DFPA, UNDERLAYMENT, GRP. 1, EXT. GLUE
STRINGERS: E = 1.8 × $10^6$ psi
BOTTOM SKIN: ⅜" EXT-DFPA, A-C, GROUP 1

48"

| PANEL NO. | WEIGHT (psf) / PANEL DEPTH | DESIGN CRITERIA | | ALLOWABLE SPANS TOTAL LOAD (LL + DL) (psf) | | | | | | |
|---|---|---|---|---|---|---|---|---|---|---|
| | | | | 40 | 45 | 50 | 55 | 60 | 65 | 70 |
| FA | 5.09 | STRENGTH | SCARFED | 20'-4" | 19'-2" | 18'-2" | 17'-4" | 16'-7" | 15'-11" | 15'-4" |
| | | | SPLICED | 16'-5" | 15'-6" | 14'-8" | 14'-0" | 13'-5" | 12'-10" | 12'-5" |
| 6 | 6⅜" | DEFLECTION | UNPLASTERED | 19'-6" | 18'-7" | 17'-9" | 17'-1" | 16'-6" | 16'-0" | 15'-6" |
| | | | PLASTERED | 17'-0" | 16'-2" | 15'-6" | 14'-10" | 14'-4" | 13'-11" | 13'-6" |
| FA | 5.89 | STRENGTH | SCARFED | 26'-1" | 24'-7" | 23'-4" | 22'-4" | 21'-3" | 20'-5" | 19'-8" |
| | | | SPLICED | 20'-5" | 19'-10" | 18'-10" | 17'-11" | 17'-2" | 16'-6" | 15'-11" |
| 8 | 8⅜" | DEFLECTION | UNPLASTERED | 25'-1" | 23'-10" | 22'-10" | 21'-11" | 21'-2" | 20'-6" | 19'-11" |
| | | | PLASTERED | 21'-11" | 20'-10" | 19'-11" | 19'-2" | 18'-6" | 17'-11" | 17'-5" |
| FA | 6.69 | STRENGTH | SCARFED | 31'-3" | 29'-6" | 27'-11" | 26'-8" | 25'-6" | 24'-6" | 23'-7" |
| | | | SPLICED | 24'-11" | 23'-6" | 22'-3" | 21'-3" | 20'-3" | 19'-6" | 18'-10" |
| 10 | 10⅜" | DEFLECTION | UNPLASTERED | 30'-4" | 28'-10" | 27'-7" | 26'-6" | 25'-7" | 24'-10" | 24'-1" |
| | | | PLASTERED | 26'-6" | 25'-2" | 24'-1" | 23'-2" | 22'-4" | 21'-8" | 21'-0" |

**Fig. 602.1*C*.**
Load-span table for flat stressed skin roof panels.

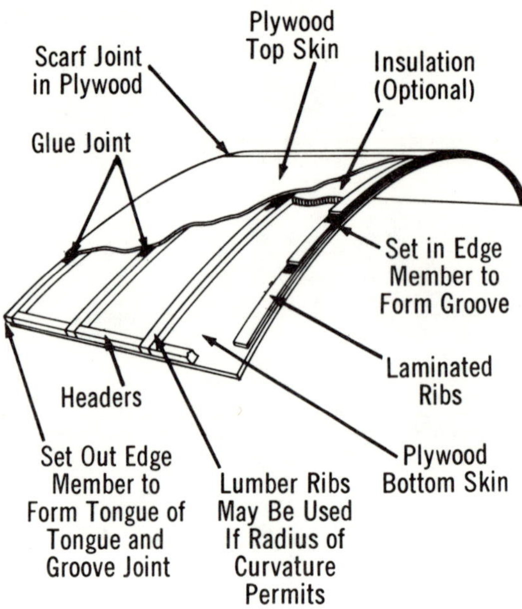


**Fig. 602.2*A*.**
Panel with curved plywood ribs.

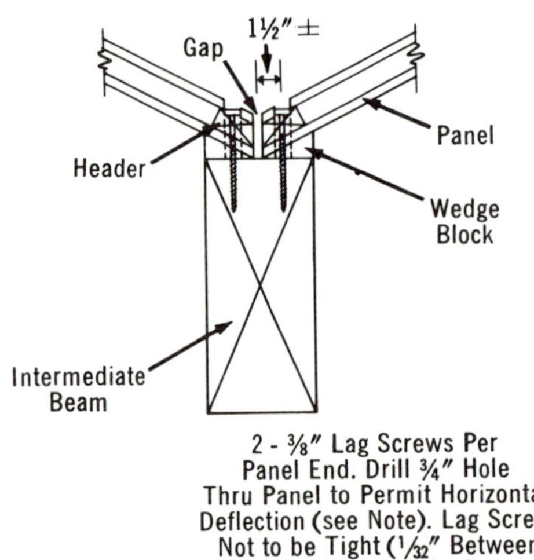


**Fig. 602.2*B*.**
Lag screw connection.

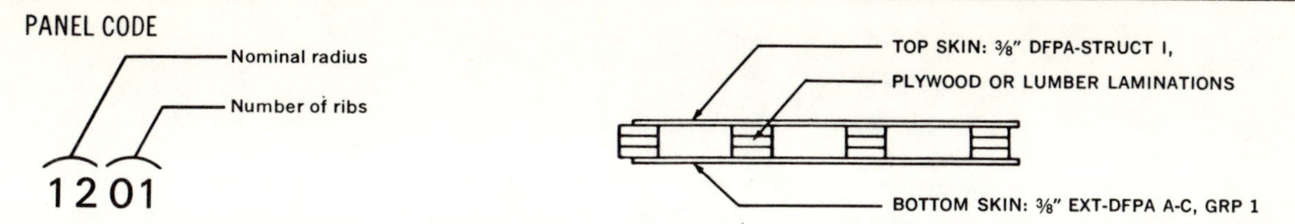


## Flexural panels

**Series PFS 3-F** (Plywood Ribs, 3/8" Laminations)

| NOMINAL RADIUS | Panel Code | Finished Radius (ft) | Weight (psf) | Panel Depth (in.) | Max. Allowable Spans —Live Load (psf) 15 | 20 | 25 | 30 | 35 | 40 |
|---|---|---|---|---|---|---|---|---|---|---|
| | 1001 | 11.71 | 2.37 | 1⅛ | 3′-5″ | 3′-5″ | 3′-5″ | 3′-5″ | 3′-5″ | 3′-5″ |
| | 1002 | 10.79 | 2.54 | 1½ | 5′-4″ | 5′-4″ | 5′-4″ | 5′-4″ | 4′-9″ | 4′-3″ |
| | 1003 | 10.32 | 2.72 | 1⅞ | 6′-11″ | 6′-11″ | 6′-11″ | 6′-10″ | 6′-6″ | 6′-3″ |
| **10** | 1004 | 10.23 | 2.89 | 2¼ | 8′-8″ | 8′-8″ | 8′-6″ | 8′-0″ | 7′-7″ | 7′-4″ |
| | 1005 | 10.17 | 3.06 | 2⅝ | 10′-5″ | 10′-4″ | 9′-8″ | 9′-1″ | 8′-7″ | 8′-3″ |
| | 1006 | 10.13 | 3.23 | 3 | 12′-1″ | 11′-7″ | 10′-9″ | 10′-2″ | 9′-8″ | 9′-3″ |
| | 1007 | 10.10 | 3.40 | 3⅜ | 13′-8″ | 12′-8″ | 11′-8″ | 11′-2″ | 10′-7″ | 10′-2″ |
| (6 & 8) | 1008 | 10.09 | 3.58 | 3¾ | 15′-0″ | 13′-9″ | 12′-9″ | 12′-2″ | 11′-7″ | 11′-1″ |
| | 1009 | 10.08 | 3.75 | 4⅛ | 16′-1″ | 14′-8″ | 13′-7″ | 13′-2″ | 12′-6″ | 12′-0″ |
| | 1010 | 10.08 | 3.92 | 4½ | 17′-2″ | 15′-8″ | 14′-6″ | 14′-3″ | 13′-6″ | 12′-11″ |
| | 1011 | 10.07 | 4.09 | 4⅞ | 18′-1″ | 16′-6″ | 15′-3″ | 15′-2″ | 14′-5″ | 13′-8″ |
| | 1012 | 10.06 | 4.26 | 5¼ | 19′-1″ | 17′-5″ | 16′-1″ | 16′-1″ | 15′-2″ | 14′-5″ |
| | 1013 | 10.05 | 4.43 | 5⅝ | 20′-0″ | 18′-3″ | 16′-11″ | 16′-11″ | 16′-0″ | 15′-2″ |
| | 1014 | 10.04 | 4.61 | 6 | 20′-1″ | 19′-2″ | 17′-9″ | 17′-9″ | 16′-9″ | 15′-11″ |

**Series PFS 5-F** (Lumber Ribs, 5/8" Laminations)

| NOMINAL RADIUS | Panel Code | Finished Radius (ft) | Weight (psf) | Panel Depth (in.) | Max. Allowable Spans —Live Load (psf) 15 | 20 | 25 | 30 | 35 | 40 |
|---|---|---|---|---|---|---|---|---|---|---|
| | 1201 | 14.60 | 2.48 | 1⅜ | 4′-7″ | 4′-7″ | 4′-7″ | 4′-7″ | 4′-7″ | 4′-7″ |
| **12** | 1202 | 12.70 | 2.77 | 2 | 7′-6″ | 7′-6″ | 7′-6″ | 7′-4″ | 7′-0″ | 6′-8″ |
| | 1203 | 12.41 | 3.05 | 2⅝ | 11′-0″ | 10′-9″ | 10′-0″ | 9′-5″ | 8′-11″ | 8′-6″ |
| | 1204 | 12.28 | 3.34 | 3¼ | 14′-1″ | 12′-10″ | 11′-11″ | 11′-4″ | 10′-9″ | 10-′4″ |
| (16 & 20) | 1205 | 12.20 | 3.62 | 3⅞ | 16′-3″ | 14′-10″ | 13′-9″ | 13′-1″ | 12′-6″ | 11′-11″ |
| | 1206 | 12.16 | 3.91 | 4½ | 18′-2″ | 16′-7″ | 15′-5″ | 15′-0″ | 14′-3″ | 13′-7″ |
| | 1207 | 12.12 | 4.19 | 5⅛ | 20′-3″ | 18′-6″ | 17′-1″ | 16′-9″ | 15′-11″ | 15′-3″ |
| | 1208 | 12.10 | 4.48 | 5¾ | 22′-3″ | 20′-4″ | 18′-10″ | 18′-9″ | 17′-9″ | 16′-11″ |
| | 1209 | 12.08 | 4.76 | 6⅜ | 24′-1″ | 22′-4″ | 20′-9″ | 20′-5″ | 19′-5″ | 18′-7″ |

## Arch panels

**Series PFS 3-A** (Plywood Ribs, 3/8" Laminations)

| NOMINAL RADIUS | Panel Code | Finished Radius (ft) | Weight (psf) | Panel Depth (in) | Max. Allowable Spans —Live Load (psf) 15 | 20 | 25 | 30 | 35 | 40 | Min. Span |
|---|---|---|---|---|---|---|---|---|---|---|---|
| **6** | 0601 | 7.03 | 2.37 | 1⅛ | 11′-3″ | 11′-3″ | 11′-3″ | 11′-3″ | 11′-3″ | 11′-0″ | 5′-5″ |
| | 0602 | 6.47 | 2.54 | 1½ | 12′-11″ | 12′-11″ | 12′-11″ | 12′-11″ | 12′-11″ | 12′-11″ | 5′-0″ |
| **8** | 0801 | 9.37 | 2.37 | 1⅛ | 10′-10″ | 10′-10″ | 10′-10″ | 10′-10″ | 10′-10″ | 10′-10″ | 7′-3″ |
| | 0802 | 8.63 | 2.54 | 1½ | 15′-9″ | 15′-9″ | 15′-9″ | 15′-4″ | 14′-11″ | 14′-6″ | 6′-8″ |
| | 1001 | 11.71 | 2.37 | 1⅛ | 10′-6″ | 10′-6″ | 10′-6″ | 10′-6″ | 10′-6″ | 10′-6″ | 9′-1″ |
| **10** | 1002 | 10.79 | 2.54 | 1½ | 19′-3″ | 18′-4″ | 17′-4″ | 16′-7″ | 15′-11″ | 15′-5″ | 8′-4″ |
| | 1003 | 10.47 | 2.72 | 1⅞ | 20′-3″ | 19′-11″ | 19′-6″ | 19′-1″ | 18′-6″ | 18′-0″ | 8′-1″ |
| | 1004 | 10.32 | 2.89 | 2¼ | 20′-7″ | 20′-7″ | 20′-2″ | 19′-9″ | 19′-4″ | 18′-11″ | 8′-0″ |

**Series PFS 5-A** (Lumber Ribs, 5/8" Laminations)

| NOMINAL RADIUS | Panel Code | Finished Radius (ft) | Weight (psf) | Panel Depth (in) | Max. Allowable Spans —Live Load (psf) 15 | 20 | 25 | 30 | 35 | 40 | Min. Span |
|---|---|---|---|---|---|---|---|---|---|---|---|
| **12** | 1201 | 14.60 | 2.37 | 1⅜ | 15′-3″ | 15′-3″ | 15′-3″ | 15′-3″ | 15′-3″ | 15′-2″ | 11′-3″ |
| | 1202 | 12.70 | 2.54 | 2 | 24′-0″ | 23′-3″ | 22′-4″ | 21′-4″ | 20′-7″ | 20′-0″ | 9′-10″ |
| **16** | 1601 | 18.03 | 2.37 | 1⅜ | 14′-7″ | 14′-7″ | 14′-7″ | 14′-7″ | 14′-7″ | 14′-7″ | 13′-10″ |
| | 1602 | 16.94 | 2.54 | 2 | 27′-6″ | 25′-3″ | 23′-11″ | 22′-9″ | 21′-9″ | 20′-11″ | 13′-1″ |
| **20** | DO NOT USE 2001 FOR ARCH PANEL | | | | | | | | | | |
| | 2002 | 21.17 | 2.54 | 2 | 27′-7″ | 26′-5″ | 24′-9″ | 23′-5″ | 22′-4″ | 21′-4″ | 16′-4″ |

**Fig. 602.2*C*.**
Load-span tables for curved panels.

**Fig. 602.2*D*.**
Typical curved panel application.

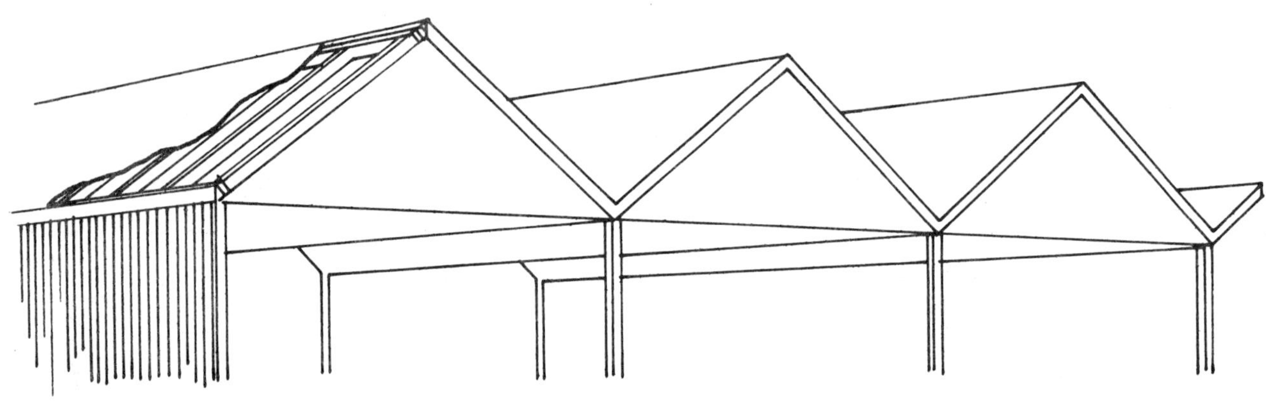

**Fig. 602.3*A*.**
Essential elements of plywood folded plates.

**There are almost an unlimited number of bay width-plate slope combinations. Therefore, certain standard plate slopes have been selected by Plywood Fabricator Service and load-span tables have been produced for these slopes. They are available from PFS. Steeper slopes allow longer spans and may be more economical. Spans range from 50′ + for an A slope to 100′ + for an F slope.**

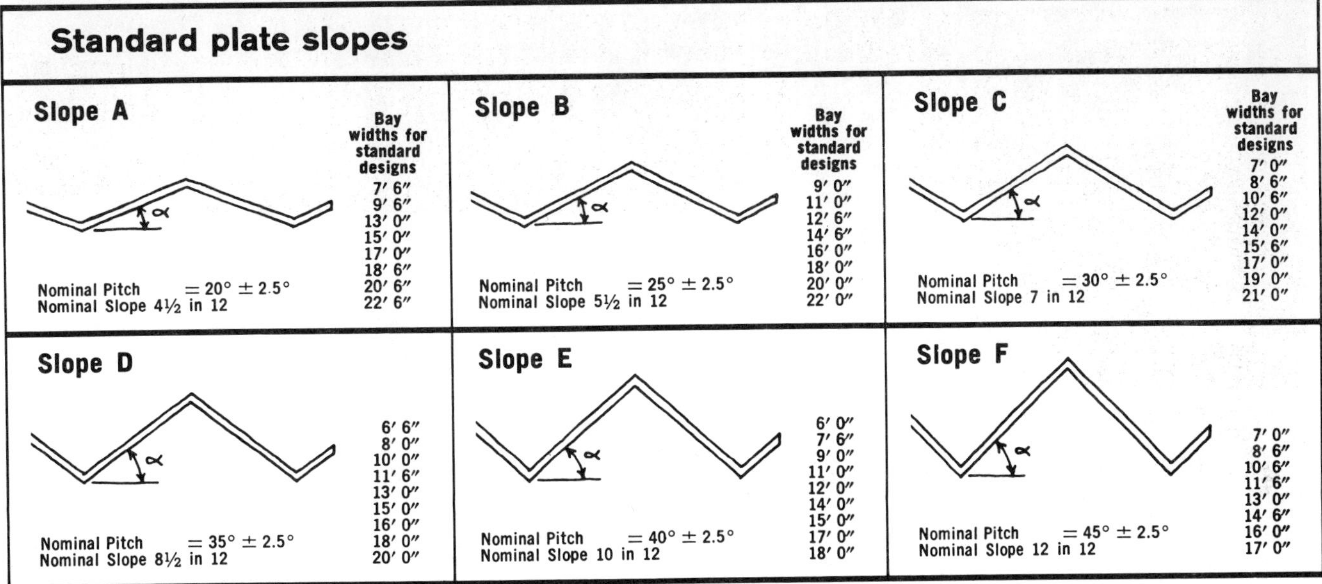


**Certain bay sizes also offer economies through standard plate widths and by limiting maximum shipping widths. The following list indicates some of these sizes. Maximum span is governed by design loads of 25 psf to 50 psf.**

| Bay | Slope | Max. Span | Bay | Slope | Max. Span |
|---|---|---|---|---|---|
| 6′-0″ | 10/12 | 76′-88′ | 12′-0″ | 5/12 | 56′-64′ |
| 6′-6″ | 8/12 | 68′-76′ | 12′-0″ | 7/12 | 56′-64′ |
| 7′-0″ | 7/12 | 56′-64′ | 12′-0″ | 10/12 | 80′-92′ |
| 7′-6″ | 4/12 | 40′-48′ | 12′-0″ | 11/12 | 96′-100′ |
| 8′-0″ | 4/12 | 40′-48′ | 12′-6″ | 5½/12 | 76′-88′ |
| 8′-0″ | 6/12 | 56′-64′ | 12′-6″ | 10/12 | 100′ |
| 8′-0″ | 9/12 | 72′-88′ | 12′-6″ | 12/12 | 100′ |
| 8′-0″ | 11/12 | 50′-64′ | 13′-0″ | 7/12 | 56′-64′ |
| 10′-0″ | 5/12 | 56′-64′ | 13′-0″ | 8½/12 | 96′-100′ |
| 10′-0″ | 8/12 | 72′-88′ | 14′-6″ | 5½/12 | 72′-88′ |
| 10′-0″ | 10/12 | 88′-96′ | 15′-0″ | 4½/12 | 56′-72′ |
| 10′-0″ | 12/12 | 96′-100′ | | | |

**Fig. 602.3*B*.**
Technical data folded plates.

**Fig. 602.3*C*.**
Junior High School Library provides attractive use of plywood folded plate.

**Fig. 602.3*D*.**
Radial folded plate roof. Accents credit union office building.

602.4 **Plywood Box Beams.** The fourth basic plywood structural component is the box beam. This is a hollow structural framing member made up of two or more vertical plywood webs bonded to lumber flanges which are further separated at intervals by spacers or stiffeners. (See Fig. 602.4*A*.)

The flanges are designed to carry com-

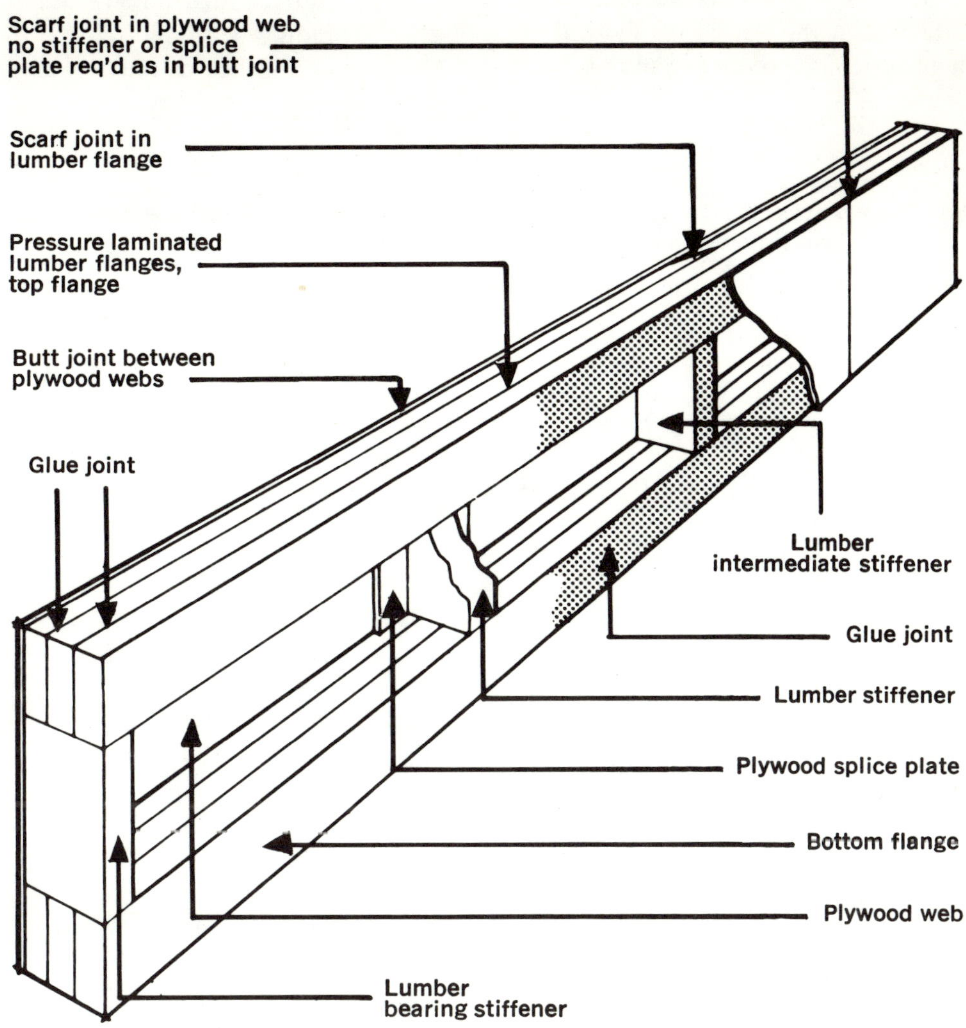


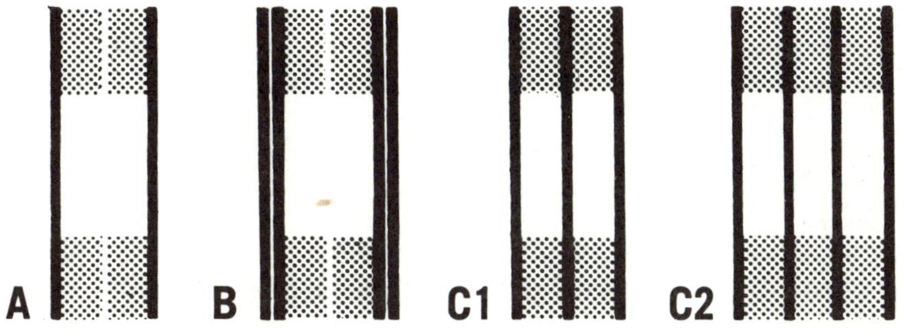


**Fig. 602.4*A*.**
Essential elements of plywood box beam.

pression and tension stresses with the plywood webs taking the shear. In addition, moderate shear stresses must be resisted in the flange-web connection which requires a calculation of minimum flange-web connection area in the design.

An alternate type of plywood beam relies on a single plywood web (I section) with flange attached in various ways. Typical of this is a proprietary product manufactured by Trus-Joist Corporation. On a high speed production line, the plywood web is inserted into a groove routed into the face of 2" × 4" flat flanges and into which a waterproof adhesive has been spread. These beams, 8" to 24" deep, are designed for spans up to about 30′, and are promoted primarily as a more dimensionally stable substitute for 2" lumber framing.

Box beams may be designed for spans of

## Figure 602.4b. Box Beams.

**Load-span tables represent a few typical size box beams. The almost infinite number of box beam configurations make it impossible to list all combinations.**

**The beam code is: type of beam, -depth in inches, -plywood web thickness, -and number of/and size of 2x members in the chords. The allowable load listed is for the more critical of shear, moment or deflection (1).**

| Beam Code | Plywood (2) (3) | Allowable load (plf) on various spans (ft) (4) | | | | | | | |
|---|---|---|---|---|---|---|---|---|---|
| | | 16′ | 18′ | 20′ | 22′ | 24′ | 26′ | 28′ | 30′ |
| A-24-3/8-2/4 | A-C | 389 | 346 | 311 | 283 | 260 | 240 | 222 | 207 |
| A-24-3/8-2/4 | STR I | 478 | 418 | 376 | 342 | 314 | 290 | 250 | 217 |
| A-24-1/2-2/4 | A-C | 509 | 452 | 407 | 370 | 339 | 290 | 250 | 218 |
| A-24-1/2-2/4 | STR I | 720 | 640 | 532 | 440 | 369 | 315 | 271 | 236 |
| A-24-1/2-3/4 | A-C | 541 | 481 | 433 | 394 | 361 | 333 | 309 | 273 |
| A-24-1/2-3/4 | STR I | 681 | 605 | 543 | 495 | 454 | 389 | 353 | 292 |
| A-24-1/2-2/6 | A-C | 530 | 471 | 424 | 385 | 353 | 326 | 303 | 282 |
| A-24-5/8-3/6 | A-C | 612 | 544 | 490 | 445 | 408 | 377 | 350 | 326 |
| C1-24-3/8-2/4 | | 600 | 533 | 443 | 366 | 307 | 262 | 226 | 197 |
| C1-24-3/8-2/6 | | 564 | 502 | 452 | 410 | 376 | 334 | 288 | 251 |
| C2-24-3/8-3/4 | | 828 | 736 | 662 | 552 | 464 | 395 | 341 | 297 |
| C2-24-3/8-3/6 | | 785 | 698 | 628 | 571 | 523 | 483 | 435 | 379 |
| C2-24-1/2-3/6 | | 1171 | 1041 | 908 | 750 | 631 | 537 | 463 | 403 |
| **Beam Code** | | **32′** | **36′** | **40′** | **44′** | **48′** | **52′** | **56′** | **60′** |
| A-48-1/2-2/6 | A-C | 549 | 488 | 439 | 399 | 338 | 288 | 248 | 216 |
| A-48-3/4-3/6 | A-C | 728 | 648 | 583 | 508 | 426 | 363 | 313 | 273 |
| C2-48-3/8-3/8 | | 793 | 705 | 635 | 565 | 473 | 403 | 349 | 304 |
| A-48-1-4/6 | A-C | 915 | 815 | 728 | 602 | 506 | 437 | 372 | 324 |
| **Beam Code** | | **44′** | **48′** | **52′** | **56′** | **60′** | **64′** | **68′** | **72′** |
| C2-48-3/8-6/6 | | 647 | 592 | 547 | 507 | 447 | 394 | 348 | 311 |
| C2-48-3/8-6/8 | | 614 | 563 | 520 | 483 | 450 | 422 | 397 | 376 |
| C2-48-1/2-6/8 | | 911 | 835 | 768 | 663 | 577 | 507 | 449 | 401 |

(1) Normal roof deflection criteria
(2) Type A beams use A-C EXT Group 1 or STRUCTURAL I sheathing webs
(3) Type C-1 and C-2 beams use A-C EXT Group 1 outer webs and STRUCTURAL I sheathing inner webs.
(4) Normal loading

Note: All flange material No. 1 Douglas Fir-Larch or Southern Pine. The above tables will enable the designer to obtain approximate beam sizes for such purposes as architectural planning. Final design must be made in accordance with American Plywood Association publication "Supplement No. 2 to the Plywood Design Specification—Design of Plywood Beams"—Form No. 68-812. Glued plywood box beams must be fabricated to rigid specifications under controlled conditions.

**Fig. 602.4*C*.**
Attractive church design uses plywood box beam framing.

100′ or more, although spans in the 30′ to 60′ range are more common. A typical load-span table is shown in Fig. 602.4*B*. and a typical application in construction is shown in Fig. 602.4*C*.

603 **Manufacturing Requirements**

To properly manufacture plywood components requires a substantial investment in plant and equipment. With today's adhesive technology, fabrication in other than a controlled factory situation is not recommended.

603.1 **Basic Equipment.** Mechanical glue mixers are essential since a near perfect glue line is required to provide the desired structural strength. Mixers come in sizes from two to several hundred gallons. They should not be purchased too large for ordinary production since not much glue is needed and pot life is limited.

Mixer speed should not exceed 65 to 70 rpm in order to avoid foam in the glue. Mixers come in portable and stationary versions. In hot climates they require cooling because high outside temperatures decrease the pot life of the glue.

Glue spreaders of the small hand or bench type are acceptable as long as they produce a uniform spread meeting at least the minimum spread requirements. In the interests of both material and labor savings, however, stationary heavy production-type spreaders are highly desirable.

Lumber surfacing equipment is necessary for practically all production classifications. A double surfacer or four sider is recommended. The four sider is recommended since it is more versatile. A surfacer which can plane two sides at once is necessary to insure parallelism between sides.

Lumber and plywood scarfing equipment is not always necessary, but most components longer than available material lengths require scarf joints to hold down material cost.

A radial saw equipped with a hollow-ground blade having a high population of carbide teeth and proper holddowns has proved satisfactory for scarfing lumber through 8" widths and plywood through 3/4" thickness.

Fork lifts of at least 6,000-lb. capacity can be used to move lumber, stacks of plywood, and finished components.

Conveyor sections of simple roller type, approximately 24" wide and adjustable in height, can serve most production machinery. These sections are necessary to support the material to infeed and outfeed ends of the machine.

Hoists, either hand operated, electric, or pneumatic, can be used advantageously in the box beam assembly area.

Stapling and nailing equipment can be employed to hold the lumber and plywood members in position until pressure has been applied even if pressure gluing is used.

Dust removal equipment should be connected with all dust and shavings-producing woodworking equipment in a modern plant.

Air compressors provide efficient sources of power to operate impact wrenches, stapling and nailing guns, and a variety of other air-operated hand tools. They can be used to generate pressure for cylinders or fire hoses and for cleaning machinery and equipment.

Impact wrenches come in both electric and pneumatic versions. The electric ones are less expensive than the pneumatic ones, but in some instances the electric wrenches have been found to require more maintenance, and they are subject to overheating in continuous use. Air-operated impact wrenches also usually allow more accurate torque settings. These wrenches can be used with the laminating jig for lumber and for several other pressure applications.

### 603.2 Hot Pressing vs. Cold Pressing.

In planning for production, many have assumed that nail gluing, or using nails to apply pressure during curing, at room temperature, is the only available technique. In this connection two things should be emphasized: first, there are other techniques for pressing that are inexpensive, practical, and flexible enough to meet the need. Second, these other techniques are most important because nail gluing has serious drawbacks which make it an interim solution at best. Nail-gluing creates an appearance problem on exposed surfaces which can only be solved by an expensive and time-consuming nail setting and hole filling. Also, the quality of bond obtained with nail-gluing is erratic. Nail-gluing pressures are far short of those recommended and adequate bonds are dependent on unusually strict control of other related variables. This kind of control frequently doesn't exist.

However, economics is the real clincher. The fabricator simply cannot afford to drive all those nails or staples.

First attempts at alternates to nail gluing were simple chain-clamp presses. Cross beams on today's chain-clamp presses are normally pairs of 6 inch channels welded back-to-back with a spacer, and pressure is applied through high-strength chains with a bolt welded on the end. Bolts are tightened with impact wrenches and subsequently adjusted accurately with torque wrenches for the desired pressure. Components of the same size and interior configuration can be stacked as high as glue assembly time and ceiling height will permit with this system.

Curing with chain-clamps is normally accomplished at room temperature. This means that ambient conditions must be carefully controlled, and curing times on available adhesives will vary from 4 to 8 hours.

Curing times in chain-clamp assemblies are sometimes speeded by mounting the assembly on rollers, and after clamping, rolling it into a so-called "hot room" where temperatures of 100 ° F. to 100 ° F. are maintained. Also, hoods can be placed over a clamped assembly and hot air circulated to reduce the cure time.

Production of curved panels provided the earliest need for faster curing using some type of conduction method of applying heat to the glue line. By their very nature, curved panels could not be laid up in stacks as in the case of flat members, and the fabricator simply couldn't wait 4 to 8 hours for one or two panels to cure in a clamp.

Various materials and techniques have been used, but the most frequently used technique employs metal bands which are inserted on the face of the platten in the jig to coincide with glue line areas. After pressure is applied, the metal bands are heated with electrical energy to some temperature short of that which will char the wood. Cure time is reduced to 10–20 minutes, depending on the distance from the platten to the farthest glue line. Other ingenious variations include a technique in which rib laminates are made 1/2″ wider than required structurally, and a groove routed in the face of individual laminates. Inserted in this goove at the time of layup is a 1/2″ steel banding strip which again is heated electrically after pressure is applied. The bands are subsequently pulled out and reused.

Box beams, folded plates, and stressed skin panels are all pressed flat, and the same pressing set up with slight variation will serve for all three. Since flat stressed skin panels account for 80 to 85 percent of the sales volume, presses are normally designed for efficient production of these units.

Much of the production continues to be cold pressed, and much of the clamping labor and time can be eliminated by making one of the cauls between the units a double caul with fire hoses between the two layers. After snugging up the assembly, the fire hoses are inflated with air to quickly and very uniformly apply pressure.

On the other hand, there appears to be a definite trend to hot pressing of flat panels. The advantages are perhaps intangible, but they are substantial nonetheless and increased usage of hot pressing can be expected.

Three different heat sources are used for the industry's presses—steam, hot oil, and electrical energy. All work very well, Plattens are heated at temperatures of 285 ° F. to 430 ° F. with the highest temperatures being used with hot-oil heated presses.

At least one manufacturer of stressed skin panels uses a technique involving a small wire embedded in the glueline at the time of panel lay-up. While the panel is under pressure in a large cold press, the wire is heated electrically to effect a rapid cure of the adhesive adjacent to the wire. Pressing schedules are comparable to those used with presses having heated plattens. The wire is not removed from the panel.

To achieve an adequate bond between two wood surfaces requires pressure of 100–150 PSI on the glue line. Pressures in this range can be obtained by one of two methods: (1) hydraulic cylinders or (2) air inflated fire hoses embedded beneath the platten. Typical cold press and hot press equipment is shown in Figs. 603.2*A* and *B*. Fig. 603.2*C* shows a stationary glue spreader.

604 **Building Codes, Standards, and Certifications.** Plywood structural components are acceptable in practically all building codes and by other regulatory bodies when evidence is provided that they are properly designed and fabricated. Design methods upon which structural engineers can base their calculations are well recognized and available. Published load-span tables are also available covering a wide range of normal design requirements. The seal of a registered engineer will normally satisfy design requirements of codes.

Fabrication specifications for these components have been published by the American Plywood Association and are readily available. Many codes and regulatory bodies require that production be under the regular supervision of an approved independent testing agency to assure proper fabrication. Providing such an inspection, testing, and certification service is Plywood Fabricator Service, Inc., a non-profit affiliate of the American Plywood Association.

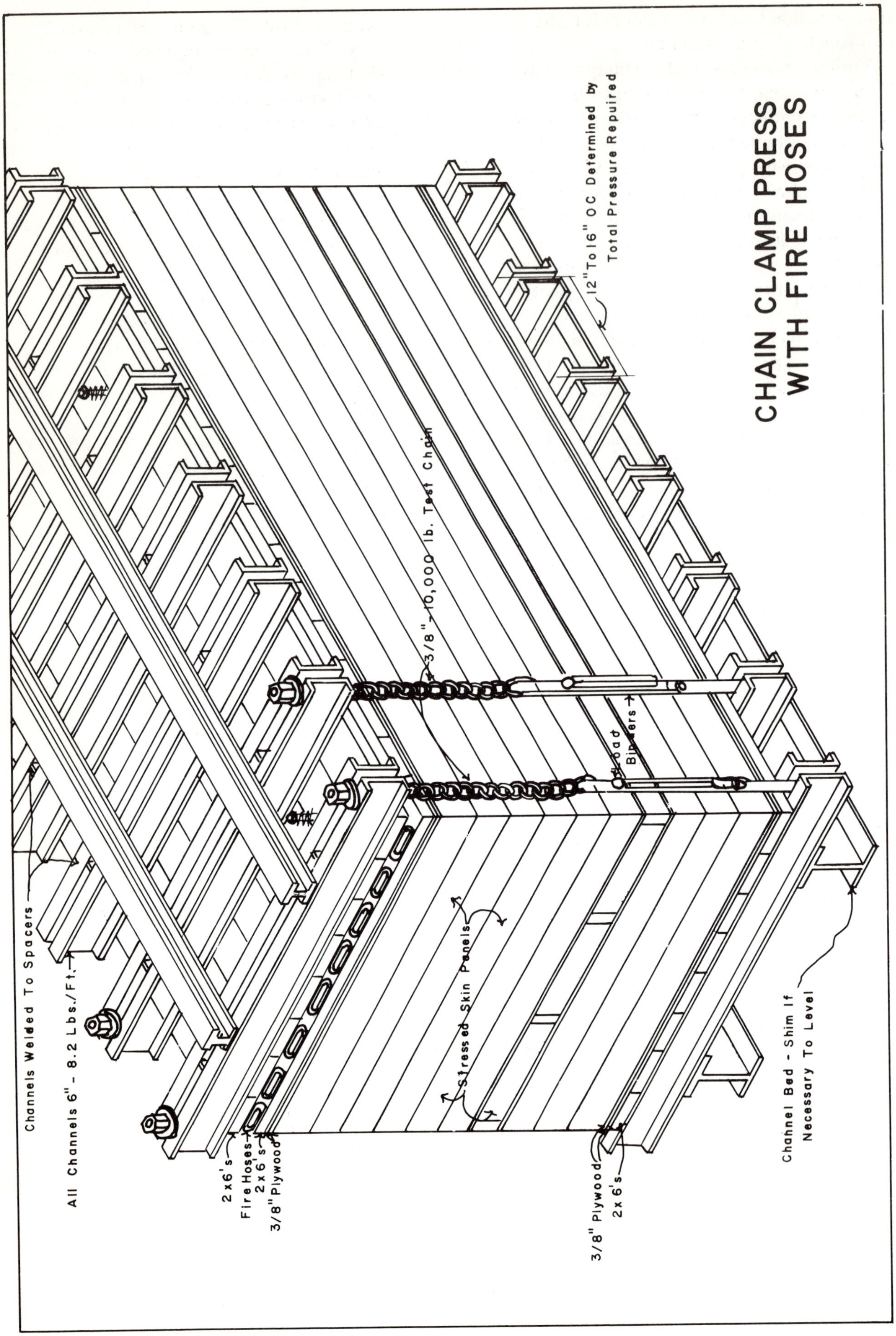

**Fig. 603.2A.**
Typical cold press for stressed skin panel production.

**Fig. 603.2*C*.**
Preassembled stressed skin panel frame has glue spread in large stationary spreader.

**Fig. 603.2*B*.**
8′ × 32′ hot press produces 256 sq. ft. of panels every 5–12 minutes.

# CHAPTER VII

## Prehung Door Units

700 **Definition.** A prehung door unit is a precut and assembled unit consisting of the door with the lock and hinges that is installed in the door frame. The door frame includes both sides of door trim. The interior or exterior door frame, trim and door, with hardware installed are delivered to the job site in a preassembled unit. Door units are inserted into openings and completely installed in a few minutes. Exterior units frequently contain the combination or screen door and sill. Units can be fully assembled or with some parts "knocked down."

700.1 **Advantages.** Time saving is the dominant advantage of prehung door units over conventional methods. Interior units can be installed in 15–20 man minutes as compared to 180–240 man minutes. In addition, the time saved in the elapsed time to complete the on-site structure must be considered. This is also a factor in modular manufacture, accelerating the flow of the modular units on the production line.

Higher and more uniform quality usually results when prehung units are used. Less of the highly skilled "finish" type of carpenters are needed on site.

Estimating is simplified and made more accurate as the use of pre-hung units gives a nearly installed cost with hardware included.

701 **Classification.** Door units may be classified as interior and exterior. Interior door units can be further classified by jamb type as follows (Commercial standard).

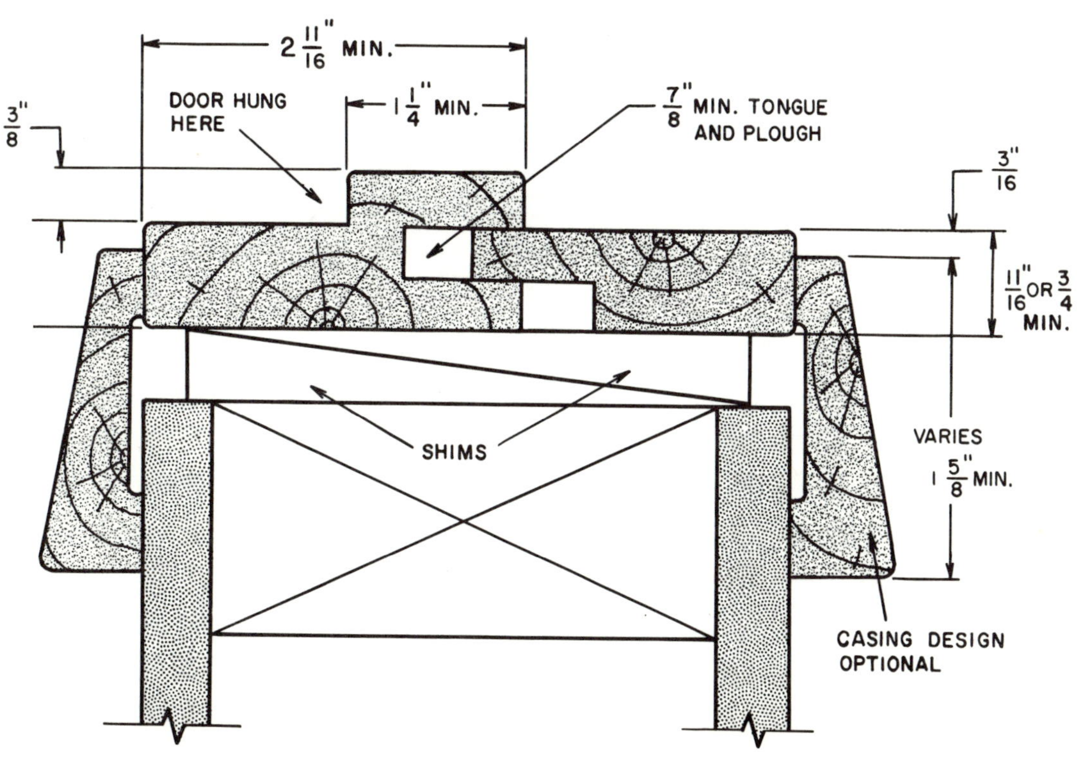


**Fig. 701.1.**
Type 1, 2 piece adjustable (split) jamb unit, full size detail.

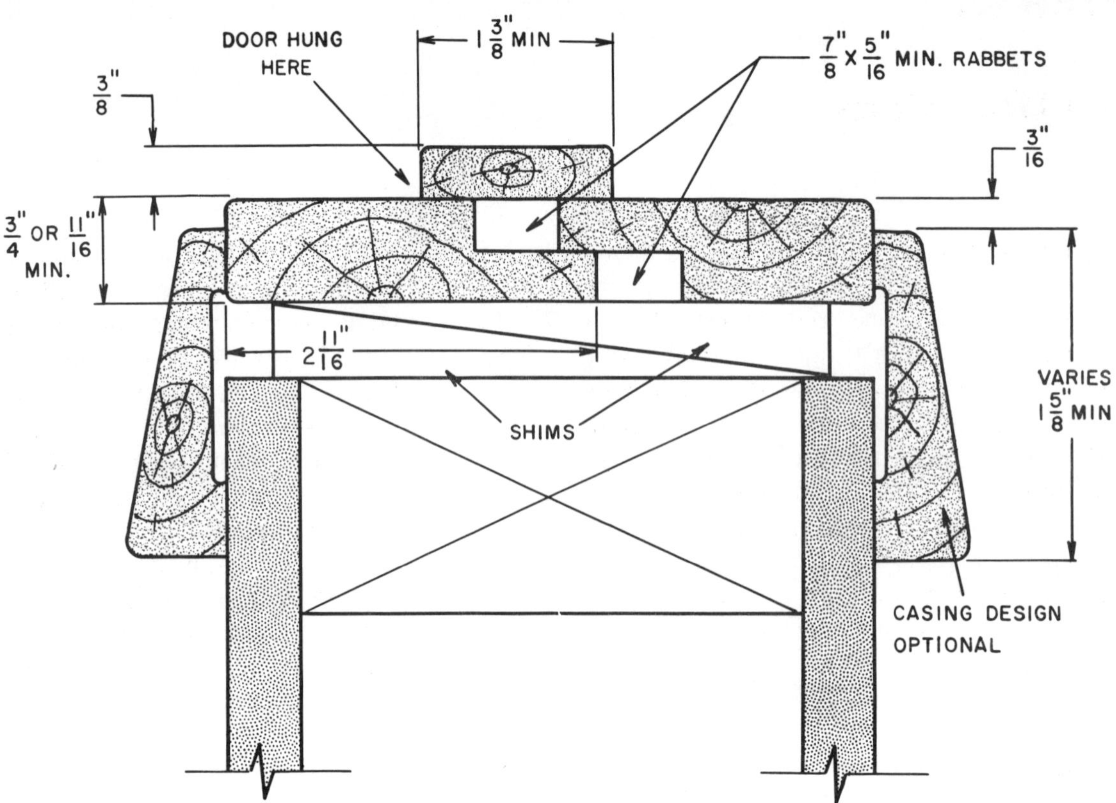


**Fig. 701.2.**
Type 2, 3 piece adjustable (split) jamb unit, full size detail.

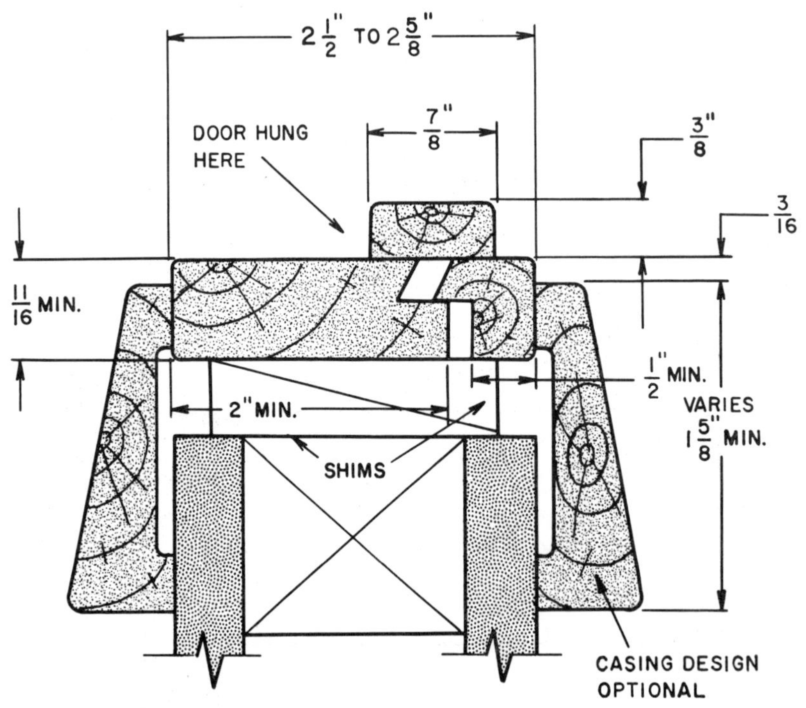


**Fig. 701.3.**
Type 2A, 3 piece adjustable (split) jamb unit, full size detail.

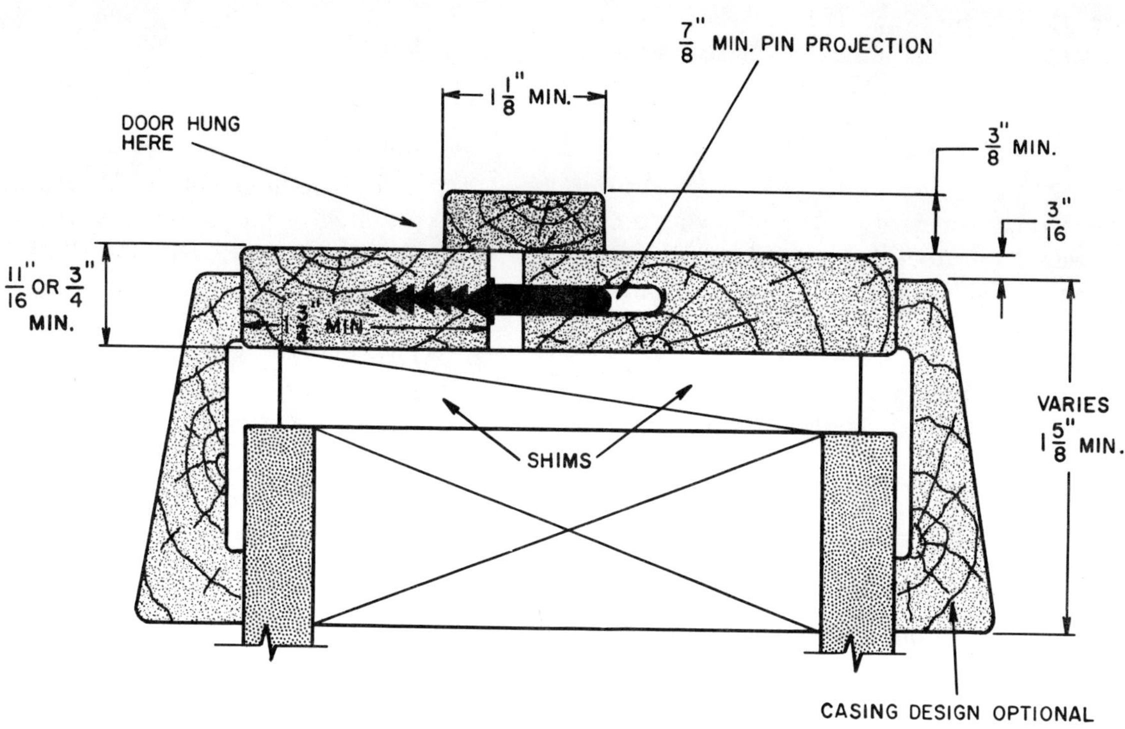


**Fig. 701.4.**
Type 3, 3 piece adjustable (split) jamb unit, full size detail.

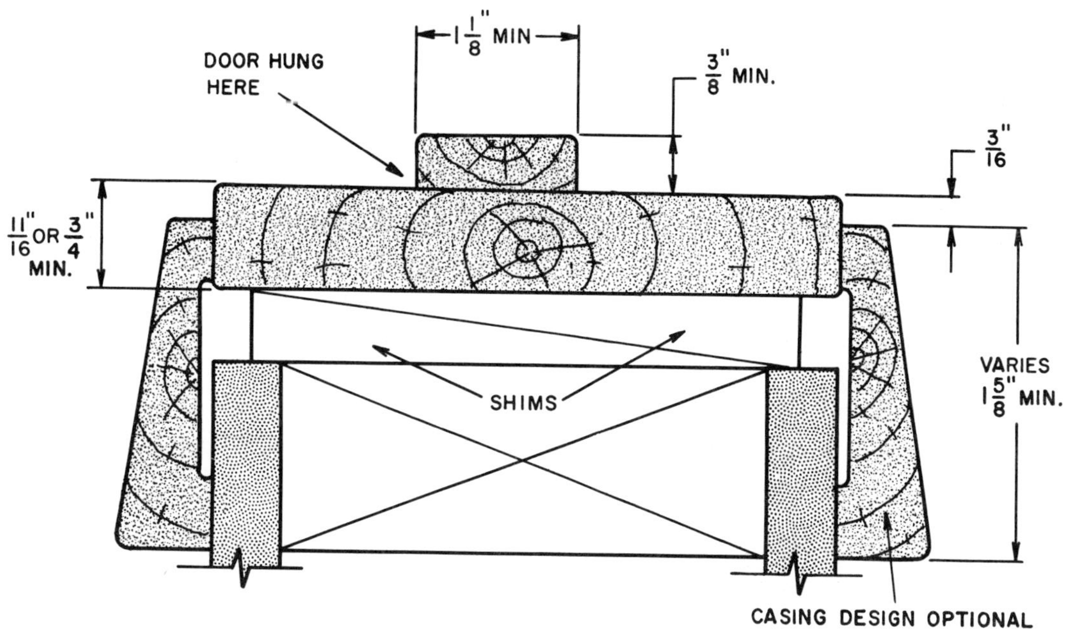


**Fig. 701.5.**
Type 4, non-adjustable jamb unit (solid jamb), full size detail.

701.6 **Split jambs** have the advantage of being adjustable for different wall thicknesses such as 3/8" drywall, 1/2" drywall, 7/8" plaster, or irregular wall thicknesses. They are more expensive then the solid or one piece jamb.

702 **Commercial Standards.** The following are excerpts from the Product Standard for Hinged Interior Wood Door Units." PS 32-70

**2.2.3** *Jamb Widths (see 3.2)*
*Jamb Width "S"—2 1/2" to 2 5/8" (Type 2A only)*
*Jamb Width "M"—3 1/8" to 3 5/8"*
*Jamb Width "L"—4 to 4 5/8"*
*Jamb Width "W"—4 1/2" to 5 1/8"*

**2.2.4** *Jamb Thicknesses (Minimum) 11/16"'*

**3.1.3** *Casing—When door units are trimmed with casing, the casings shall be at least 1/4 inch thick at point of fastening to the jamb sections, not less than 9/16" thick at its thickest part, and not less than 1 5/8" wide. All machining of casings shall be clean and smooth with sharp profile.*

**3.1.5** ***Hinges.*** *The hinges shall be brass or steel full mortise type with a minimum thickness of 0.095 in. and may have round or square corners.*

*Each half of each shall have solid full size leaves with at least three screws and shall be at least 3 1/2" in vertical dimension and at least 1 5/8" from center of pin to edge of each leaf.*

**3.3** ***Assembly-Jambs.*** *The side jambs and head jambs shall be joined together with a dado or notch at least 3/16" deep. The width of the dado or notch should be not more than 1/32" wider than the receiving member. The joints between the side jambs and head jambs shall be fastened as follows:*

*A. If solid one piece side and head jambs are used in the fabrication of the unit, and joint between the side and head jamb is a dado, any of the following may be used to fasten the joint:*

*Four 1 3/4 in. (5 penny) box or common nails.*

*Four 1 3/4 in. Tee nails 16 gauge, any finish.*[5]

*Two 1 1/2 in. staples 16 gauge, any finish.*

*Five 1 1/4 in. Tee nails 16 gauge, plastic finish.*

*B. If solid one piece side and head jambs are used in the fabrication of the unit, and the joint between the side of the head jamb is a notch, any of the above may be used for fastening one way and in addition, shall be fastened the cross direction by any one of the following:*

*Two 1 3/4 in. (5 penny) box or common nails.*

*Two 1 3/4 in. Tee nails 16 gauge, any finish.*

*One 1 1/2 in. staple 16 gauge, any finish.*

*Two 1 1/4 in. Tee nails 16 gauge, plastic finish.*

*C. If either two piece or three piece split side and head jamb are used in the fabrication of the units, and the joint between the side and the head jamb is a dado, any of the following may be used to fasten the joint of the wider section:*

*Three 1-3/4 in. (5 penny) box or common nails.*

*Three 1-3/4 in. Tee nails 16 gage, any finish.*

*Three 1-1/2 in. staples 16 gage, any finish.*

*Four 1-1/4 in. Tee nails 16 gage, plastic finish.*

*Any of the following may be used to fasten the narrower section:*

*Two 1-3/4 in. (5 penny) box or common nails.*

*Two 1-3/4 in. Tee nails 16 gage, any finish.*

*Two 1-1/2 in. staples 16 gage any finish.*

*Three 1-1/4 in. Tee nails 16 gage, plastic finish.*

*D. If either two piece or three piece split side and head jambs are used in the fabrication of the unit, and the joint between side and head jamb is a notch, any of the methods listed above in "C" may be used for fastening one way and in addition, each section shall be fastened in the cross direction by any one of the following:*

*One 1-3/4 in. (5 penny) box or common nail.*

*One 1-3/4 in. Tee nail 16 gage, any finish.*

*One 1-1/2 in. staple 16 gage, any finish.*

*One 1-1/4 in. Tee nail 16 gage, plastic finish.*

*E. If the face of the narrow jamb section of split jambs is less than 1 in., the sections shall be fastened (in) two directions with any of the following:*

*One 1-3/4 in. (5 penny) box or common nail.*

*One 1-3/4" in. Tee nail 16 gage, any finish.*

*One 1-1/2 in. staple 16 gage, any finish.*

*One 1-1/4 in. Tee nail 16 gage, plastic finish.*

**3.4** ***Assembly-casing to jamb.*** *The side casing trim as specified in 3.1.3 shall be mitered with the head casing. These miter joints shall have a blind saw kerf in each end and shall receive a metal spline at least 1 in. long. Miter and saw kerf shall be accurate so that finished joint will be true and tight with faces in alignment. Casing shall be cut square and even with bottom of side jamb section. Each casing member shall have one fastener within 3 in. of each end and fasteners shall be spaced not more than 11 in. apart. All of these fasteners shall be set approximately 1/16 in. below the surface. The casing shall be recessed 3/16 in. from face of jamb plus or minus 1/16 in. but shall have uniform offset the length of the recess. Casing trim not over 3/8 in. thick at fastening point may be fastened to the jambs by any of the following methods:*

*1-1/4 in. (3 penny) casing or finish nails.*

*1-1/4 in. Tee nails 16 gage, any finish.*

*7/8 in. 3/16 in. wide staples 18 gage, any finish.*

*For casing up to and including 5/8 in. thick at fastening point, any of the following may be used:*

*1-1/2 in. (4 penny) casing or finish nails*

*1-1/2 in. Tee nails 16 gage, any finish.*

*1-1/8 in. 3/16 in. wide staples 18 gage, any finish.*

*1-1/4 in. Tee nails 16 gage, plastic finish.*

*For casing up to and including 3/4 in. thick at fastening point, any of the following may be used:*

*1-3/4 in. (5 penny) casing or finish nails.*

*1-3/4 in. Tee nails, 16 gage, any finish.*

*1-1/2 in. Tee nails, 16 gage, plastic finish.*

**3.6** ***Installation of hinges and door.*** *Both the door and the jamb shall be routed for flush installation of hinge with hinge pin center as least 1/2 in. from the edge of the jamb to afford a swing of 180 degrees for the door. The hinge route on the door edge shall not extend the full thickness of the door, but shall leave at least 1/4 in. of wood on the back edge. Screws for hinges shall be slotted or cross head and at least 3/4 in. long with full screw threads. All screws shall be installed with a tight firm grip into the door and the jamb. Each hinge shall have at least three screws per side. The center of the top and bottom hinges shall be not more than 12 in. from the top and the bottom of the door. Doors weighing less than 50 pounds shall have at least two hinges. Doors weighing 50 pounds or more, shall have at least three hinges with the center hinge located an equal distance from the other two. Hinges shall be applied to jamb and to square edge of door in such a manner as to give a 1/16 in. clearance between jamb and door edge; a 1/16 in. clearance between the face of the door and the edge of door stops; 1/8 in. clearance between the top of the door and the head jamb; and a 1/8 in. clearance between the lock edge of the door and the jamb* (see Figure 702). *Clearance between the bottom of the door and the bottom of the jambs to accommodate variations of finish floor and/or floor coverings shall be not less than 3/8 in. A tolerance of 1/32 in. will be allowed on each of these dimensions.*

**3.6.1** ***Installation of latch set.*** *The beveled edge of the door shall be machined for the latch set (see 3.1.6). The center of the bore for the latch shall be not less than 36 in. from the bottom of the jamb nor more than 40 in. from bottom of door. Where required, the edge of the door, and the side jamb shall be machined for the insertion of the face plate and the keeper plate in true alignment with the latch. Plates shall be installed flush with the edge of the door and with the face of the jamb.*

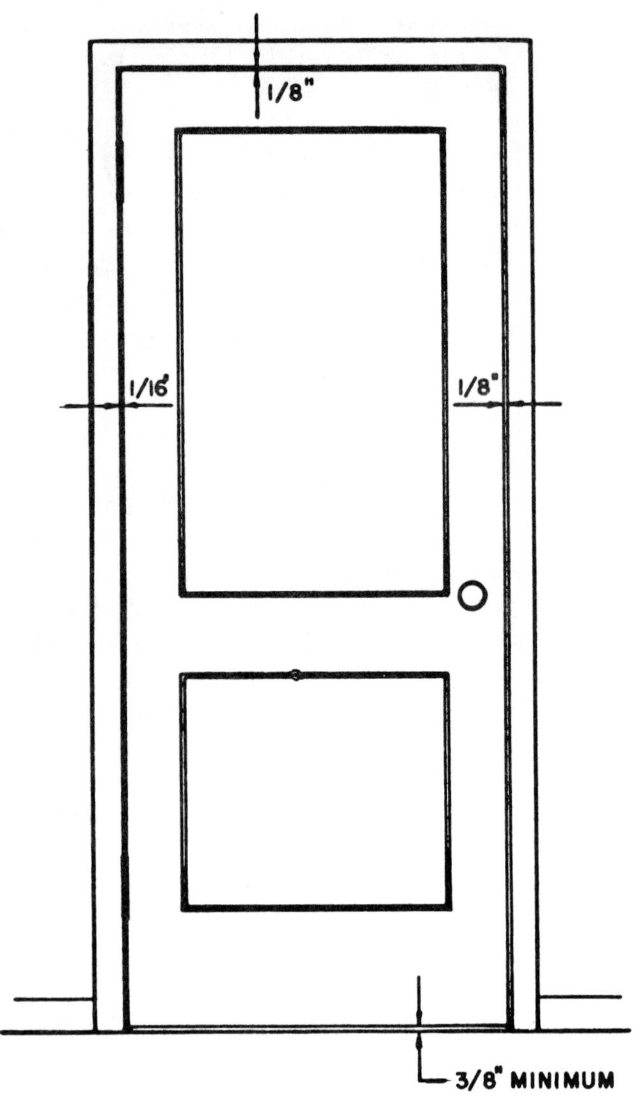


**Fig. 702.**
"Elevation of Door Unit" showing clearances around the door.

***3.6.2 Installation of door.*** *Door openings shall be within limits as outlined in 3.6. All measurements shall be taken from the bottom of the rabbet where the door is hung. Edges of both jamb sections that receive the casing may be either square with the face of the jamb or be beveled. Corners on the face of both jamb sections may be either square or eased.*

***3.7 Door Unit Bracing.*** *Each door unit shall be secured across the bottom to insure safe handling until delivery to construction site. Either a wood brace or steel, fabric, or filament tape shall be used. The wood brace shall be fastened with 1-1/2 in. box nails, or staples, or Tee nails driven into jamb sections to space the jambs the proper distance apart. One-eighth in. thick space wafers may be tacked to the edge of the door near the bottom on the lock side; one near the top and one on the top near the lock edge; each fastened with 1 in. nail, or a staple, or a Tee nail. These spacer wafers shall provide a tight compact unit for easy handling and prevent racking damage to miter joints and shall assist installation of the unit into the wall with proper clearance. A closure block with one 1 in. nail, or a staple, or a Tee nail shall be used near the center to keep the door in a closed position. As an alternate to the closure block a 1-3/4 in. (five penny) nail or 1-3/4 in. Tee nail may be driven through the jamb securely into the top rail or the lock stile of door, but not driven home so that it may be removed before installation. Where one or both sides of casing are applied, casing shall be adequately supported or protected.*

---

*Copies of this Commercial Standard are available from the Superintendent of Documents, U.S. Government Printing Office, Washington, D.C. 20402*

703 **"Hand" of Door Units.** Some manufacturers are the opposite but the consensus is that the hand is described as follows:

Standing on the hinge side of the door and facing the door, if the lock is on your right, it is a right hand door. This may also be described as: Standing with your back to the hinge jamb, if the door is hinged on your right, it is right hand; left, left hand.

704 **Reversible Construction.** Some manufacturers manufacture their flush door units and the subcomponents so that they may be used either right or left. This is done by boring for the lock in the center of the door (40″) for a 6′ 8″ door; applying butts equidistant from the ends of the jambs; dadoing the head jamb instead of the side jambs and arranging the stop so that it will miter with or butt the head jamb on either end of the side jamb. Thus, these components can be used to assemble a right or left hand door. Reduction and simplification of inventory may make this desirable.

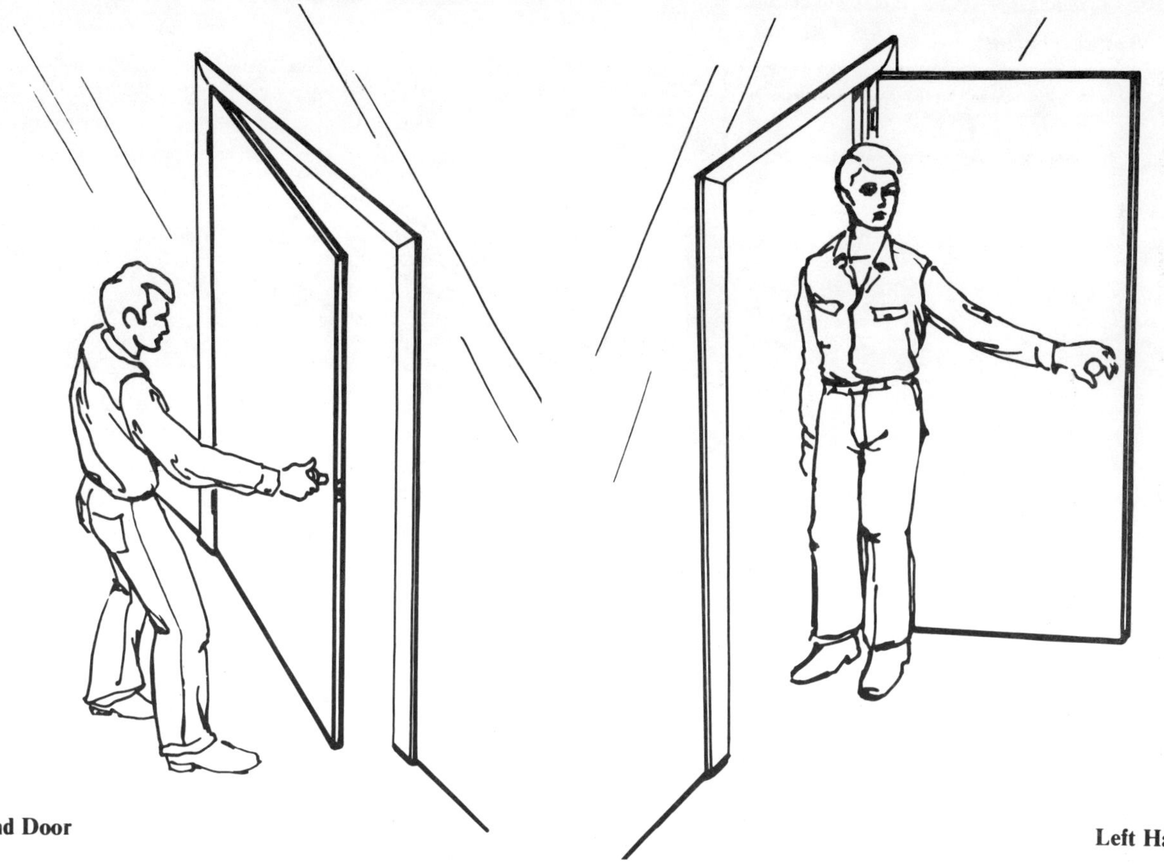

Right Hand Door

Left Hand Door

Fig. 703.

705 **Make or Buy.** Most areas in the country have several highly developed prehung door manufacturing specialists. After considering the factors of investment in equipment, inventory, plant space, costs, and availability, many package, component, and modular manufacturers have found out it is advantageous to purchase prehung door units from one of these specialists on a long term contract basis.

706 **Investment Required.** As a general guide the investment required for setting up a prehung door operation is as follows:

| Size Operation | Units/ Day | Equipment | Space | Inventory |
|---|---|---|---|---|
| Small | up to 50 | $ 7–10,000 | 1200′ | $10–12,000 |
| Medium | 100+ | 11–15,000 | 2500′ | 25,000 |
| Large | 200+ | 15–30,000 | 20,000′ | 75,000 |

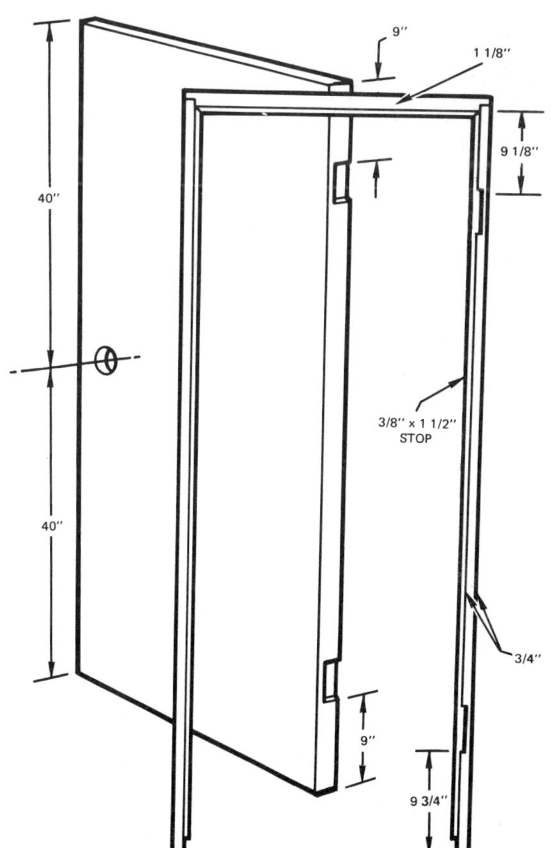


Fig. 704.
Reversible type construction.

## 707 Manufacturing:

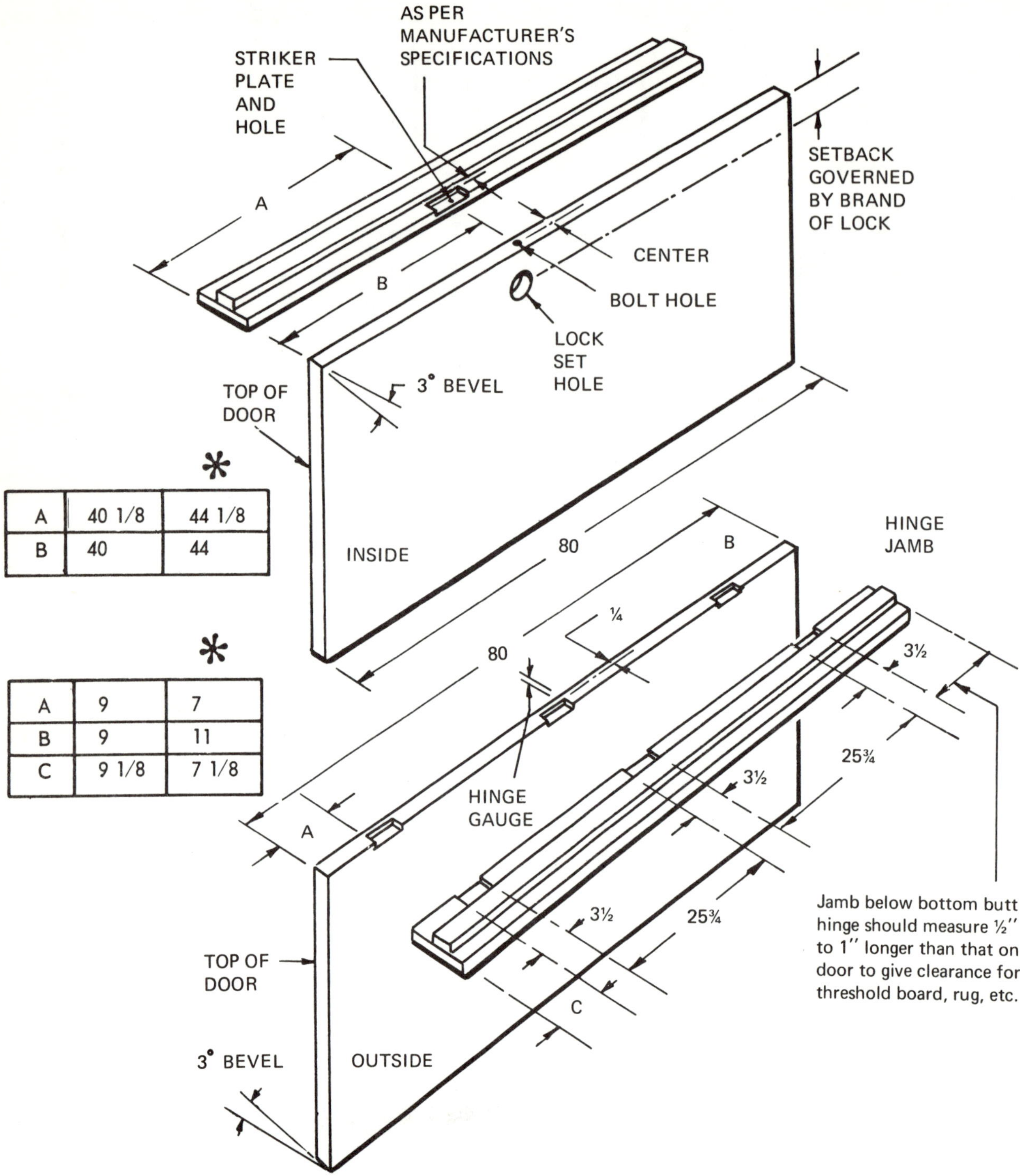


| | | |
|---|---|---|
| A | 40 1/8 | 44 1/8 |
| B | 40 | 44 |

*

| | | |
|---|---|---|
| A | 9 | 7 |
| B | 9 | 11 |
| C | 9 1/8 | 7 1/8 |

NOTE – In routing for butt hinges, on jamb, the distance should be 5/16" and always measured from jamb stop out. On the door, the routing should be 1/4" in from inside edge of door. This will allow 1/16" clearance between door and stop. Jamb above top butt hinge should measure 1/8" longer than that on door to insure clearance on door.

* These dimensions most commonly used in the door unit industry.

**Fig. 707.**
Door & jamb layout.

*(Clary)*

707.1 **Operations**

**a.** "Stitching" stop to jamb (except 2 piece adjustable jamb) Some operations use an S4S rectangular stop on the head jamb with a molded stop on side jambs. This eliminates the need to miter or cope the joints at the head. The molded side stop simply butts to the head.

**b.** Sizing and beveling the door. (3°= bevel on lockside of door) Doors can now be purchased, sized, and beveled from the manufacturer.

**c.** Door machine operation, routing for butts on jamb and door, and bores for latch. Setting is slightly different for exterior doors. When doors and jambs are run separately, accuracy should be such that jambs and doors should match whether run on same batch or not.

**d.** Route and apply strike plate on jamb. In some equipment, this is done on the door machine.

**e.** Apply butts to door and jamb. (Can be done on some door machines.)

**f.** Mitering and splining trim.

**g.** Assembly of unit

**h.** Bracing of unit.

707.2 **Equipment.** (See Figs. 707.2*A*–*J*.)

**Fig. 707.2*A*.**
Hinge butt template for smaller operations.

*(Stanley)*

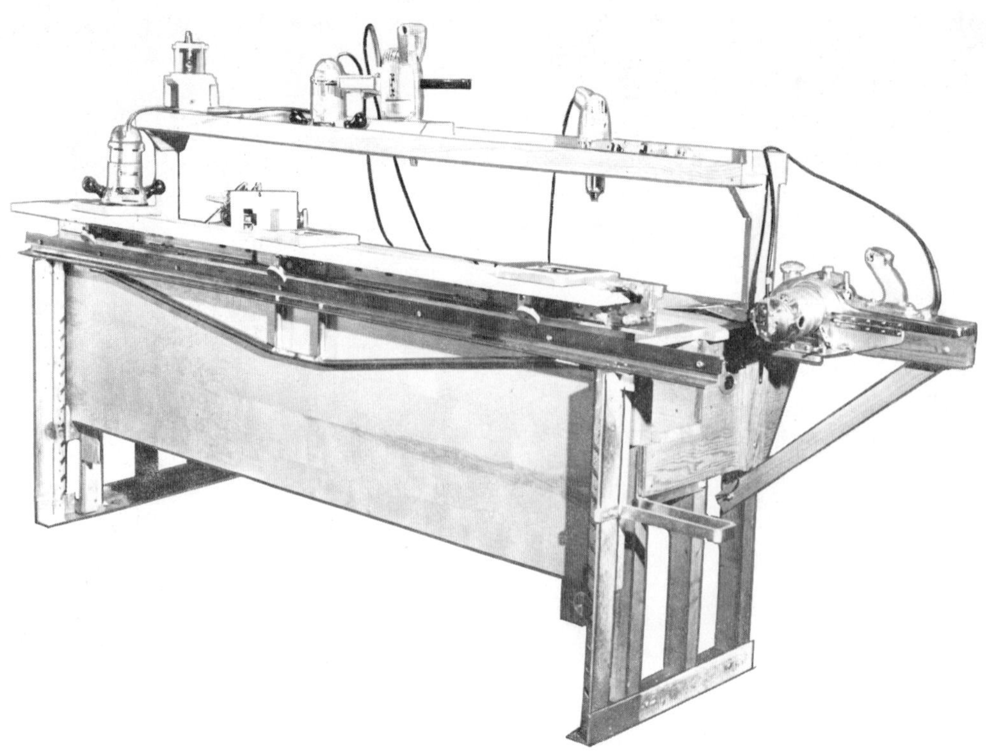

**Fig. 707.2*B*.**
Simple, low cost door jig for small operations, door and jamb machined together.
*(Master Hung Door Equipment Co.)*

**Fig. 707.2*C*.**
Automatic Door Machine. Three doors per minute can be machined on this equipment.
*(Kval Machinery)*

**Fig. 707.2*D*.**
Automatic hinge jamb machine. Actuating foot switch starts automatic sequence. Machines five jambs per minute.
*(Kval Machinery)*

**Fig. 707.2*E*.**
Door sizer for sizing, beveling, and sanding edge of door.
*(General Construction Automation)*

**Fig. 707.2*F*.**
Door machine incorporating sizer.

*(Norfield)*

**Fig. 707.2*G*.**
Jamb assembly unit automatically stitches stop to jamb.

*(General Construction Automation)*

**Fig. 707.2*H*.**
Automatic double end trim saw. Cuts, miters and kerfs for spline.

*(Norfield)*

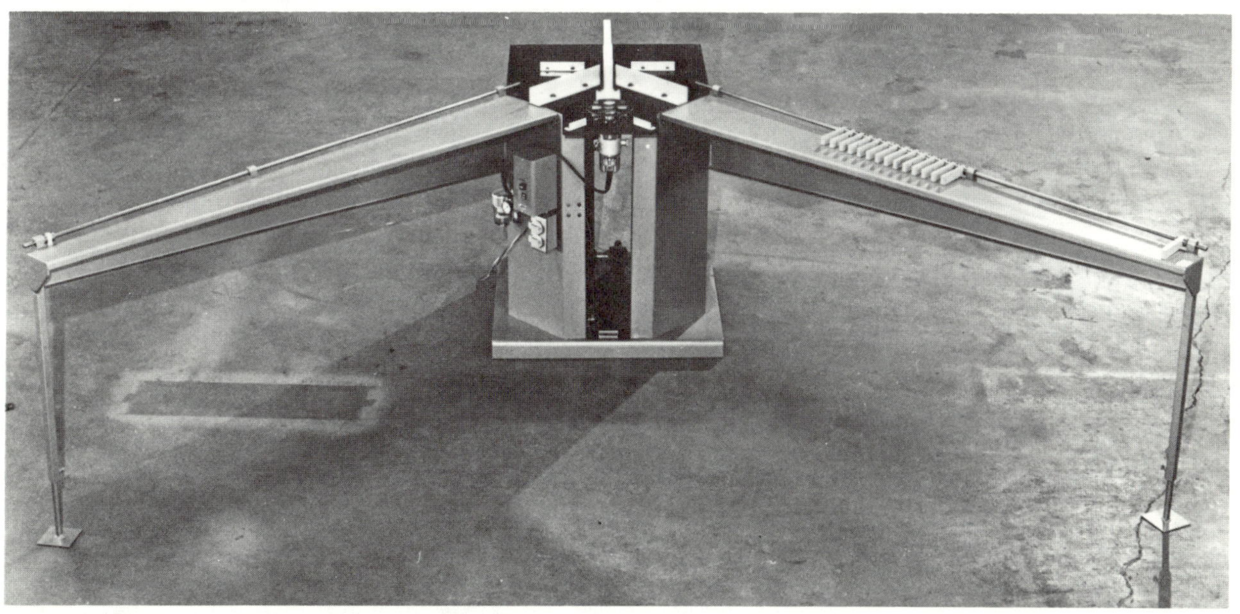

**Fig. 707.2*I*.**
Miter saw miters and kerfs for spline.

*(General Construction Automation)*

WITHDRAWN

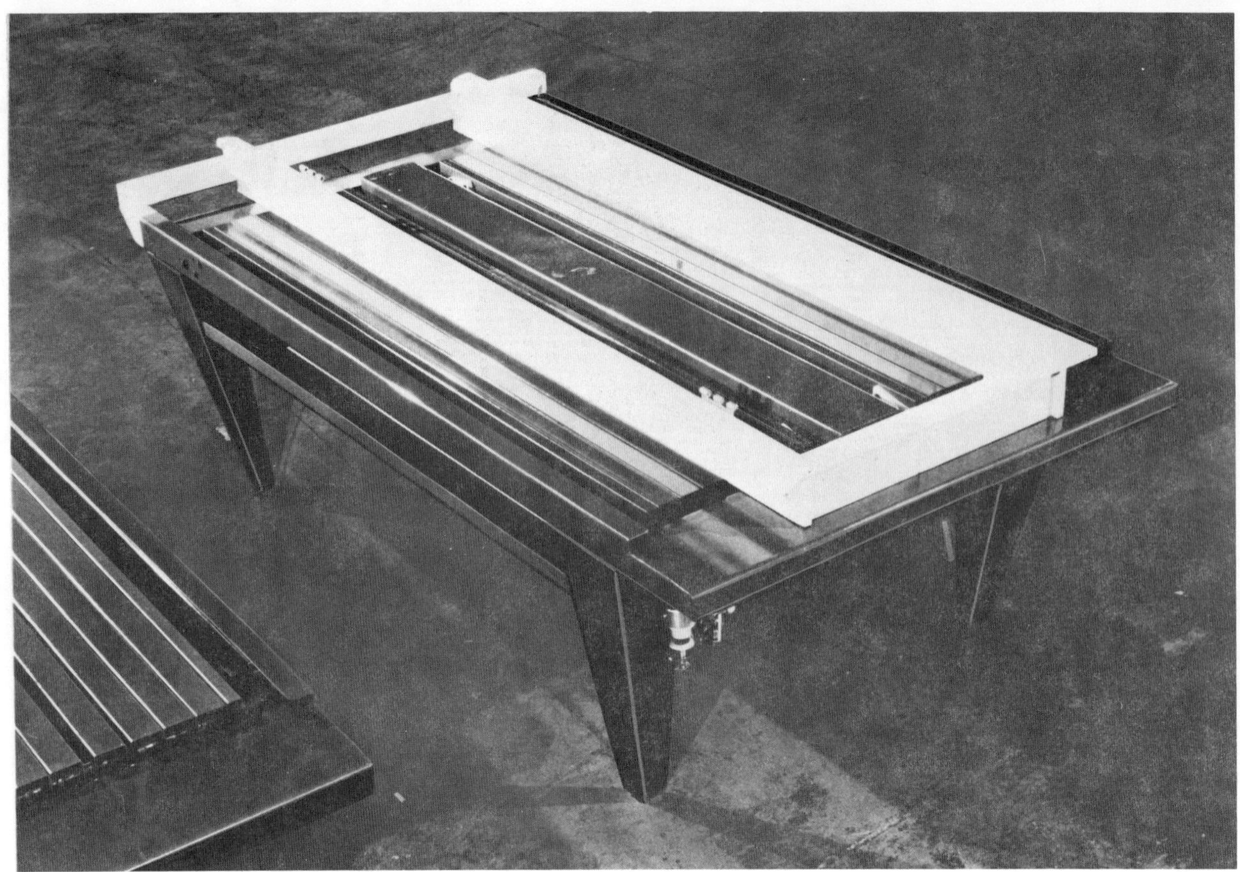

**Fig. 707.2*J*.**
Unit assembly machine.

*(General Construction Automation)*

707.3 **Plant Layout.** As in any manufacturing operation, plant layout is important for efficiency. Consideration must be given to materials handling, flexibility, and elimination of unnecessary movements. A typical layout is shown in Fig. 707.3.

707.4 **Storage and handling of completed units.** Completed door units should be stored so that they are readily available for shipment but at the same time will minimize handling damage. Fig. 707-4 shows a pallet-rack for in plant movement of door units.

707.5 **Bi-Fold Doors**—Assembling fixtures are important in the assembly of these doors. Fig. 707.5 *A* and *B* show typical methods.

707.6 **Steel Entrance Doors.** These doors are usually stocked blank and then routed for installation of lites or feature panels. Decorative plastic plant-on's of various sizes and shapes and are used on steel doors to give patterns such as panel doors, colonial doors, etc. Typical equipment is shown in Fig. 707.6.

708 **Prefinishing.** Doors and trim can be purchased completely prefinished either with spray or dip liquid finished or with vinyl or other plastic films laminated to the wood. Prefinished doors are usually wrapped in plastic film. The film is left in place through the machinery operations, delivery and until the building is ready for occupancy.

709 **Delivery.** Component manufacturers usually deliver prehung units in enclosed trucks, standing (leaning) in racks secured by canvas straps. In order to minimize damage to casing, some manufacturers do not apply the casing in the plant, furnishing it precut or in pre-assembled units shipped separately on the same truck.

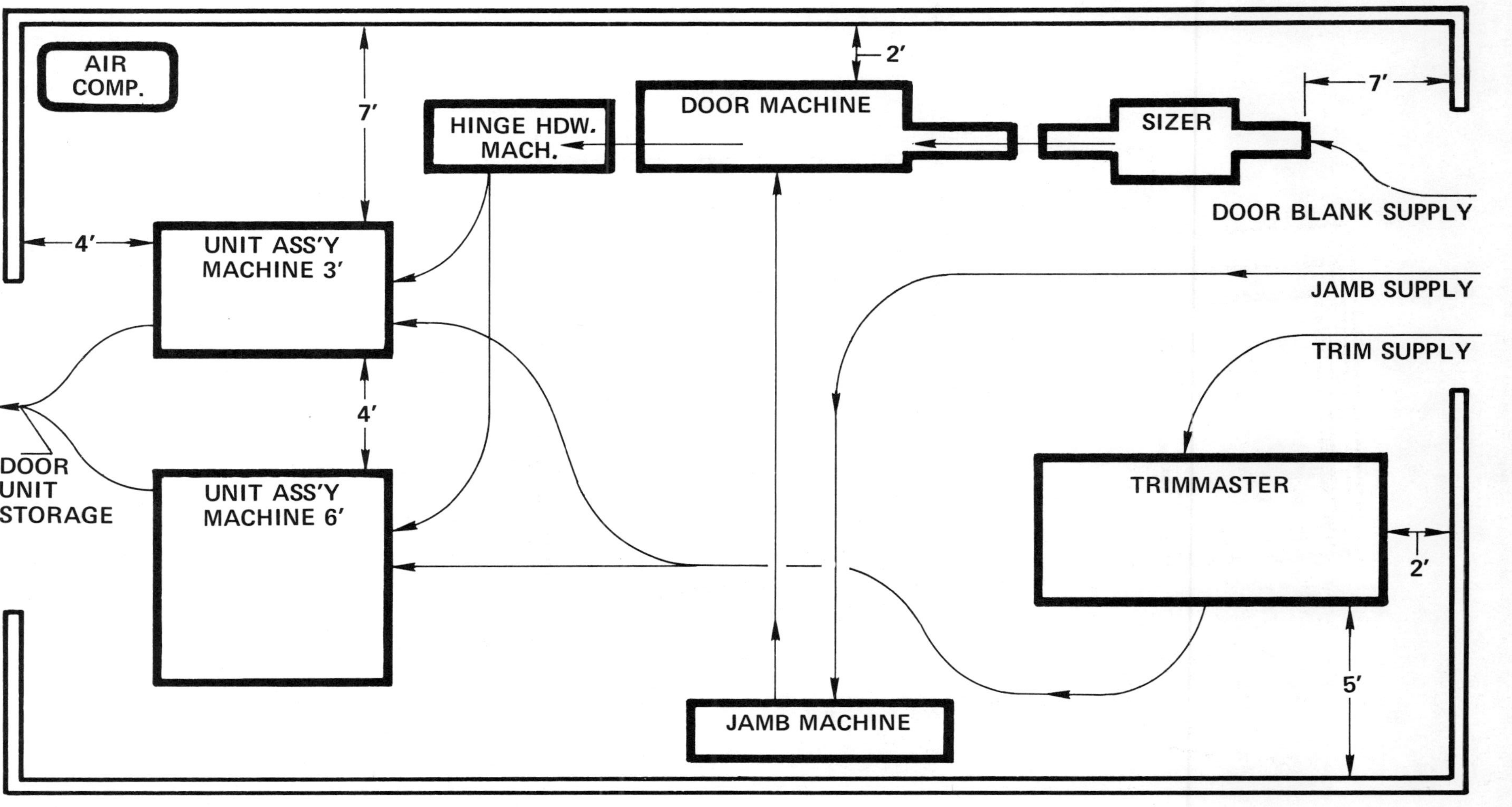


THE AREA ABOVE IS 25' x 55'. AN ALIGNMENT ON THIS PATTERN WILL GET THE MOST EFFICIENT RESULTS FROM THE MACHINES.

**Fig. 707.3.**
Typical plant layout.

*(After Clary)*

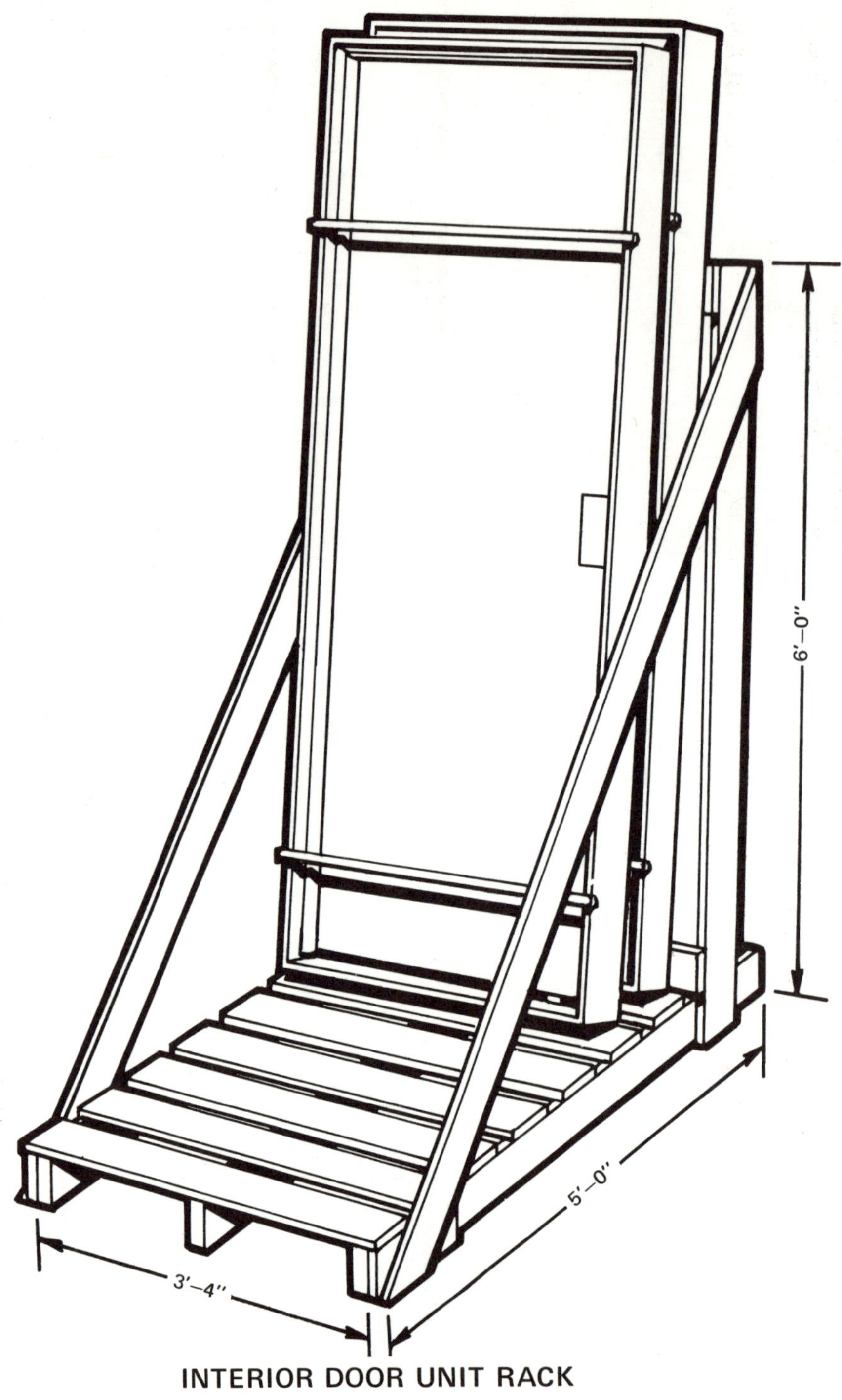


**Fig. 707.4.**
Simple pallet for in-plant handling of job quantities of door units.
*(After Pease)*

**Fig. 707.5*A*.**
Applying hinge screws thru bushings in fixture.

*(Stanley)*

**Fig. 707.5*B*.**
Boring holes for pivot and guide hardware with template.

*(Stanley)*

**Fig. 707.6.**
Equipment for routing steel doors.

*(After Pease)*

**710 Installation.**

**710.1 Adjustable (split) Jambs.** The door side of the unit is placed in the opening, plumbed and the casing nailed. Then the jamb is shimmed and nailed through the shims into the stud.

The remaining section of the jamb is now installed. The casing is nailed to the wall. The door is opened and the split jamb squeezed together and nailed through the door stop into the stud.

**710.2 Nonadjustable Jamb** (solid jamb). The door is placed in the opening, plumbed as above, and if casing has been applied to one side, the casing is nailed to the wall. The jamb is then shimmed, nailed, and casing applied to the other side.

Some manufacturers use metal clips to eliminate the shimming operation. To use the clips, no casing is plant installed. The door is plumbed and the "ears" of the clips are nailed to the wall. This method eliminates hammer marks and the necessity of puttying nail holes on the face of the jamb.

Five clips are recommended on each side jamb.

Fig. 710.2 shows one of these clips.

**711 Order Form.** Fig. 711 shows a typical form used to record prehung doors.

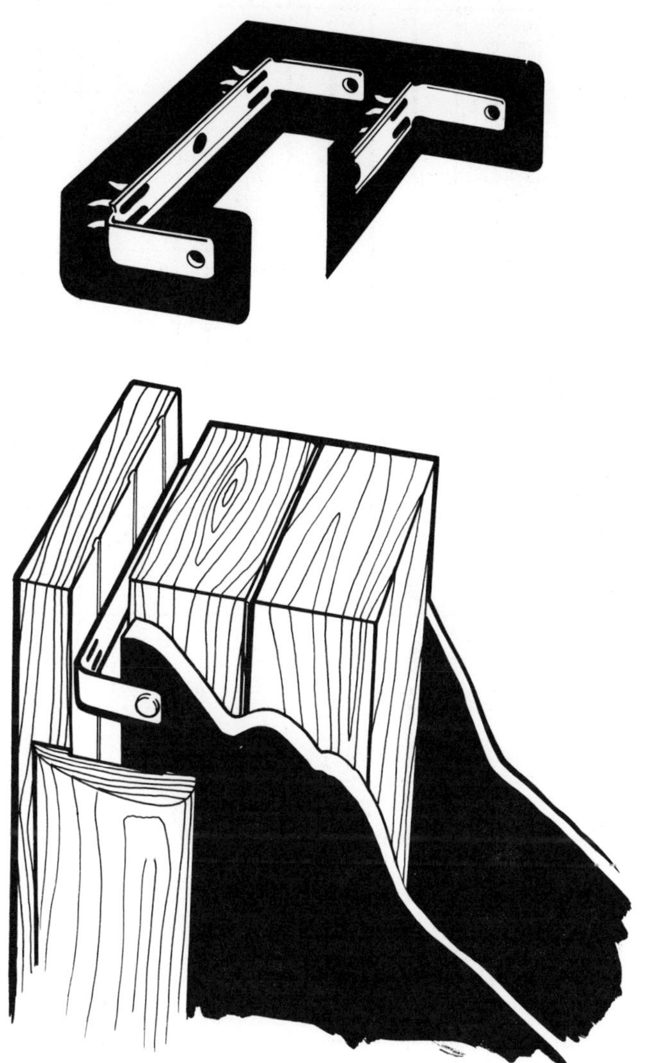

**Fig. 710.2.**
Clips may be installed with a hammer or with air operated press. For odd-sized jambs, clips can be snapped in two.

*(Panel-Clip)*

# PRE-HUNG DOOR ORDER FORM

FORM NO. A-100

SOLD TO: ______________________

ADDRESS: ______________________

CITY: ______________ STATE: ______

JOB: ______________________ Job Phone No. ______________

Date Sold ______________

Date Needed ______________

Sold By ______________

Charge ______________

C.O.D. ______________

| INTERIOR | | THICK | | CORE | | SPECIE | | | | | TRIM | | SWING | | LOCK | | JAMB WIDTH | | |
|---|---|---|---|---|---|---|---|---|---|---|---|---|---|---|---|---|---|---|---|
| Amount | Size | 1 3/8" | 1 3/4" | Hollow | Solid | Mahog. | Birch | Ash | Masonite | Other | 1 5/8" | 2 1/4" | Left | Right | Weiser | Kwikset | | Completed | Other |
| | | | | | | | | | | | | | | | | | | | |
| | | | | | | | | | | | | | | | | | | | |
| | | | | | | | | | | | | | | | | | | | |
| | | | | | | | | | | | | | | | | | | | |
| | | | | | | | | | | | | | | | | | | | |
| | | | | | | | | | | | | | | | | | | | |
| | | | | | | | | | | | | | | | | | | | |
| | | | | | | | | | | | | | | | | | | | |

| EXTERIOR | | | | | | TYPE DOOR | JAMB WIDTH | BACKSET | EXT. TRIM | SILL | | | |
|---|---|---|---|---|---|---|---|---|---|---|---|---|---|
| | | | | | | | | | | | | | |
| | | | | | | | | | | | | | |
| | | | | | | | | | | | | | |
| | | | | | | | | | | | | | |
| | | | | | | | | | | | | | |
| | | | | | | | | | | | | | |

NOTE: Make in duplicate. Send one copy to Prehunq Department. Keep other copy for your files.

DELIVERED BY: ______________________

ACCEPTED BY: ______________________

**Fig. 711.**
Order form for prehung doors.

*(Norfield Mfg. Co.)*

# CHAPTER VIII

## Prefinishing *

800 **General.** Completely finished panels or modular units are more attractive to the cutomer, can result in substantial cost savings in the turn-key price, and speed up the on-site delivery time. Finished units can result from the use of prefinished materials or from finishing operations in the manufacturer's plant. As a minimum, most fabricators provide for the priming of all exterior materials. This protects finished units from the weather during construction and permits color choice in on-site painting.

801 **Unfinished Units.** Unfinished (or primed only) units are frequently used in otherwise complete structures on which financing with a "sweat-equity" provision is employed. Under this arrangement the consumer does painting, interior and exterior, and possibly other items of finish such as floor laying. The labor thus expended is considered part of the down payment. Wall board and exterior trim application are basically the same as completely finished units.

Except for primed exterior trim, packages of custom component manufacturers are unfinished. Component package manufacturers have varying degrees of finish in their package.

802 **Prefinished Materials.** The majority of modular or complete package manufacturers tend to use a maximum of prefinished or preprimed materials. This is advantageous if a regular supply can be assured, as it eliminates the need for any finishing operations in the fabricator's plant. These operations can be dangerous from the fire standpoint, where high flash solvents are used. In addition, material finishing operations are highly specialized and require personnel, supervision, and space which can often be devoted to more profitable operations.

Examples of prefinished materials are:

802.1 **Floor Materials** such as asphalt, vinyl, and linoleum tile and sheet goods. Considerable care must be exercised in the design and application of the subfloors under these materials. A minimum of 5/8" plywood with either tongue and grooved joints or cross blocking is used. Floors are glued and nailed or, in many cases, screwed to the substructure. Screws or nails should be countersunk. Plywood is then "touch-sanded" at joints after holes or cracks have been filled with a rapid setting filler.

802.2 **Prefinished Plywood** or hardboard paneling is often used. Material is usually both glued and nailed. When proper procedures are used, these materials can be counted on to add materially to the rigidity of modular units, particularly stack-on units which must provide a great deal of their own resistance to handling stresses. See Fig. 802.2.

802.3 **Upson Board.** This material is applied with concealed clips and, because it is available prefinished in full wall sizes, does not usually present joint problems. Details are shown in Fig. 802.3

803 **Gypsum Wallboard**

803.1 **Gypsum wallboard** and the allied joint treatment products are not structural materials, therefore certain factors must be carefully considered during application and finishing of wallboard, movement of components within the factory, assembly of components, and shipment and placement of the housing unit at its final destination.

Proper application methods, techniques, etc., and dimensional accuracy can lend some strength to wall, partition, and ceiling components, and the completed housing unit.

*Much of the material in this chapter, particularly relating to applying and finishing gypsum drywall, was furnished by the National Gypsum Company.

**Fig. 802.2.**
Application of interior plywood with panels in horizontal position.

*(Wausau Homes)*

803.1A **Dimensional Accuracy of Components.** Basically, an industrialized structure is the construction of a cube, or series of cubes, made up of flat plane elements, generally of wood frame construction. The success or failure of finished gypsum wallboard is highly dependent upon these elements (walls, partitions, ceilings, etc.) manufactured as true squares or rectangles (not parallelograms), held to the most stringent tolerances which the manufacturer is capable of maintaining.

This means the employment of proper machines, jigs, clamps, and squaring devices to assure squareness and to keep dimensional accuracy within tolerance. Failure to maintain this dimensional accuracy usually requires force fitting components during assembly, which will result in drywall problems by placing severe stresses on the wallboard and finished joints.

These stresses may result in immediate failure of the wallboard and treated joints, or since the stresses are "built in," wallboard and joint failures may not be noticed until the unit is in the field and occupied. Repairs are costly and time consuming, defeating the purpose of building in the factory.

803.1B **In-Plant Handling of Components.** Methods of, and devices, for in-plant handling of components (walls, partitions and ceilings) must be carefully considered especially when confronted with the movement of an outside wall section that may be 8′ × 40′ to 60′ long, with various weakened sections such as door and window openings, and gypsum wallboard applied to one side, with the joints finished.

Keeping in mind that wallboard lends only minimal strength to the components, the method of pick up, pick up points, etc., become extremely important if the wallboarded and finished components are to be successfully moved. The pick up, whether

**Fig. 802.3.**
Application of interior wallboard. Water filled roller imbeds clips (inset) in back of wallboard.
*(The Upson Company)*

from a horizontal or vertical position of the component, must be uniform and not allow damaging stresses to be placed on the wallboard.

The most common method of picking up a wall or partition section is the attaching of a lifting device to the top plate, at a minimum number of points and making the lift. By doing this, the entire weight of wallboard, studs and sill are placed on the integrity of the mechanical attachment of top plate to studs, and mechanical-adhesive fastening of, and tensile strength of the wallboard itself. The wallboard (and finished joints) are placed in tension, a situation which gypsum wall board is not designed for.

It would be best to devise a method of pick up whereby the partition, wall, or ceiling assembly is kept as close to its natural state as possible, i.e., resting on a solid surface. While this may not be totally practical in all cases, attachment of lifting devices should at least be made to the primary structural elements of the wall, partition or ceiling assembly, such as the studs or bottom chords of trusses.

Pick up points for any given partition, wall or ceiling assembly probably should not exceed 10′ O.C., with a maximum of 5′ cantilever at the ends of the component. Lifting devices should be equipped to insure even pick up at each point, and should be free of sag or bow under load.

Unless a reasonable pick up system is employed, gypsum wallboard and finished joints are subject to fracturing, no matter what "drywall system" is used. See Fig. 803.1*B*.

803.1*C* **Assembly of Walls and Partitions on Floor Deck.** Generally, when a modular floor deck or section is completed (subflooring, rough plumbing, etc.) it is placed on rolling beams or other devices to facilitate movement of the unit down the final assembly line.

Prior to setting the partitions and walls,

**Fig. 803.1*B*.**
Lifting device used to lift panels from jig, insuring even pickup.
*(Deluxe Homes)*

the deck must be flat and true. Many times, the number of, or placement of rolling beams is not adequate to initially support the floor deck in a flat plane, or continue to support it as it gains weight.

If the floor deck is cantilevered too far, or too little intermediate support is used, causing a bowed, sagged or wavy floor, the wall and partition sections will not fit properly. Thus all of the care and attention that went into the accuracy of these elements is lost.

When this condition prevails, the wall and parition sections are usually forced into position, in an attempt to cause them to conform to the untrue line of the floor deck. This again results in severe and "built in" stresses on the wallboard and joints, resulting in fractures, some of which may not be noticed until the unit is in the field.

Another common practice during assembly is the placement of carpeting and pad, and other finish floor materials of unlike thickness prior to setting walls and partitions. This method may be valid from a time-saving point of view; however, it can lead to serious wallboard and joint problems.

Usually wall and partition sections are designed and produced to a uniform height, and when installed over uneven finish floor levels, it results in unevenness at the top of adjoining walls and partitions. The typical remedy for this condition is to force fit the offending wall or partition by compressing the floor material, thus placing severe compression stresses on the wallboard and joints.

Placement of wall or partitions directly over carpeting or other resilient floor materials creates a flexible joint between these elements and the floor deck, where good design calls for as rigid a joint as possible.

**803.1*D*** **Structural Considerations.** This system recommends the horizontal application of gypsum wallboard to walls and partitions, since fewer joints need to be finished and butt joints (which require skill to finish properly) can be designed to occur behind intersecting partitions.

With this application of wallboard, it is strongly recommended that a continuous 1" × 4" girt be let into the framing (studs), to occur behind and centered on the wallboard joint. The girt should be adhesively and mechanically fastened to the framing members.

The let-in girt serves several important purposes; it provides a stiffening action to the basic frame which greatly helps to maintain squareness, and it also provides additional surface contact area to which the wallboard is adhered.

This additional surface contact area for adhesive is extremely significant relative to overall strength of the components and the entire unit.

The girt should be allowed to run continuously through window and door openings, which will strengthen those weakened sections during movement of the component. The girt can be cut out after placement of the component on the floor deck.

The easiest and fastest method of placing wallboard on the bottom chord of joists or other ceiling framing, is to place it parallel to the frame. This will eliminate butt joints which require skill to finish.

If the ceiling framing is over 16" O.C., a let-in 1" × 4" girt should be placed at the third points (in 12' overall) for the very same reasons as mentioned for walls and partitions.

While the vertical application of gypsum wallboard to trusses or other framing with let-in girts at the third points is not currently approved FHA ceiling construction, FHA approval of this construction has been applied for, and is expected to be granted shortly.

**803.1*E*** **Use of Adhesives.** The overall use of proper adhesives during all phases of assembly is strongly recommended, since it is known that adhesives will lend significant strength to components and the entire unit. The choosing of an adhesive should be given as much thought and attention as is given to structural design and structural strengths of the materials used. In other words, selecting an adhesive is more than just specifying a "glue."

Most structural failures of an industrialized housing unit is due to some form of shear caused by racking or other torsional stresses incurred during movement of components within the factory or shipment and placement of the unit. Therefore, adhesives should display developed shear strengths at least equal to the materials being joined.

In the case of gypsum wallboard, which has a shear strength of approximately 80 PSI, we should be using an adhesive which will develop at least 80 PSI minimum shear strength within a short period of time, and continue to develop additional strength without becoming brittle. The same approach is valid with other materials; i.e., there is a parallel between developed shear strength of the adhesive and the shear strengths of the materials to be joined.

MC (Modified Contact) adhesive is designed to develop 80 PSI shear strength within 24 hours. It is also designed to develop early stiffness properties, and when augmented with mechanical fastening, allows immediate movement of components, prior to the adhesive attaining full strength.

MC adhesive should be applied to all wall, partition, and ceiling framing surfaces that will come in contact with the wallboard. The adhesive should be applied in continuous beads (1/4″ to 3/8″ diameter). At the girt lines, on solid headers, and where wallboard butts, the adhesive should be applied in a serpentine pattern.

Do not apply more adhesive to framing than that which will exceed approximately 10 minutes open (exposure) time before wallboard is applied, since a skin will form over the adhesive bead and seriously impair the bond between wallboard and frame.

Those adhesives which allow more open or exposure time generally do not have the immediate stiffness properties and require longer periods of time to gain full strength, thereby not contributing to structural strength at the proper time.

Mechanical fastening (nails or screws) is required to augment the immediate stiffness characteristics and contribute to strength of the component.

Consideration should be given to the application of adhesive at the juncture of walls and partitions to floor decks, intersecting partitions and walls, and ceiling assemblies as they are placed on the unit, since it is known that this practice also contributes greatly to overall strength of the unit.

**803.1*F*** **Recognition of Stress Points in the Structure.** The sectional or modular structure is unique in that a great deal of consideration must be given to the ability of the unit to absorb strain without harmful effect to finished surfaces.

In conventional residential construction, we normally ignore expansion and relief joints or "planned cracking" in small buildings such as these. However, in commercial construction, much consideration is given to potential building movement and some means are provided to relieve stresses.

A successful structural design anticipates where and how a crack in the structure will occur and then structurally reinforces these areas *or* provides a relief joint to absorb the movement.

We have previously recognized that door and window cut outs are weakened sections of a wall or partition. Minimal amounts of structure are available over these weakened areas, and they are highly susceptible to cracking. Therefore, consideration must be given to providing a mechanical (but architecturally acceptable) relief joint over door and window cut outs, since they are most difficult to structurally reinforce.

**803.2** **Application of Gypsum Wallboard.** In addition to the above considerations relating to factory built construction, application of drywall should be made in accordance with the manufacturer's instructions. Using the adhesive nail-on method, when wall or ceiling assemblies must be moved before the adhesive is set (normally 24 hours) the wall board is both perimeter and field nailed with nail spacing of 12″ O.C. or screw spacing of 16″ O.C. On long walls, it may be desirable to apply the fastenings 8″ O.C. to insure minimum cracking problems. On small partitions, mechanical fastenings may be minimized.

For 7′-6″ ceiling, gypsum wallboard is available in 45″ widths to minimize cutting. 3/8″, 1/2″, or 5/8″ board may be used.

803.3 **Hardening Type Joint Compound.** Use of this material permits the completion of drywall taping is one day vs. the 3 or 4 days required for conventional joint finishing. Manufacturer's instructions should be followed. This material is not suitable for use with mechanical tools, because of cleanup difficulties.

803.4 **The Thermo-Weld Drywall System** is a new system designed exclusively for use in the factory. The system has been designed for faster application with unskilled or semi-skilled labor and finishing of drywall joints in one hour.

Cove or crown mouldings are recommended for interior corners such as wall-ceiling angles. Careful design will eliminate many exterior corners and those remaining can be taped or covered with a moulding.

A feature of this system is the use of an iron-on joint tape. The application is shown in Fig. 803.4.

The Thermo-Weld system envisages a two coat finish which serves to cover the minor imperfections which are a by product of speed and semi-skilled labor. First, a water-based texture is applied followed by a water-based latex finish (poly-vinyl acetate or acrylic). The texture is usually spray applied and the finish either spray or roller applied.

The manufacturer estimates total labor for this system on a 44′ × 24′ split modular unit with about 4000 square feet of wall and ceiling area at 48 man hours including drywall application, taping, spray and cleanup.

804 **Prime Coating.** As stated earlier, most of the items involved may be purchased preprimed. However, occasions will arise where some materials must be factory primed by the fabricator. Most manufacturers will use a water based latex primer for this purpose. There will be some slight grain raising but this is not believed to be important on cornice material, soffit plywood, etc.

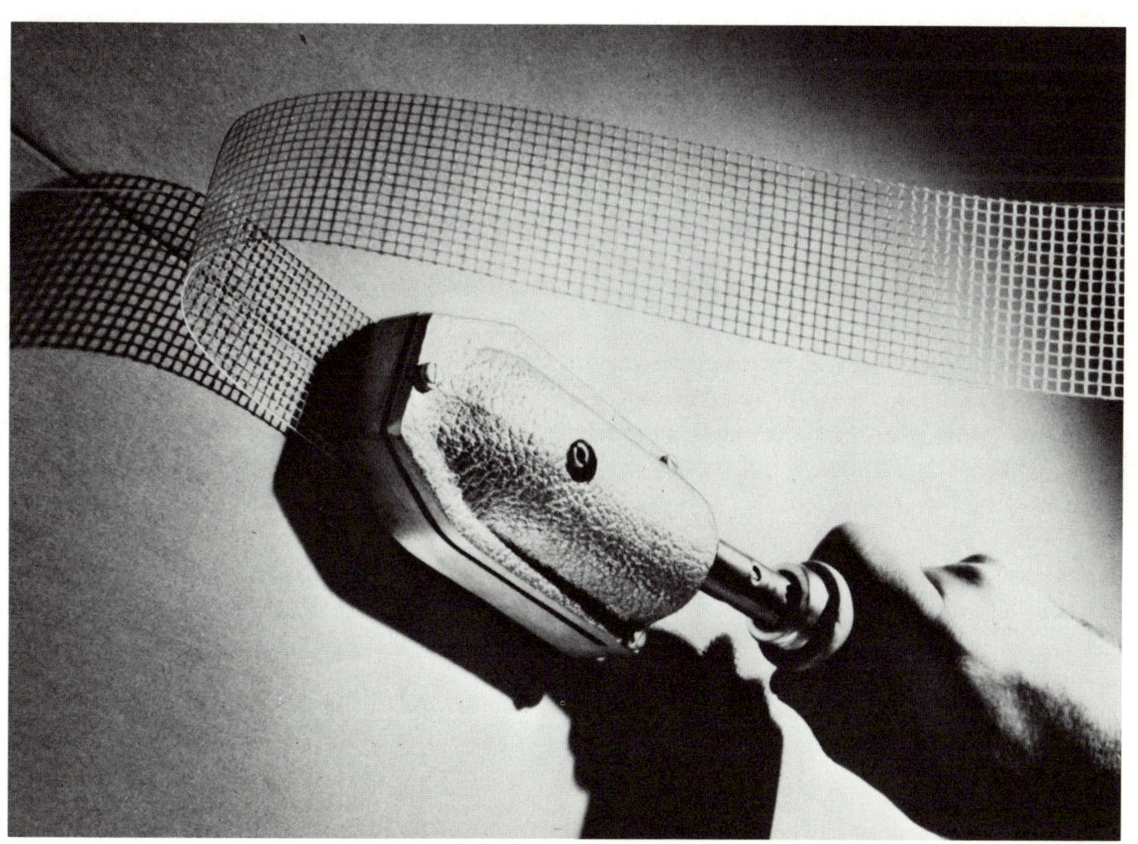

**Fig. 803.4.**
Tape Activator being used with Gold Bond's Thermo-Weld System.

804.1 **Drywall** (meaning gypsum wallboard or other paper surfaced material). Except as above, where a special texture is used, latex primer-sealers are recommended.

804.2 **Wood, Interior.** In most interior situations, wood may be primed with the same latex material used on the walls, if some slight-grain raising is not objectionable.

For clear finishes, a clear wood sealer is required preceeded by a filler if necessary.

805 **Finish Coating.** Interior and exterior water based or latex paints are generally used because of safety requirements. Where "Odorless" Alkyd flat paints are used good ventilation must be used because of the presence of oil vapors.

For detailed information, consult "Selection of Paint" #796 by National Paint, Varnish & Lacquer Assn., 1500 Rhode Island Avenue., N.W., Washington, D.C. 20005.

806 **Methods of Application.** The selection of the method of application of paints and finishes should be influenced by the manufacturer of the material. Some of the most common methods:

806.1 **Dipping.** Dipping is probably the simplest method. Paint use is efficient and labor cost is low, particularly on mouldings. A long dip tank is used with drying racks positioned to return drippings to the tank.

806.2 **Compressed Air Spray.** Inexpensive to install, but has high overspray. Adequate safety provisions must be used to insure fire safety where solvent based materials are used. See Fig. 806.2.

806.3 **Airless Spray.** Paint is under high pressure. There is less overspray in comparison to conventional air spraying. Film is prone to sagging.

806.4 **Roll Coating.** Roll coating may be used in a mechanized setup for quantity production of primed or finished flat parts. Hand operated rollers may be used on walls or ceilings or for occasional priming of flat materials normally purchased pre-primed.

806.5 **Curtain Coating.** On flat or nearly flat wood surfaces this method has advantages in speed and uniform film thickness.

807 **Laminated Plastic Films and Vinyl Clad Units.** Several manufacturers are now producing vinyl wrapped mouldings and prehung door units to eliminate any need for finishing of wood. These vinyl-wrapped mouldings can be worked in standard prehung door machinery without film separation.

808 **Vinyl Film For Walls and Ceilings.** Congoleum now has a film and a machine for applying it which will apply a film to plywood, gypsum and other substrates with a minimum joint preparation. Textured surface masks minor substrate imperfections. The material is available in 8′ and 12′ widths. (See Fig. 808.)

809 **Field Touch Up Kit.** Provision should be made for touchup of finished units which may be damaged in the delivery or installation process. Aerosol paint cans or small jars of the various finishes may be sent with the unit or installation personnel.

**Fig. 806.2.**

Spray paint setup . . . at right, paint cans; center is castered cart for moving spray drum about; at left castered platform to give spray operator mobility for spray painting the ceiling roof sections, part of which are shown in back of the platform. Note also the lift device to minimize stresses on completed sections and plastic drop to cover finished work. Both joint work and painting are done in this position.

*(Deluxe Homes) (Reschke Photo)*

**Fig. 807.1.**
Vinyl-wrapped prehung door units and moulding.
*(Caradco)*

**Fig. 807.2.**
Vinyl clad window unit.
*(Caradco)*

**Fig. 808.**
Machine for applying vinyl film to wall and ceiling sections.
*(Congoleum Industries)*

# CHAPTER IX

## Plumbing & Heating

*Steve Sabo*
*Slayter Associates**
*Elkhart, Indiana*

900 **General.** Plumbing and heating installation in industrialized buildings represent a greater opportunity for cost saving than any other part of the structure to be produced in the factory. At the same time, proper design, and higher quality installation procedures can result in greatly improved plumbing and heating installation over what is usually experienced in on-site construction.

901 **Codes.** To the industrialized housing manufacturer, code compliance plays a prime role in the manufacturing of the total plumbing system. Manufacturers must contend with the different rules and regulations established by various municipal administrative authorities. As a general rule, most administrative authorities require that a manufacturer submit for approval, plans and specifications regarding the particular structure to be erected in their area. There are national codes which most local municipalities use as their basic plumbing code. This chapter does not intend to go into detail on the many plumbing codes. After a survey of the codes in the market area, compliance with those codes which are controlling should be insured.

901.1 **National Plumbing Code.** At the present time there is not one specific national plumbing code available to the industrialized housing manufacturer such as the National Electric Code published by the National Fire Protection Association; however, there are model codes which are used by many state and local authorities. These codes are:

1. BOCA Basic Plumbing Code
   BOCA (Building Officials Conference of America)
   1313 East 60th Street
   Chicago, Illinois 60637

2. Uniform Plumbing Code
   IAPMO (International Association of Plumbing and Mechanical Officials)
   5032 Alahambre Avenue
   Los Angeles, California 90032

3. SBCC Southern Standard Plumbing Code
   SBCC (Southern Building Code Congress)
   1116 Brown-Marks Building
   Birmingham, Alabama 35203

4. USAS - A119.1 Standards for Mobile Homes
   USASI (United States of America Standards Institute)

   Mobile Homes Manufacturers' Association
   20 North Wacker Drive
   Chicago, Illinois 60606

   National Fire Protection Association
   60 Battery March Street
   Boston, Massachusetts 02110

   Trailer Coach Association
   1340 West Third Street
   Los Angeles, California 90017

*Slayter Associates provides a full range of consulting services to those interested in entering the mass-produced structures industry. Steve Sabo has an ME degree and is a former chief engineer for Richardson Homes Corporation. Steve joined Slayter Associates in 1969 as a project manager and is now a principal with the firm.

5. Federal Housing Administration Minimum Property Standards

901.2 **State Plumbing Code.** In general, states have building codes which apply to plumbing; however, the state authority is usually concerned only with multiple family dwellings projects. Therefore, if industrialized manufacturers are considering building multiple family dwelling units the state authority should be contacted so that all plumbing requirements will be met. As for single family dwellings and mobile homes, the administrative authority responsible for plumbing is generally at a local level, although in some states the state code covers areas where no municipal code exists.

901.3 **Local Codes.** In smaller cities (population less than 50,000) throughout the United States the local authority responsible for administration of plumbing code compliance may rely on one of the model codes or a state plumbing code. In rural areas plumbing codes may not exist. In this case it is up to the home manufacturer to use the minimum standards set forth within the model codes, such as BOCA.

902 **Materials.** Materials used in plumbing can be broken into four categories. They are: pipe, fixtures, fittings, and equipment. The industrialized building manufacturer should be aware that there are several types of materials utilized for plumbing today. Lightweight materials, such as fiberglass and plastic, are now being used in place of cast iron, copper, and steel. Lightweight materials when used in place of cast iron and copper, are used primarily because of lower cost, reduced weight, and increased flexibility.

902.1 **DWV (Drain, Waste, and Vent) Pipe**

**Cast Iron.** Cast iron is not considered to be an industrialized manufacturer's standard product for DWV systems. The weight of the material makes it difficult for the manufacturer to fabricate and handle the product for quick and rapid installation. Cast iron is used only when local codes require its use.

**Copper.** Copper provides many of the convenience features which the industrialized manufacturer needs, but the economics of copper are questionable. As a rule, copper is more desirable than cast iron DWV, because of its lightweight characteristics and ease of assembly. When local requirements present a choice, copper should be the choice over cast iron for DWV requirements.

**ABS and PVC Plastic Pipe DWV.** Plastic pipe products are presently being used by many industrialized housing manufacturers and are exclusively used by manufacturers of mobile homes. It is the most desirable DWV product for the industrialized manufacturer. Plastic DWV is lightweight and easily fabricated. Repairs can be made quickly in the event corrections should be required to relocate DWV lines.

**Table 1. Weights (lbs.) Per 100′ of Pipe**

| Nominal Size, Inches | ABS | PVC | Copper DWV | Sched. 40 Galv. & Black | Cast Iron Single Hub |
|---|---|---|---|---|---|
| 1-1/4 | 31 | 42 | 65 | 227 | |
| 1-1/2 | 37 | 51 | 81 | 272 | |
| 2 | 50 | 68 | 107 | 365 | 550 |
| 3 | 103 | 141 | 169 | 757 | 950 |
| 4 | | 201 | 287 | 1,079 | 1,300 |
| 5 | | | | 1,460 | 1,500 |
| 6 | | | 610 | 1,800 | 2,000 |

**Table 2. Support Centers for Horizontal ABS Pipe**

| Nominal Pipe Size, Inches | Distance Between Centers (Feet): SDR & Sch. 40 | Sch. 80 |
|---|---|---|
| 1/2 | 4 | 5 |
| 3/4 | 4 | 5 |
| 1 | 4-1/2 | 5-1/2 |
| 1-1/4 | 4-1/2 | 5-1/2 |
| 1-1/2 | 5 | 6 |
| 2 | 5 | 6 |
| 3 | 6 | 7 |
| 4 | 6-1/4 | 7-1/2 |
| 6 | 6-3/4 | 8-1/2 |

*Source:* Plastic Pipe Institute

902.2 **Water Supply Line.** Presently both copper and galvanized pipe are used in the industrialized building industry. Where straight runs in excess of 10′ are found, galvanized pipe may be the choice for the industrialized manufacturer because of cost considerations. However, where a floor plan requires flexibility in the location of fixture outlets copper should be selected. Plastic water supply lines such as ABS, PE, and PVC, at the present time have not been widely accepted by the industrialized manufacturer. They have not been reliable under the extreme temperature and pressure conditions that water supply lines are subject to. Within the near future, plastic water supply lines will be playing a greater role in the water supply system.

903 **Floor Plan Design Considerations.** Plumbing system design originates with the designer, and it is left to the engineer to work out the details of providing a waste and supply system that will meet the needs of the basic floor plan set by the designer. It is important that during the floor planning stage of a new product, the designer and engineer work very closely to eliminate any problems which might arise. For example, a consideration the designer should make when planning floors is the location of wet components. The bathroom, kitchen, and other areas requiring water should be adjacent so that the building manufacturer may reduce the amount of plumbing material and also confine his plumbing system to one or two walls. This practice can eliminate unnecessary runs through ceilings, floors, and walls. Fig. 903 shows two typical floor plans, the upper one designed without consideration being given to the problems which production might encounter with the plumbing of the homes. While the second floor plan defines the same basic floor plan, the rooms are arranged in such a manner that all wet components join each other, simplifying the plumbing of the home.

The designer will do well to follow one basic rule—attempt to locate all plumbing systems as close as possible. This is not only a good idea because of the savings in materials but also is important because it results in a plumbing system that is easier to install during the manufacturing process. Spreading out the plumbing system can only lead to the production problems. The designer can floor plan his homes, working around a basic plumbing core. Mobile home manufacturers have been quite successful in this attempt. While they are able to provide several hundred variations in floor plan design, it may be necessary to have only two or three different types of plumbing systems.

904 **Schematic Drawing and Kit Drawings.** Fig. 904*A* illustrates a typical schematic DWV riser diagram of a drain system. While this drawing is sufficient information for an experienced plumber, the information, as presented, is not in a desirable form for the average production worker.

Fig. 904*B* shows a typical kit drawing. This drawing lists various components of a plumbing system, which is easily understood by the average housing production worker. We must keep in mind that in the industrialized housing atmosphere, a skilled craftsman may not be available to complete the plumbing system; therefore, simplification of drawings is of prime importance. The kit drawing breaks the basic plumbing system into the various components which may be fabricated on a bench and later assembled into the home.

905 **Methods.** The methods used for fabricating plumbing systems in the industrialized building field is generally based on the number of homes produced in a plant. A plant with a capacity of one to two homes per day, may subcontract the plumbing to a local shop and simply assemble components of the plumbing system into the home as the units go down the line. Plants producing from three to eight homes per day have enough volume to warrant a fabrication shop for all plumbing components. Plants producing only three homes per day may utilize one man specifically for both bench fabrication and installation of components. There are drawbacks in this particular case because if the man either quits or is absent, it is very difficult to replace him and generally results in many problems for the production department. Beyond three homes per day, there may be two men primarily responsible for the fabrication of plumbing. They should be completely familiar with the bench operations of fabricating small subcomponents for the plumbing systems and be familiar with the installa-

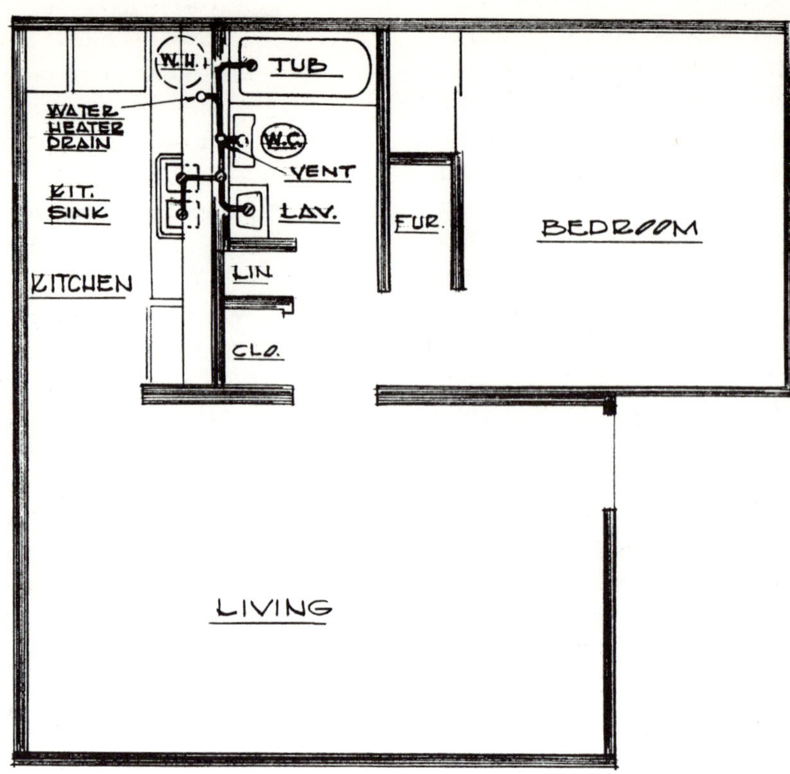

Optimum bath/kitchen layout to facilitate plumbing installation in common plumbing wall.

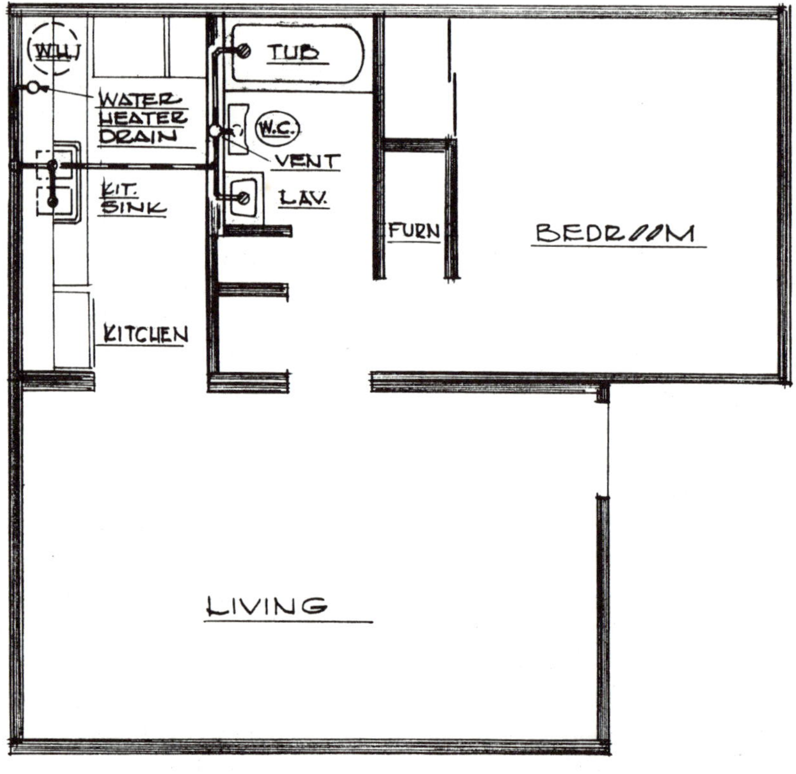


**Fig. 903.**
Poor bath/kitchen layout.

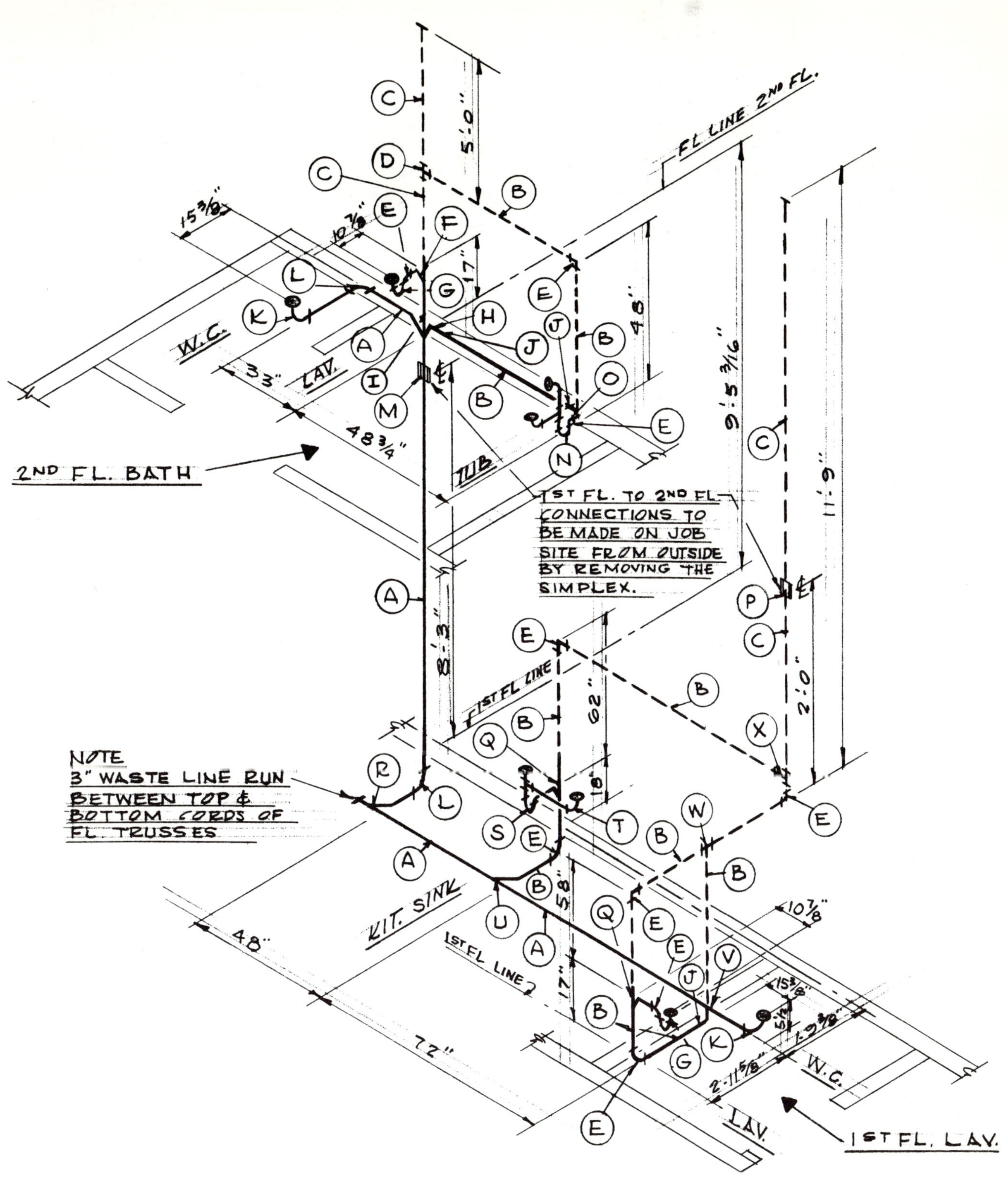


Fig. 904*A*.
Waste riser diagram (no scale).

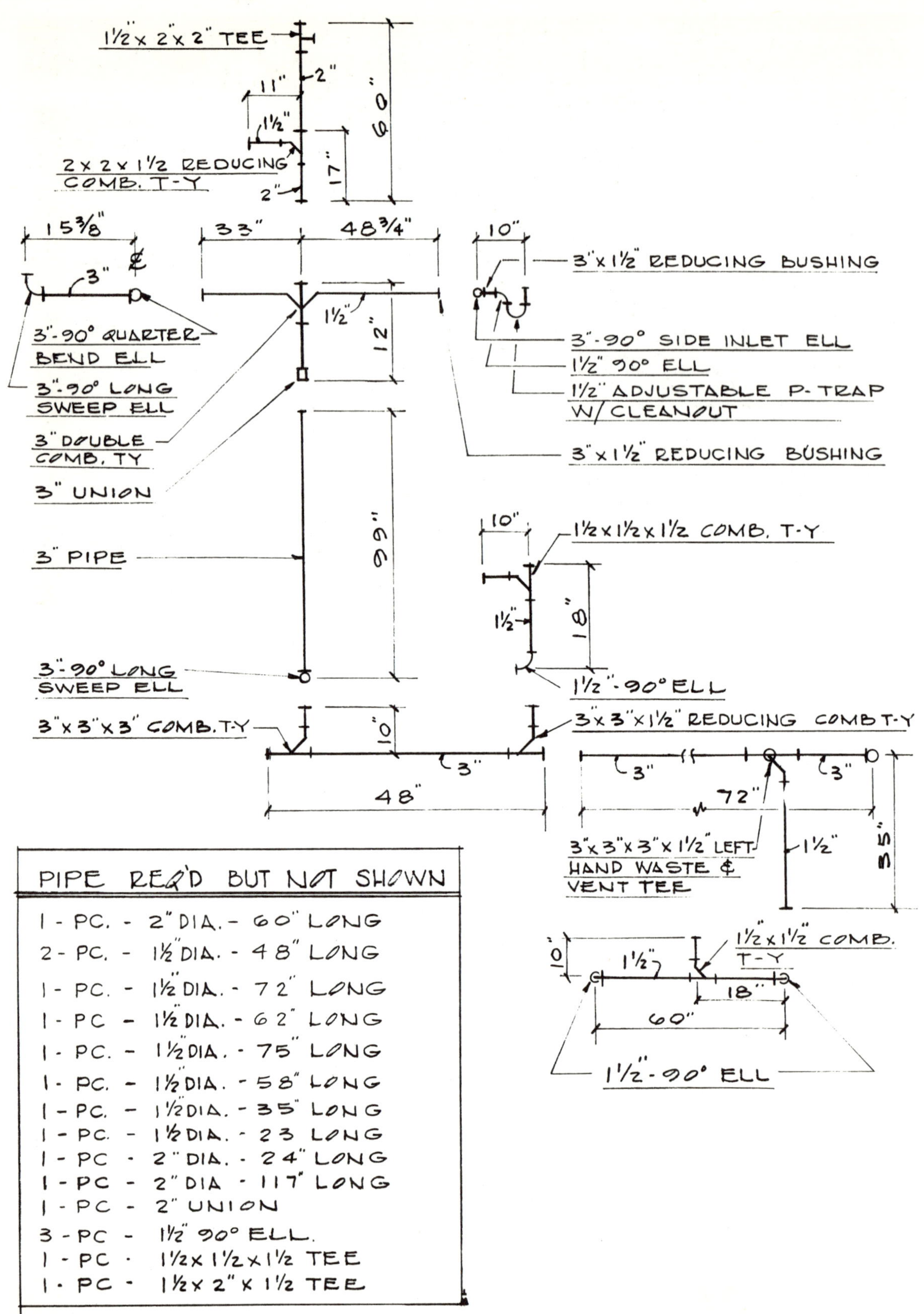


**Fig. 904*B*.**
Kit drawing for use by production personnel.

**Fig. 904*C*.**
Bench fabricated plumbing component can be easily handled by one man and installed into wet core.
*(Wausau Homes)*

**Fig. 905.**
Typical plumbing wall purchased from an outside source. Provides for both kitchen and bath with wall hung water closet.
*(Tyler Pipe)*

tion procedures of these components. Consideration should always be given to having plumbing components subcontracted based on the volume within any particular plant.

905.1 **Typical Fabrication Area.** Considerations given to the fabrication areas for the plumbing department are that:

1. Material flow from supplier to the main plant. This is of prime importance due to long lengths of pipe.
2. The proximity of the fabrication department to the production line. It would be unwise to locate the plumbing department in another building, or even a position more than 50′ away from the position where plumbing components are normally installed into the home. (See Figure 904*C* illustrating a typical plumbing fabrication shop and the associated production line area.)

905.2 **Equipment.** A typical plumbing shop requires the following pieces of equipment.

1. Abrasive shop saw.
2. Butane torch and tank.
3. DWV plumbing bench. (See Fig. 905.2*A*.)
4. Water supply plumbing bench.
5. Vertical storage racks (See Fig. 905.2*B*.)
6. Bench mounted grinder and wire wheel brush.
7. Vise
8. Components
9. Pipe threader
10. Pipe vise and stand
11. Pipe rack

Jigs and fixtures used in the fabrication of plumbing are usually not warranted, due the low volume. Normally, a steel rule tape is attached to the plumbing bench to cut lengths of pipe. A fabricator may cut several lengths ahead and store these at his bench for future assembly. The sophistication and quality of the equipment is generally based on the volume of homes pro-

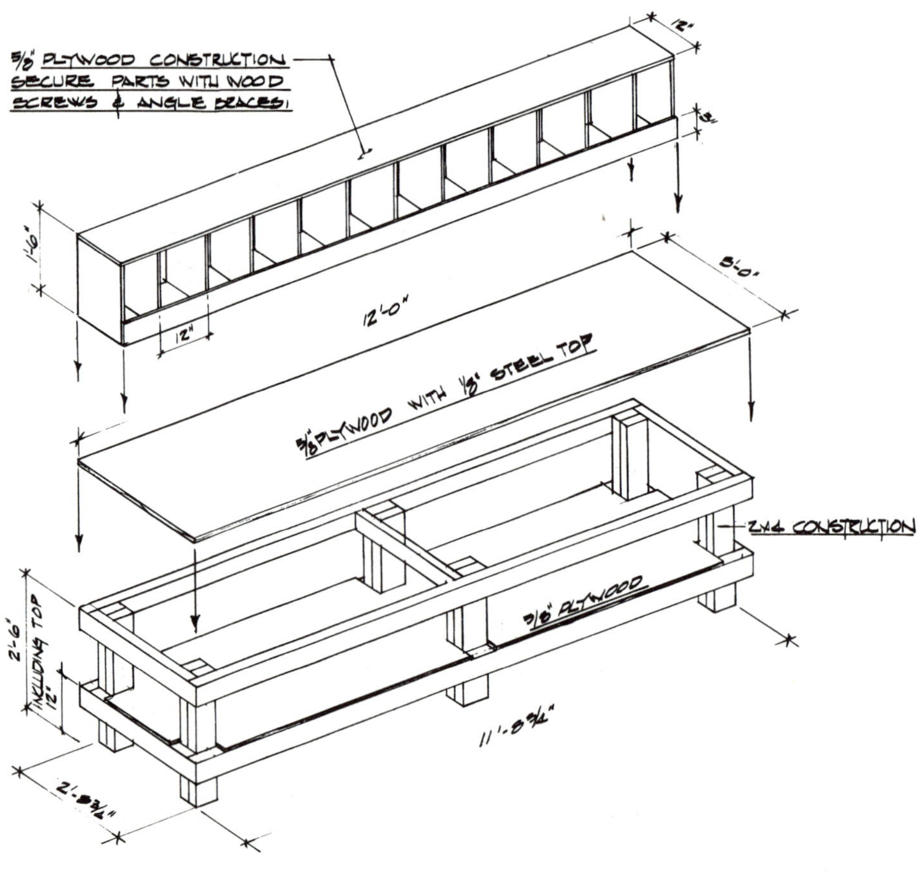


**Fig. 905.2*A*.**
Plumbing Shop Bench, no scale.

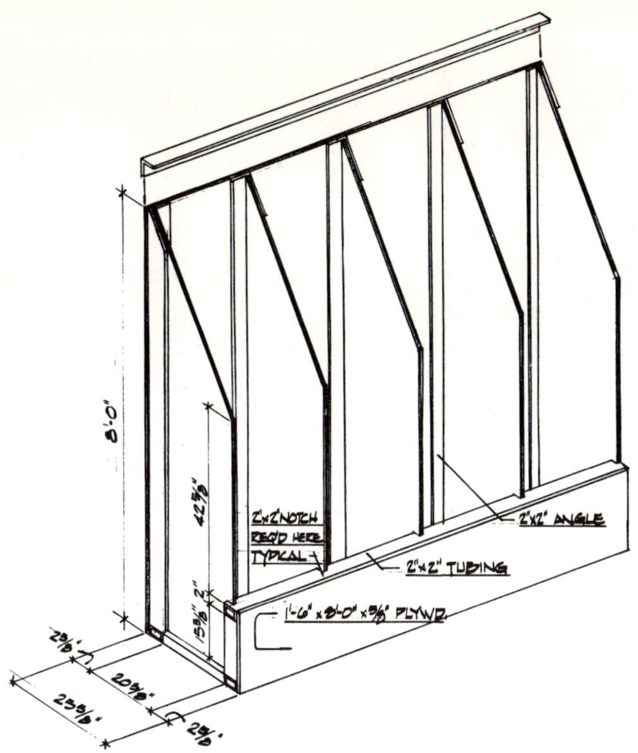


**Fig. 905.2*B*.**
Vertical Pipe Rack, no scale.

duced. Production of one to three homes per day does not warrant high quality equipment; whereas plants producing four or more homes per day will place great demands on the equipment being used.

905.3 **Installation.** There are two general methods of installing plumbing systems. The first is to prefab components into small subassemblies and complete the fabrication after the floor of the home has been completed. A second method is to prefab the bulk of the plumbing system into a plumbing wall. However, the decision on how the particular plumbing system is to be assembled, is primarily based on the lead times within the line cycle and the arrangement and complexity of the plumbing trees and water supply harnesses. Normal practice will allow enough time to install the rough plumbing system on the production line. Installation of fixtures takes place throughout the line, as time permits. It is important for all plumbing to be completed by the time the home is approximately three-fourths complete. This procedure will allow enough time for proper inspection and any tests which are required.

905.4 **Inspection.** Many inspection tests have been developed for plumbing systems, and some are outlined in plumbing code books. The water supply lines are normally tested under air pressure at approximately 100 PSI and let set for approximately 15 minutes. If there is no drop in pressure, then the system has passed the test. An alternative to this test, is to apply air pressure to the water solution. However, this does not indicate the condition of any concealed fittings; therefore, the primary test utilizing 100 lbs. of air pressure for 15 minutes without a fall in pressure should always be conducted. The drain system can be tested by capping off the main outlet and filling all fixtures with water to an adequate level so that all connections can be inspected. The water should remain for approximately 30 minutes and a reading of the water level taken. If the DWV system is properly installed then the water level will not have dropped. At the completion of this test, the water should be drained from all lines, especially in colder climates, and an anti-freeze solution added. When utilizing plastic pipe, for DWV, be sure to use a type of anti-freeze which will not attack the plastic pipe.

905.5 **Field Connections.** The well engineered industrialized house will limit the number of field connections to be made. There are several types of connections which may be encountered and some are outlined below:

Connection of water service to unit. The designer should locate this entrance as near as possible to the rear and outside walls of a home. Field connection may be made in a conventional manner by the local water department. The same holds true with the waste system. The location of the main drain should be again, as close as possible to the outside wall and located in a position accessible to the field workmen. Avoid installations which set the main water outlet in the center of the home. Connections between modules are generally made by couplings. However, there are some approved flexible connectors which can be used. These connectors work well when alignment problems occur. Small knockouts, utility closets are ideal places to run vertical runs between modules, first and

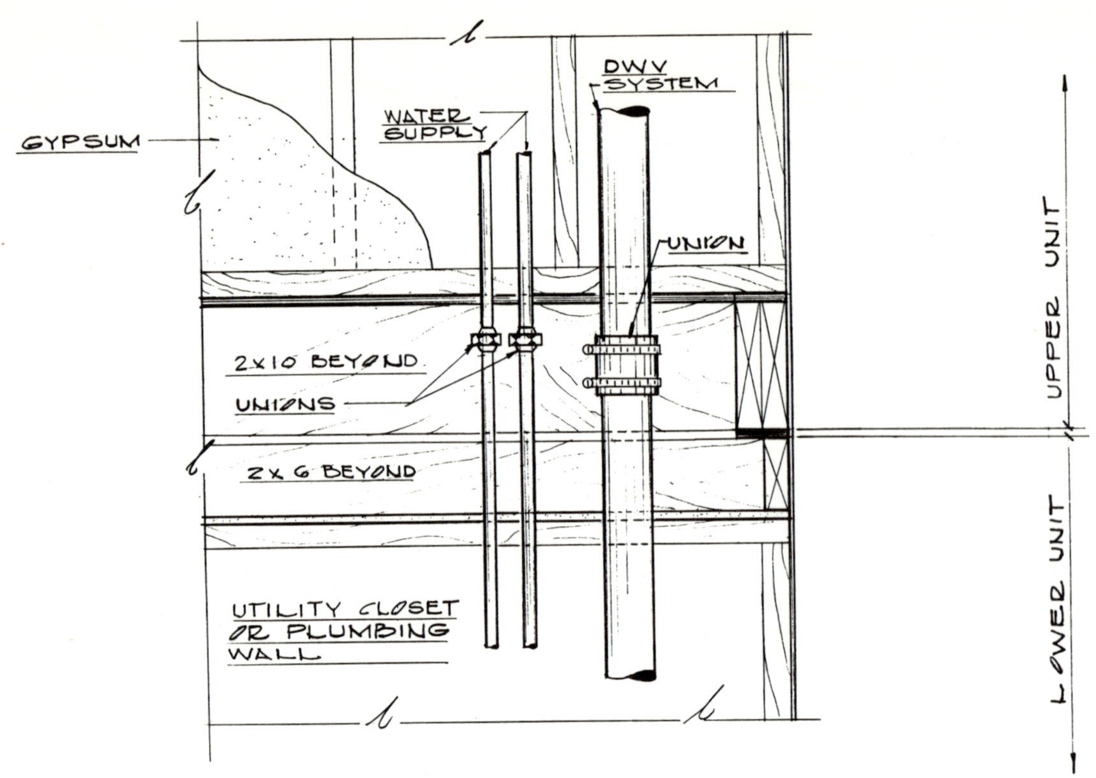


**Fig. 905.5.**
Field connection between two stack on units. Access from below provided for connections.

second floors. Connections can be made in these areas quite easily by the field installation crew. (See Fig. 905.5.)

906 **Fixtures.** The most conventional types of fixtures are those fixtures which we find in our present homes. While mobile homes utilize some fixtures smaller than the conventional units that we are accustomed to, they still have the same basic construction and require the same installation procedures.

The trend seems to be to special wall draining tubs and water closets to minimize under-floor work.

910 **Forced Air Heating Systems.** Forced air heating is the predominant heating system used in modular construction. The system consists of a package heating unit with combustion chamber and motor power. Fuels for these systems may be natural gas, LP, fuel oil and electric resistance coil. For details on electric heating see Chapter X, "Electric Wiring and Heating."

The heating units for all the above systems are basically the same except that electric systems do not require a flue. Fig. 910 shows a typical small package heating unit. Units are compact and measure approximately 24″ × 21″× 5′ high. This type of heating unit is produced by a number of manufacturers throughout the entire country. The particular advantage to this type of unit is that it can be easily installed. Connection can be made below the furnace base for warm air discharge or in some cases can be made though the top for an up-flow furnace.

The choice of which type of furnace is to be used, upflow or downflow, is dependent on the location of the furnace in the home. A two story module with the furnace located on the first floor would require an up-flow unit, whereas the downflow unit would be used for single story units. With stacking modules, locating the furnace on the second floor is most desirable as all connections can be made relatively easy with the flue stack connection made on the production line.

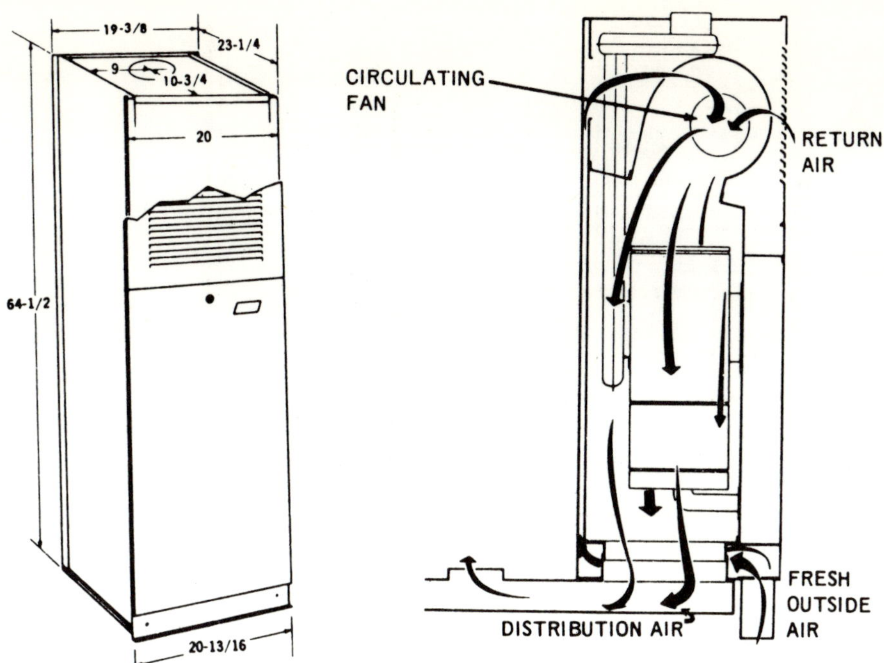


**Fig. 910.**
Typical packaged forced air heating unit.

911 **Forced Air Distribution Systems.** Fig. 911.1 shows the typical heat duct layout. Note, in this particular case, that the majority of the heat duct runs are at 90° to the floor joists.

The modular manufacturers can take advantage of an open web floor truss which is shown in Fig. 911.2. This particular floor joist is open through the center with staggered gusset plates utilizing 2 × 3's above and below. The heat duct may then pass through each floor joist.

912 **Heat Duct Materials.** Fibreglass, galvanized sheet metal, and aluminum are materials presently being used for heat duct runs. These materials all have their specific advantages and disadvantages.

*Fibreglass heat duct* is easily handled. Ducts can be fabricated from sheet stock with the use of a small knife and duct tape. They are easily installed and light in weight. Economics are questionable.

*Galvanized heat ducts* are relatively low in cost; however, connections between ducts are more difficult than in the fibreglass system.

*Aluminum heat ducts* are low in cost, light weight, easily cut and formed to fit heat duct off-shoots and collars. They tend to damage easily and the result may be a collapsed heat duct.

913 **Floor Plan Design Considerations.** The designer of the modular unit should work closely with the engineer when setting up his floor plan. Utilizing the open web joist shown in Fig. 911.2 can be very valuable. The heating system can be installed in a single unit with the heat ducts run thru the joist. Accessibility to the furnace compartment will determine the ease of installation in the production situation. Ideally, the duct system should consist of one straight run with duct openings up into the second floor and down into the first floor. This procedure can eliminate many costly field connections. When it is necessary to run heat from one unit to another laterally, connections can be made as shown in Fig. 913.

914 **Shop Drawings.** The industrialized housing manufacturer may have several heat duct layouts. Generally, the information required by the production worker may be like that shown in Fig. 911.1, Heat Duct Layout. Note that the only information

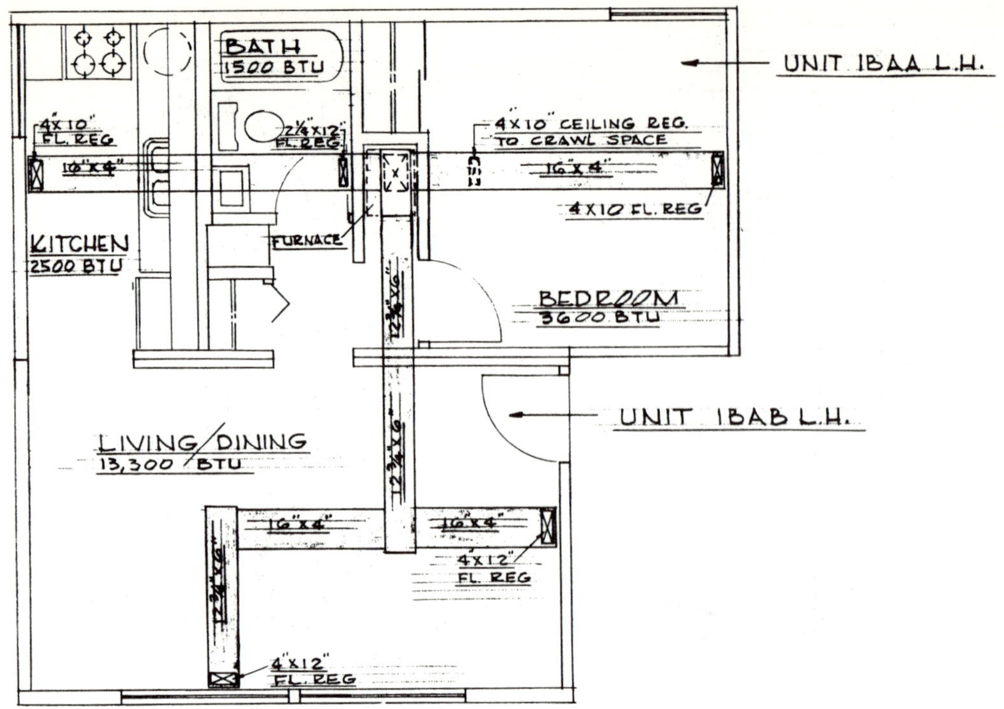


**Fig. 911.1.**
Heat duct layout.

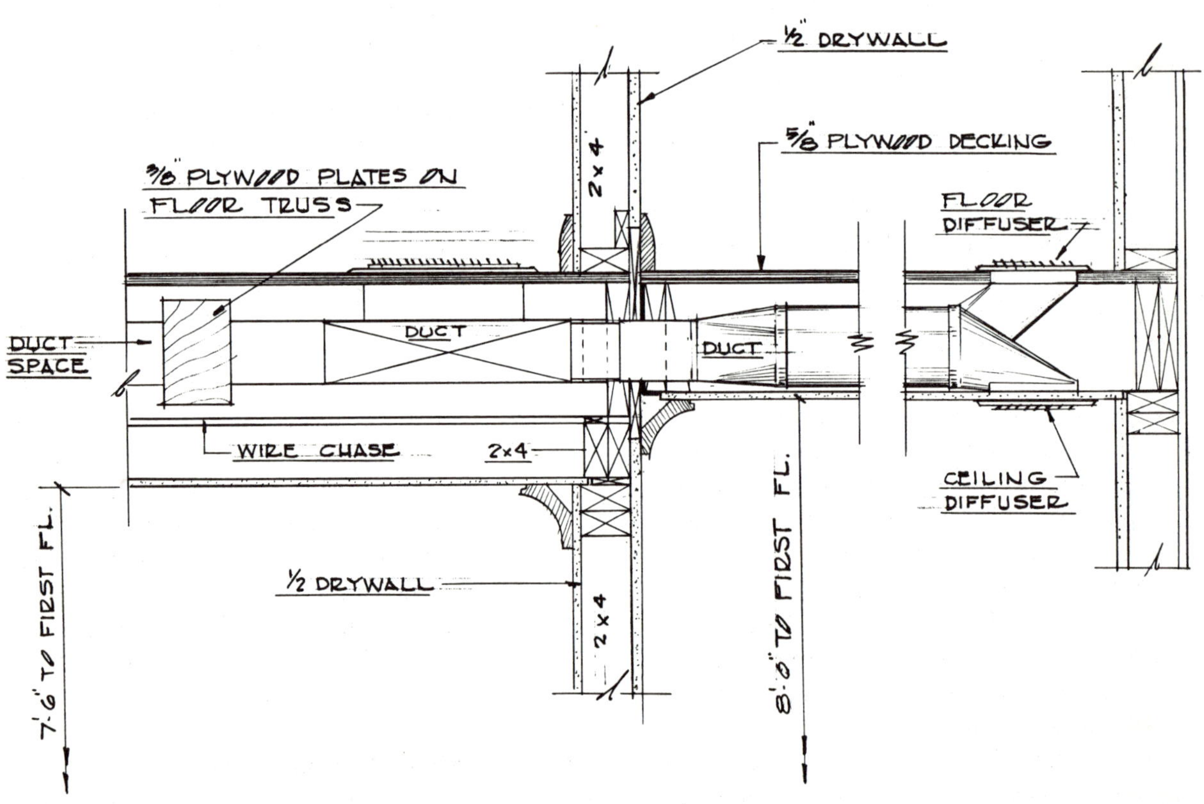


**Fig. 911.2.**
Detail showing use of open web truss.

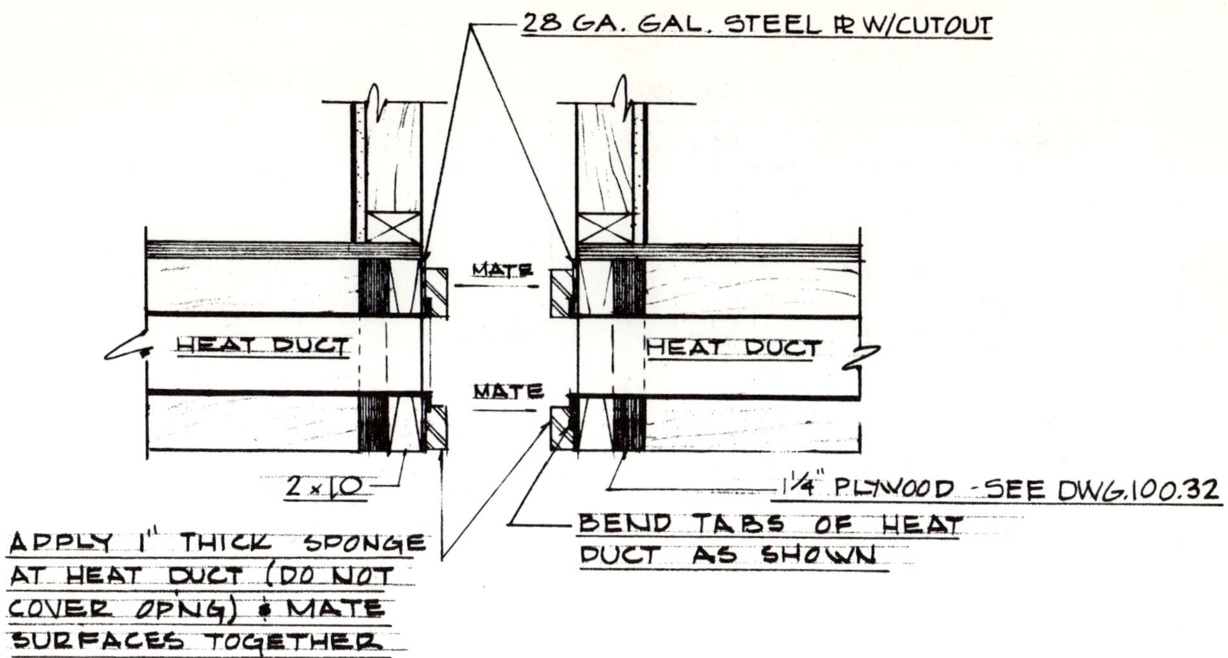


**Fig. 913.**
Mating heat ducts.

given here is the location of the lateral heat duct outlet and the position of the main heat duct from the edge of the floor.

The manufacturer should attempt to standardize his components into an assortment of lengths ranging from five to six on the main run and three to four lengths of heat duct offshoot. Doing this, the ducts can be purchased from local fabricators and should come in by truck without creating inventory problems. Information on the floor plan gives the location of the main heat duct, location of off shoots and also location of warm air outlets. This information is used by the production worker when the floor is fabricated to position the duct and cut the heat outlet hole.

915 **Production methods.** The method for installing the heating system in the modular unit is as follows:

915.1 **Install the Main Heat Duct Run.** This is normally done just after all lateral floor joists have been positioned in the floor. After the floor has been decked, an electric handsaw is used to cut openings for the furnace base and heat duct outlets. Fig. 915.1 illustrates a typical drawing used when cutting the floor decking.

After all cutouts have been made, the floor is sanded and rollgoods and carpeting are installed. The production worker may utilize a razor-knife like the one shown in Fig. 915.2 to cut roll goods and carpeting where the floor decking has been cut.

Attach collars to the main heat duct run. Collars are generally precut and the production worker simply folds them into shape the size of the opening in the floor and attaches the collar to the heat duct using sheet metal screws and heat duct tape.

The small heat loss at these connections is not considered to be critical in that any loss will be thrown into the floor cavity and, eventually, returned to the heating system by the cold air return.

Install the furnace base. Fig. 915.3 shows a typical furnace base installation. The heat duct is marked using a template which is sized by the duct connector. The heat duct is cut for the collar attachment. The collar is attached to heat duct by simply bending the small metal tabs around the main heat duct opening. Then the furnace base is placed over the collar.

When the home is nearly completed, the furnace is rolled into the home utilizing a small hand pushcart and is slid onto the furnace base. At this time, connect the flue stack, fuel line, and electrical connections

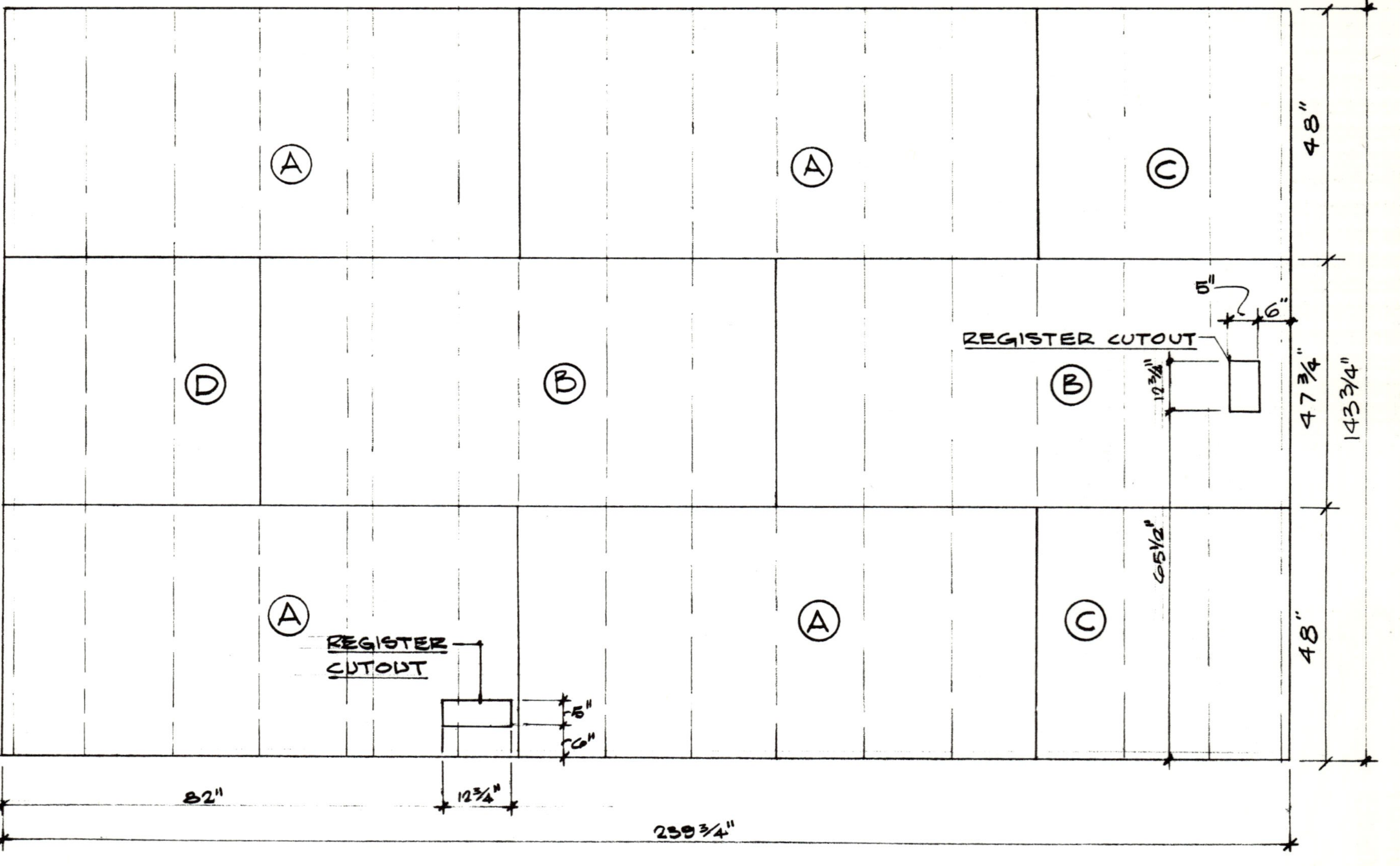


Fig. 915.1.
Floor decking. Cutout drawing.

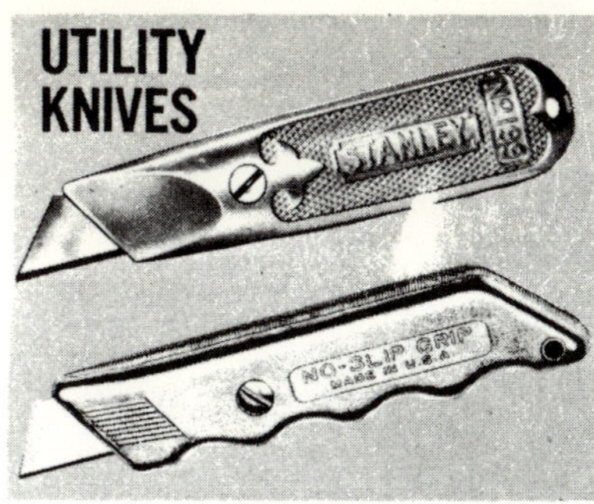


Fig. 915.2.
Razor knife.

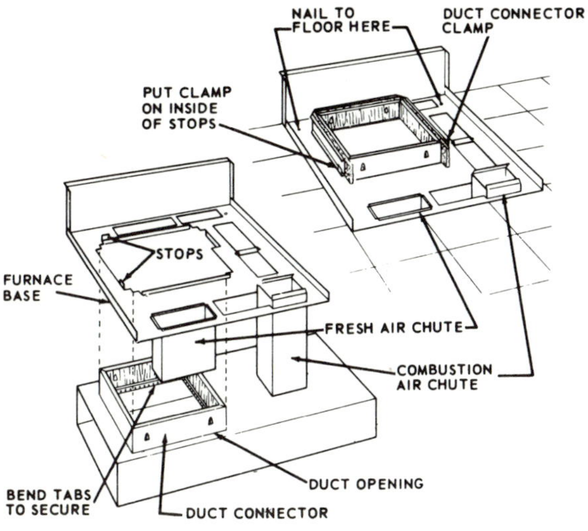


Fig. 915.3.
Furnace base.

for the blower motor and thermostat control wires.

916 **Fabrication Areas.** Off line fabrication areas are generally not required. Most of the fabrication takes place within the home except for minor packaging and assembly of small components of the main heating unit. All assembly takes place within the flow of the line. Storage areas are required for heat ducts, miscellaneous collars and air diffusers. Also, a large storage area is required for heating units. Units are normally received in closed van trucks and may be handled from deck level and stored on roller conveyor track as shown in Fig. 916.

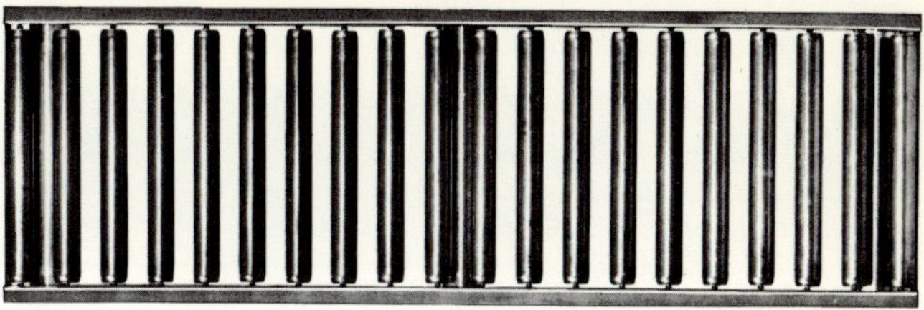

Fig. 916.
Roller conveyor.

917 **Inspection.** The inspection of the heating system generally takes place throughout the line cycle. After the heat duct assembly has been installed in the floor, a check of all connections should be made to insure that heat duct off shoots are airtight and sealed properly. The most critical inspection is at the point of installation itself. Inspection should check to see that all connections have been made properly, especially those connections on the flue stack. A special note of caution should be made to insure that proper clearances are maintained. Clearances of the furnace stack are normally recommended by the furnace manufacturer in his installation literature. The final inspection of the heating unit will normally be left to the field erection crew or, if natural gas is being used, the local gas company will inspect for proper installation and operation.

# CHAPTER X

## Electrical Wiring & Heating*

1000 **General.** In the initial planning of a manufactured building system, it is important to determine the feasibility of the electrical installation with the proposed structural method. For example, the need to provide electrical boxes containing a certain number of cubic inches in accordance with the code, may limit the use of "thin" walls. The need to effect connections between panels or modules may affect the structural planning.

Most of the electrical installations in manufactured buildings are installed using conventional methods, materials and equipment. There has been little development of specialized techniques, hence there is much that can and will be done in the future.

Building manufacturers should have on their staff a competent, licensed master electrician or, at least one should be available on a consulting basis. Should this individual be licensed in a number of cities, counties, or states in which the buildings are sold, code obstacles will be more easily overcome.

Provision for electrical service to the building should be more than adequate for all present and projected needs. In homes, a minimum service of 100 Amps should be used with 150 Amps preferred. A 200 Amp service should be provided for units having electric heat.

1001 **Codes.** The National Electrical Code is the dominant code in the field. There are some varying local requirements, but basically, a thorough knowledge of this code is adequate. The 1968 version of this code is available as *NFPA #70* for $2.00 from the National Fire Protection Association, 60 Battery March Street, Boston, Mass. 02110. They also publish an excerpt for one and two family dwellings, *NFPA #70A*, $1.75.

There are two valuable adjuncts to this code published by Wing Publishing Company, 3940 Grand River Ave., Detroit, Mich. 48208:

1. *Code Interpretations of the 1968 National Electrical Code Book,* $5.00
2. *Criss-Cross Index of the 1968 National Electrical Code Book,* $4.00

For planning electrical installations in dwelling units a helpful publication is *American Standard Requirements for Residential Wiring, C91.1—1958.* This is available from the Industry Committee on Interior Wiring Design, Room 1650, 750 Third Ave., New York, New York for 25¢.

A new National Electrical Code (1971) is in preparation. The major change affecting manufactured buildings will be a provision calling for only one ground wire entering a box to be counted in determining the size of the box. The resulting smaller box sizes will be important to this industry as it will permit the use of thin walls and smaller junction boxes.

At least one state, Minnesota, requires that the walls of prefabricated units be open for inspection after wiring is installed. This arbitrary requirement can only be overcome by having one of the local inspectors come to the fabricator's factory to inspect the wiring before it is covered. It is hoped that the future will eliminate unreasonable requirements such as these.

1002 **Materials.** The major materials that building manufacturers are concerned with are wire, boxes, and fixtures.

*Material in this chapter was largely gleaned from interviews with two individuals who are charged with supervision of electrical installations of their respective companies: We gratefully acknowledge their help:
*Raleigh Fisher,* Mechanical Designer, Wausau Homes, Wausau, Wisconsin. He has over 30 years experience as both an electrician and a plumber. He holds over 15 electrical licenses. Mr. Fisher has been in the manufactured home field for eleven years.
*Clare Lefler,* Chief Engineer, Active Homes Corp. Mr. Lefler has also had mobile home experience.

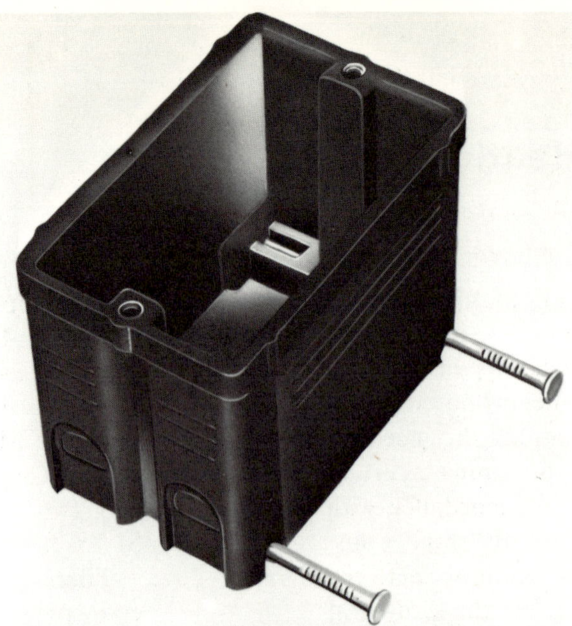

**Fig. 1002-2*A*.**
Typical nail-on outlet box of plastic.
*(Union Insulating Co.)*

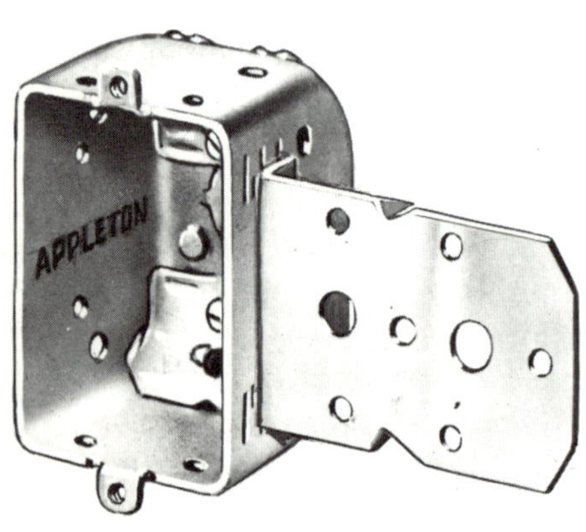


**Fig. 1002-2*B*.**
Steel nail-on outlet box with cable clamps.
*(Appleton)*

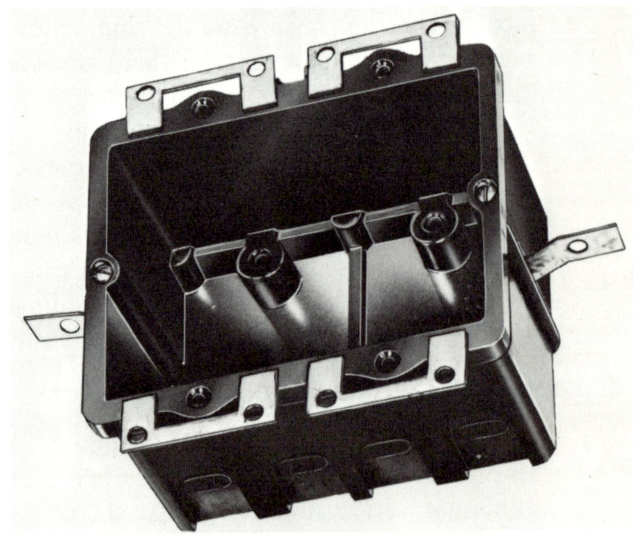

**Fig. 1002-2*C*.**
Double outlet box in plastic. The metal ears lock themselves on the back of the wall board, thus eliminating the need for attachment to the stud.
*(Union Insulating Co.)*

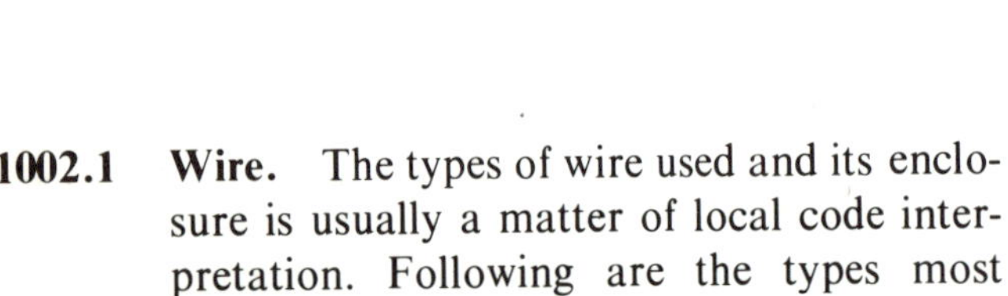

**1002.1 Wire.** The types of wire used and its enclosure is usually a matter of local code interpretation. Following are the types most frequently encountered.

**1002.1A Nonmetallic Sheathed Cable** (ROMEX) is the least expensive and the easiest to work with.

**1002.1B Metal Clad Cable** (**BX**) has a flexible metal covering.

**1002.1C Flexible Metal Conduit** (**Greenfield**) contains no wires and can be used where local codes require wiring to be done on the site. The conductors are pulled through with the aid of pull wires. An expensive operation.

**1002.1D Rigid Metal Conduit** is used similarly to the flexible but is difficult to use unless complete wiring is done at the factory. Most expensive.

1002.1E Single and double conductor rubber or plastic insulated wires are used for thermostats, entrance chimes, etc.

1002.2 **Boxes.** Electrical outlet and junction boxes are available in both steel and plastic. Typical boxes are shown in Figs. 1002.2A, B, and C.

Several manufacturers attach their boxes to the wallboard with "Hold it" clips or by using boxes of the self-attaching type shown in Fig. 1002-2C. This method saves labor but may be ruled out by a strict code interpretation.

1002.3 **Fixtures.** The minimum requirement for fixtures is that they be Underwriters Laboratory (UL) approved. They should be selected for ease of installation and minimum likelihood of shipping damage to globes, pendants, etc.

1003 **Layouts.** A wiring layout should be prepared for each model built by a manufacturer. This is not usually done in conventional construction but is of considerable importance in manufactured buildings. A typical layout is shown in Fig. 1003.

1004 **Techniques.** As mentioned earlier, the wiring techniques used in manufactured buildings are very nearly the same as those used in conventional construction.

1004.1 **Modular Construction.** Wall panels for these units are frequently jig-fabricated with the interior finish applied and the exterior open to receive wiring, etc., before application of exterior siding. Studs are often pre-drilled as a part of the cutting operations.

Some manufacturers dado the studs so that wiring can be placed in the 7/8" by 2" pocket thus formed, without threading the wire through numerous holes in the studs. When this is done, wires are required to be protected against nails driven into them by metal shields as shown in Fig. 1004.1.

1004.2 **Precut Wires.** Wire meters are available to meter and cut to length up to five pieces of cable at a time. These pieces are then stripped and stocked on racks near the point of use. Wiring layout specifies the length required for each application.

**Fig. 1004.1**
Metal shields for protection during wall assembly. The U-shield provides two sided protection, and flat shield is available for one sided protection.

*(Truswal)*

1004.3 **Pre-Wiring Circuit Breakers.** Where construction permits, the cables going to the circuit breaker can be attached and coded as a bench operation, removed from the production line, resulting in a labor saving.

1004.4 **Connections Between Units.** The connection between two panels can be effected by the use of pull wires installed at the plant. Connections between modular units can be done by the use of junction boxes over the ceiling as shown in Fig. 1004.4.

1005 **Electric Heating.** Electric heating is frequently used in manufactured buildings where utility rates permit because of the simplicity of installation and the fact that no flue is required.

1005.1 **Types of Electric Heat**

*A.* Baseboard radiation—probably the most frequently used.

*B.* Electric boiler—with hot water baseboard.

*C.* Radiant ceiling.

*D.* Hot air with or without air conditioning.

*E.* Heat pump, including air conditioning in warmer climates.

1005.2 **Layout.** As in the wiring, a layout of the electric heating system is essential. An example is shown in Fig. 1005.2.

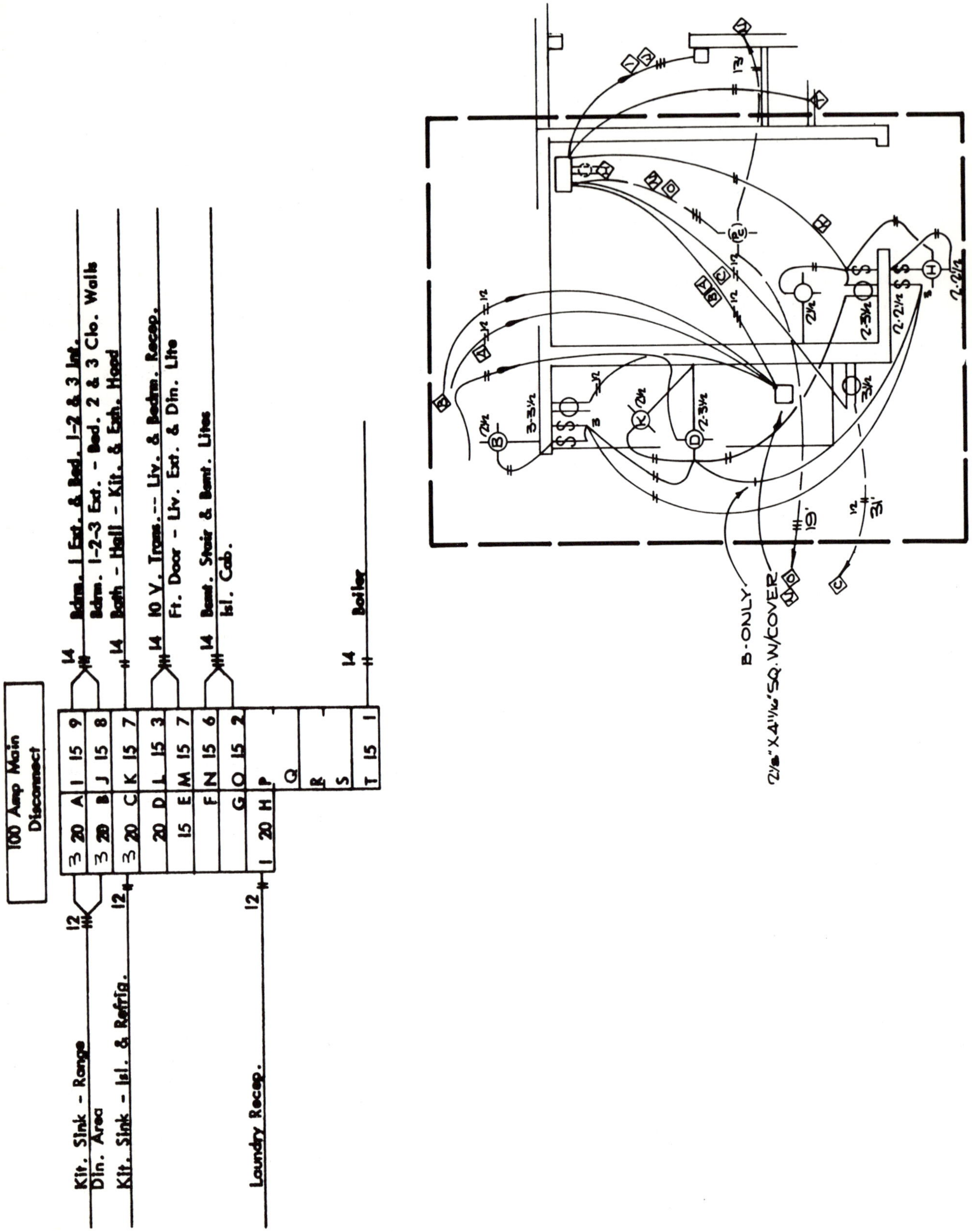

100 Amp Main Disconnect

| Circuit (left) | Wire | | | | | | Wire | Circuit (right) |
|---|---|---|---|---|---|---|---|---|
| Kit. Sink - Range / Din. Area | 12 | 3 20 A | 3 20 B | I 15 9 | J 15 8 | | 14 | Bdrm. 1 Ext. & Bed. 1-2 & 3 Int. / Bdrm. 1-2-3 Ext. - Bed. 2 & 3 Clo. Walls |
| Kit. Sink - Isl. & Refrig. | 12 | 3 20 C | | K 15 7 | | | 14 | Bath - Hall - Kit. & Exh. Hood |
| | | 20 D | 15 E | L 15 3 | M 15 7 | | 14 | 10 V. Trans.-- Liv. & Bedrm. Recep. / Ft. Door - Liv. Ext. & Din. Lite |
| | | F | G | N 15 6 | O 15 2 | | 14 | Bsmt. Stair & Bsmt. Lites / Isl. Cab. |
| Laundry Recep. | 12 | 1 20 H | | P | Q | R S | | |
| | | | | T 15 1 | | | 14 | Boiler |

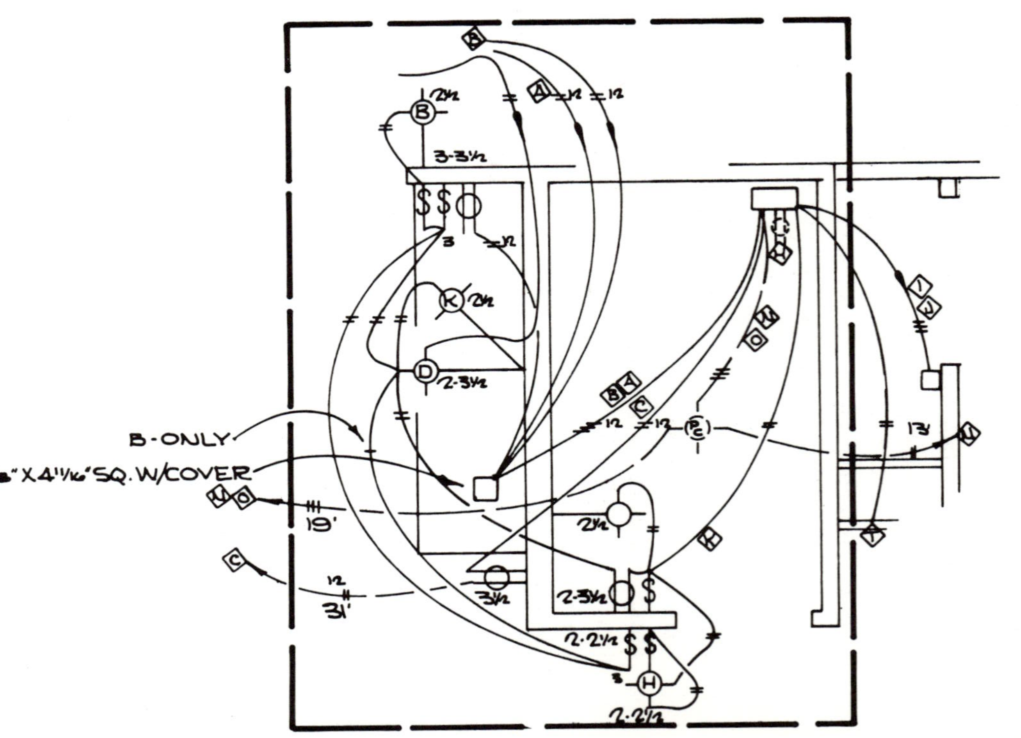

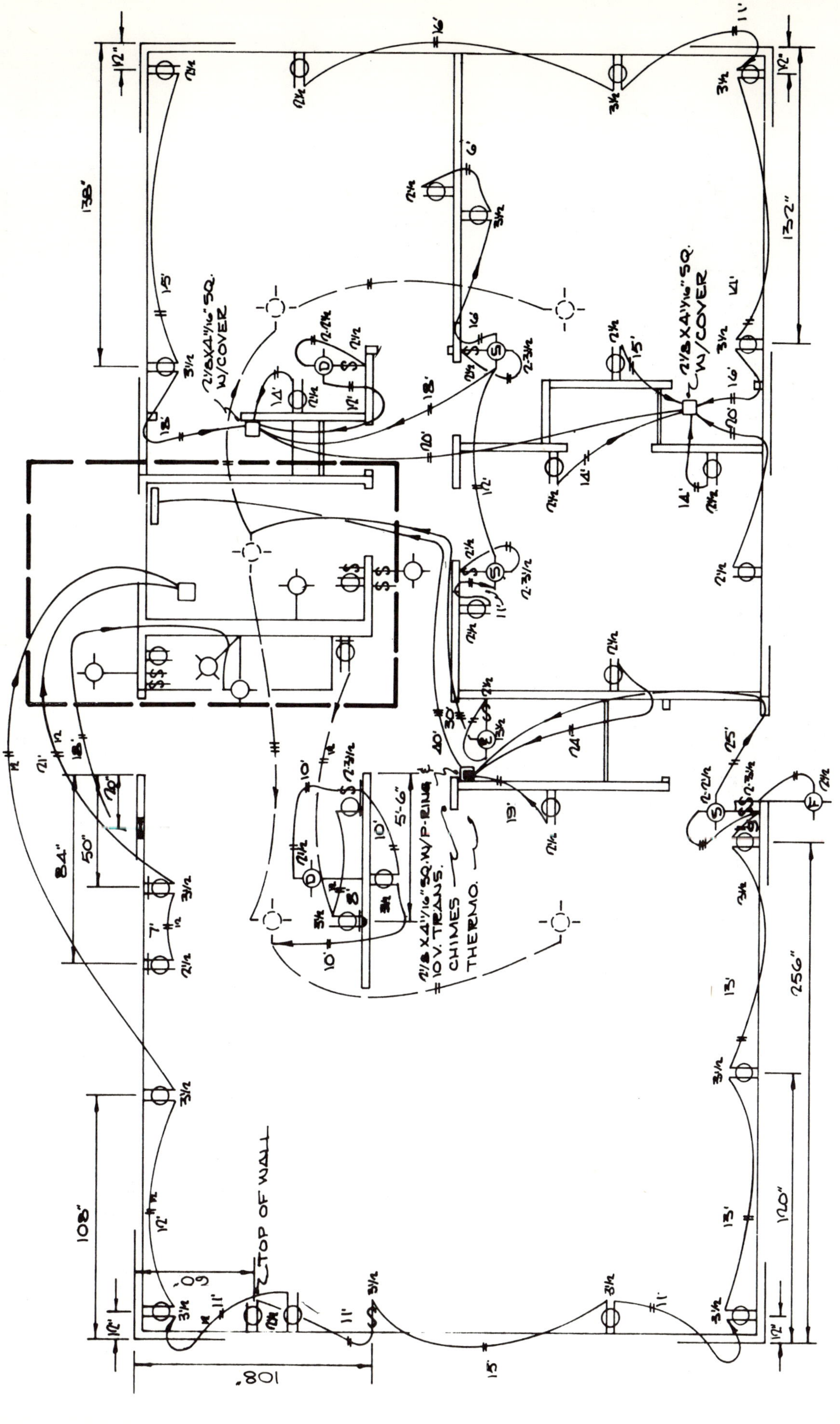

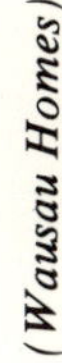

**Fig. 1003.**
A typical wiring layout for a panelized house with a central utility module. The lengths shown on the runs are the actual wire lengths which are precut and stripped for use on the assembly line.

*(Wausau Homes)*

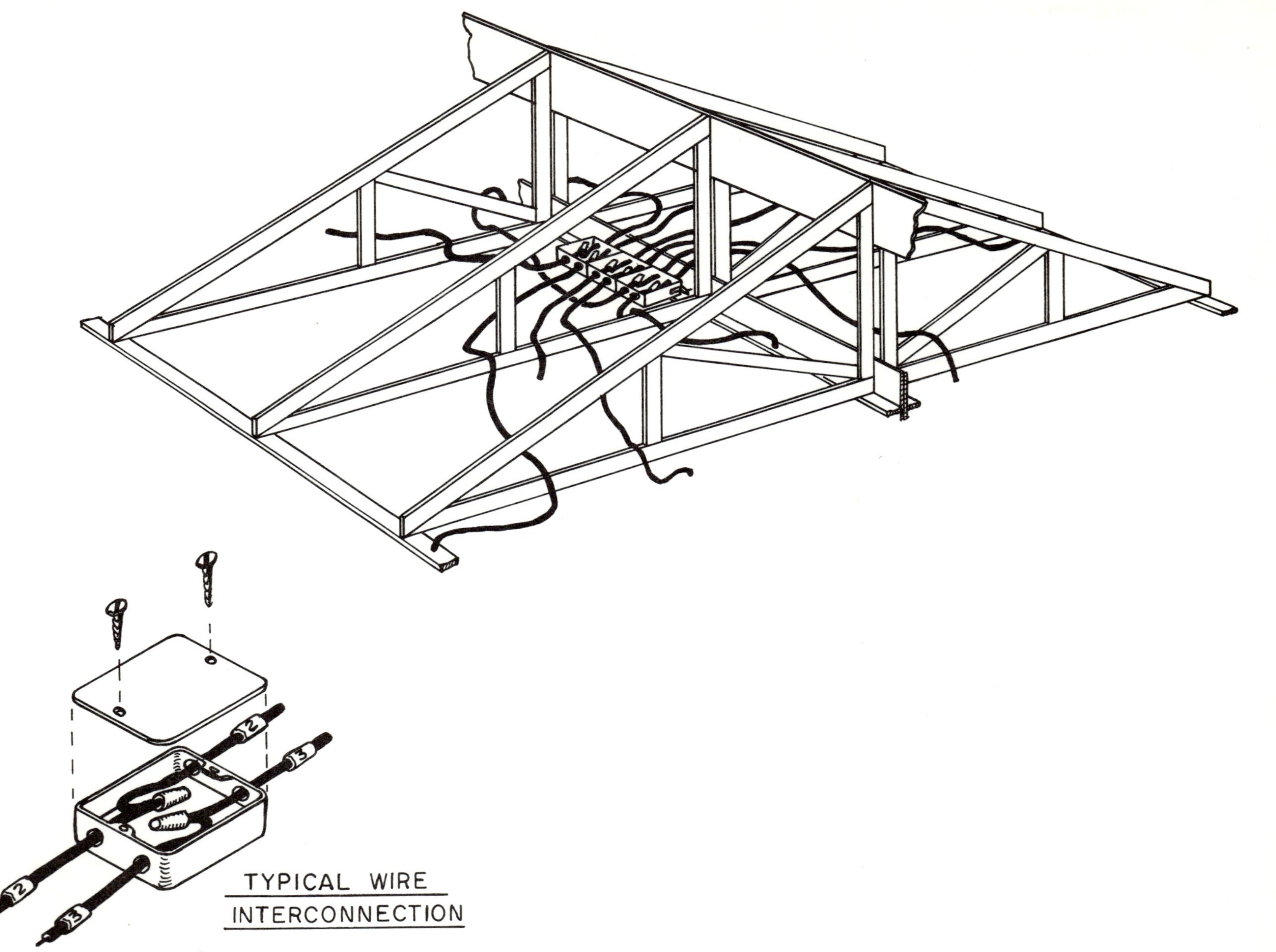


**Fig. 1004.4.**
Wiring between modules takes place above the hall thru scuttle in ceiling. Wiring is numbered when installed in each section. On site, wires are matched by number, spliced into box, and cover installed.

*(Continental Homes)*

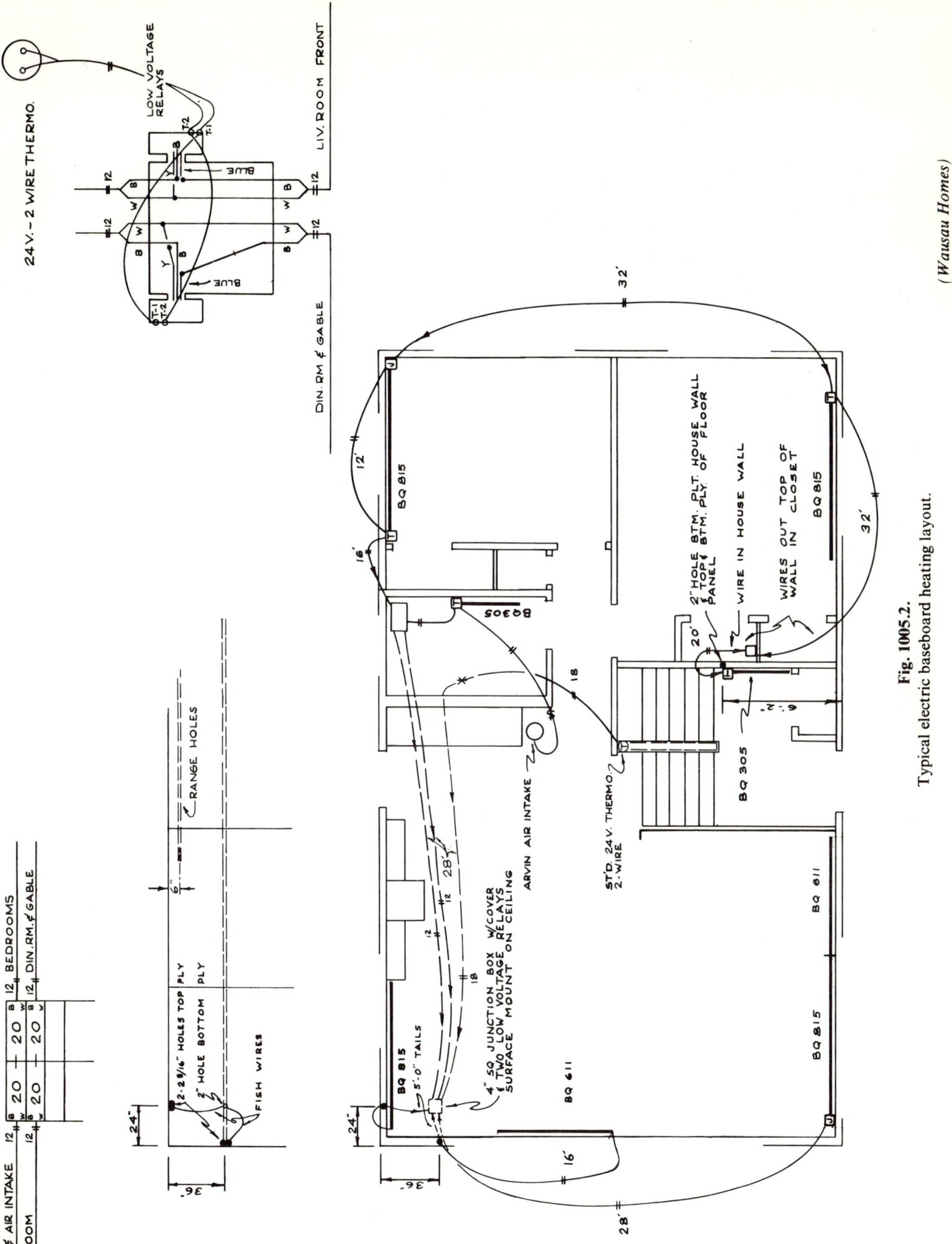


**Fig. 1005.2.**
Typical electric baseboard heating layout.

*(Wausau Homes)*

# CHAPTER XI

# Modular Units

*J. A. (Al) Reidelbach, Jr.**

**1100** **Typical Construction Details.** The basic construction details currently employed by a majority of manufacturers of modular housing frequently parallel those of conventional wood framed housing. Although the size and spacing of floor joists, exterior wall studs, interior partitions, window and door framing, and other integral parts are similar, there are certain details which vary to accommodate special loadings, connections and other requirements of these specialized housing forms. Because of the predominance of wood as the primary construction material of the modular industry, no attempt is made in this section to show construction details for other materials.

The rigors of plant handling, over-the-highway transportation, and erection of the units create certain stresses and strains which the typical site-built house does not undergo. Accordingly, it is essential that special consideration be given in the design and fabrication in order to avoid damage to finish materials or the structure itself. Modular housing must also be built in such a manner that the units can be efficiently joined to one or more other units at the job site, with joint details structurally adequate to meet local building codes and to effectively perform during the intended life of the structure. Certain additional details must be incorporated to improve aesthetics, and all such details must work in harmony with one another.

While these special construction considerations may vary from one geographical area to another and may even vary from one plant to the next, certain recurrent design features emerge which merit inclusion in a general category. The construction details described on the following pages are those considered most common within the industry. There are other requirements besides these, and they can vary greatly. In all cases, a qualified engineer should be retained to prepare final structural details consistent with building requirements in the marketing area. To meet the requirement that the highest point of a transported unit not exceed the 13′-6″ limit, it has become almost commonplace in the modular industry to utilize roof systems with flat pitches. In this regard, roof slopes generally range from 2 1/2 to 3 in 12, but where the manufacturer wishes to increase ceiling heights by a few inches, an even lesser slope may be employed. All such trusses are of the monopitch variety, with a spacing truss at 24″ O.C. This results in the gable roof which has become associated with this housing form. See Fig. 1101.

**1101.1** **Trusses.** For the most part, metal truss plates are used for these low slope trusses, although some manufacturers will occasionally employ the plywood glue-nailed or nailed gusset systems. Since the span of these trussed rafters is typically equivalent to the 12′-0″ half the house width, individual members of the truss are 2″ × 4″s and 2″ × 3″s. Designers will find that stress graded lumber is generally required for the top chords of such units, whereas lower rated, ungraded materials may be totally acceptable for the rest of the truss. See Fig. 1101.1.

*Al Reidelbach has been employed by a number of home manufacturers and is president of a North Carolina company formed to build modular homes. For ten years he was technical director and Executive Vice President of the Home Manufacturer's Association (now National Association of Building Manufacturers). Al is also a housing industry consultant in the Washington, D.C. area. Recently published and authored by Reidelbach is *Modular Housing in the Real* (Modco, Inc., P.O. Box 425, Annandale, Virginia 22003) A study of all the aspects of the emerging modular industry.

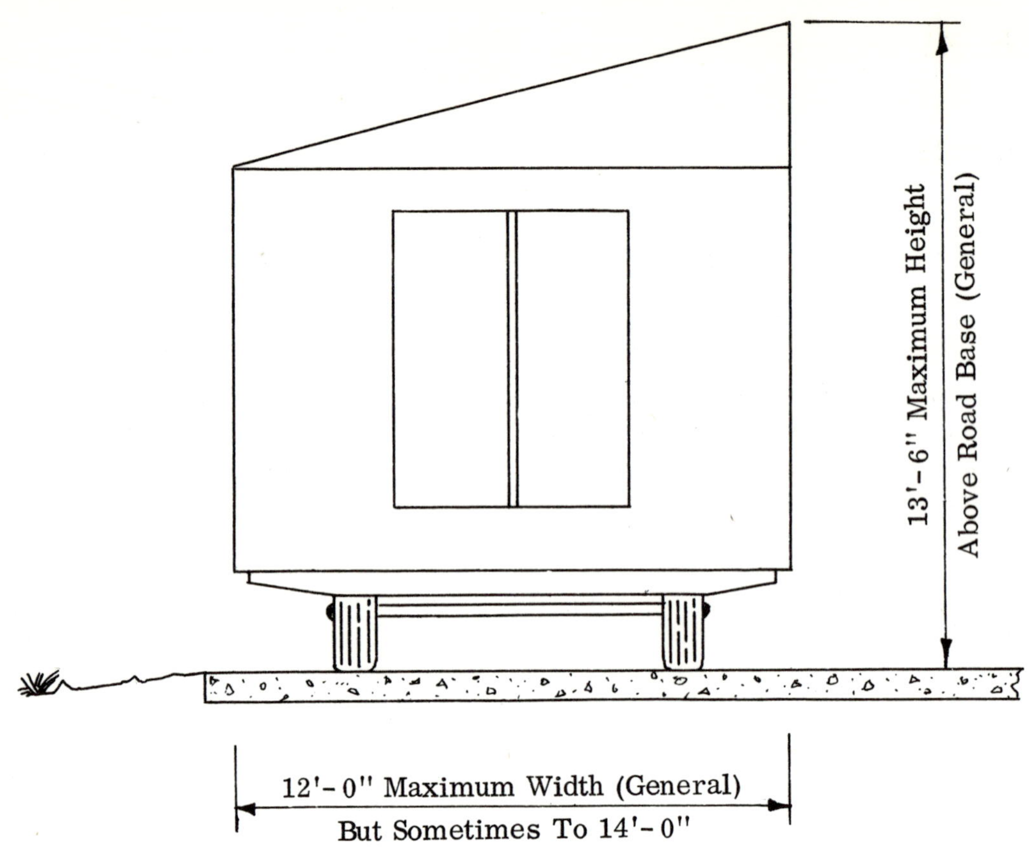


**Fig. 1101.**
Typical maximum shipping dimensions of modular housing units NOTE: Dimensions will vary with each state. Those shown are the most prevalent.

1101.2 **Folding Roof.** To obtain a steeper pitched roof, which may be desired to improve public acceptance, a folding type of trussed rafter roof system may be employed. With this method and the same 13'-6" height limitation, a 4 in 12 roof pitch can be obtained without the requirement of extensive on-site labor to finish out the roof. A typical application would have the upper half of the top chord member lap and bolt to the side of the lower half. At the ridge, the vertical truss member is similarly bolted to the lapped top chord member.

The bolts act as hinges and enable the upper part of the top chord and the vertical portion to fold and rest for shipment on the bottom chord and diagonal members. Plywood roof sheathing is factory applied to the folding portion, while shingles are applied to all roof areas except at the ridge, which is field applied after the sections have been tied together. In lieu of bolts and field nailing, some manufacturers make use of split rings for linking and load transfer at the joints.

Some modular manufacturers will simply provide a flat panel roof component which spans from about the midpoint of the unit to the ridge. During shipment from factory to job site it will rest on the trussed roof portion, which is fabricated and permanently attached on the production line. Once this unit is in place on the foundation, the flat roof panel is raised and nailed to the trussed rafter portion and at the ridge to the adjacent roof panel. Intermediate column supports under the ridge may also be added. See Fig. 1101.2*A*.

A variation is where the rafter portion is hinged at the eave line and cut short so it will not project beyond the module. Hinging is accomplished by nailing the rafter with only one nail to the ceiling member. (Additional nails are applied on site).

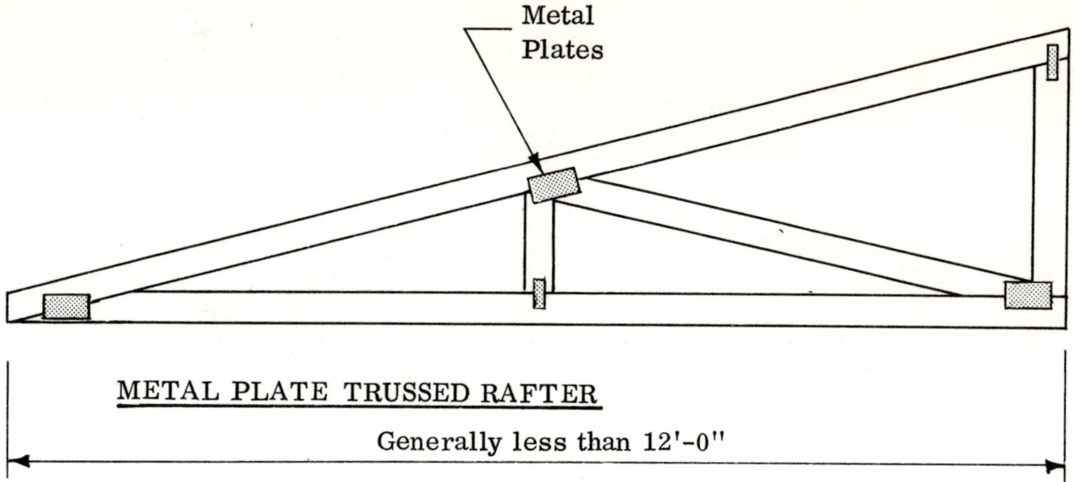


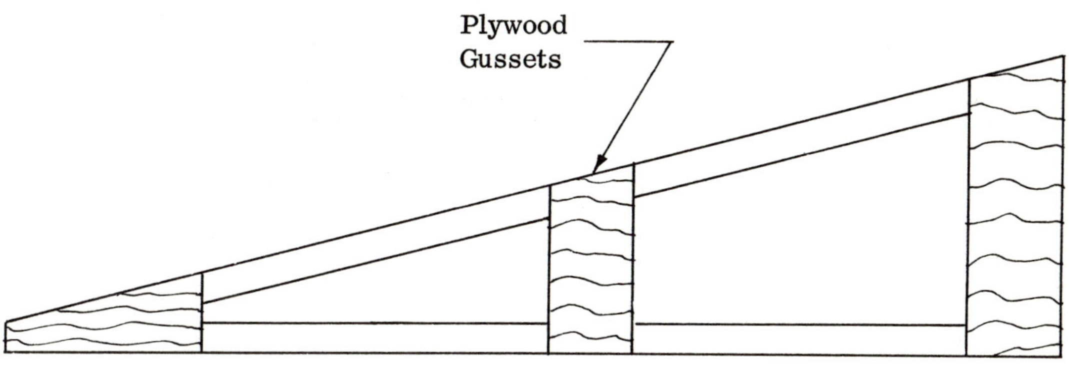


**Fig. 1101.1.**

After installation the roof sections are raised and a center filler section is installed at the peak. See Fig. 1101.2*B*.

**1101.3** To achieve pitched roofs steeper than 4 in 12, it becomes almost mandatory to employ a sectional box modular system in combination with regular trussed rafter or conventional joist and rafters which are framed at the site after the individual modular sections are joined together. In addition to providing more typical roof lines, use of this system enables local labor to participate on a greater scale, and may provide the incentive needed in certain markets to obtain labor for finishing out modular houses. When the conventional approach is employed, rafter and joists may be precut at the factory and included as part of total modular package, with roofing paper, nails, and shingles also included. If roof framing materials are purchased locally, the use of trussed rafters may prove economical from the standpoint of cost and time. See Fig. 1101.3

While less than the low slope gable roof, other roof configurations are also employed. These would include hip, flat, and mansard types, with the latter two becoming more popular for use with the stack-on sectional units.

**1102** **Eave Overhangs.** In an effort to provide housing units with the characteristics of conventionally built housing, yet remain within the 12′ shipping limit, modular

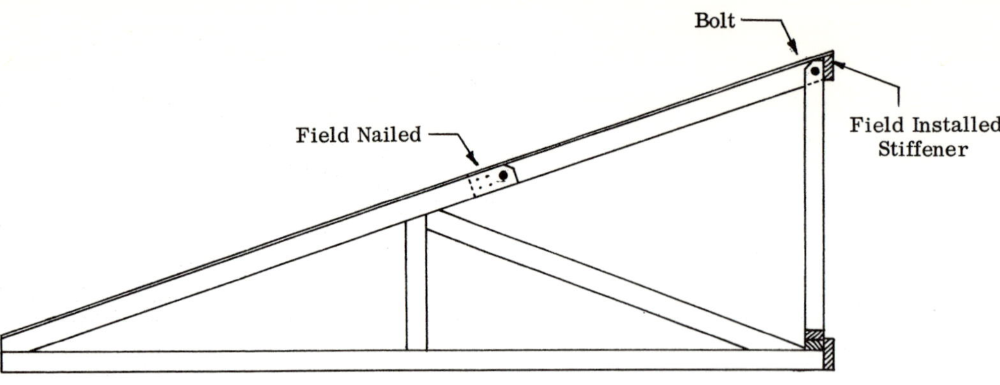


UNFOLDED POSITION

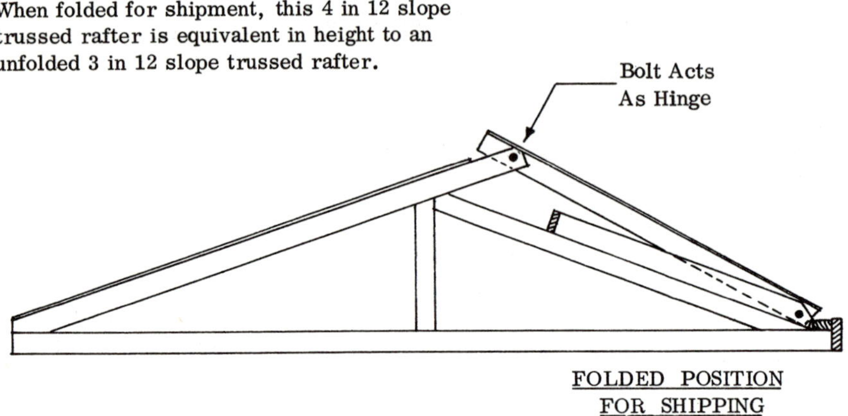


FOLDED POSITION
FOR SHIPPING

**Fig. 1101.2*A*.**

**Fig. 1101.2*B*.**
Ridge filler being installed on site.

*(Suburban Homes)*

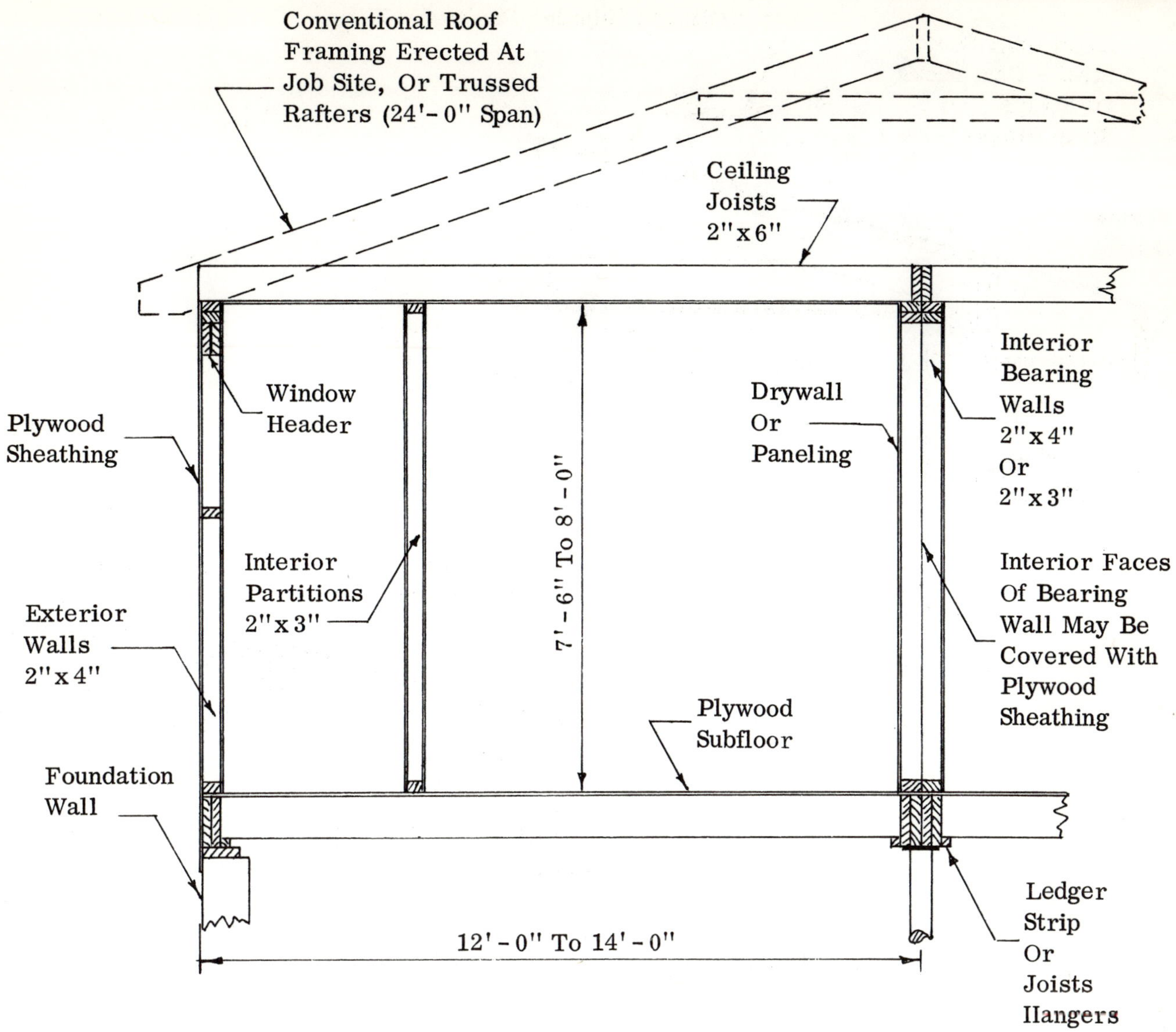


**Fig. 1101.3.**
Typical cross section sectional box—single story.

manufacturers have designed ingenious methods of providing overhangs at the factory which do not add to the overall shipping width. These eave overhangs are attached to the modular unit in the factory with light gage galvanized steel straps generally at each trussed rafter location, or a continuous sheet of light gage galvanized steel may be attached along the length of the unit.

The overhang is first built as a component and attached to the eave of the roof during production. The typical overhang, 12″ wide, can then be folded back to rest on the roof, where it is temporarily fastened for shipping. At the job site, it is simply flipped down and nailed in final position. This portion of the roof surface is not shingled at the factory, but must be field applied.

Rather than rely on light gage steel to act as both a hinge and as part of the permanent structural support for the overhang unit, some manufacturers will use strap hinges with a fewer number even using piano type hinges. Other manufacturers use aluminum instead of galvanized steel for this detail. Still others will ship the overhang as a separate component to be applied at the job site. This architectural trim treatment adds to the overall appearance of the finished modular house, and most manufacturers today include it as an integral part of their unit. See Fig. 1102.

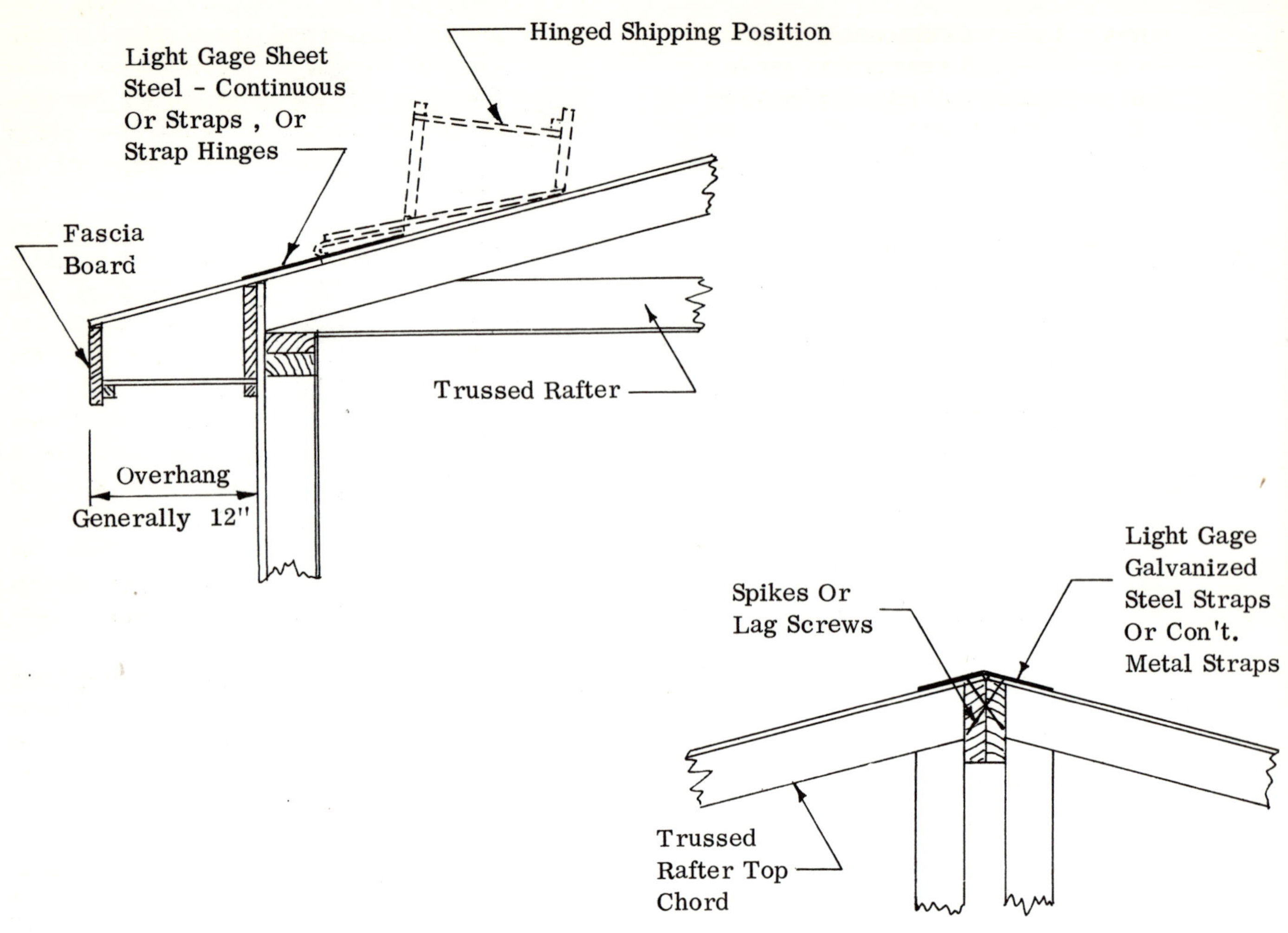


**Fig. 1102.**
Typical detail hinged eave overhand and typical ridge joint detail.

1103 **Bearing Walls.** Of all structural elements, bearing walls are perhaps the most important. The methods used to connect framing members, the methods of framing and locating door and window openings, can greatly affect the unit during highway shipment and job site erection. Large window and door openings are points of weakness, and though adequate transporters may be provided to eliminate flex and warp during over the road shipment, the erection process may still create finish and/or structural failures in these areas. Proper design is therefore essential.

While exterior bearing walls are typically 2″ × 4″, the interior or center bearing wall studs are generally 2″ × 3″, with both spaced 16″ O.C. as in conventional framing. The interior bearing wall, can become a double wall when adjacent modular units are joined together. Because of this, six or eight inch nominal wall thickness results, and a few manufacturers have accordingly reduced the stud size in the interior wall to 2″ × 2″, which they feel is equivalent to the normal 2″ × 4″ stud wall. Generally speaking, this smaller size stud should not be employed unless a structural glue and plywood sheathing is used in conjunction with close quality control on the production line. Plywood is the most common sheathing used; but some manufacturers utilize insulation board for this semi-structural wall covering material.

When proper nailing is made, particularly in conjuction with a good adhesive, wall sheathing material in combination with studs and cross partitions can act as a deep girder to provide more than adequate strength to resist shipment and erection stresses. Unfortunately, some manufacturers are not totally cognizant of the important part proper wall fastenings can play in reducing drywall cracks and other finish failures, the net result being that costly on-site repairs must be made.

1104 **Beams and Girders.** Unlike conventional framing, in the case of sectional housing units, two band or ribbon joists are typically provided in the longitudinal direction of the unit. These occur along the exterior wall and also along the center bearing wall. When modular units are joined together, the latter form a four member girder along the center of the finished house.

The double ribbon joists along the exterior wall are generally two 2″ × 10″s. Although they play little or no structural role once the module is resting on foundations walls, during plant fabrication, transportation and erection they must be capable of providing intermediate and at times sizeable load carrying ability. Because these members run the full length of the house, they can be considered as a continuous girder or beam, particularly if designed and fabricated to resist the stresses imposed during plant handling and the erection sequence. Butt joints in such beams are staggered, with individual adjacent members well nailed to each other. For added strength and rigidity, glue is sometimes also applied, enabling the double ribbon joists to act more as a solid continuous beam. The double ribbon joists configurations in the case of stack-on sectional units, when properly designed, can act as a header or lintel over door and window openings.

When trussed rafters are used, as in conventional construction, one half of the roof load goes to each exterior wall. In the case of sectional housing units, with half truss roof systems resting on the center bearing wall, a substantially greater load is transmitted to the basement, or center girder. Because of height restrictions, manufacturers have reduced beam depths by fabricating this important structural element as a continuous beam. The same system of staggering butt joints as explained for the exterior double ribbon joist is followed, but because the loading is more critical the location and type of splices is more specific. Similarly, higher stress grade lumber is typically employed for this continuous beam with nails, metal truss plates and/or glue also being employed to increase its structural performance.

The maximum span betweeen columns supporting the center girder does not as a rule exceed 8′-0 for normal loadings, with all such spans generally being equal. For heavier loadings, as can occur with the stack-on units, and in the case of wide door openings with jamb studs located at mid-span of the girder, a shorter span may be in order. The center girder, which is bolted together at the job site to form a four member thick beam, also acts as one of the primary structural constituents during transportation and field erection of sectional units.

It is rather common practice to employ headers and beams over window and door openings which are consistent in size and lumber grade to their counterparts in conventional framing. An exception to this, of course, would be wide openings for window banks or larger than normal openings in the center bearing wall, as between rooms in adjacent halves of the house. In such cases, some manufacturers utilize flat trusses located above the ceiling line. In so doing, headroom clearance is greatly improved inasmuch as all structural elements are raised above the ceiling line. See Figs. 1104.1 thru 1104.5.

1105 **Erection Details.** In single story sectional housing, the primary structural connections made during erection are those at the ridge, center wall, center girder wall, and along the foundation walls. Once the units are in place, and prior to placement of shingles along the ridge of roof, light gage galvanized metal straps, or continuous sheet metal, with or without angle driven spikes or lag screws, may be used to effectively tie the two halves together. See Fig. 1102. For door openings in the center bearing wall, as well as where the half sections meet in the end walls, light gage metal plates are generally used, but some modular manufacturers simply recommend nails or lag screws at these locations prior to trim-out. Galvan-

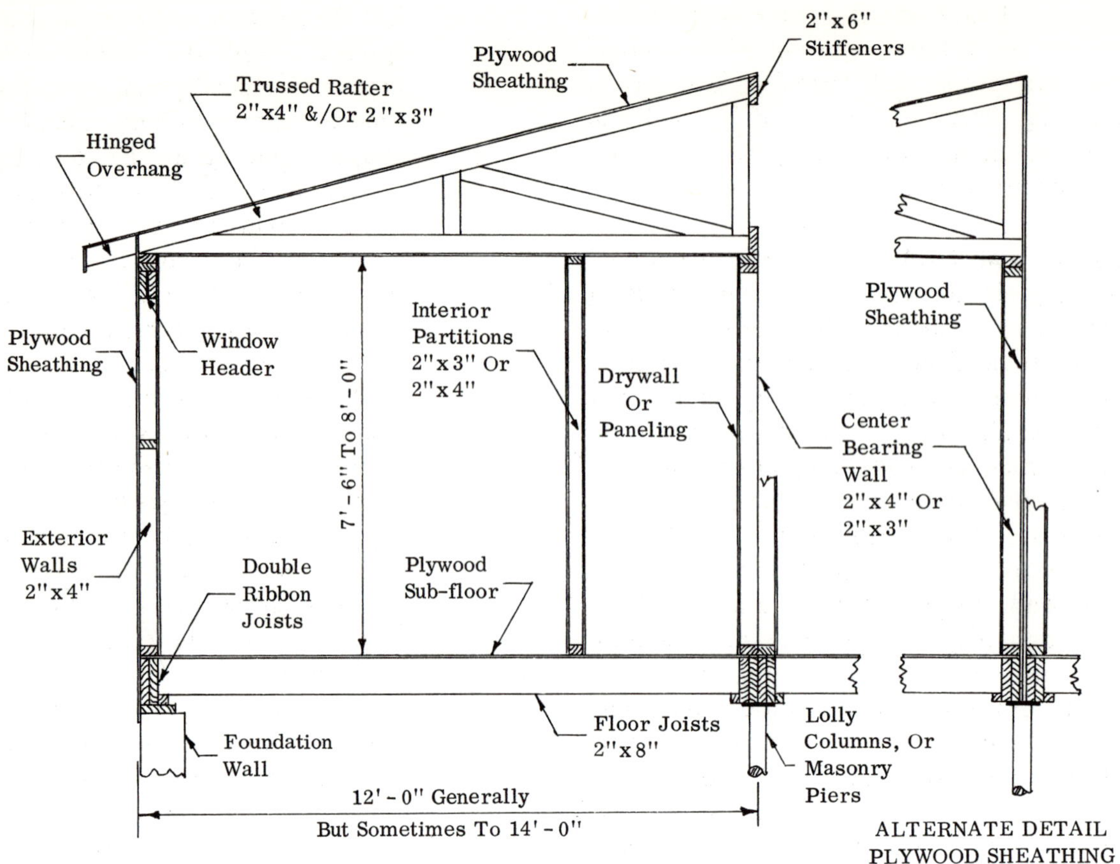


**Fig. 1104.1.**
Typical cross section single family-sectional house.

ized steel trussed rafter plates with integral nails or prepunched nail holes and special nails are ideally suited for these types of field connections.

Individual halves of the center girder are almost always drawn together with bolts spaced four to six feet apart along the full length of house. When steel lolly columns are used as intermediate supports, they are lag screwed to the bottom of the four member thick girder. Proper anchoring of the units to foundation walls requires that space be left at the bottom of the modular unit to make this connection on the outside of the building. When factory applied wall material and trim do not allow this type of connection, metal straps nailed to the sides of the floor joist and to the wall plate and foundation wall are sometimes used. Because of the ease of accessibility, field connections on the outside of units are always preferable. See Fig. 1105.1.

The erection details for stack-on units are basically identical to all joint connections of the single story sectional house, with the exception of the connection between the first and second floors. Two primary connections are made at the center bearing wall and along the exterior walls. At the center wall, manufactureres will leave an access area opening the ceiling adjacent to the intersection of ceiling and center wall. This opening, which is later covered with wood trim or drywall, enables the workmen, albeit with some difficulty, to mechanically join the four units together. Bolts and/or lag screws are typically used at this important joint. See Fig. 1105.2.

1106 **Floor Framing.** The framing system used by a majority of modular manufacturers is essentially identical to conventional framing. Floor joists, which are spaced 16″ O.C. are generally 2″ × 8″. Where they frame into the center girder beam and at the exterior ribbon joists, either a 2″ × 2″ ledger strip or galvanized metal framing hangers are used to transfer floor load. Double

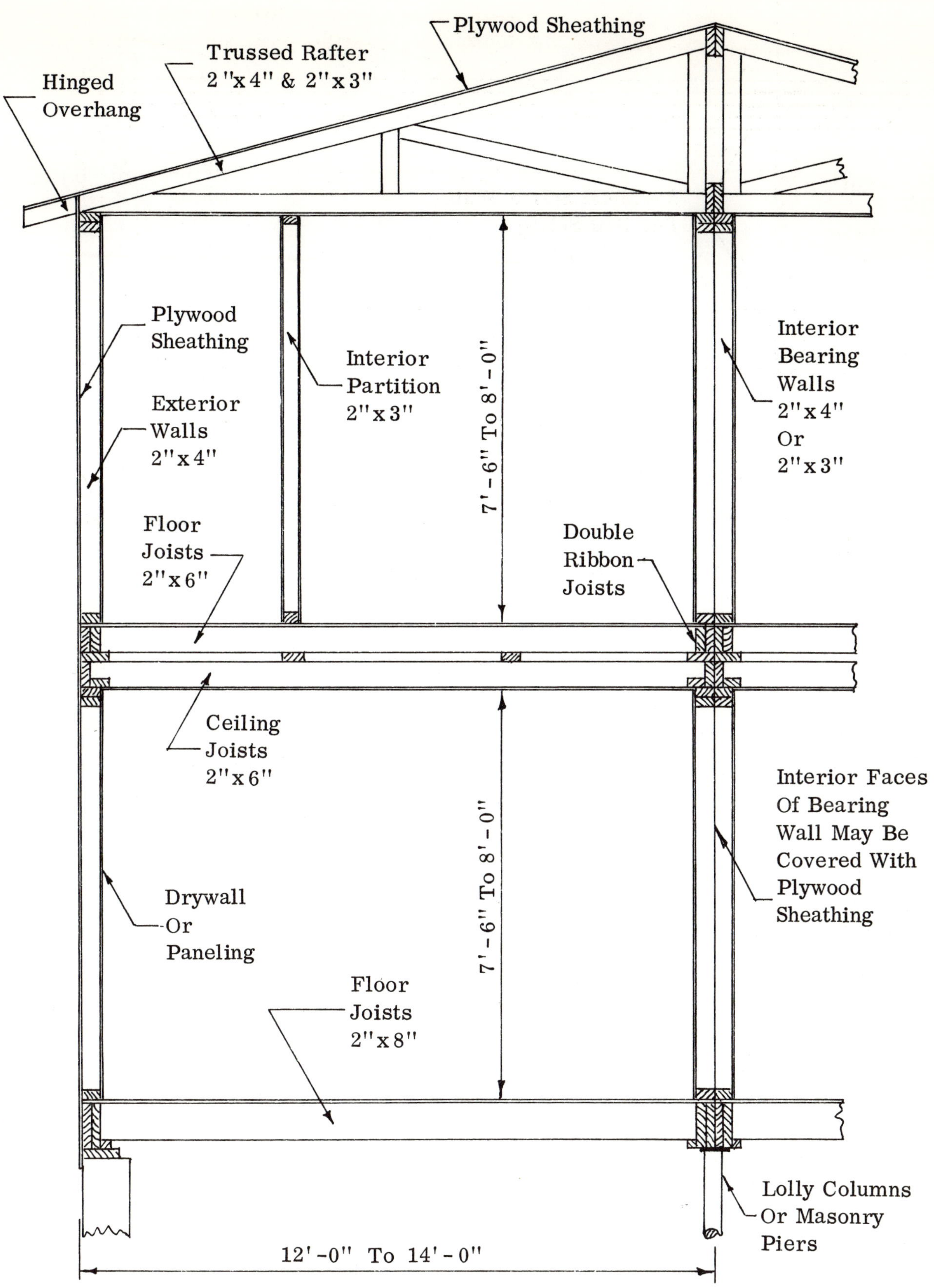


**Fig. 1104.2.**
Typical cross section two story stack-on units.

2 - Metal Splice Plates
Per Butt Splice
Half Girder
2 - 2"x 10" Per Half Girder
Generally 8'-0" Maximum

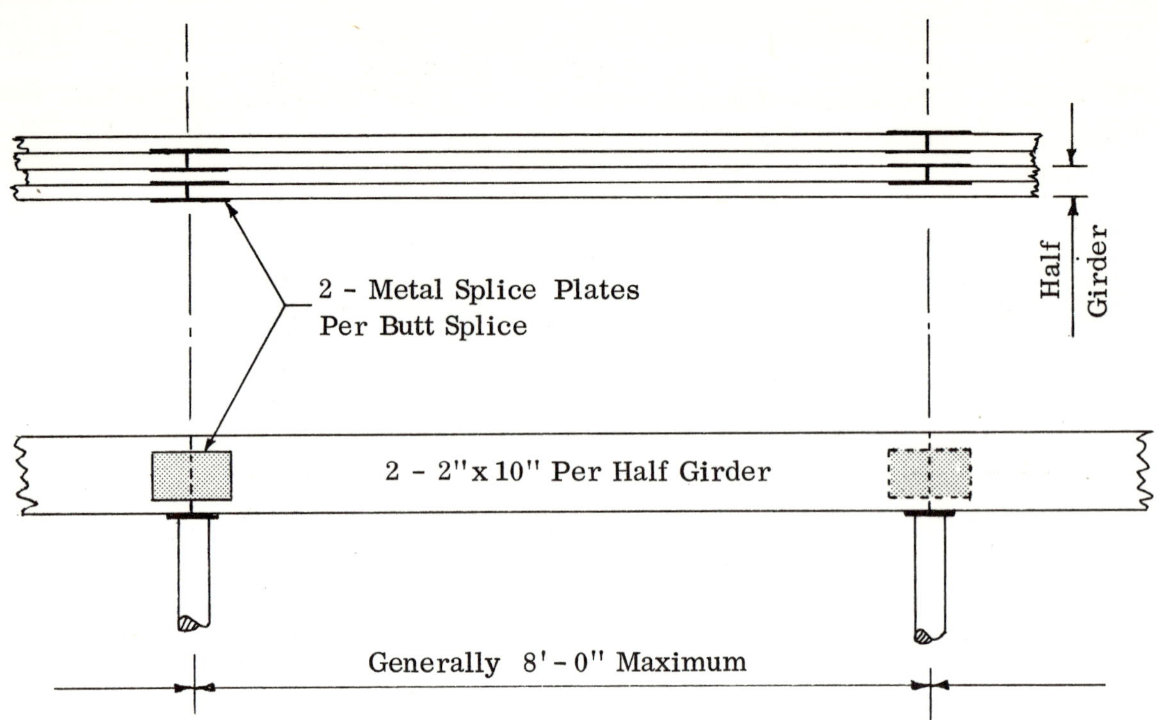

**Fig. 1104.3.**
Typical metal plate type continuous center girder [for single story units only].

2 - 2"x10" Per Half Girder
Half Girder
Half Girder
2"x 8"
Floor
Joist
Double
2"x 10"
Band Joists
Lolly Column
Or Masonry
Pier Ctr. Line
Sub-floor
2"x2" Ledger
Or Joist Hangers
L/4
L/4
L/4
L/4
Span "L"
Span "L"
Generally 8'-0" Or Less

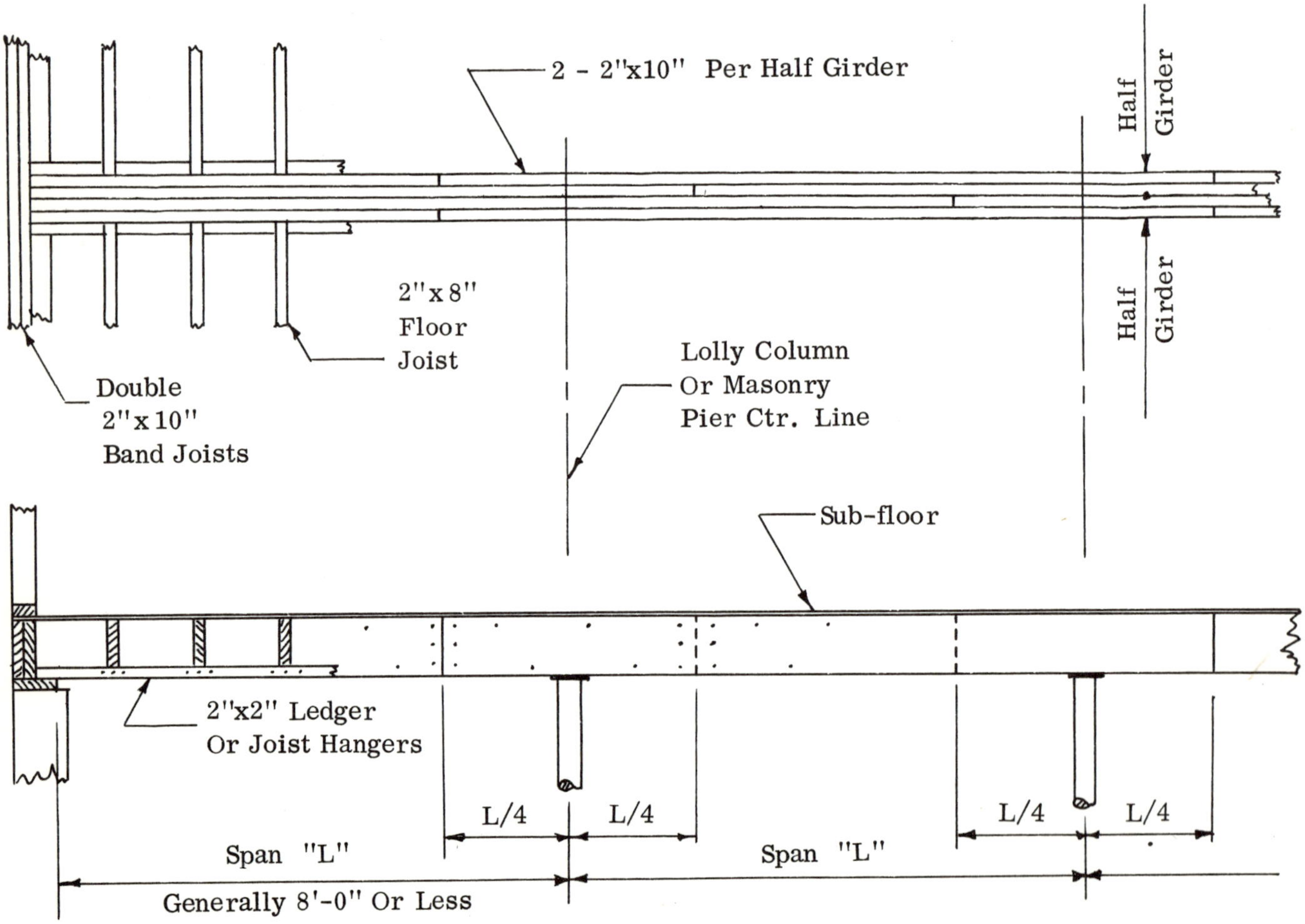

**Fig. 1104.4.**
Typical glued and nailed type continuous center girder [for single story units only].

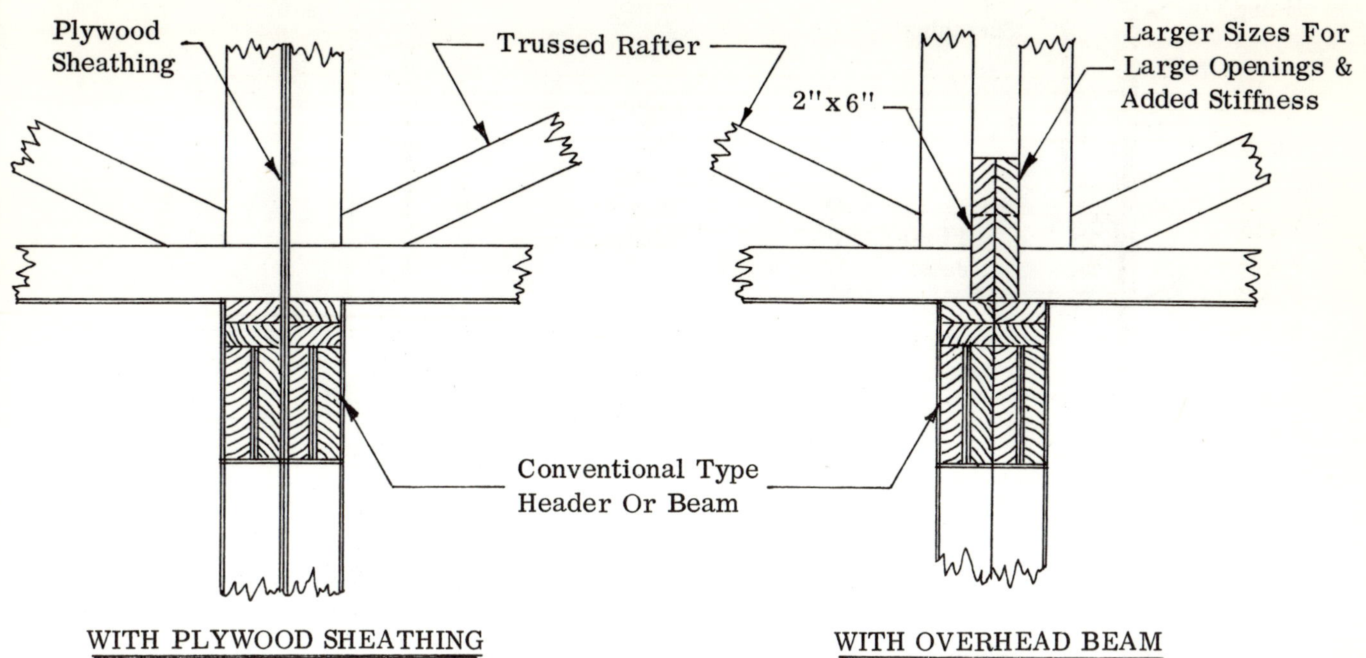


**Fig. 1104.5.**
Typical details—center bearing wall headers.

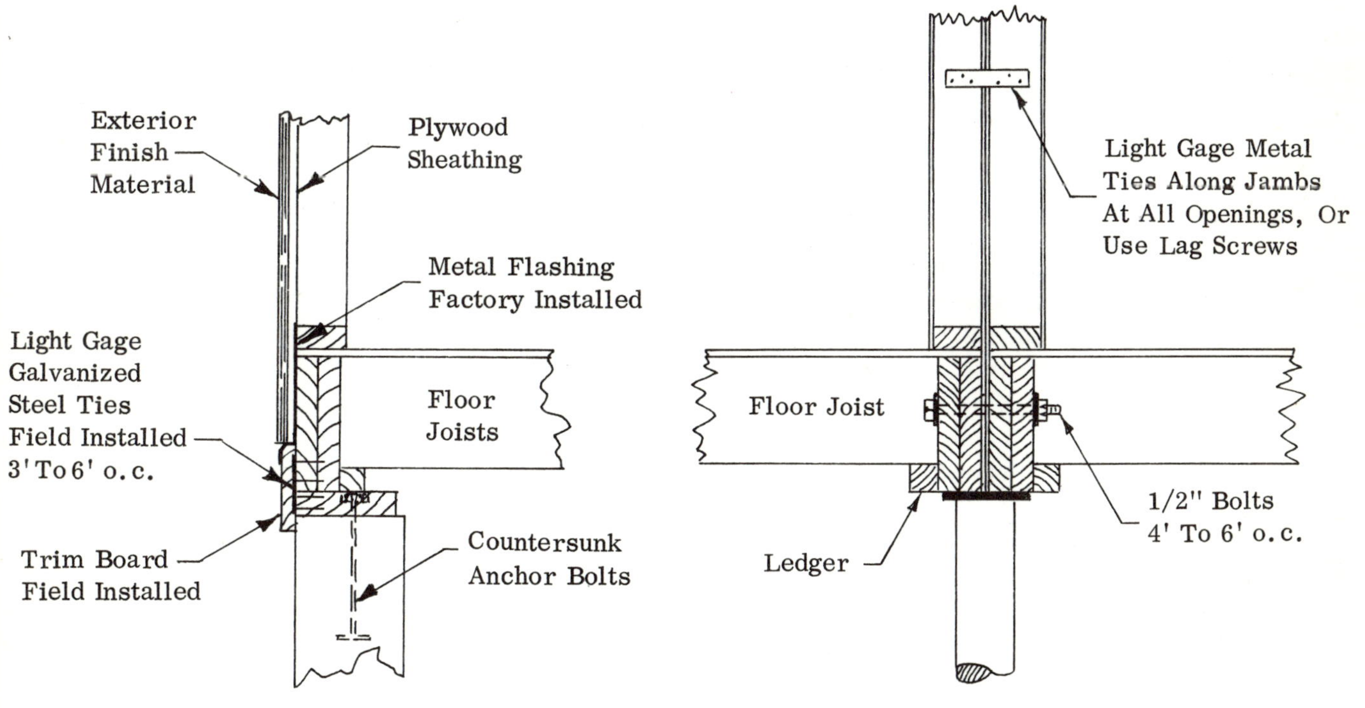


**Fig. 1105.1.**

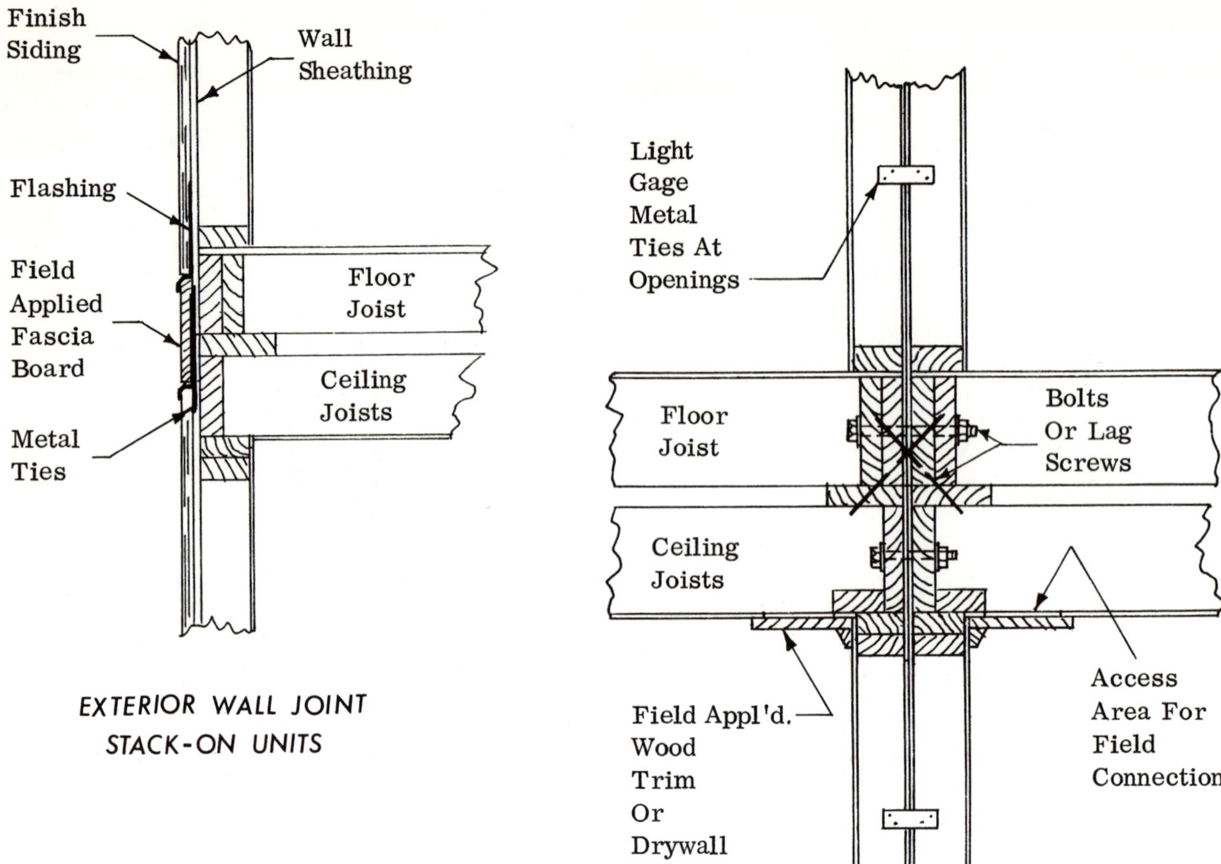


Fig. 1105.2.

joists are typically located under interior partitions, but since these partitions in most cases are not load bearing due to trussed rafter roof construction, some manufacturers eliminate the double joists. The subfloor covering is generally plywood, with many modular producers using 5/8″ thick tongue and groove plywood. To impart additional stiffness and strength to the floor system, glue may be used in combination with regular nailing.

In order to drop the modular unit closer to the roadway and thus provide more leeway for the roof design and height considerations, manufacturers can make use of floor framing systems with wheel wells. This permits the overall height of the housing units being shipped to be increased 6″ or more, and still remain within the maximum shipping height of 13′-6″. Recessing of transporter wheels into the floor system requires that proper headers be designed to accomodate the floor joists framing into the sides of the wheel well area.

Along the exterior walls, metal straps or plates are used to connect the upper and lower halves together. This area, which would not have wall finish material applied at the factory, is then covered over with an appropriate trim or fascia board. Proper flashing and caulking at this junction and others are important to eliminate weather leaks. See Fig. 1106.

Erection details will vary considerably with method of erection, type of modular unit and the type of exterior finish materials being applied. These connection details must be designed so that field joints will provide:

1. Structural adequacy to enable individ-

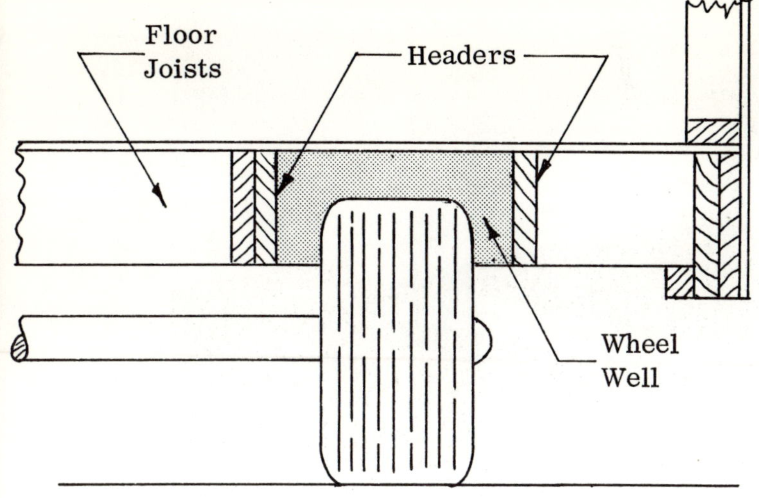


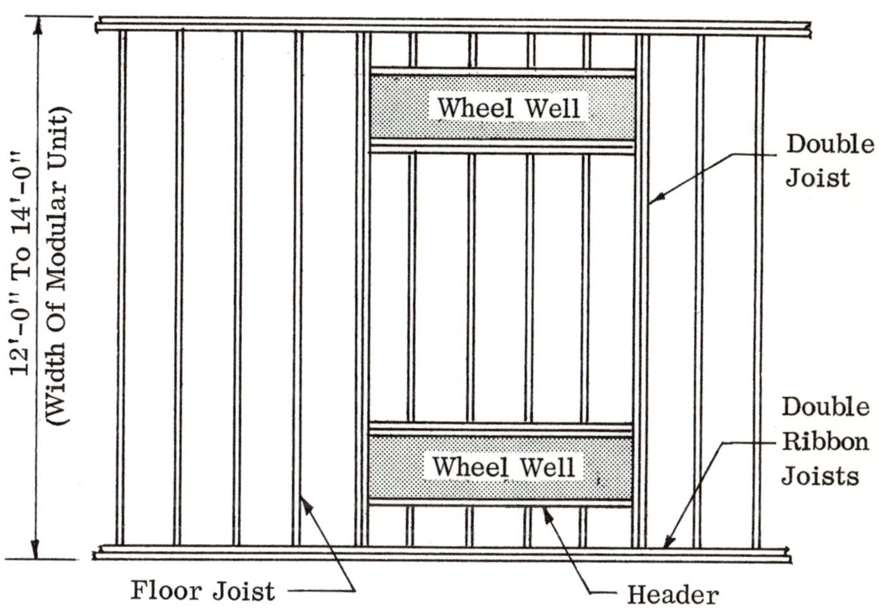


**Fig. 1106.**
Section showing wheels recessed in floor system and typical framing for wheel wells.

ual units to perform as if they were one complete unit.

2. Proper flashings, caulking, insulation as required for weather-tight joints at eaves, foundations and between individual sections.

3. Aesthetic appeal with fastening devices which do not detract from the final appearance.

4. Fast and trouble free methods to eliminate costly on-site labor.

5. Accessibility for inspection of erected unit.

6. Details conforming to local building and other requirements.

It is significant to note that there are several instances on record where field crews have failed to make all of the manufacturers prescribed connections. The results have not been pleasing to the homeowner nor to the manufacturers. The more difficult and inaccessible a connection, the more easily it may be overlooked during final inspection of the erected unit. It is best, therefore, to keep all erection details as simple as possible, and also in plain view to facilitate inspection.

1108 The following photographs show further details in modular housing plants and techniques.

**Fig. 1108.1.**
Job data card on carrier hitch tells plant personnel the specifications of this particular module.
*(Deluxe Homes) (Reschke Photo)*

**Fig. 1108.2.**
Jig for manufacturing and finishing ceiling/roof sections.
*(Deluxe Homes) (Reschke Photo)*

**Fig. 1108.3.**
Not all modules are made the long way of the building. These townhouse units are fabricated across the units.
*(Modular Housing System, Inc.)*

**Fig. 1108.4.**
Plant view showing modules in various stages of fabrication.
*(Modular Housing Systems, Inc.)*

**Fig. 1108.5.**
Upper floor module of townhouse ready to be lifted into place by crane. When hoisted, wheel-axle under carriage and front trailer-hitch assembly will be removed by unfastening a few bolts.

*(Scholz Homes) (Reschke Photo)*

**Fig. 1108.6.**
Detail of assembled townhouse. Rigid skin of side walls permits handling and shipping like a box without full length trailer.

*(Scholz Homes) (Reschke Photo)*

**Fig. 1108.7.**
Detail show rail-roller method of moving modules thru production.
*(Missouri Continental Homes)*

**Fig. 1108.8.**
Floor systems in various stages of fabrication.
*(Winston Modular Homes)*

**Fig. 1108.9.**
Electric-hydraulic jacks used to lift modules in plant and on site.
*(Westran Corporation)*

# CHAPTER XII

## Miscellaneous: Safety, Inventory Control, Material Handling, and Fireplaces

1200 **Safety.** The implementation of safety training, safety rules, and safety procedures can contribute a great deal in helping employees produce. Accidents cause personal loss and injury, lost time from the job, and damaged property.

Accident prevention measures include design of equipment so it can be safely operated, carefully developed work methods, safety equipment (glasses, goggles, shoes, etc.), safety rules, safety training, safety campaigns, and management support to develop safety consciousness and good attitudes. Because many accidents occurring off the job also cause lost time from work, training programs should emphasize safe work habits at home as well as on the job.

Most safety training, unfortunately, is soon forgotten. Therefore, it is necessary to have periodic campaigns and safety programs to remind both employees and supervisors to follow safe practices.

1201 **Workmen's Compensation Insurance.** Since the manufactured building industry is construction-related, the insurance rates for Workmen's Compensation insurance are usually high initially. Rates are then usually adjusted based on experience and claims, either higher or lower. A good safety record will result in lower insurance costs. More importantly, it will be reflected in increased output per hour because of better morale.

Insurance companies are usually in a position to give advice about loss prevention and to provide training materials, including posters. The National Safety Council also has posters available. Posters should be changed frequently to insure continuing interest.

1202 **Safety Officer.** One individual, preferably not connected with actual production, should be charged with preparation and implementation of safety programs, and the training and supervision. Two possibilities include the Purchasing Agent or Personnel Officer.

1203 **Noise Control.** Noise control has received increasing attention in recent years. The harmful effects of unduly loud industrial noise include lowered production rates and potential employee hearing losses.

Should the plant be involved in government contracts covered by the Walsh-Healey Public Contracts Law, a recent U.S. Labor Department ruling sets maximum noise levels. The ruling requires that employees' hearing be safeguarded by adequate personal protection equipment in the event that maximum noise levels cannot be achieved.

1204 **Safety Equipment.** About one-half of the plants surveyed required the use of safety glasses by all personnel, including visitors. Some had experimented with hard hats and safety shoes but had abandoned them. Safety glasses would seem to be essential for all personnel in building manufacturing plants.

1205 **Nailing Machines.** The largest source of injuries in all plants seems to be from the use of 16d air-operated nailers. Although these devices are equipped with safety equipment which prevents their being fired unless held against the work, the nail's path is sometimes diverted by a knot or poor aim. The nail can go through the wood and into the workman's hand. In a few cases nails have actually gone through the board to strike a man on the other side of the jig.

1205.1 **Precautions in Use.** When nailing machines are used in wall panel fabrication, the following precautions are suggested:

**a.** Adequatedly instruct new personnel in the dangers involved.

**b.** Construct jigs so it is not necessary to hold studs to the plate with one hand while operating the nailer with the other.

**c.** Where possible mount nailing machines on a track as shown in Fig. 306.2D. This will limit the location of firing points and direction for the guns.

**d.** Where machines must be used by men on each side of the jig at the same time, require them to offset themselves.

**e.** When nailing machines are used to fabricate subcomponents, provide for their use in a compartment to prevent the chance firing of a nail into other areas of the plant.

1206 **Electric Tools.** Electric tools should meet the requirements of Underwriter's Laboratory Standard UL 45-1969. All tools should be grounded. Tools in fixed locations should be wired in accordance with the National Electrical Code.

Extension cords should be of the sizes listed in the table (Appendix) "Minimum Cord Wire Sizes" for the distance involved.

1206.1 **"Cordless" or Belt-Battery Tools.** Consideration should be given to the use of these tools in certain operations where cords tend to become entangled or get in the way of operations.

1206.2 **"Portable Electric Tools,"** the detailed discussion in the appendix should be read by all supervisiory personnel.

1207 **Fire Safety.** Provisions for preventing and stopping fires are of great importance in manufactured building operations. Although losses may be covered by insurance, the cost of interruption of your business usually is not.

Depending on investment, fire insurance, and other costs, the following considerations are important:

1. Have a sprinkler system installed.

2. Install hoses at strategic points, connected to an adequate water supply *not* dependent on the plant's electrical system.

3. Provide fire extinguishers of the type and at locations recommended by your fire department or insurance company.

4. Hold a fire drill every six months or oftener.

5. Have a separate, segregated area for the storage of flammables.

6. Where possible, use water-based paints instead of solvent based.

7. Provide adequate ventilation in areas where solvent-based paints and adhesives are used.

8. Dispose of the residue from paint spray booths daily. Spontaneous combustion can occur in these materials.

1208 **Housekeeping.** Keep the plant clean with a place for everything and everything in its place.

1209 **Clothing and Hair.** Loose, flapping clothing can catch in moving machinery. Saw and other machine operators should wear short sleeved shirts or roll their sleeves up. Long hair, male or female, should be in a net.

1230 **Inventory Control.** Building manufacturing plants handle large quantities of materials both in dollars and in physical bulk. The number of times the inventory turns over annually is a dominant factor in the profit/investment ratio.

Production delays caused by poor materials management become a very costly matter. Assuring that the right items reach the point of manufacture, assembly or shipping in the correct quantities and at the proper moment can result in considerable savings in time and money normally lost to delays, shutdowns, etc.

1230.1 **Inventory Turnover.** There is considerable variation in the plants studied as to inventory turnover. Here are some of the operations and their reported turnover:

**a.** Large truss manufacturer—6X year.

**b.** Large custom component operator—4–6X year.

**c.** Large component package manufacturer (4–5 homes per day)—10X year.

**d.** Small component package manufacturer. 8X—year. (Buys considerable quantities of materials from large distributors in nearby big city, thus reducing inventory of some items to only one week's supply.)

**Fig. 1280.**
Installation of prefabricated fireplace and flue with imitation brick housing.
*(Vega)*

**e.** Another small component package manufacturer—12–14X year. (This manufacturer is even more dependent on distributors and is within trucking distance of supplying lumber mills.)

**f.** Large component package manufacturer—3X year. (Uses a computer.)

**g.** Non-residential modular producer—6–7X year.

**1230.2 Methods.** Inventory control methods are numerous and in every case seem to have been adapted by trial and error. The key seems to be having a strong purchasing agent and frequent physical inventories. One manufacturer counts certain items daily with the result that the entire inventory and purchasing program is checked weekly. This may be an over-emphasis but does result in one of the highest turnovers.

**1260 Material Handling.** The large tonnage of materials to be moved in a manufactured building operation demands constant improvement to accomplish one or all of these objectives:

**1260.1 Increased Productive Capacity.** Capacity of facilities, equipment, and labor is increased by: increasing productivity per man hour; increasing machine efficiency through reduction of down time; smoothing out work flow in the plant and improving production control.

**1260.2 Reduced Waste.** To accomplish this, material handling must maintain proper control over in-and-out-of-stock handling and eliminate damage of material by better handling and storage during the process.

**1260.3 Improved Working Conditions.** This objective can be met by providing safer working conditions, reducing employee fatigue, and improving personnel comfort.

**1260.4 Reduced Costs.** This means an overall cost reduction, not a reduction in one area and an increase in another. This is done done by: Increasing productivity; decreasing or controlling inventories; utilizing space to a better advantage; reducing stray shipments; and cutting pilferage through planned package handling.

**1261 Lift Trucks.** Manufacturers seem to increasingly shift to heavier duty lift trucks. Capacities found were from 5 to 12 tons with 8 to 12 ton predominating.

**1280 Fireplaces.** Prefabricated fireplaces are increasingly being used in manufactured buildings. These can be of the gas, electric, or all-fuel with corresponding flue. Brick facing and mantel applied later give the unit the traditional look.

# CHAPTER XIII

## Delivery and Installation

1300 **General.** The fabrication of panels, trusses, component packages, and modules in a factory involves the application of existing industrialization techniques to the construction of buildings. Getting these fabricated parts or modules to the site and putting them in place is the final step in the process and must be considered in every design and system selected. Ingenious pieces of building, reflecting a high degree of industrialization, are of little value if they cost too much to deliver and install.

1300.1 **Investment Considerations.** The cost of delivery equipment is substantial, and unless it is to be utilized full time, it may be best to use a common carrier. The carriers with experience in the mobile home field are now being widely used in the shipment of modules. There are several carriers with a good supply of flat bed and open top vans that can be used by custom component and component package manufacturers. These carriers have the experience, governmental permits, and other authorizations to handle or supplement manufacturer's delivery program.

1300.2 **Demurrage.** Demurrage is desirable to insure the rapid turnaround of expensive delivery and installation equipment. The manufacturer should first have a system of checks to be sure that the job is ready on the date specified and then, should the equipment be held up for any reason a substantial charge per hour or day should be made. It is best that the foundation actually be installed and ready before the building is placed on the manufacturing and shipping schedule. This may mean a delay of weeks in the on site schedule but is better than the manufacturer having to close his plant because all his delivery equipment is tied up.

1300.3 **Role of the Driver.** Skilled and dependable drivers are the utmost importance. The expense of repairing damaged in transit units can be considerable even though repair costs may be covered by the carrier's insurance. The neccessity of such repairs will result in customer dissatisfaction and inconvenience to the manufacturer.

The judgment of the driver must be depended upon in getting the unit across the difficult terrain surrounding most foundations without getting stuck or damaging the equipment.

Unless the installation personnel accompany the unit, the driver is in effect the representative of the manufacturer at the time of delivery. As such, his relationship with the customer is of great importance to continuing customer satisfaction.

1301 **Truss Manufacturers.** Trusses are delivered with several types of equipment. The selection of the method and equipment to be used is a function of the size and types of trusses to be delivered; the probable sales volume; highway regulations; whether or not delivery is made "FOB the top plate" (in place on the building); the investment required; and funds available.

Damage free delivery is important because, in some areas, the customer backcharge for repairing trusses on the job site is $11.00 an hour or more. Strapping "truss packages" together will minimize unloading damage.

Customers usually demand that trusses be on the job site well in advance of their need. Cost considerations dictate that self-unloading equipment be used to accomplish this objective.

Equipment used:

1301.1 **Flat Bed Trailer** with or without crank-off roller unloading attachments. Rollers may be so arranged that trusses on one side may

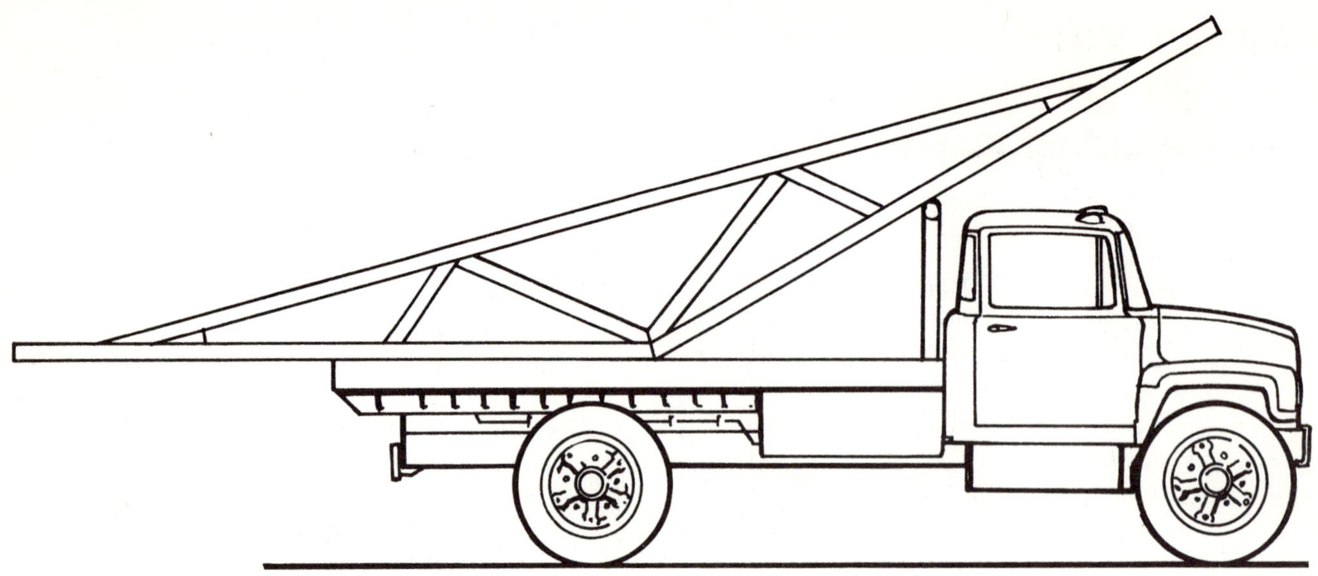

**Fig. 1301.2.**
Platform truck used to deliver roof trusses. Note pipe rack to rest trusses on and protect cab. A roller bed can also be used.

be rolled off without disturbing those on the other side having a different destination.

1301.2 **Platform Truck.** The standard stake or flatbed truck with or without dumping equipment is an effective delivery method for shorter trusses. (See Fig. 1301.2)

1301.3 **Pole Type Trailer.** This equipment is good for general use, particularly for longer trusses. (See Fig. 1301.3)

1301.5 **Long Span Trusses.** Longer spans or odd shaped trusses are frequently shipped in halves and assembled on the job site with nail on truss plates or bolts.

1301.6 **Cranes.** Cab or trailer mounted cranes of types shown elsewhere in this chapter are frequently used to provide the customer

**Fig. 1301.3.**
Dump-O-Matic pole type trailer has provision for push button side unloading. Several models available with truss capacity up to 80 feet. Patented.

*(Trailer division Barns Lumber & Mfg. Co.)*

**Fig. 1301.4.**
*Straddle Truck* may be used for truss and other component delivery on short hauls.

*(Hyster)*

service of placing trusses on the building. A tower type crane of the type shown in Fig. 1301.5 is valuable for higher and longer reaches.

1301.7 **Trailer Loads** of trusses may be left on the job site for later placement directly from trailer to building by crane. This may be done with a fifth wheel dolly (Fig. 1303.10) to permit movement of the trailer by a bulldozer through otherwise impassable terrain.

1301.8 **Additional Details** about truss installation may be found in Chapter IV.

1302 **Prehung Door Manufacturers.** When delivered as part of a component package, prehung units should be in a carton or covered by a plastic bag with corrugated blocking at weak points.

1303 **Custom Component and Component Package Manufacturers.** Depending on the distance from the site, components may be unitized (shipped with each load containing all or nearly all of the package for one

**Fig. 1301.5.**
Tower type crane placing roof trusses. Manufacturer claims single trusses can be set every 70–90 seconds with this equipment.

*(Pettibone)*

unit—trusses, panels, plywood, etc.) or components may be bulked (loads of all roof trusses, loads of all wall panels, etc.) The bulk shipments are often more desirable for apartment projects.

Unitized loads require more ingenuity and planning to get the maximum material on the load and at the same time have it in "last on, first off" order.

Analysis of shipping costs should always be made on longer hauls. It may be desirable to purchase some of the non-manufactured materials locally or ship roof trusses knock-down to eliminate an extra load.

1303.1 **Covers.** The investment in high quality tarpaulins and their regular maintenance will save time and money.

1303.2 **Hold for Future Delivery.** Provision should be made by manufacturers to store units on which the delivery has been postponed or units made in advance of desired delivery date. Custom component manufacturers should have a definite delivery schedule, providing for payment when components are ready for delivery according to that schedule whether or not the project is ready. When stored outside, packages of wall and partition panels should be stacked so they may be handled by lift truck. All components should be covered if they are to be stored outside for more than a few days.

**Fig. 1303.3.**

Wall panels on the outside are supported by stakes in the trailer bed; center core contains, from top to bottom, rake overhangs, floor materials, oak flooring. Floor may be installed on the foundation within the free time allowed so that wall panels need be handled only once.

*(Imperial Homes)*

**Fig. 1303.4.**
Roller bed dump truck carries two stacks of wall panels.

*(Pease)*

**Fig. 1303.5.**
Tractor converts to lift truck to unload trailer.

*(Advance Lift Truck Corp.)*

**Fig. 1303.6.**
Automatic dump trailer for wall panels.

*(Barns Lumber & Mfg. Co.)*

**Fig. 1303.7.**
Tractor mounted crane installing wall panels.
*(Hydraulic Materials Handling Division, Omark Industries)*

**Fig. 1303.8.**
Loading finished wall panel.
*(Wausau Homes)*

**Fig. 1303.9.**
Finished wall panel being installed.

*(Wausau Homes)*

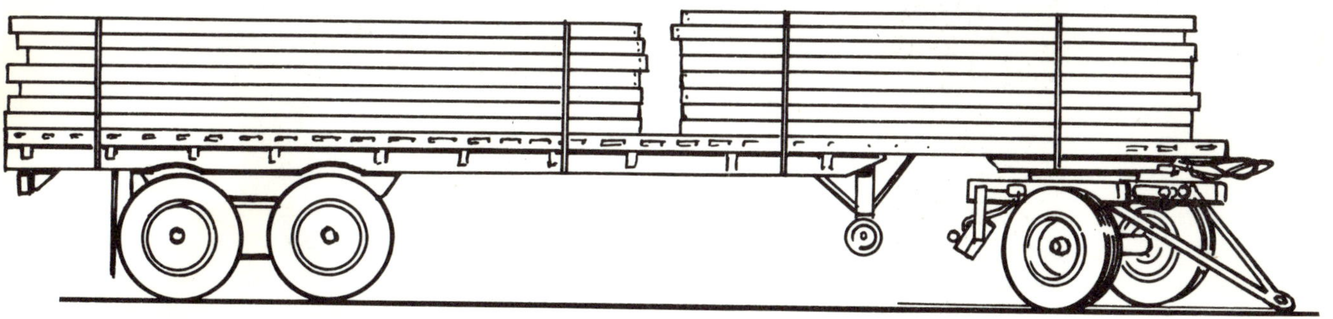

**Fig. 1303.10.**
Fifth wheel dolly permits trailers to be moved through mud at site by bulldozer.

**Fig. 1303.11.**
Useful device for lining up wall panels.

*(Proctor Products Company, Inc.)*

1304 **Modular Manufacturers.** The width and height of modular units requires special loading and delivery equipment.

Some manufacturers use the delivery trailer as the production platform that moves through the plant. Others construct units so that they need only an undercarriage and a detachable drawbar assembly. Still others manufacture the units so they are placed on the delivery trailer after manufacturing is complete.

1304.1 **Fourteen Wides.** Most modular production is at present with units 12′ wide or less. However, at this writing, 19 states allow movement of 14′ wides over their highways. These are:

| | |
|---|---|
| Arizona | New Mexico |
| Colorado | North Dakota |
| Idaho | Oklahoma |
| Iowa | Oregon |
| Kansas | South Dakota |
| Louisiana | Texas |
| Minnesota | Washington |
| Montana | Wisconsin |
| Nebraska | Wyoming |
| New Hampshire | |

Fourteen wides are usually transported with the load offset two feet over the shoulder of the road. This places an eccentric load on the undercarriage which must be considered in design.

1304.2 **Routing.** The shortest distance may not always be the distance modular units may have to travel. State highway regulations can require a round-about routing substantially increasing the mileage. Estimation of delivery costs should be done only after a review of all highway and permit limitations.

1304.3 **Return of Trailers.** Equipment should be so constructed that it may return permit free (not overwidth and overlength). Telescoping or folding components can be used to accomplish this.

**Fig. 1304.4.**
Straddle-Gantry for use in loading modular units.

*(Modular Housing Systems)*

**Fig. 1304.5.**
Trailer with telescoping frame and arms.

*(Lakeside Manufacturing Co.)*

**Fig. 1304.6.**
26,000 lbs. capacity trailer has low profile and wheel clearance must be provided in floor framing.
*(Bock Industries)*

**Fig. 1304.7.**
Roller installation of modules from trailer to foundation.

*(Suburban Homes)*

**Fig. 1304.8.**
Crane installation of modules. Suspension rods extend through unit to underside floor and may be removed later.
*(Modular Housing Systems)*

# CHAPTER XIV

## New Systems Techniques

*Robert C. Reschke**

**1400 General.** Nearly all the advances being made in construction are based on the principle of doing as much preparatory and assembly work as possible in a well-planned factory where lesser-skilled workers apply themselves in repetitive fashion under better working conditions and at lower wage rates.

**1400.1 Styles.** Two major factory "styles" are merging as the predominant forms of the near future:

**a.** *Modular* 3-dimensional factory-produced units that assemble at the site needing minimal site finishing work.

**b.** *Panelized* components for floors, walls, and roof incorporating to some degree provisions for mechanical elements and supplemented by central 3-dimensional "cores" involving kitchen, bath, or other utility functions.

**1400.2 Application.** With some exceptions, the above developments are occurring in such a way that the prefinished modular style factory building is being applied almost entirely in the field of low-rise light construction while urban inner-core buildings are favoring panelized developments in pre-cast concrete which is more acceptable to officials because of more stringent code requirements and fire-resistive values.

**1400.3 Trends.** While the general process of urbanization continues, there are well established counter-trends in which housing, commercial and industrial occupancies are moving outward towards urban fringes and it is these kinds of buildings that are more important from the standpoint of industrialized new construction. This is borne out by buildings in the low- and mid-rise classes (5 stories or less) that are being built in suburban fringes regardless of city size.

A second applicable generalization about industrialization and systems building that seems likely to remain the same for some time is of dual nature: 1. New development work in light-frame construction and pre-finished 3-dimensional modular units is being done predominantly by domestic organizations while; 2. A high proportion of the newer systems approaches involving pre-cast panels for multi-story construction have origins or ties to foreign, particularly European, building techniques.

**1400.4 Modular Pre-Cast** 3-dimensional units of the Montreal-Habitat type have not reached much beyond the experimental stage in the U.S. and this investigator's opinion is that such box-like pre-casting will advance very slowly, its volume in the seventies likely remaining very small in comparison with that of either the light-frame modulars or the pre-cast panel systems.

**1400.5 New Technology Directions** are emerging as the modular and systems building methods are finding broader and more rapid acceptance. As might be expected in such a favorable industrialization climate, the new directions are overwhelmingly related to plant or factory production. Evidence of this is apparent in the rapidity with which growing numbers of architectural firms are getting directly involved or becoming allied with industrialized building systems. It almost seems as if a sudden shift in empha-

*Mr. Reschke has for years been a columnist and consulting editor for *Professional Builder* magazine. A graduate economist, Mr. Reschke, through his R & C Associates, provides counseling, guidance, and marketing services relating to building systems, components, prefabrication, modular housing, and other industrialized building techniques.

sis has occurred, switching technology's major thrusts from the *materials* of construction to the industrialized *techniques* of construction. The major observable new directions are:

a. Combining different kinds of basic materials in the same assembly or component and a greater inclination to use composite materials such as laminates or sandwiches having a combination of superior properties;

b. Increasing regard for the *flow* of materials in a plant thereby increasing efficiency as a greater amount of work (mechanical and sub trades) is done in the plant than ever before;

c. Concentration of mechanical or utility elements in centralized components or modules both in rough forms and in prefinished complete modules;

d. An extension of the flow concept beyond the plant so that more attention and ingenuity is being applied to handling, transport, and placement.

The above new directions will be dealt with in more detail in the sections immediately following (1401 through 1403) that cover the light-frame class of construction generally used in low- and mid-rise buildings. Then, section 1404 will deal with handling and transport developments and especially those related to the heavier panelized or combination systems designed for urban-core applications.

1401 **Growth of Composite Construction.** A sizable number of building manufacturers are experimenting with light-frame modular systems that employ steel in one form or another for its special properties. Some companies are already producing modules using steel teamed up with other materials. One is Guerdon Industries whose Vicksburg, Miss., plant is turning out modules

**Fig. 1401A.**
Guerdon panel production showing steel column framing in combination with wood materials.

**Fig. 1401B.**
Finished 2-story office building built with 16 12′ × 40′ modules and erected in a half-day's time.

with a column type of steel frame that permits stacking of the modules up to five stories in height.

Guerdon's initial order involved 12′ × 36′ steel-and-concrete modules for a college dormitory whose finished cost was about $14 per sq. ft. The concrete portion of the modules was a thin slab factory-poured on the steel-framed floor of the units. Exterior walls were sheathed in gypsumboard and after placement at the site, brick veneer finish was applied. Since this initial project, the company has furnished similar modules for apartment projects and commercial buildings and a contract has been signed for supplying military housing overseas.

1401.1 **HUD's Operation Breakthrough** program acts as a healthy and confidence-instilling stimulus for quite a large number of new companies and groups to propose factory-built components or modules for prototype housing projects around the country. The aim: aid in getting mass production. One of the twenty-two proposals selected from an original 550 submissions was that of a consortium led by the Republic Steel Co. Involved in this proposal was a system of factory-made modules using a simple set of standard steel-framed components. Steel box-beams were designed as foundations for the modules. Floor, wall, and roof panels used steel facing on both sides of a foam or honeycomb-paper core. In addition to the living area modules, the Republic designs called for a garage module and two types of connector modules to give flexibility in site arrangements as well as in unit sizes.

1401.2 **Jones & Laughlin—Donn Products**
A steel box-frame with gypsumboard is the combination used in a modular townhouse system devised as a joint venture between Jones & Laughlin Steel and Donn Products Inc., a steel fabricator in Westlake, Ohio. The system is being adapted by Modfac Industries of Cleveland. In the prototype structure, modules used light steel structurals (a specialty of J & L trade-name "Junior Beams") with light rolled-steel studs to form a box-frame for the application of gypsum wallboard and enameled steel siding. Steel-framed floor sections had plywood decking plus finished floor coverings.

1401.3 **Foam Core.** In addition to combining materials of different kinds during the factory assembly process, some companies have developed composite or laminate panels having structural properties. An early forerunner of this kind of building

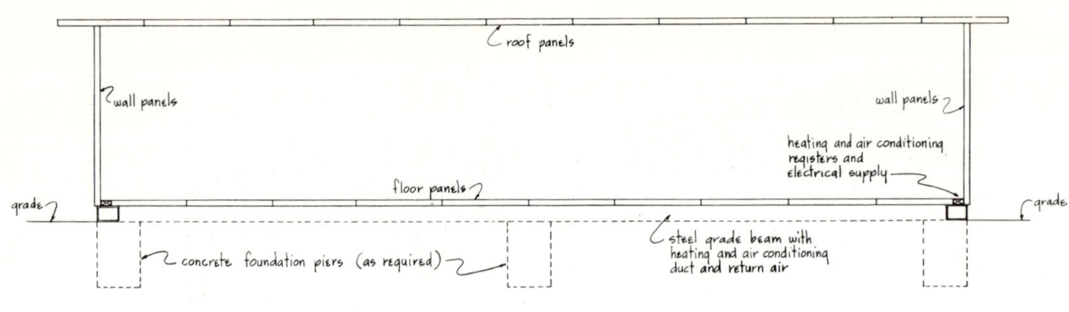


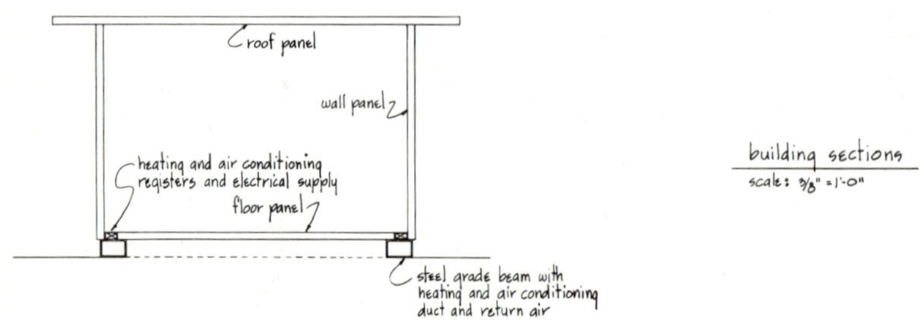


**Fig. 1401.1A.**
Steel box members as a foundation atop piers also serve as runs for heating or air-conditioning.
*(Republic Steel)*

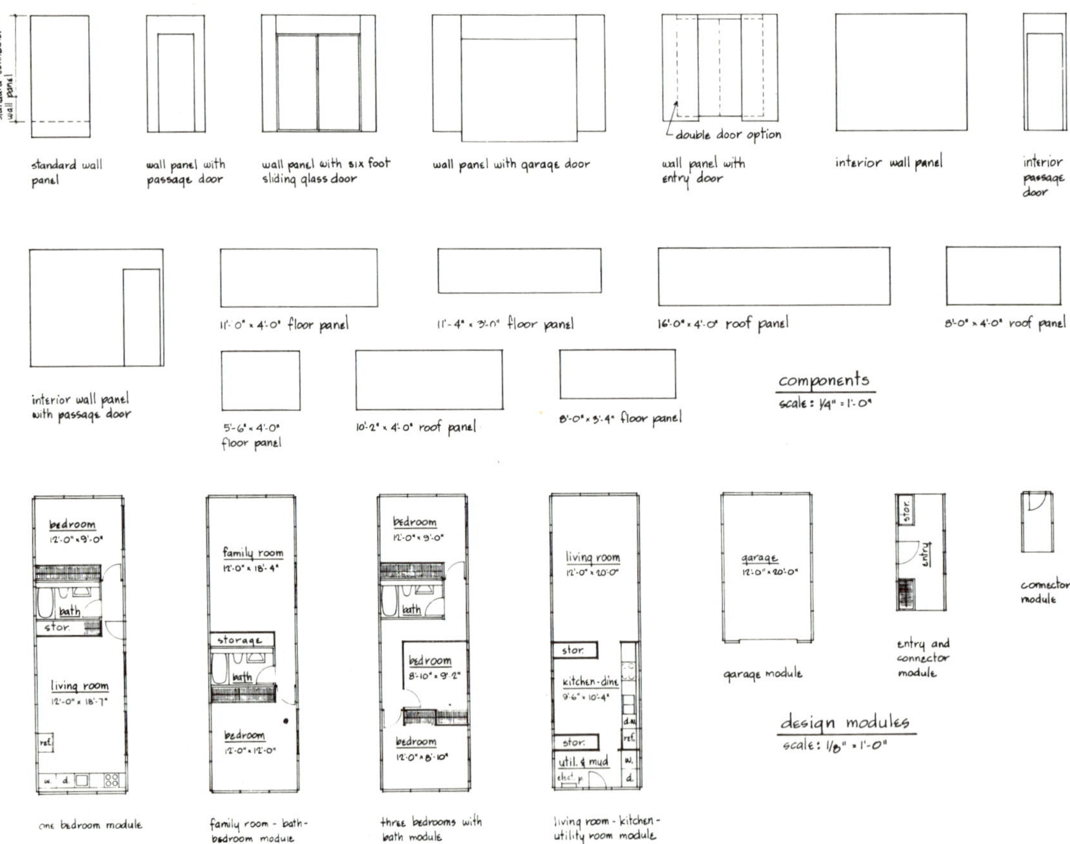


**Fig. 1401.1B.**
Steel-faced panel units and supplementary modules comprise the system proposed by Republic.
*(Republic Steel)*

**Fig. 1401.2.**
Prototype project uses steel box-frame modules, gypsumboard interiors, and steel siding.

system was the styrene foam-core experiments of Dow Chemical and the factory-produced urethane foam-core plywood panels made by the Koppers Co. and used in a research house erected by the National Association of Home Builders.

The foam-core or honeycomb-core principle is still attractive to a few companies. One Florida firm has had some success in furnishing packaged residential and commercial buildings using cored panels. However, with the industry trending towards 3-dimensional modular construction, the outlook for the use of core-panel products is improving.

Typical of the new sophistication involved in core-type panels is the basis panel material developed by Ball Bros. Research Corp. (branch of the pioneer glass jar firm) of Boulder, Colo. As indicated in the accompanying sketch, the foam core is faced with asbestos-cement board on the outside and by hardboard on the interior. Exterior surfacing consists of an aggregate material applied by an epoxy adhesive over the asbestos-cement board. The panels have outer frames of aluminum that furnish a panel interlock. Non-combustible wiring raceways are within the core.

1401.4 **General Electric.** Aerospace organizations have shown more than a passing interest in the possible housing applications for their systems techniques. A few have gone into active development work, and one such organization now having a forward-looking housing system is General Electric's Re-Entry & Environmental Systems Division in Philadelphia.

The GE housing system is a flexible one consisting of three unusual material combinations:

a. Heating-plumbing-electrical services centralized in utility chases pre-assembled for insertion with other components.

b. Walls and ceilings panelized using light rolled-steel studs and pre-cast plaster.

c. Floor system using a resin-impreg-

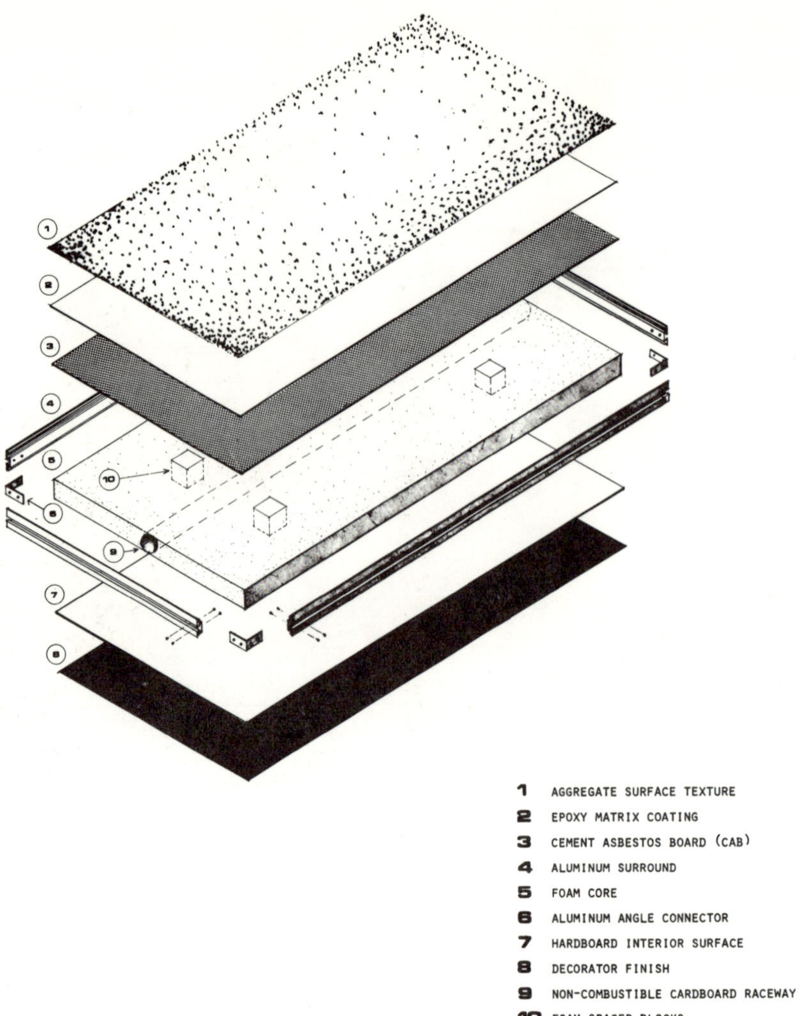


**Fig. 1401.3.**
Composition of research-developed Ball Bros. panel.

nated paper honeycomb core bonded to plywood facings.

The cast plaster factory technique involves the assembly of framing members plus expanded metal lath. A special plaster formula is then poured into a flat mold and the wall or ceiling frame is lowered into the plaster which then sets around the lath.

1401.5 **Dukor Modular Systems.** Working with a team of architects and engineers plus some University of California consultants, Dukor Modular Systems Inc. of Redwood City has started production on housing designs involving a "moment-resistant frame" of steel. In finished form, the modules are combinations of the steel frame, wood infill assemblies, and glass in a contemporary style with roof overhangs and cantilevered decks.

The Dukor steel frame uses tubular steel columns welded top and bottom to light-gauge steel channels to frame the floor and the roof-ceiling. Production is in progress in a 170,000 sq. ft. plant in Gilroy, California.

While the initial work of this company has been aimed at residential applications, the design and construction details are such that the buildings are readily adaptable with only minor changes to such commercial uses as stores, offices, banks, professional buildings and other special occupancies.

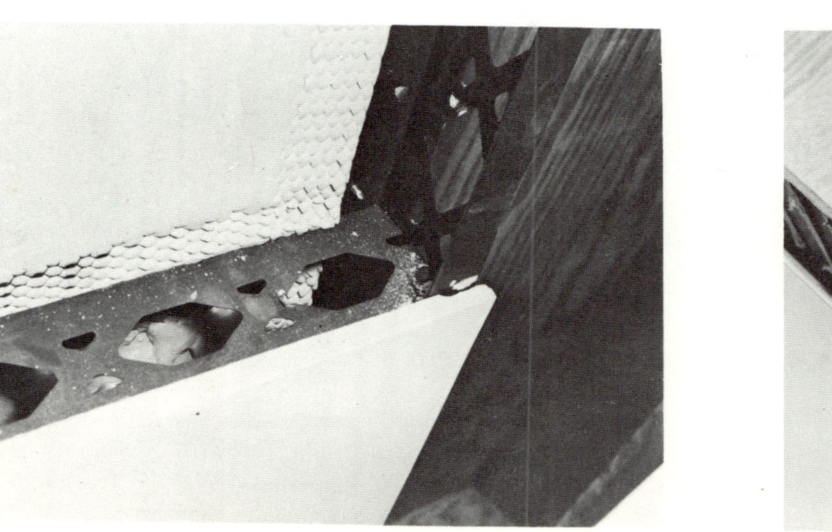


**Fig. 1401.4*A*.**
The three technology innovations in General Electric's new component housing system.

**Fig. 1401.4*B*.**
Prototype GE townhouses; lefthand unit is complete housing unit while remaining serve as GE's Housing technology lab.

**Fig. 1401.5*A*.**
Steel-frame modules by Dukor Modular Systems being assembled at the building site.

Fig. 1401.5*B*.
Steel framing system provides for easy extension of joists for roof overhang or patio deck support.

1402 **Factory Production Flow.** As large manufacturing companies enter the housing production field, a change in both factory and management procedures is seen. Factory planning is much more comprehensive and detailed. Special emphasis is given to material flow techniques. The factory process is quickly growing into a substantially automated production process, a far cry from merely building a house under a factory roof.

One example of a new plant so planned is the 68,000 sq. ft. facility of Urban Systems Development Corp. (a subsidiary of Westinghouse Electric) at Fredericksburg, Va. This production plant is going on stream in the fall of 1970 producing factory-finished modules 12′ wide, 9′ high and up to 52′ in length. The 6- and 9-ton modular sections are trucked to the site and assembled by crane into townhouses and garden apartments.

Material flow starts in such a planned plant with the in-feed facilities—rail sidings, truck docks, and multiple large doors convenient to storage and subassembly areas. The flow aspects continue with proper equipment and suitable methods of moving the subassemblies to the main line. The main assembly and its feeders must be planned to accomodate varying flow rates as crews or shifts are expanded or curtailed.

1402.1 **Levitt**

The newly-built housing production plant by Levitt Building Systems Inc. (a subsidiary of the world's largest site-building organization) in Battle Creek, Mich. is the result of extensive investigation and research. The 135,000 sq. ft. facility has 30′ clear interior heights in the manufacturing area which is flanked by two warehouse areas served by rail sidings and truck unloading facilities. Large outdoor storage space is provided to accomodate raw materials and completed modules. Initial production will be on townhouse modules.

Materials flow in the plant is well automated with two subassembly flow lines, one for floor construction and the other for wall, ceiling and roof subassemblies (see sketches). Overhead monorails are used to move the subassemblies to the main line. Production is gauged to reach 2,000 units a year by 1972 on single-shift operation employing about 450 people.

**Fig. 1402*A*.**
How modules by USDC will be plant-produced and site-assembled into townhouses and apartments.

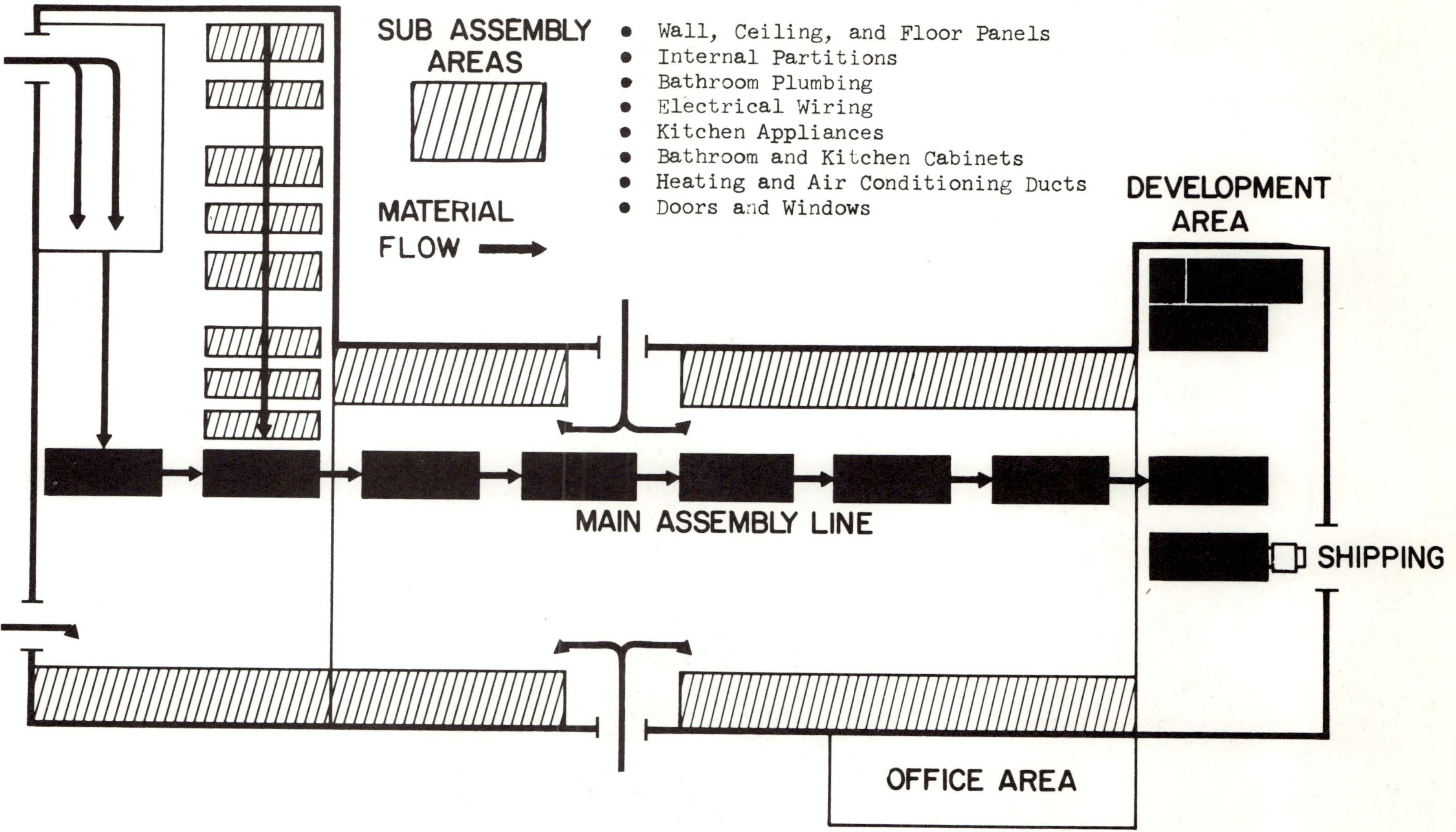


**Fig. 1402*B*.**
Various departments in USDC plant are arranged for efficient flow of materials and subassemblies.

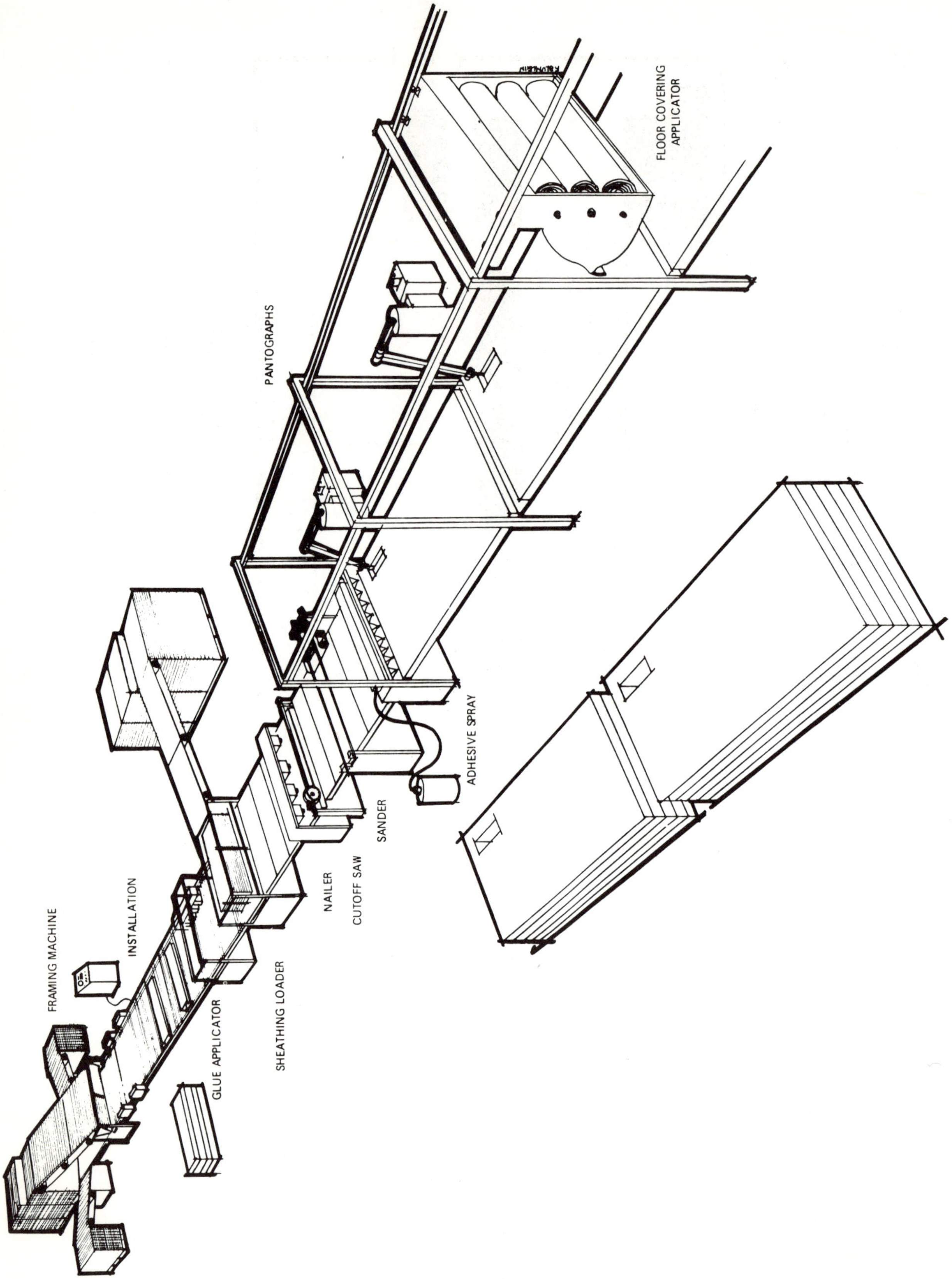

**Fig. 1402.1*A*.**
Automated assembly line for floor panel subassemblies is a continuous flow procedure.

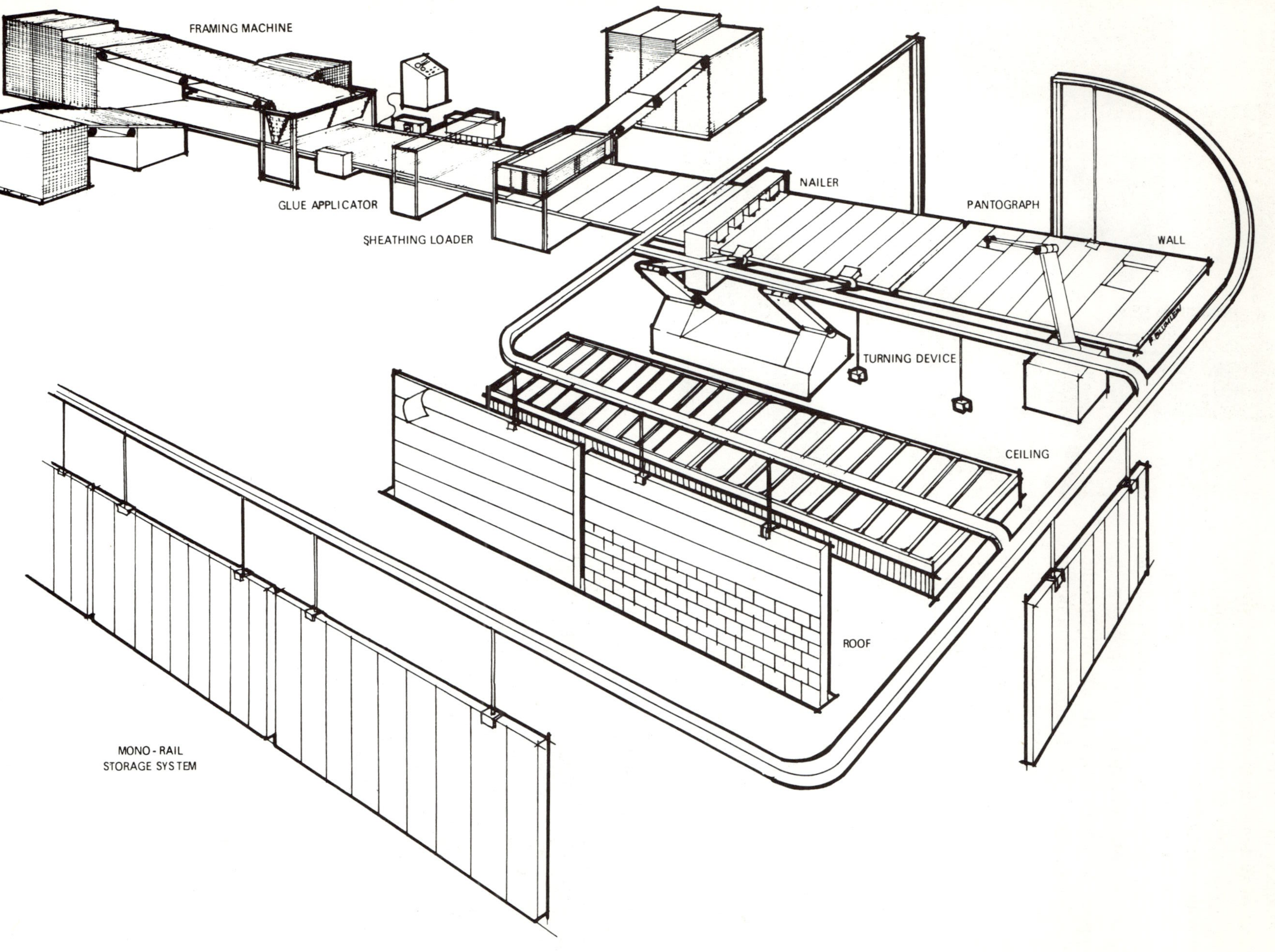


**Fig. 1402.1*B*.**
Subassemblies for walls-ceilings-roof are made on this line which can be adapted for one- or two-sided applications.

1402.2 **Computers.** Along with material flow techniques for plant production, another facet of systems development is the expanding application of computer technology to provide management information.

These are rapidly changing times. It's not practical to list all the various possible functions of computers as they might be applied to production methods. At present, computerization in housing production facilities is well established for purchasing-inventory-bookkeeping uses. A growing feature of the factory building industry, however, is the provision for time-sharing of computers through the use of standardized software programs. Such programs are now available to a limited degree for certain applications in design and feasibility analyses, in critical path scheduling, and in saw cutting schedules. New computer methods are being devised for site evaluations and other develop-and-build forecasts. A growing number of home manufacturers will make direct use of these methods or make them available to co-venturers or dealers.

**Fig. 1402.2*B*.**
Computer software marketed to housing producers and developers is in a growth-and-test period with many new management-info methods being worked out.

**Fig. 1402.2*A*.**
Technican from Co/Data Corp., a programming firm, takes plan details to feed computer for cost estimates.

1403 **Variations on the Core Concept.** More than two decades ago, the Ingersoll Products Division of Borg-Warner introduced a revolutionary building product—a mechanical heating-plumbing-electrical core that was really a wall section thickened to about 2′ in width. It accomodated a compact furnace, a water heater, all plumbing connections for kitchen and bath and an electrical distribution center. Though extensive marketing efforts support the Ingersoll core, the stumbling blocks in the form of code restraints, union objections, and homebuilder resistance were too much and production was halted. The core was ahead of its time. Today comparable and in some cases more elaborate cores and complete factory-finished bathrooms are giving every indication that the core concept is here to stay.

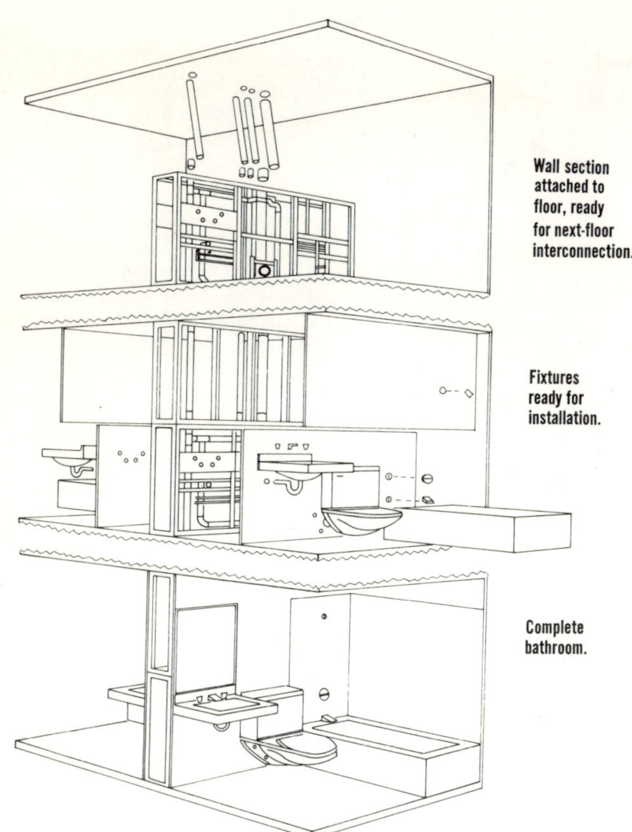


**Fig. 1403*A*.**
Sketch of component plumbing system.

*(American Standard)*

One plumbing core concept, pioneered by an Indiana plumbing-supply firm, is now in the process of start-up marketing by American Standard's Mechanical Systems Dept. It is a very flexible component that consists of thickened wall assembly that has rough plumbing completed and is designed to fit a variety of back-to-back kitchen/bath floor plan arrangements and is also suited to stacking in multiple-floor construction.

Perhaps a significant fact in the future outlook for such core and component modules is evident in the recent acceptance of these assemblies by certain unions and local building officials.

**1403.2 Wausau Homes.** One way of employing the mechanical core idea in single- or multi-family housing is to design a floorplan having a reasonably compact centrally-located bath and kitchen. Then, the complete bathroom with a one-wall backup of the kitchen can be factory-built as a pre-finished module. The balance of the house or apartment can be panelized for fast site assembly. This procedure has been in operation for a few years by Wausau Homes of Wausau, Wis., on single-family dwellings of wood-frame construction.

The core-plus-panel system will undoubtedly enjoy steady growth as new companies come on the scene with specialized forms of building panels or modules that are designed to coordinate with standardized core assemblies. See Fig. 904*C*.

**1403.3 Fidelity Homes.** In Nashville, Tenn., Fidelity Homes of America has introduced a line of pre-packaged single-family homes using kitchen-bath modules and a wall panel construction of particle-board in sandwich form. The sandwich panels can be varied in thickness to meet structural and climatic needs or fire-resistive requirements by filling, treating, adding layers, laminating or coating the board at time of manufacture.

**1403.4 Ball Brothers.** Another core-plus-panel system just taking form as the company works on a HUD contract award for prototype construction is that developed by Ball Bros. Research Corp. This company's composite foam-core panels (see earlier illustration this chapter) are to be used in conjunction with kitchen-bath modules. Details of the modules and the typical sequence of erection are shown in the accompanying sketches.

**1403.5. Speedspace.** There are a few designers and their companies who have done experimental work on the use of core-module principles with another consideration in mind—that of reducing the number of shipping units or reduction of empty space involved in shipping pre-finished modules.

Some early work was done a few years ago in this respect by the Speedspace Corp., of Santa Rosa, Cal., in some relocatable school buildings. The classroom units were built with hinged sections that unfolded into place once the basic module has been positioned.

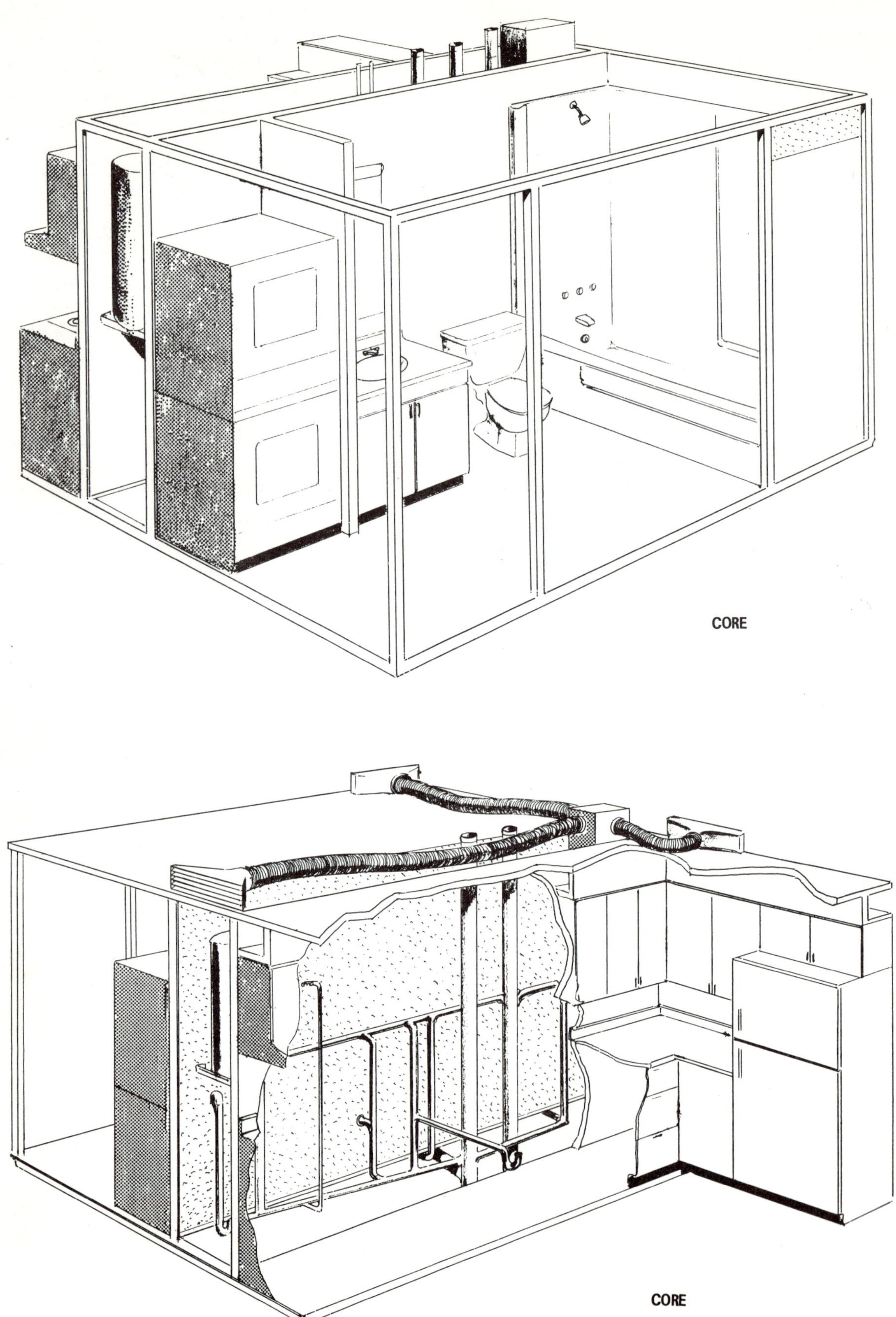


**Fig. 1403.1A.**
Bathroom side view and cut-away kitchen in the new single-family modules of Ball Bros.

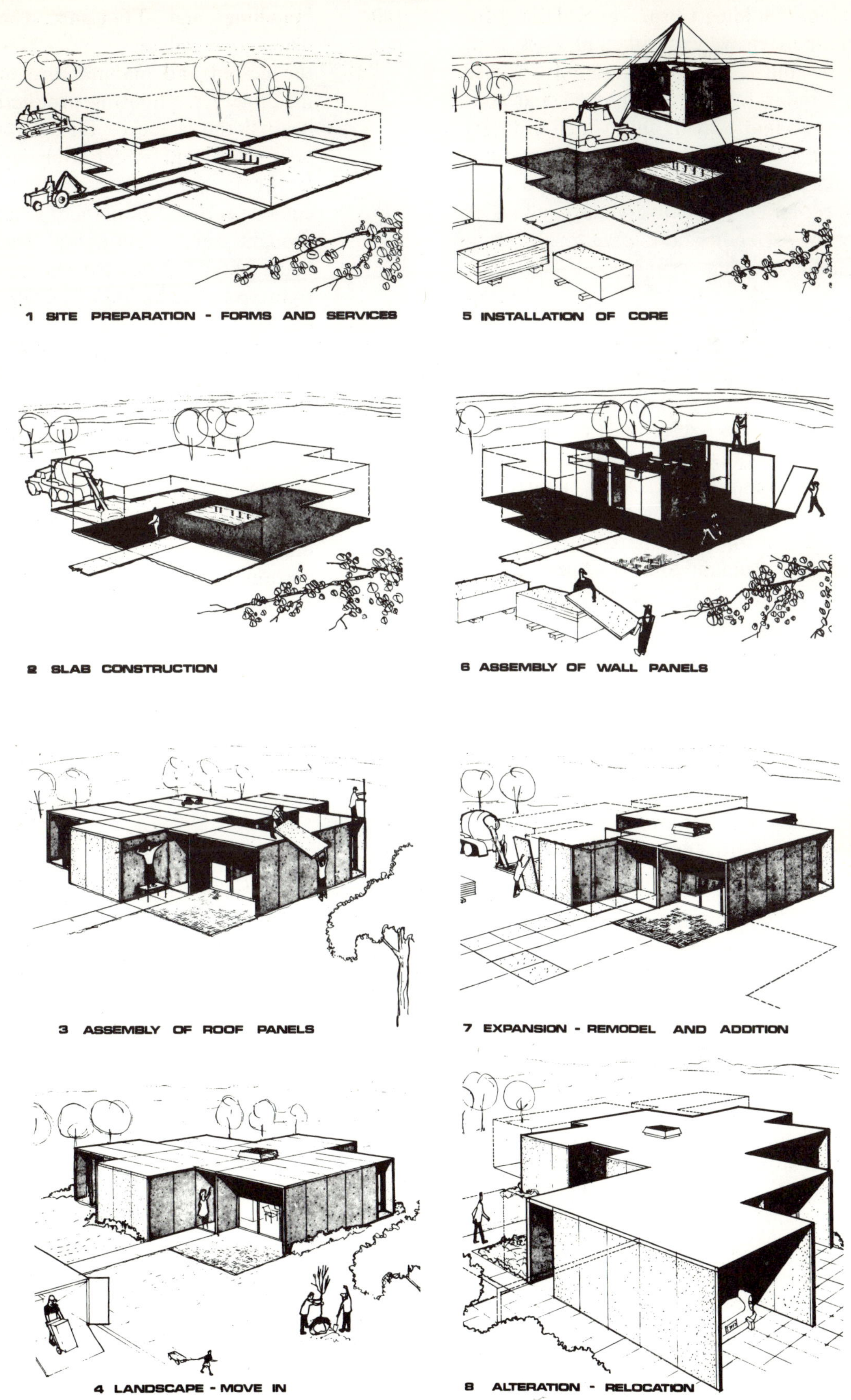


**Fig. 1403.1B.**
Eight sketches showing the sequence of construction combining core-modules with panels.

1403.6 **The Home Building Corp.** of Sedalia, Mo. has done extensive experimental work with both 1- and 2-story single-family homes using similar fold-out floor, wall and roof sections so that a living unit which ordinarily might need shipments of 2 or 3 modules on separate trailers could be shipped on a single trailer cutting delivery costs in half or more—or extending the practicable shipping radius.

1403.7 **Leischner Const. Co.** On the West Coast, the G. R. Leischner Construction Co. has applied this folding-section principle to its Evergreen Homes operation. For the HUD Breakthrough program, Leischner designed a 3-story modular stack-up apartment complex of 18 units using the same fold-up idea. The core in these apartment homes is the central module that includes a U-kitchen at one end and a bathroom at the other. The in-between hall space is used for shipping closet components. Upon placement at the site, floor, wall and roof sections fold out to form the living-dining rooms on one side of the central module and two bedrooms on the other side. Other new ideas for factory production of core units are coming, and more can be expected as designers learn more about what the other fellow is doing.

1403.8 **General Housing Industries.** One final core-plus-panel development might be briefly described to give one example of the new thinking. General Housing Industries Inc., in State College, Pa., is an outgrowth of Harlan Wall's architectural firm. The company calls its core the "Action Center." It is a 2-story factory-fabricated and finished module that includes a fully-equipped kitchen, 1-1/2 baths, a 2nd-floor laundry with washer and dryer, and a stairway adaptable to different floorplan designs and available in carpeted or hardwood finishes. Core walls are drywall. Teaming with the core are pre-finished panels for floors, walls, and roof. The system is FHA approved and has been used on a total of 514 living units in three separate townhouse complexes in Eastern Pennsylvania cities.

1404 **Handling and Transport Considerations.** The rapid advancements being made in the design and manufacture of specialized machinery for housing production lines are beyond the scope of this chapter, but this new equipment is definitely a contributing factor in the "materials flow" ideas discussed earlier. But there's an additional thought worth mentioning. The flow line is being extended beyond the factory's walls right up to the building site wherever it may be.

Although efforts are made to keep module weights down, the plain fact is that modules built to normal construction standards such as FHA are a little different item with which to cope with a typical mobile home delivered to and remaining on its wheeled undercarriage. As modular manufacturers seek transport-design information, the transportation field is beginning to sit up and take notice of the housing producer's problems. Both trucking and railroad interests are becoming actively engaged in helping solve these problems. In addition, two major corporations already sophisticated in rail and shipping containers have decided to venture with that know-how into the housing production business.

1405 **Concrete Building Systems.** For inner-core urban use and certain other applications, there's much appeal to building sponsors in the fire-resistant characteristics and durability of concrete construction. With a strong and rapid trend to factory production in this country, pre-cast concrete structural systems are being investigated and in the past 18 months, there's been a quick adaptation of European systems techniques by entrepreneurs in this country who have obtained licenses from the Euro-systems' originators.

While a small handful of companies are becoming active in pre-cast 3-dimensional boxes, by far the most experienced companies are those having structural panel systems. For example, the Tracoba system is being developed in this country by Module Communities Inc. of Yonkers, N.Y. The system covers the following structural elements: load-bearing cross walls, floor panels, non-bearing sandwich-type facade

**Fig. 1404.**
View in Berwick, Pa., plant of CoManCo Inc., shipping container manufacturer, showing experiments with modular housing units; the company ran tests on the adaption of standard TTX railcars-for-containers for housing module purposes.

panels, gable panels, and special components such as shear walls, shaft walls, and stairs. These structural elements are factory-cast on steel tables and yard-cured. For extra large projects, the factory is established at the site. For other projects, the procedure of inventory, shipment-loading, transport, unload, and placement becomes a vital part of the factory-production chain.

1405.1 **Descon-Concordia.** A Canadian joint venture of two construction management firms won a HUD Breakthrough contract and is bringing the Descon/Concordia system of reinforced concrete panels, prestressed or post-tensioned as needed, to this country. The system's components may be cast in a plant or at the site, and an unusual feature is the use of dry mechanical joints for component assembly. Thus, weather conditions are not a critical element in the assembly process. Complementary to the D/C structural elements are other components and subassemblies designed for local fabrication: kitchen sections, cabinets, closets, partitions, and bathroom.

1405.2 **Other Systems.** Balency-MBM is an English system now being marketed in this country through Building Systems International Inc. England's "Bison" system is being applied here through a series of joint-venture firms. Several French systems are seeking U.S. connections, distributors and markets.

What may well prove to be the most noteworthy development in heavy engineering construction techniques for high-rise buildings, however, are coming from two companies whose experience has been almost exclusively in light-frame low-rise buildings—National Homes Corp. of Lafayette, Ind. and Stirling Homex Corp. of Avon, N.Y.

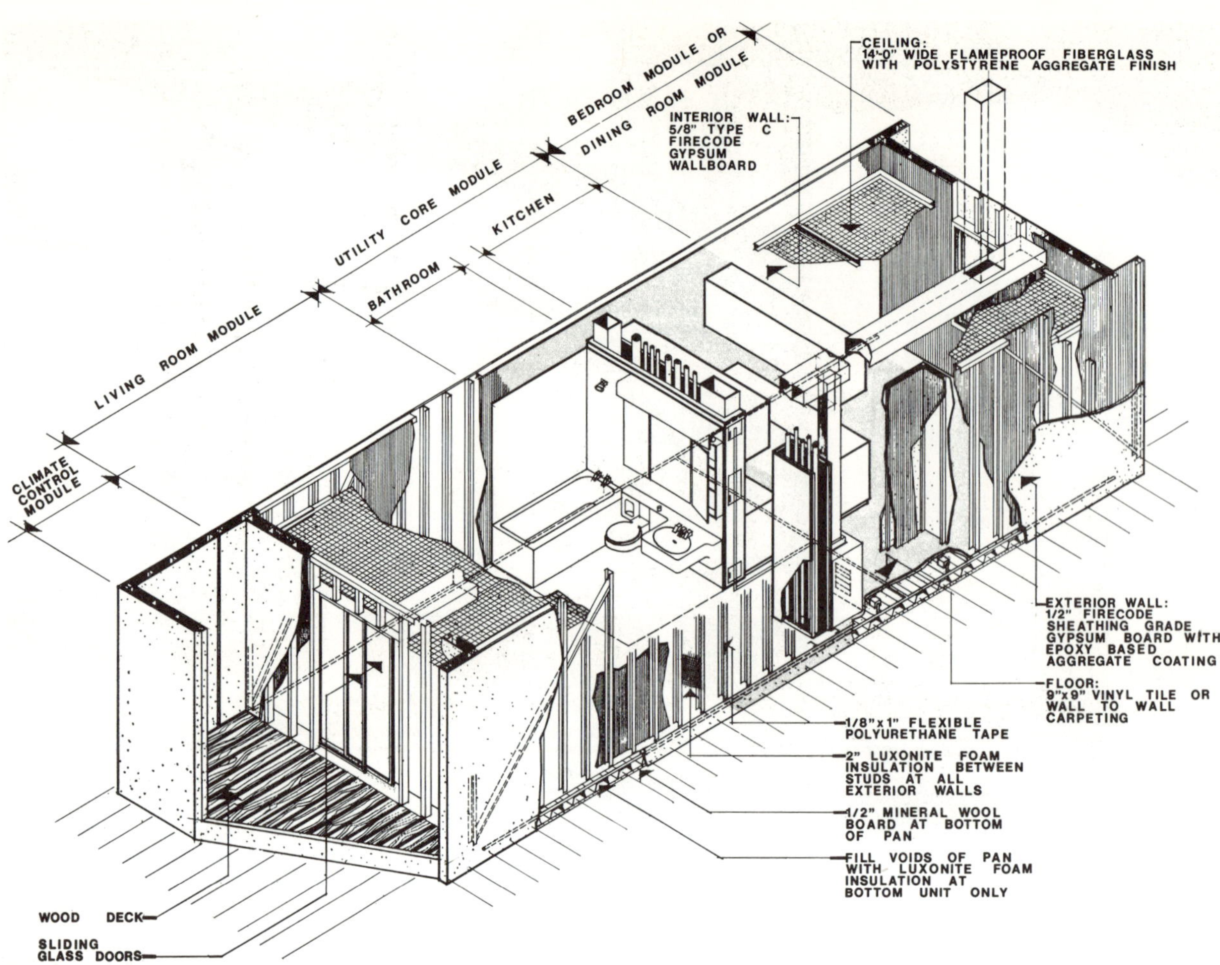


**Fig. 1405.3.**
Features of modular living units in the high-density non-combustible-materials design of National Homes.

1405.3 **National Homes.** A modular building system using non-combustible materials which has the capacity to rise 26 stories high has been developed by National Homes. The system uses pre-cast foamed concrete weighting about 30 lbs. per cu.ft. in both floor and wall construction. Exterior finish is a sprayed mixture of resin and natural granules to give the desired texture-color plus a monolithic surface at low cost. Ceilings are of stretched fabric with flame-proofing treatment and an adhesive coating in which small particles of polystyrene aggregate are embedded to furnish an attractive surface. The modular designs are divided into wet and dry modules (with or without plumbing) plus a facade module whose varying arrangements of balcony and sun control appendages have given it the name of "Climate control module."

1405.4 **Stirling-Homex.** Probably the most stimulating and provocative design to come along recently for high-density applications is the modular system being worked out by the Stirling Homex Corp. It's unique in that the factory-made modules incorporate integral structural frame elements. Construction begins with the top-level modules being moved into position at grade level and then being jacked up to make room for the next-to-top-floor modules to come in below at grade level. Again, jacking hoists the completed assembly to allow moving in of the next lower modules. And so on. The modules, the steel beams and concrete floor are all raised as a unit. About 90 percent of the overall work in the high-rise building—which can go up as high as 20 stories—is done in the factory.

**Fig. 1405.4.**
This modular high rise uses hydraulic and mechanical jacks to lift the top floor for insertion of modules that form the next floor. The system is capable in installing a floor a day up to 20 levels.

*(Stirling-Homex)*

1406 **Steel & Aluminum.** Recently major manufacturers have shown interest in greater application of their materials in the manufactured building field. Figs. 1406.1 & 1406.2 show two examples.

**Fig. 1406.1.**
Alumiframe building system substitutes punched aluminum extrusions for standard framing.
*(Alcoa)*

**Fig. 1406.2.**
Homaday wall panel system. Wall panels are produced on high speed production lines. A hydraulic press drives galvanized steel studs, fabricated with 32 barbs per stud into exterior wall sheathing with one stroke. Interior gypsum board is attached with adhesive.
*(U.S. Steel)*

## BIBLIOGRAPHY


*Design Criteria for Trussed Rafters,* U.S. Dept. of Housing & Development FHA-G 4541.1

*Hinged Interior Wood Door Units,* U.S. Govt. Printing Office, Washington, D.C. 20260 Voluntary Product Standard PS 32-70

*Modular Housing in the Real,* 1970 $22.50
Modco, Inc.
Box 425
Annandale, Virginia 22003

*Manufacturing Management, Introduction to,*
Ivan R. Vernon, Editor
Society of Manfacturing Engineers
20501 Ford Rd.
Dearborn, Michigan 48128 $10.65

*Material Handling, An Introduction to,*
Material Handling Institute, Inc.
1326 Freeport Road
Pittsburgh, Pennsylvania 15238 $2.00

*Modular Housing in the Real,*
J.A. Reidelbach, Jr.
P. E. Modco, Inc.
P.O. Box 425
Annandale, Virginia 22003 $22.50

*National Electrical Code,*
NFPA #70, National Fire Protection Assn.
60 Battery March Street,
Boston, Massachusettts 02110 $2.00

*Electrical Code for One and Two Family Dwellings,*
(Excerpts of the above) $1.75

*National Electrical Code, 1968, Criss-Cross Index,* $4.00
and
*National Electrical Code, 1968, Code Interpretations*
by: $5.00
C. W. Shufflebarger
Wing Publishing Co.
3940 Grand River
Detroit, Michigan 48208

*Residential Wiring,* American Standard Requirement for Industry Committee on Interior Wiring Design, Room 1650, 750 Third Ave. New York, New York 14301 .25

*"Selection of Paint" #796,*
National Paint Varnish & Lacquer Assn.
1500 Rhode Island Ave., N.W.
Washington, D.C. 20005

*Steel Construction, Manual of, 6th Edition*
American Insitute of Steel Construction
101 Park Avenue
New York, New York 10017

*TPI 68,* AIA File No. 19B-3, Truss Plate Institute
Suite 800, 919 Eighteenth St. N.W.
Washington, D.C. 22006

# Appendix

## BOARD MEASURE

| NOMINAL SIZE OF PIECE | BOARD FEET CONTENT WHEN LENGTH IN FEET OR NUMBER OF LINEAR FEET EQUALS | | | | | | | | | | | |
|---|---|---|---|---|---|---|---|---|---|---|---|---|
| | **1** | **2** | **3** | **4** | **5** | **6** | **7** | **8** | **9** | **10** | **11** | **12** | **14** |
| 1 x 1 | 1/12 | 1/6 | 1/4 | 1/3 | 5/12 | 1/2 | 7/12 | 2/3 | 3/4 | 5/6 | 11/12 | 1 | 1- 1/6 |
| 1 x 2 | 1/6 | 1/3 | 1/2 | 2/3 | 5/6 | 1 | 1- 1/6 | 1- 1/3 | 1- 1/2 | 1- 2/3 | 1- 5/6 | 2- | 2- 1/3 |
| 1 x 3 | 1/4 | 1/2 | 3/4 | 1 | 1- 1/4 | 1- 1/2 | 1- 3/4 | 2 | 2- 1/4 | 2- 1/2 | 2- 3/4 | 3 | 3- 1/2 |
| 1 x 4 | 1/3 | 2/3 | 1 | 1- 1/3 | 1- 2/3 | 2 | 2- 1/3 | 2- 2/3 | 3 | 3- 1/3 | 3- 2/3 | 4 | 4- 2/3 |
| 1 x 5 | 5/12 | 5/6 | 1- 1/4 | 1- 2/3 | 2- 1/12 | 2- 1/2 | 2-11/12 | 3- 1/3 | 3- 3/4 | 4- 1/6 | 4- 7/12 | 5 | 5- 5/6 |
| 1 x 6 | 1/2 | 1 | 1- 1/2 | 2 | 2- 1/2 | 3 | 3- 1/2 | 4 | 4- 1/2 | 5 | 5- 1/2 | 6 | 7 |
| 1 x 8 | 2/3 | 1- 1/3 | 2 | 2- 2/3 | 3- 1/3 | 4 | 4- 2/3 | 5- 1/3 | 6 | 6- 2/3 | 7- 1/3 | 8 | 9- 1/3 |
| 1 x 10 | 5/6 | 1- 2/3 | 2- 1/2 | 3- 1/3 | 4- 1/6 | 5 | 5-5/6 | 6- 2/3 | 7- 1/2 | 8- 1/3 | 9- 1/6 | 10 | 11- 2/3 |
| 1 x 12 | 1 | 2 | 3 | 4 | 5 | 6 | 7 | 8 | 9 | 10 | 11 | 12 | 14 |
| 1 x 14 | 1- 1/6 | 2- 1/3 | 3- 1/2 | 4- 2/3 | 5- 5/6 | 7 | 8- 1/6 | 9 1/3 | 10- 1/2 | 11- 2/3 | 12- 5/6 | 14 | 16- 1/3 |
| 1 x 16 | 1- 1/3 | 2- 2/3 | 4 | 5- 1/3 | 6- 2/3 | 8 | 9- 1/3 | 10 2/3 | 12 | 13- 1/3 | 14- 2/3 | 16 | 18- 2/3 |
| 1-1/4x 1 | 5/48 | 5/24 | 5/16 | 5/12 | 25/48 | 5/8 | 35/48 | 5/6 | 15/16 | 1- 1/24 | 1- 7/48 | 1- 1/4 | 1-11/2 |
| 1-1/4x 2 | 5/24 | 5/12 | 5/8 | 5/6 | 1- 1/24 | 1- 1/4 | 1-11/24 | 1- 2/3 | 1- 7/8 | 2- 1/12 | 2- 7/24 | 2- 1/2 | 2-11/1 |
| 1-1/4x 3 | 5/16 | 5/8 | 15/16 | 1- 1/4 | 1- 9/16 | 1- 7/8 | 2- 3/16 | 2- 1/2 | 2-13/16 | 3- 1/8 | 3- 7/16 | 3- 3/4 | 4- 3/8 |
| 1-1/4x 4 | 5/12 | 5/6 | 1- 1/4 | 1- 2/3 | 2- 1/12 | 2- 1/2 | 2-11/12 | 3- 1/3 | 3- 3/4 | 4- 1/6 | 4- 7/12 | 5 | 5- 5/6 |
| 1-1/4x 5 | 25/48 | 1- 1/24 | 1- 9/16 | 2- 1/12 | 2-19/48 | 3- 1/8 | 3-31/48 | 4- 1/6 | 4-11/16 | 5- 5/24 | 5-35/48 | 6- 1/4 | 7- 7/2 |
| 1-1/4x 6 | 5/8 | 1- 1/4 | 1- 7/8 | 2- 1/2 | 3- 1/8 | 3- 3/4 | 4- 3/8 | 5 | 5- 5/8 | 6- 1/4 | 6- 7/8 | 7- 1/2 | 8- 3/4 |
| 1-1/4x 8 | 5/6 | 1- 2/3 | 2- 1/2 | 3- 1/3 | 4- 1/6 | 5 | 5- 5/6 | 6- 2/3 | 7- 1/2 | 8- 1/3 | 9- 1/6 | 10 | 11- 2/3 |
| 1-1/4x 10 | 1- 1/24 | 2- 1/12 | 3- 1/8 | 4- 1/6 | 5- 5/24 | 6- 1/4 | 7- 7/24 | 8- 1/3 | 9- 3/8 | 10- 5/12 | 11-11/24 | 12- 1/2 | 14- 7/1 |
| 1-1/4x 12 | 1- 1/4 | 2- 1/2 | 3- 3/4 | 5 | 6- 1/4 | 7- 1/2 | 8- 3/4 | 10 | 11- 1/4 | 12- 1/2 | 13- 3/4 | 15 | 17- 1/2 |
| 1-1/4x 14 | 1-11/24 | 2-11/12 | 4- 3/8 | 5- 5/6 | 7- 7/24 | 8- 3/4 | 10- 5/24 | 11- 2/3 | 13- 1/8 | 14- 7/12 | 16- 1/24 | 17- 1/2 | 20- 5/1 |
| 1-1/4x 16 | 1- 2/3 | 3- 1/3 | 5 | 6- 2/3 | 8- 1/3 | 10 | 11- 2/3 | 13- 1/3 | 15 | 16- 2/3 | 18- 1/3 | 20 | 23- 1/3 |
| 1-1/2x 1 | 1/8 | 1/4 | 3/8 | 1/2 | 5/8 | 3/4 | 7/8 | 1 | 1- 1/8 | 1- 1/4 | 1- 3/8 | 1- 1/2 | 1- 3/4 |
| 1-1/2x 2 | 1/4 | 1/2 | 3/4 | 1 | 1- 1/4 | 1- 1/2 | 1- 3/4 | 2 | 2- 1/4 | 2- 1/2 | 2- 3/4 | 3 | 3- 1/2 |
| 1-1/2x 3 | 3/8 | 3/4 | 1- 1/8 | 1- 1/2 | 1- 7/8 | 2- 1/4 | 2- 5/8 | 3 | 3- 3/8 | 3- 3/4 | 4- 1/8 | 4- 1/2 | 5- 1/4 |
| 1-1/2x 4 | 1/2 | 1 | 1- 1/2 | 2 | 2- 1/2 | 3 | 3- 1/2 | 4 | 4- 1/2 | 5 | 5- 1/2 | 6 | 7 |
| 1- 1/2x 5 | 5/8 | 1- 1/4 | 1- 7/8 | 2- 1/2 | 3- 1/8 | 3- 3/4 | 4- 3/8 | 5 | 5- 5/8 | 6- 1/4 | 6- 7/8 | 7- 1/2 | 8- 3/4 |
| 1-1/2x 6 | 3/4 | 1- 1/2 | 2- 1/4 | 3 | 3- 3/4 | 4- 1/2 | 5- 1/4 | 6 | 6- 3/4 | 7- 1/2 | 8- 1/4 | 9 | 10- 1/2 |
| 1-1/2x 8 | 1 | 2 | 3 | 4 | 5 | 6 | 7 | 8 | 9 | 10 | 11 | 12 | 14 |
| 1-1/2x 10 | 1- 1/4 | 2- 1/2 | 3- 3/4 | 5 | 6- 1/4 | 7- 1/2 | 8- 3/4 | 10 | 11- 1/4 | 12- 1/2 | 13- 3/4 | 15 | 17- 1/2 |
| 1-1/2x 12 | 1- 1/2 | 3 | 4- 1/2 | 6 | 7- 1/2 | 9 | 10- 1/2 | 12 | 13- 1/2 | 15 | 16- 1/2 | 18 | 21 |
| 1-1/2x 14 | 1- 3/4 | 3- 1/2 | 5- 1/4 | 7 | 8- 3/4 | 10- 1/2 | 12- 1/4 | 14 | 15- 3/4 | 17- 1/2 | 19- 1/4 | 21 | 24- 1/2 |
| 1-1/2x 16 | 2 | 4 | 6 | 8 | 10 | 12 | 14 | 16 | 18 | 20 | 22 | 24 | 28 |
| 2 x 2 | 1/3 | 2/3 | 1 | 1- 1/3 | 1- 2/3 | 2 | 2- 1/3 | 2- 2/3 | 3 | 3- 1/3 | 3- 2/3 | 4 | 4- 2/3 |
| 2 x 3 | 1/2 | 1 | 1- 1/2 | 2 | 2- 1/2 | 3 | 3- 1/2 | 4 | 4- 1/2 | 5 | 5- 1/2 | 6 | 7 |
| 2 x 4 | 2/3 | 1- 1/3 | 2 | 2- 2/3 | 3- 1/3 | 4 | 4- 2/3 | 5- 1/3 | 6 | 6- 2/3 | 7- 1/3 | 8 | 9- 1/3 |
| 2 x 5 | 5/6 | 1- 2/3 | 2- 1/2 | 3- 1/3 | 4- 1/6 | 5 | 5- 5/6 | 6- 2/3 | 7- 1/2 | 8- 1/3 | 9- 1/6 | 10 | 11- 2/3 |
| 2 x 6 | 1 | 2 | 3 | 4 | 5 | 6 | 7 | 8 | 9 | 10 | 11 | 12 | 14 |
| 2 x 7 | 1- 1/6 | 2- 1/3 | 3- 1/2 | 4- 2/3 | 5- 5/6 | 7 | 8- 1/4 | 9- 1/3 | 10- 1/2 | 11- 2/3 | 12- 5/6 | 14 | 16- 1/ |
| 2 x 8 | 1- 1/3 | 2- 2/3 | 4 | 5- 1/3 | 6- 2/3 | 8 | 9- 1/3 | 10- 2/3 | 12 | 13- 1/3 | 14- 2/3 | 16 | 18- 2/3 |
| 2 x 9 | 1- 1/2 | 3 | 4- 1/2 | 6 | 7- 1/2 | 9 | 10- 1/2 | 12 | 13- 1/2 | 15 | 16- 1/2 | 18 | 21 |
| 2 x 10 | 1- 2/3 | 3- 1/3 | 5 | 6- 2/3 | 8- 1/3 | 10 | 11- 2/3 | 13- 1/3 | 15 | 16- 2/3 | 18- 1/3 | 20 | 23- 1/ |
| 2 x 12 | 2 | 4 | 6 | 8 | 10 | 12 | 14 | 16 | 18 | 20 | 22 | 24 | 28 |
| 2 x 14 | 2- 1/3 | 4- 2/3 | 7 | 9- 1/3 | 11- 2/3 | 14 | 16- 1/3 | 18- 2/3 | 21 | 23- 1/3 | 25- 2/3 | 28 | 31- 2/ |
| 2 x 16 | 2- 2/3 | 5- 1/3 | 8 | 10- 2/3 | 13- 1/3 | 16 | 18- 2/3 | 21- 1/3 | 24 | 26- 2/3 | 29- 1/3 | 32 | 37- 1/ |
| 2 x 18 | 3 | 6 | 9 | 12 | 15 | 18 | 21 | 24 | 27 | 30 | 33 | 36 | 42 |
| 2 x 20 | 3- 1/3 | 6- 2/3 | 10 | 13- 1/3 | 16- 2/3 | 20 | 23- 1/3 | 26- 2/3 | 30 | 33- 1/3 | 36- 2/3 | 40 | 46- 2/ |
| 3 x 3 | 3/4 | 1- 1/2 | 2- 1/4 | 3 | 3- 3/4 | 4- 1/2 | 5- 1/4 | 6 | 6- 3/4 | 7- 1/2 | 8- 1/4 | 9 | 10- 1/ |
| 3 x 4 | 1 | 2 | 3 | 4 | 5 | 6 | 7 | 8 | 9 | 10 | 11 | 12 | 14 |
| 3 x 5 | 1- 1/4 | 2- 1/2 | 3- 3/4 | 5 | 6-1/4 | 7- 1/2 | 8- 3/4 | 10 | 11- 1/4 | 12- 1/2 | 13- 3/4 | 15 | 17- 1/ |
| 3 x 6 | 1- 1/2 | 3 | 4- 1/2 | 6 | 7- 1/2 | 9- | 10- 1/2 | 12 | 13- 1/2 | 15 | 16- 1/2 | 18 | 21 |
| 3 x 7 | 1- 3/4 | 3- 1/2 | 5- 1/4 | 7 | 8- 3/4 | 10- 1/2 | 12- 1/4 | 14 | 15- 3/4 | 17- 1/2 | 19- 1/4 | 21 | 24- 1/ |
| 3 x 8 | 2 | 4 | 6 | 8 | 10 | 12 | 14 | 16 | 18 | 20 | 22 | 24 | 28 |
| 3 x 9 | 2- 1/4 | 4- 1/2 | 6- 3/4 | 9 | 11- 1/4 | 13- 1/2 | 15- 3/4 | 18 | 20- 1/4 | 22- 1/2 | 24- 3/4 | 27 | 31- 1/ |
| 3 x 10 | 2- 1/2 | 5 | 7- 1/2 | 10 | 12- 1/2 | 15 | 17- 1/2 | 20 | 22- 1/2 | 25 | 27- 1/2 | 30 | 35 |
| 3 x 12 | 3 | 6 | 9 | 12 | 15 | 18 | 21 | 24 | 27 | 30 | 33 | 36 | 42 |
| 3 x 14 | 3- 1/2 | 7 | 10- 1/2 | 14 | 17- 1/2 | 21 | 24- 1/2 | 28 | 31- 1/2 | 35 | 38- 1/2 | 42 | 49 |
| 3 x 16 | 4 | 8 | 12 | 16 | 20 | 24 | 28 | 32 | 36 | 40 | 44 | 48 | 56 |
| 3 x 18 | 4- 1/2 | 9 | 13- 1/2 | 18 | 22- 1/2 | 27 | 31- 1/2 | 36 | 40- 1/2 | 45 | 49- 1/2 | 54 | 63 |
| 3 x 20 | 5 | 10 | 15 | 20 | 25 | 30 | 35 | 40 | 45 | 50 | 55 | 60 | 70 |
| 4 x 4 | 1- 1/3 | 2- 2/3 | 4 | 5- 1/3 | 6- 2/3 | 8 | 9- 1/3 | 10- 2/3 | 12 | 13- 1/3 | 14- 2/3 | 16 | 18- 2/ |
| 4 x 5 | 1- 2/3 | 3- 1/3 | 5 | 6- 2/3 | 8- 1/3 | 10 | 11- 2/3 | 13- 1/3 | 15 | 16- 2/3 | 18- 1/3 | 20 | 23- 1/ |
| 4 x 6 | 2 | 4 | 6 | 8 | 10 | 12 | 14 | 16 | 18 | 20 | 22 | 24 | 28 |
| 4 x 7 | 2- 1/3 | 4- 2/3 | 7 | 9- 1/3 | 11- 2/3 | 14 | 16- 1/3 | 18- 2/3 | 21 | 23- 1/3 | 25- 2/3 | 28 | 32- 2/ |
| 4 x 8 | 2- 2/3 | 5- 1/3 | 8 | 10- 2/3 | 13- 1/3 | 16 | 18- 2/3 | 21- 1/3 | 24 | 26- 2/3 | 29- 1/3 | 32 | 37- 1/ |
| 4 x 9 | 3 | 6 | 9 | 12 | 15 | 18 | 21 | 24 | 27 | 30 | 33 | 36 | 42 |
| 4 x 10 | 3- 1/3 | 6- 2/3 | 10 | 13- 1/3 | 16- 2/3 | 20 | 23- 1/3 | 26- 2/3 | 30 | 33- 1/3 | 36- 2/3 | 40 | 46- 2/ |
| 4 x 12 | 4 | 8 | 12 | 16 | 20 | 24 | 28 | 32 | 36 | 40 | 44 | 48 | 56 |
| 4 x 14 | 4- 2/3 | 9- 1/3 | 14 | 18- 2/3 | 23- 1/3 | 28 | 32- 2/3 | 37- 1/3 | 42 | 46- 2/3 | 51- 1/3 | 56 | 65- 1/ |
| 4 x 16 | 5- 1/3 | 10- 2/3 | 16 | 21- 1/3 | 26- 2/3 | 32 | 37- 1/3 | 42- 2/3 | 48 | 53- 1/3 | 58- 2/3 | 64 | 74- 2/ |
| 4 x 18 | 6 | 12 | 18 | 24 | 30 | 36 | 42 | 48 | 54 | 60 | 66 | 72 | 84 |
| 4 x 20 | 6- 2/3 | 13- 1/3 | 20 | 26- 2/3 | 33- 1/3 | 40 | 46- 2/3 | 53- 1/3 | 60 | 66- 2/3 | 73- 1/3 | 80 | 93- 1/ |
| 5 x 5 | 2- 1/12 | 4- 1/6 | 6- 1/4 | 8- 1/3 | 10- 5/12 | 12- 1/2 | 14- 7/12 | 16- 2/3 | 18- 3/4 | 20- 5/6 | 22-11/12 | 25 | 29- 1/ |
| 5 x 6 | 2- 1/2 | 5 | 7- 1/2 | 10 | 12- 1/2 | 15 | 17- 1/2 | 20 | 22- 1/2 | 25 | 27- 1/2 | 30 | 35 |
| 5 x 7 | 2-11/12 | 5- 5/6 | 8- 3/4 | 11- 2/3 | 14- 7/12 | 17- 1/2 | 20- 5/12 | 23- 1/3 | 26- 1/4 | 29- 1/6 | 32- 1/12 | 35 | 40- 5/ |
| 5 x 8 | 3- 1/3 | 6- 2/3 | 10 | 13- 1/3 | 16- 2/3 | 20 | 23- 1/3 | 26- 2/3 | 30 | 33- 1/3 | 36- 2/3 | 40 | 46- 2/ |
| 5 x 9 | 3- 3/4 | 7- 1/2 | 11- 1/4 | 15 | 18- 3/4 | 22- 1/2 | 26- 1/4 | 30 | 33- 3/4 | 37- 1/2 | 41- 1/4 | 45 | 52- 1/ |
| 5 x 10 | 4- 1/6 | 8- 1/3 | 12- 1/2 | 16- 2/3 | 20- 5/6 | 25 | 29- 1/6 | 33- 1/3 | 37- 1/2 | 41- 2/3 | 45- 5/6 | 50 | 58- 1/ |
| 5 x 12 | 5 | 10 | 15 | 20 | 25 | 30 | 35 | 40 | 45 | 50 | 55 | 60 | 70 |
| 5 x 14 | 5- 5/6 | 11- 2/3 | 17- 1/2 | 23- 1/3 | 29- 1/6 | 35 | 40- 5/6 | 46- 2/3 | 52- 1/2 | 58- 1/3 | 64- 1/6 | 70 | 81- 2/ |
| 5 x 16 | 6- 2/3 | 13- 1/3 | 20 | 26- 2/3 | 33- 1/3 | 40 | 46- 2/3 | 53- 1/3 | 60 | 66- 2/3 | 73- 1/3 | 80 | 93- 1/ |
| 5 x 18 | 7- 1/2 | 15 | 22- 1/2 | 30 | 37- 1/2 | 45 | 52- 1/2 | 60 | 67- 1/2 | 75 | 82- 1/2 | 90 | 105 |
| 5 x 20 | 8- 1/3 | 16- 2/3 | 25 | 33- 1/3 | 41- 2/3 | 50 | 58- 1/3 | 66- 2/3 | 75 | 83- 1/3 | 91- 2/3 | 100 | 116- 2/ |
| 6 x 6 | 3 | 6 | 9 | 12 | 15 | 18 | 21 | 24 | 27 | 30 | 33 | 36 | 42 |
| 6 x 8 | 4 | 8 | 12 | 16 | 20 | 24 | 28 | 32 | 36 | 40 | 44 | 48 | 56 |
| 8 x 8 | 5- 1/3 | 10- 2/3 | 16 | 21- 1/3 | 26- 2/3 | 32 | 37- 1/3 | 42- 2/3 | 48 | 53- 1/3 | 58- 2/3 | 64 | 74- 2/ |

## BOARD MEASURE

| NOMINAL SIZE OF PIECE | BOARD FEET CONTENT WHEN LENGTH IN FEET OR NUMBER OF LINEAR FEET EQUALS | | | | | | | | | | | | |
|---|---|---|---|---|---|---|---|---|---|---|---|---|---|
| | 16 | 18 | 20 | 22 | 24 | 26 | 28 | 30 | 32 | 34 | 36 | 38 | 40 |
| 1 x 1 | 1- 1/3 | 1- 1/2 | 1- 2/3 | 1- 5/6 | 2 | 2- 1/6 | 2- 1/3 | 2- 1/2 | 2- 2/3 | 2- 5/6 | 3 | 3- 1/6 | 3- 1/3 |
| 1 x 2 | 2- 2/3 | 3 | 3- 1/3 | 3- 2/3 | 4 | 4- 1/3 | 4- 2/3 | 5 | 5- 1/3 | 5- 2/3 | 6 | 6- 1/3 | 6- 2/3 |
| 1 x 3 | 4 | 4- 1/2 | 5 | 5- 1/2 | 6 | 6- 1/2 | 7 | 7- 1/2 | 8 | 8- 1/2 | 9 | 9- 1/2 | 10 |
| 1 x 4 | 5- 1/3 | 6 | 6- 2/3 | 7- 1/3 | 8 | 8- 2/3 | 9- 1/3 | 10 | 10- 2/3 | 11- 1/3 | 12 | 12- 2/3 | 13- 1/3 |
| 1 x 5 | 6- 2/3 | 7- 1/2 | 8- 1/3 | 9- 1/6 | 10 | 10- 5/6 | 11- 2/3 | 12- 1/2 | 13- 1/3 | 14- 1/6 | 15 | 15- 5/6 | 16- 2/3 |
| 1 x 6 | 8 | 9 | 10 | 11 | 12 | 13 | 14 | 15 | 16 | 17 | 18 | 19 | 20 |
| 1 x 8 | 10- 2/3 | 12 | 13- 1/3 | 14- 2/3 | 16 | 17- 1/3 | 18- 2/3 | 20 | 21- 1/3 | 22- 2/3 | 24 | 25- 1/3 | 26- 2/3 |
| 1 x 10 | 13- 1/3 | 15 | 16- 2/3 | 18- 1/3 | 20 | 21- 2/3 | 23- 1/3 | 25 | 26- 2/3 | 28- 1/3 | 30 | 31- 2/3 | 33- 1/3 |
| 1 x 12 | 16 | 18 | 20 | 22 | 24 | 26 | 28 | 30 | 32 | 34 | 36 | 38 | 40 |
| 1 x 14 | 18- 2/3 | 21 | 23- 1/3 | 25- 2/3 | 28 | 30- 1/3 | 32- 2/3 | 35 | 37- 1/3 | 39- 2/3 | 42 | 44- 1/3 | 46- 2/3 |
| 1 x 16 | 21- 1/3 | 24 | 26- 2/3 | 29- 1/3 | 32 | 34- 2/3 | 37- 1/3 | 40 | 42- 2/3 | 45- 1/3 | 48 | 50- 2/3 | 53- 1/3 |
| 1-1/4 x 1 | 1- 2/3 | 1- 7/8 | 2- 1/2 | 2- 7/24 | 2-1/2 | 2-17/24 | 2-11/12 | 3- 1/8 | 3- 1/3 | 3-13/24 | 3- 3/4 | 3-23/24 | 4- 1/6 |
| 1-1/4 x 2 | 3- 1/3 | 3- 3/4 | 4- 1/6 | 4-11/24 | 5 | 5- 5/12 | 5- 7/12 | 6- 1/4 | 6- 2/3 | 7- 1/12 | 7- 1/2 | 7-11/12 | 8- 1/3 |
| 1-1/4 x 3 | 5 | 5- 5/8 | 6- 1/4 | 6- 7/8 | 7-1/2 | 8- 1/8 | 8- 3/4 | 9- 3/8 | 10 | 10- 5/8 | 11- 1/4 | 11- 7/8 | 12- 1/2 |
| 1-1/4 x 4 | 6- 2/3 | 7- 1/2 | 8- 1/3 | 9- 1/6 | 10 | 10- 5/6 | 11- 2/3 | 12- 1/2 | 13- 1/3 | 14- 1/6 | 15 | 15- 5/6 | 16- 2/3 |
| 1-1/4 x 5 | 8- 1/3 | 9- 3/8 | 10- 5/12 | 11-11/24 | 12-1/2 | 13-13/24 | 14- 7/12 | 15- 5/8 | 16- 2/3 | 17-17/24 | 18- 3/4 | 19-19/24 | 20- 5/6 |
| 1-1/4 x 6 | 10 | 11- 1/4 | 12- 1/2 | 13- 3/4 | 15 | 16- 1/4 | 17- 1/2 | 18- 3/4 | 20 | 21- 1/4 | 22- 1/2 | 23- 3/4 | 25 |
| 1-1/4 x 8 | 13- 1/3 | 15 | 16- 2/3 | 18- 1/3 | 20 | 21- 2/3 | 23- 1/3 | 25 | 26- 2/3 | 28- 1/3 | 30 | 31- 2/3 | 33- 1/3 |
| 1-1/4 x 10 | 16- 2/3 | 18- 3/4 | 20- 5/6 | 22-11/12 | 25 | 27- 1/12 | 29- 1/6 | 31- 1/4 | 33- 1/3 | 35- 5/12 | 37- 1/2 | 39- 7/12 | 41- 2/3 |
| 1-1/4 x 12 | 20 | 22- 1/2 | 25 | 27- 1/2 | 30 | 32- 1/2 | 35 | 37- 1/2 | 40 | 42- 1/2 | 45 | 47- 1/2 | 50 |
| 1-1/4 x 14 | 23- 1/3 | 26- 1/4 | 29- 1/6 | 32- 1/12 | 35 | 37-11/12 | 40- 5/6 | 43- 3/4 | 46- 2/3 | 49- 7/12 | 52- 1/2 | 55- 5/12 | 58- 1/3 |
| 1-1/4 x 16 | 26- 2/3 | 30 | 33- 1/3 | 36- 2/3 | 40 | 43- 1/3 | 46- 2/3 | 50 | 53- 1/3 | 56- 2/3 | 60 | 63- 1/3 | 66- 2/3 |
| 1-1/2 x 1 | 2 | 2- 1/4 | 2- 1/2 | 2- 3/4 | 3 | 3- 1/4 | 3- 1/2 | 3- 3/4 | 4 | 4- 1/4 | 4- 1/2 | 4- 3/4 | 5 |
| 1-1/2 x 2 | 4 | 4- 1/2 | 5 | 5- 1/2 | 6 | 6- 1/2 | 7 | 7- 1/2 | 8 | 8- 1/2 | 9 | 9- 1/2 | 10 |
| 1-1/2 x 3 | 6 | 6- 3/4 | 7- 1/2 | 8- 1/4 | 9 | 9- 3/4 | 10- 1/2 | 11- 1/4 | 12 | 12- 3/4 | 13- 1/2 | 14- 1/4 | 15 |
| 1-1/2 x 4 | 8 | 9 | 10 | 11 | 12 | 13 | 14 | 15 | 16 | 17 | 18 | 19 | 20 |
| 1-1/2 x 5 | 10 | 11- 1/4 | 12- 1/2 | 13- 3/4 | 15 | 16- 1/4 | 17- 1/2 | 18- 3/4 | 20 | 21- 1/4 | 22- 1/2 | 23- 3/4 | 25 |
| 1-1/2 x 6 | 12 | 13- 1/2 | 15 | 16- 1/2 | 18 | 19- 1/2 | 21 | 22- 1/2 | 24 | 25- 1/2 | 27 | 28- 1/2 | 30 |
| 1-1/2 x 8 | 16 | 18 | 20 | 22 | 24 | 26 | 28 | 30 | 32 | 34 | 36 | 38 | 40 |
| 1-1/2 x 10 | 20 | 22- 1/2 | 25 | 27- 1/2 | 30 | 32- 1/2 | 35 | 37- 1/2 | 40 | 42- 1/2 | 45 | 47- 1/2 | 50 |
| 1-1/2 x 12 | 24 | 27 | 30 | 33 | 36 | 39 | 42 | 45 | 48 | 51 | 54 | 57 | 60 |
| 1-1/2 x 14 | 28 | 31- 1/2 | 35 | 38- 1/2 | 42 | 45- 1/2 | 49 | 52- 1/2 | 56 | 59- 1/2 | 65 | 66- 1/2 | 70 |
| 1-1/2 x 16 | 32 | 36 | 40 | 44 | 48 | 52 | 56 | 60 | 64 | 68 | 72 | 76 | 80 |
| 2 x 2 | 5- 1/3 | 6 | 6- 2/3 | 7- 1/3 | 8 | 8- 2/3 | 9- 1/3 | 10 | 10- 2/3 | 11- 1/3 | 12 | 12- 2/3 | 13- 1/3 |
| 2 x 3 | 8 | 9 | 10 | 11 | 12 | 13 | 14 | 15 | 16 | 17 | 18 | 19 | 20 |
| 2 x 4 | 10- 2/3 | 12 | 13- 1/3 | 14- 2/3 | 16 | 17- 1/3 | 18- 2/3 | 20 | 21- 1/3 | 22- 2/3 | 24 | 25- 1/3 | 26- 2/3 |
| 2 x 5 | 13- 1/3 | 15 | 16- 2/3 | 18- 1/3 | 20 | 21- 2/3 | 23- 1/3 | 25 | 26- 2/3 | 28- 1/3 | 30 | 31- 2/3 | 33- 1/3 |
| 2 x 6 | 16 | 18 | 20 | 22 | 24 | 26 | 28 | 30 | 32 | 34 | 36 | 38 | 40 |
| 2 x 7 | 18- 2/3 | 21 | 23- 1/3 | 25- 2/3 | 28 | 30- 1/3 | 32- 2/3 | 35 | 37- 1/3 | 39- 2/3 | 42 | 44- 1/3 | 46- 2/3 |
| 2 x 8 | 21- 1/3 | 24 | 26- 2/3 | 29- 1/3 | 32 | 34- 2/3 | 37- 1/3 | 40 | 42- 2/3 | 45- 1/3 | 48 | 50- 2/3 | 53- 1/3 |
| 2 x 9 | 24 | 27 | 30 | 33 | 36 | 39 | 42 | 45 | 48 | 51 | 54 | 57 | 60 |
| 2 x 10 | 26- 2/3 | 30 | 33- 1/3 | 36- 2/3 | 40 | 43- 1/3 | 46- 2/3 | 50 | 53- 1/3 | 56- 2/3 | 60 | 63- 1/3 | 66- 2/3 |
| 2 x 12 | 32 | 36 | 40 | 44 | 48 | 52 | 56 | 60 | 64 | 68 | 72 | 76 | 80 |
| 2 x 14 | 37- 1/3 | 42 | 46- 2/3 | 51- 1/3 | 56 | 60- 2/3 | 65- 1/3 | 70 | 74- 2/3 | 79- 1/3 | 84 | 88- 2/3 | 93- 1/3 |
| 2 x 16 | 42- 2/3 | 48 | 55- 1/3 | 58- 2/3 | 64 | 69- 1/3 | 74- 2/3 | 80 | 85- 1/3 | 90- 2/3 | 96 | 101-1/3 | 106-2/3 |
| 2 x 18 | 48 | 54 | 60 | 66 | 72 | 78 | 84 | 90 | 96 | 102 | 108 | 114 | 120 |
| 2 x 20 | 53- 1/3 | 60 | 66- 2/3 | 73- 1/3 | 80 | 86- 2/3 | 93- 1/3 | 100 | 106-2/3 | 113-1/3 | 120 | 126-2/3 | 133-1/3 |
| 3 x 3 | 12 | 13- 1/2 | 15 | 16- 1/2 | 18 | 19- 1/2 | 21 | 22- 1/2 | 24 | 25- 1/2 | 27 | 28- 1/2 | 30 |
| 3 x 4 | 16 | 18 | 20 | 22 | 24 | 26 | 28 | 30 | 32 | 34 | 36 | 38 | 40 |
| 3 x 5 | 20 | 22- 1/2 | 25 | 27- 1/2 | 30 | 32- 1/2 | 35 | 37- 1/2 | 40 | 42- 1/2 | 45 | 47- 1/2 | 50 |
| 3 x 6 | 24 | 27 | 30 | 33 | 36 | 39 | 42 | 45 | 48 | 51 | 54 | 57 | 60 |
| 3 x 7 | 28 | 31- 1/2 | 35 | 38- 1/2 | 42 | 45- 1/2 | 49 | 52- 1/2 | 56 | 59- 1/2 | 63 | 66- 1/2 | 70 |
| 3 x 8 | 32 | 36 | 40 | 44 | 48 | 52 | 56 | 60 | 64 | 68 | 72 | 76 | 80 |
| 3 x 9 | 36 | 40- 1/2 | 45 | 49- 1/2 | 54 | 58- 1/2 | 65 | 67- 1/2 | 72 | 76- 1/2 | 81 | 85- 1/2 | 90 |
| 3 x 10 | 40 | 45 | 50 | 55 | 60 | 65 | 70 | 75 | 80 | 85 | 90 | 95 | 100 |
| 3 x 12 | 48 | 54 | 60 | 66 | 72 | 78 | 84 | 90 | 95 | 102 | 108 | 114 | 120 |
| 3 x 14 | 54 | 63 | 70 | 77 | 84 | 91 | 98 | 105 | 112 | 119 | 126 | 133 | 140 |
| 3 x 16 | 64 | 72 | 80 | 88 | 96 | 104 | 112 | 120 | 128 | 136 | 144 | 152 | 160 |
| 3 x 18 | 72 | 81 | 90 | 99 | 108 | 117 | 126 | 135 | 144 | 153 | 162 | 171 | 180 |
| 3 x 20 | 80 | 90 | 100 | 110 | 120 | 130 | 140 | 150 | 160 | 170 | 180 | 190 | 200 |
| 4 x 4 | 21- 1/3 | 24 | 26- 2/3 | 29- 1/3 | 32 | 34- 2/3 | 37- 1/3 | 40 | 42- 2/3 | 45- 1/3 | 48 | 50- 2/3 | 53- 1/3 |
| 4 x 5 | 26- 2/3 | 30 | 33- 1/3 | 36- 2/3 | 40 | 45- 1/3 | 46- 2/3 | 50 | 53- 1/3 | 56- 2/3 | 60 | 63- 1/3 | 66- 2/3 |
| 4 x 6 | 32 | 36 | 40 | 44 | 48 | 52 | 56 | 60 | 64 | 68 | 72 | 76 | 80 |
| 4 x 7 | 37- 1/3 | 42 | 46- 2/3 | 51- 1/3 | 56 | 60- 2/3 | 65- 1/3 | 70 | 74- 2/3 | 79- 1/3 | 84 | 88- 2/3 | 93- 1/3 |
| 4 x 8 | 42- 2/3 | 48 | 53- 1/3 | 58- 2/3 | 64 | 69- 1/3 | 74- 2/3 | 80 | 85- 1/3 | 90- 2/3 | 96 | 101-1/3 | 106-2/3 |
| 4 x 9 | 48 | 54 | 60 | 66 | 72 | 78 | 84 | 90 | 95 | 102 | 108 | 114 | 120 |
| 4 x 10 | 53- 1/3 | 60 | 66- 2/3 | 73- 1/3 | 80 | 86- 2/3 | 93- 1/3 | 100 | 106-2/3 | 113-1/3 | 120 | 126-2/3 | 133-1/3 |
| 4 x 12 | 64 | 72 | 80 | 88 | 96 | 104 | 112 | 120 | 128 | 136 | 144 | 152 | 160 |
| 4 x 14 | 74- 2/3 | 84 | 93- 1/3 | 102-2/3 | 112 | 121-1/3 | 130-2/3 | 140 | 149-1/3 | 158-2/3 | 168 | 177-1/3 | 186-2/3 |
| 4 x 16 | 85- 1/3 | 96 | 106-2/3 | 117-1/3 | 128 | 138-2/3 | 149-1/3 | 160 | 170-2/3 | 181-1/3 | 192 | 202-2/3 | 213-1/3 |
| 4 x 18 | 96 | 108 | 120 | 132 | 144 | 156 | 168 | 180 | 192 | 204 | 216 | 228 | 240 |
| 4 x 20 | 106-2/3 | 120 | 133-1/3 | 146-2/3 | 160 | 173-1/3 | 186-2/3 | 200 | 213-1/3 | 226-2/3 | 240 | 253-1/3 | 266-2/3 |
| 5 x 5 | 33- 1/3 | 37- 1/2 | 41- 2/3 | 45- 5/6 | 50 | 54- 1/6 | 58- 1/3 | 62- 1/2 | 66- 2/3 | 70- 5/6 | 75 | 79- 1/6 | 83- 1/3 |
| 5 x 6 | 40 | 45 | 50 | 55 | 60 | 65 | 70 | 75 | 80 | 85 | 90 | 95 | 100 |
| 5 x 7 | 46- 2/3 | 52- 1/2 | 58- 1/3 | 64- 1/6 | 70 | 75- 5/6 | 81- 2/3 | 87- 1/2 | 93- 1/3 | 99- 1/6 | 105 | 110-5/6 | 116-2/3 |
| 5 x 8 | 53- 1/3 | 60 | 66- 2/3 | 73- 1/3 | 80 | 86- 2/3 | 93- 1/3 | 100 | 106-2/3 | 113-1/3 | 120 | 126-2/3 | 133-1/3 |
| 5 x 9 | 60 | 67- 1/2 | 75 | 82- 1/2 | 90 | 97- 1/2 | 105 | 112-1/2 | 120 | 127-1/2 | 135 | 142-1/2 | 150 |
| 5 x 10 | 66- 2/3 | 75 | 83- 1/3 | 91- 2/3 | 100 | 108-1/3 | 116-2/3 | 125 | 133-1/3 | 141-2/3 | 150 | 158-1/3 | 166-2/3 |
| 5 x 12 | 80 | 90 | 100 | 110 | 120 | 130 | 140 | 150 | 160 | 170 | 180 | 190 | 200 |
| 5 x 14 | 93- 1/3 | 105 | 116-2/3 | 128-1/3 | 140 | 151-2/3 | 163-1/3 | 175 | 186-2/3 | 198-1/3 | 210 | 221-2/3 | 233-1/3 |
| 5 x 16 | 106-2/3 | 120 | 133-1/3 | 146-2/3 | 160 | 173-1/3 | 186-2/3 | 200 | 213-1/3 | 226-2/3 | 240 | 253-1/3 | 266-2/3 |
| 5 x 18 | 120 | 135 | 150 | 165 | 180 | 195 | 210 | 225 | 240 | 255 | 270 | 285 | 300 |
| 5 x 20 | 133-1/3 | 150 | 166-2/3 | 183-1/3 | 200 | 216-2/3 | 233-1/3 | 250 | 266-2/3 | 283-1/3 | 300 | 316-2/3 | 333-1/3 |
| 6 x 6 | 48 | 54 | 60 | 66 | 72 | 78 | 84 | 90 | 96 | 102 | 108 | 114 | 120 |
| 6 x 8 | 64 | 72 | 80 | 88 | 96 | 104 | 112 | 120 | 128 | 136 | 144 | 152 | 160 |
| 8 x 8 | 85- 1/3 | 96 | 106-2/3 | 117-1/3 | 128 | 138-2/3 | 149-1/3 | 160 | 170-2/3 | 181-1/3 | 192 | 202-2/3 | 213-1/3 |

## Tables of Length, Area, Volume, and Weight

### Standard Measurements

**Measure of length (linear measure)**

| | | |
|---:|---|---|
| 4 inches | = | 1 hand |
| 9 inches | = | 1 span |
| 12 inches | = | 1 foot |
| 3 feet | = | 1 yard |
| 6 feet | = | 1 fathom |
| 5-1/2 yards–16-1/2 feet | = | 1 rod or 11 poles |
| 40 poles | = | 1 furlong |
| 8 furlongs | = | 1 mile |
| 5,280 feet—1,760 yards—320 rods | = | 1 mile |
| 3 miles | = | 1 league |

**Measure of surface (area)**

| | | |
|---:|---|---|
| 144 square inches | = | 1 square foot |
| 9 square feet | = | 1 square yard |
| 30-1/4 square yards | = | 1 square rod |
| 40 square rods | = | 1 rood |
| 4 square roods | = | 1 square area |
| 160 square rods | = | 1 acre |
| 43,560 square feet | = | 1 acre |
| 640 square acres | = | 1 square mile |
| 36 square miles | = | 1 township |

**Metric length**

| | | |
|---:|---|---|
| 1 inch | = | 2.54 centimeters |
| 1 foot | = | .305 meter |
| 1 yard | = | .914 meter |
| 1 mile | = | 1.609 kilometers |
| 1 fathom | = | 6 feet |
| 1 knot | = | 6,086 feet |
| 3 knots | = | 1 league |
| 1 centimeter | = | .394 inch |
| 1 meter | = | 3.281 feet |
| 1 meter | = | 1.094 yards |
| 1 kilometer | = | .621 mile |

**Metric weight**

| | | |
|---:|---|---|
| 1 grain | = | .065 gram |
| 1 apothecaries' scruple | = | 1.296 grams |
| 1 avoirdupois ounce | = | 28.350 grams |
| 1 troy ounce | = | 31.103 grams |
| 1 avoirdupois pound | = | .454 kilogram |
| 1 troy pound | = | .373 kilogram |
| 1 gram | = | 15.432 grains |
| 1 gram | = | .772 apothecaries' scruple |
| 1 gram | = | .035 avoirdupois ounce |
| 1 gram | = | .032 troy ounce |
| 1 kilogram | = | 2.205 avoirdupois pounds |
| 1 kilogram | = | 2.679 troy pounds |

**Liquid measure**

| | | |
|---:|---|---|
| 2 cups | = | 1 pint |
| 4 gills | = | 1 pint |
| 16 fluid ounces | = | 1 pint |
| 2 pints | = | 1 quart |
| 4 quarts | = | 1 gallon |
| 31-1/2 gallons | = | 1 barrel |
| 2 barrels | = | 1 hogshead |
| 1 gallon | = | 231 cubic inches |
| 1 cubic foot | = | 7.48 gallons |
| 1 teaspoon | = | .17 fluid ounces (1/6 oz.) |
| 3 teaspoons (level) | = | 1 tablespoon (1/2 oz.) |
| 2 tablespoons | = | 1 fluid ounce |
| 1 cup (liquid) | = | 16 tablespoons (8 oz.) |
| 1 teaspoon | = | 5 to 6 cubic centimeters |
| 1 tablespoon | = | 15 to 16 cubic centimeters |
| 1 fluid ounce | = | 29.57 cubic centimeters |

**Apothecaries' weight**

| | | |
|---:|---|---|
| 20 grains | = | 1 scruple |
| 3 scruples | = | 1 dram |
| 8 drams | = | 1 ounce |
| 12 ounces | = | 1 pound |
| 27-11/32 grains | = | 1 dram |
| 16 drams | = | 1 ounce |
| 16 ounces | = | 1 pound |
| 2,000 pounds | = | 1 ton (short) |
| 2,240 pounds | = | 1 ton (long) |

### Metric Equivalents

**Capacity**

| | | |
|---:|---|---|
| 1 U.S. fluid ounce | = | 29,573 milliliters |
| 1 U.S. liquid quart | = | .946 liter |
| 1 U.S. dry quart | = | 1.101 liters |
| 1 U.S. gallon | = | 3,785 liters |
| 1 U.S. bushel | = | .3524 hectoliters |
| 1 cubic inch | = | 16.4 cubic centimeters |
| 1 liter | = | 1,000 milliliters or 1,000 cubic centimeters |
| 1 cubic foot water | = | 7.43 gallons or 62-1/2 pounds |
| 231 cubic inches | = | 1 gallon |
| 1 millimeter | = | .034 U.S. fluid ounce |
| 1 liter | = | 1.057 U.S. liquid quarts |
| 1 liter | = | .908 U.S. dry quart |
| 1 liter | = | .264 U.S. gallon |
| 1 hectoliter | = | 2.838 U.S. bushels |
| 1 cubic centimeter | = | .061 cubic inch |

**Cubic measure (volume)**

| | | |
|---:|---|---|
| 1,728 cubic inches | = | 1 cubic foot |
| 27 cubic feet | = | 1 cubic yard |
| 2,150.42 cubic inches | = | 1 standard bushel |
| 231 cubic inches | = | 1 standard gallon (liquid) |
| 1 cubic foot | = | 4/5 of a bushel |
| 128 cubic feet | = | 1 cord (wood) |
| 7.48 gallons | = | 1 cubic foot |
| 1 bushel | = | 1.25 cubic feet |

## DECIMAL EQUIVALENTS

| DECIMAL OF A FOOT | | | | | | DECIMAL OF AN INCH | |
|---|---|---|---|---|---|---|---|
| FRACTION | DECIMAL | FRACTION | DECIMAL | FRACTION | DECIMAL | FRACTION | DECIMAL |
| 1/16 | 0.0052 | 4-1/16 | 0.3385 | 8-1/16 | 0.6719 | 1/64 | 0.015625 |
| 1/8 | 0.0104 | 4-1/8 | 0.3438 | 8-1/8 | 0.6771 | 1/32 | 0.03125 |
| 3/16 | 0.0156 | 4-3/16 | 0.3490 | 8-3/16 | 0.6823 | 3/64 | 0.046875 |
| 1/4 | 0.0208 | 4-1/4 | 0.3542 | 8-1/4 | 0.6875 | 1/16 | 0.0625 |
| 5/16 | 0.0260 | 4-5/16 | 0.3594 | 8-5/16 | 0.6927 | 5/64 | 0.078125 |
| 3/8 | 0.0313 | 4-3/8 | 0.3646 | 8-3/8 | 0.6979 | 3/32 | 0.09375 |
| 7/16 | 0.0365 | 4-7/16 | 0.3698 | 8-7/16 | 0.7031 | 7/64 | 0.109375 |
| 1/2 | 0.0417 | 4-1/2 | 0.3750 | 8-1/2 | 0.7083 | 1/8 | 0.125 |
| 9/16 | 0.0469 | 4-9/16 | 0.3802 | 8-9/16 | 0.7135 | 9/64 | 0.140625 |
| 5/8 | 0.0521 | 4-5/8 | 0.3854 | 8-5/8 | 0.7188 | 5/32 | 0.15625 |
| 11/16 | 0.0573 | 4-11/16 | 0.3906 | 8-11/16 | 0.7240 | 11/64 | 0.171875 |
| 3/4 | 0.0625 | 4-3/4 | 0.3958 | 8-3/4 | 0.7292 | 3/16 | 0.1875 |
| 13/16 | 0.0677 | 4-13/16 | 0.4010 | 8-13/16 | 0.7344 | 13/64 | 0.203125 |
| 7/8 | 0.0729 | 4-7/8 | 0.4063 | 8-7/8 | 0.7396 | 7/32 | 0.21875 |
| 15/16 | 0.0781 | 4-15/16 | 0.4115 | 8-15/16 | 0.7448 | 15/64 | 0.234375 |
| 1- | 0.0833 | 5- | 0.4167 | 9- | 0.7500 | 1/4 | 0.250 |
| 1-1/16 | 0.0885 | 5-1/16 | 0.4219 | 9-1/16 | 0.7552 | 17/64 | 0.265625 |
| 1-1/8 | 0.0938 | 5-1/8 | 0.4271 | 9-1/8 | 0.7604 | 9/32 | 0.28125 |
| 1-3/16 | 0.0990 | 5-3/16 | 0.4323 | 9-3/16 | 0.7656 | 19/64 | 0.296875 |
| 1-1/4 | 0.1042 | 5-1/4 | 0.4375 | 9-1/4 | 0.7708 | 5/16 | 0.3125 |
| 1-5/16 | 0.1094 | 5-5/16 | 0.4427 | 9-5/16 | 0.7760 | 21/64 | 0.328125 |
| 1-3/8 | 0.1146 | 5-3/8 | 0.4479 | 9-3/8 | 0.7813 | 11/32 | 0.34375 |
| 1-7/16 | 0.1198 | 5-7/16 | 0.4531 | 9-7/16 | 0.7865 | 23/64 | 0.359375 |
| 1-1/2 | 0.1250 | 5-1/2 | 0.4583 | 9-1/2 | 0.7917 | 3/8 | 0.375 |
| 1-9/16 | 0.1302 | 5-9/16 | 0.4635 | 9-9/16 | 0.7969 | 25/64 | 0.390625 |
| 1-5/8 | 0.1354 | 5-5/8 | 0.4688 | 9-5/8 | 0.8021 | 13/32 | 0.40625 |
| 1-11/16 | 0.1406 | 5-11/16 | 0.4740 | 9-11/16 | 0.8073 | 27/64 | 0.421875 |
| 1-3/4 | 0.1458 | 5-3/4 | 0.4792 | 9-3/4 | 0.8125 | 7/16 | 0.4375 |
| 1-13/16 | 0.1510 | 5-13/16 | 0.4844 | 9-13/16 | 0.8177 | 29/64 | 0.453125 |
| 1-7/8 | 0.1563 | 5-7/8 | 0.4896 | 9-7/8 | 0.8229 | 15/32 | 0.46875 |
| 1-15/16 | 0.1615 | 5-15/16 | 0.4948 | 9-15/16 | 0.8281 | 31/64 | 0.484375 |
| 2- | 0.1667 | 6- | 0.5000 | 10- | 0.8333 | 1/2 | 0.500 |
| 2-1/16 | 0.1719 | 6-1/16 | 0.5052 | 10-1/16 | 0.8385 | 33/64 | 0.515625 |
| 2-1/8 | 0.1771 | 6-1/8 | 0.5104 | 10-1/8 | 0.8438 | 17/32 | 0.53125 |
| 2-3/16 | 0.1823 | 6-3/16 | 0.5156 | 10-3/16 | 0.8490 | 35/64 | 0.546875 |
| 2-1/4 | 0.1875 | 6-1/4 | 0.5208 | 10-1/4 | 0.8542 | 9/16 | 0.5625 |
| 2-5/16 | 0.1927 | 6-5/16 | 0.5260 | 10-5/16 | 0.8594 | 37/64 | 0.578125 |
| 2-3/8 | 0.1979 | 6-3/8 | 0.5313 | 10-3/8 | 0.8646 | 19/32 | 0.59375 |
| 2-7/16 | 0.2031 | 6-7/16 | 0.5365 | 10-7/16 | 0.8698 | 39/64 | 0.609375 |
| 2-1/2 | 0.2083 | 6-1/2 | 0.5417 | 10-1/2 | 0.8750 | 5/8 | 0.625 |
| 2-9/16 | 0.2135 | 6-9/16 | 0.5469 | 10-9/16 | 0.8802 | 41/64 | 0.640625 |
| 2-5/8 | 0.2188 | 6-5/8 | 0.5521 | 10-5/8 | 0.8854 | 21/32 | 0.65625 |
| 2-11/16 | 0.2240 | 6-11/16 | 0.5573 | 10-11/16 | 0.8906 | 43/64 | 0.671875 |
| 2-3/4 | 0.2292 | 6-3/4 | 0.5625 | 10-3/4 | 0.8958 | 11/16 | 0.6875 |
| 2-13/16 | 0.2344 | 6-13/16 | 0.5677 | 10-13/16 | 0.9010 | 45/64 | 0.703125 |
| 2-7/8 | 0.2396 | 6-7/8 | 0.5729 | 10-7/8 | 0.9063 | 23/32 | 0.71875 |
| 2-15/16 | 0.2448 | 6-15/16 | 0.5781 | 10-15/16 | 0.9115 | 47/64 | 0.734375 |
| 3- | 0.2500 | 7- | 0.5833 | 11- | 0.9167 | 3/4 | 0.750 |
| 3-1/16 | 0.2552 | 7-1/16 | 0.5885 | 11-1/16 | 0.9219 | 49/64 | 0.765625 |
| 3-1/8 | 0.2604 | 7-1/8 | 0.5938 | 11-1/8 | 0.9271 | 25/32 | 0.78125 |
| 3-3/16 | 0.2656 | 7-3/16 | 0.5990 | 11-3/16 | 0.9323 | 51/64 | 0.796875 |
| 3-1/4 | 0.2708 | 7-1/4 | 0.6042 | 11-1/4 | 0.9375 | 13/16 | 0.8125 |
| 3-5/16 | 0.2760 | 7-5/16 | 0.6094 | 11-5/16 | 0.9427 | 53/64 | 0.828125 |
| 3-3/8 | 0.2813 | 7-3/8 | 0.6146 | 11-3/8 | 0.9479 | 27/32 | 0.84375 |
| 3-7/16 | 0.2865 | 7-7/16 | 0.6198 | 11-7/16 | 0.9531 | 55/64 | 0.859375 |
| 3-1/2 | 0.2917 | 7-1/2 | 0.6250 | 11-1/2 | 0.9583 | 7/8 | 0.875 |
| 3-9/16 | 0.2969 | 7-9/16 | 0.6302 | 11-9/16 | 0.9635 | 57/64 | 0.890625 |
| 3-5/8 | 0.3021 | 7-5/8 | 0.6354 | 11-5/8 | 0.9688 | 29/32 | 0.90625 |
| 3-11/16 | 0.3073 | 7-11/16 | 0.6406 | 11-11/16 | 0.9740 | 59/64 | 0.921875 |
| 3-3/4 | 0.3125 | 7-3/4 | 0.6458 | 11-3/4 | 0.9792 | 15/16 | 0.9375 |
| 3-13/16 | 0.3177 | 7-13/16 | 0.6510 | 11-13/16 | 0.9844 | 61/64 | 0.953125 |
| 3-7/8 | 0.3229 | 7-7/8 | 0.6563 | 11-7/8 | 0.9896 | 31/32 | 0.96875 |
| 3-15/16 | 0.3281 | 7-15/16 | 0.6615 | 11-15/16 | 0.9948 | 63/64 | 0.984375 |
| 4- | 0.3333 | 8- | 0.6667 | 12- | 1.0000 | 1" | 1.000 |

# NAILS

| SIZE | LENGTH INCHES | WIRE GAGE | APPROX. NO./LB. | APPROX. STRENGTH POUNDS Pull (1) | Lateral (2) |
|---|---|---|---|---|---|
| **COMMON NAILS** | | | | Douglas Fir, Larch or Southern Pine | |
| 2d | 1 | 15 | 847 | | |
| 3d | 1 1/4 | 14 | 543 | | |
| 4d | 1 1/2 | 12 1/2 | 294 | | |
| 5d | 1 3/4 | 12 1/2 | 254 | | |
| 6d | 2 | 11 1/2 | 167 | 29 | 63 |
| 7d | 2 1/4 | 11 1/2 | 150 | | |
| 8d | 2 1/2 | 10 1/4 | 101 | 34 | 78 |
| 9d | 2 3/4 | 10 1/4 | 92 | | |
| 10d | 3 | 9 | 69 | 38 | 94 |
| 12d | 3 1/4 | 9 | 63 | 38 | 94 |
| 16d | 3 1/2 | 8 | 49 | 42 | 107 |
| 20d | 4 | 6 | 31 | 49 | 139 |
| 30d | 4 1/2 | 5 | 24 | 53 | 154 |
| 40d | 5 | 4 | 18 | 58 | 176 |
| 50d | 5 1/2 | 3 | 14 | 63 | 202 |
| 60d | 6 | 2 | 11 | 68 | 223 |
| **SPIKES** | | | | | |
| 10d | 3 | 6 | 32 | 49 | 139 |
| 12d | 3 1/4 | 6 | 31 | 49 | 139 |
| 16d | 3 1/2 | 5 | 24 | 53 | 155 |
| 20d | 4 | 4 | 19 | 58 | 176 |
| 30d | 4 1/2 | 3 | 14 | 63 | 202 |
| 40d | 5 | 2 | 12 | 68 | 223 |
| 50d | 5 1/2 | 1 | 10 | 73 | 248 |
| 60d | 6 | 1 | 9 | 73 | 248 |
| 5/16 | 7 | 5/16 | 6 | 80 | 289 |
| 3/8 | 8-12 | 3/8" | 5-3 | 96 | 380 |
| **HARDENED THREADED NAILS** | | | | | |
| 6d | 2 | 12 | 190 | 80 | 69 |
| 8d | 2 1/2 | 11 | 117 | 90 | 82 |
| 10d | 3 | 10 | 78 | 100 | 94 |
| 12d | 3 1/4 | 10 | 73 | 100 | 94 |
| 16d | 3 1/2 | 9 | 57 | 110 | 107 |
| 20d | 4 | 7 | 36 | 135 | 139 |
| 30d | 4 1/2 | 7 | 31 | 135 | 139 |
| 40d | 5 | 7 | 27 | 135 | 139 |
| 50d | 5 1/2 | 7 | 23 | 135 | 139 |
| 60d | 6 | 7 | 18 | 135 | 139 |

(1) Per inch penetration of point
(2) For penetration of 11 diameters

# LAG SCREWS

| D | $D_r$ | H | W |
|---|---|---|---|
| 3/16 | .120 | 9/64 | 9/32 |
| 1/4 | .173 | 11/64 | 3/8 |
| 5/16 | .227 | 13/64 | 1/2 |
| 3/8 | .265 | 1/4 | 9/16 |
| 7/16 | .328 | 19/64 | 5/8 |
| 1/2 | .371 | 21/64 | 5/8 |
| 9/16 | .435 | 3/8 | 7/8 |
| 5/8 | .471 | 27/64 | 15/16 |
| 3/4 | .579 | 1/2 | 1-1/8 |

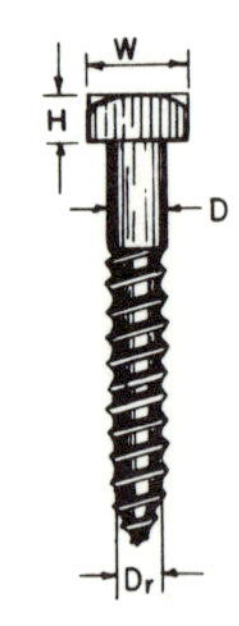


## BOLTS

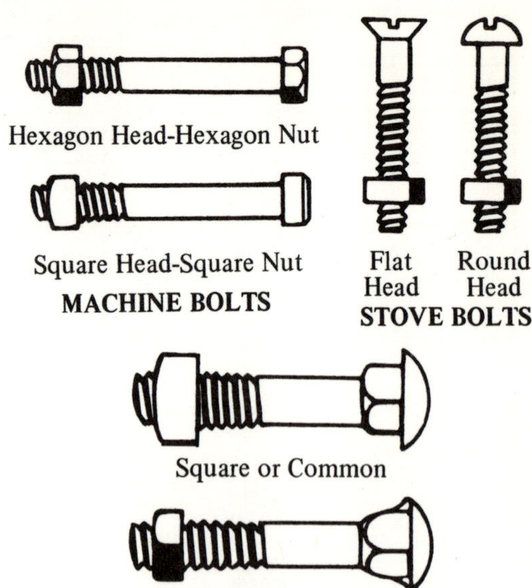

CARRIAGE BOLTS

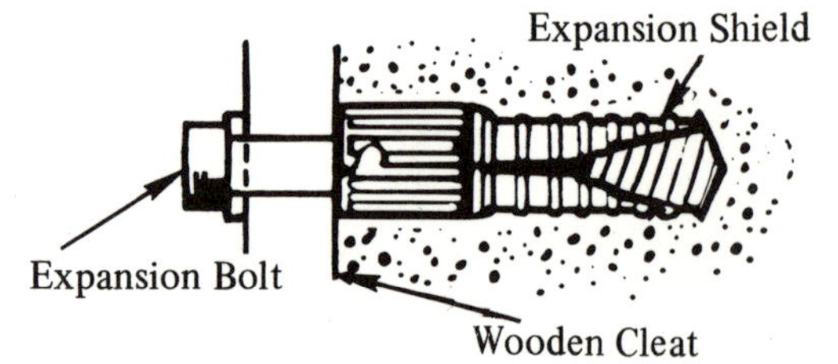


# WIRE GAGES
ACTUAL SIZE

| NO. | SIZE |
|---|---|
| 1 | .2830 |
| 2 | .2625 |
| 3 | .2437 |
| 4 | .2253 |
| 5 | .2070 |
| 6 | .1920 |
| 7 | .1770 |
| 8 | .1620 |
| 9 | .1483 |
| 10 | .1350 |
| 11 | .1205 |
| 12 | .1055 |
| 13 | .0915 |
| 14 | .0800 |
| 15 | .0720 |

# REFERENCE INFORMATION

(Not part of *American Standard Requirements for Residential Wiring,* C91.1-1958.)

## GRAPHICAL ELECTRICAL SYMBOLS FOR RESIDENTIAL WIRING PLANS

**These symbols have been extracted or adapted from ASA Standard Z32.9-1943, wherever possible.**

### General Outlets

Lighting Outlet

Ceiling Lighting Outlet for recessed fixture (Outline shows shape of fixture.)

Continuous Wireway for Fluorescent Lighting on ceiling, in coves, cornices, etc. (Extend rectangle to show length of installation.)

Lighting Outlet with Lamp Holder

PS — Lighting Outlet with Lamp Holder and Pull Switch

Fan Outlet

Junction Box

Drop-Cord Equipped Outlet

Clock Outlet

To indicate wall installation of above outlets, place circle near wall and connect with line as shown for clock outlet.

### Convenience Outlets

Duplex Convenience Outlet

3 — Triplex Convenience Outlet (Substitute other numbers for other variations in number of plug positions.)

Duplex Convenience Outlet — Split Wired

GR — Duplex Convenience Outlet for Grounding-Type Plugs

WP — Weatherproof Convenience Outlet

X" — Multi-Outlet Assembly (Extend arrows to limits of installation. Use appropriate symbol to indicate type of outlet. Also indicate spacing of outlets as X inches.)

S — Combination Switch and Convenience Outlet

R — Combination Radio and Convenience Outlet

Floor Outlet

R — Range Outlet

DW — Special-Purpose Outlet. Use subscript letters to indicate function. DW-Dishwasher, CD-Clothes Dryer, etc.

### Switch Outlets

S — Single-Pole Switch

$S_3$ — Three-Way Switch

$S_4$ — Four-Way Switch

$S_D$ — Automatic Door Switch

$S_P$ — Switch and Pilot Light

$S_{WP}$ — Weatherproof Switch

$S_2$ — Double-Pole Switch

### Low-Voltage and Remote-Control Switching Systems

S — Switch for Low-Voltage Relay Systems

MS — Master Switch for Low-Voltage Relay Systems

R — Relay—Equipped Lighting Outlet

Low-Voltage Relay System Wiring

### Auxiliary Systems

Push Button

Buzzer

Bell

Combination Bell-Buzzer

CH — Chime

Annunciator

D — Electric Door Opener

M — Maid's Signal Plug

Interconnection Box

T — Bell-Ringing Transformer

Outside Telephone

Interconnecting Telephone

R — Radio Outlet

TV — Television Outlet

### Miscellaneous

Service Panel

Distribution Panel

Switch Leg Indication. Connects outlets with control points.

a,b — Special Outlets. Any standard symbol given above may be used with the addition of subscript letters to designate some special variation of standard equipment for a particular architectural plan. When so used, the variation should be explained in the Key of Symbols and, if necessary, in the specifications.

## EXPLANATION OF TERMS

(Not part of *American Standard Requirements for Residential Wiring,* C91.1-1958.)

LIGHTING OUTLET: Means by which branch circuits are made available for connection to lampholders, to surface-mounted fixtures, to flush or recessed fixtures, or for extension to mounting devices for light sources in valances, cornices, or coves.

*CONVENIENCE OUTLET: The plug-in receptacle, as well as the outlet box in which it is housed. It shall be at least of the duplex type (two or more plug-in positions) except as otherwise specified. Multi-outlet assembly may be substituted, if desired, for the convenience outlets mentioned in these standards. Convenience outlets installed on 15- or 20-ampere branch circuits shall be of the grounding type.

WALL SWITCH: A switch on the wall, not part of any fixture, for the control of one or more lighting or convenience outlets.

SPECIAL-PURPOSE OUTLET: A point of connection to the wiring system for a particular equipment, which is normally reserved for the exclusive use of that equipment. Special-purpose outlets may be installed in or on the walls and equipped with suitable wiring devices, or may be enclosures which are an integral part of the equipment to be served, within which the appliance is permanently connected to the house wiring system.

Clock, range and laundry outlets are examples of the first type of connection. Furnace, ventilating fan, built-in space heater, and water-heater outlets are examples of the second.

BRANCH CIRCUIT: That portion of a wiring system extending beyond the final overcurrent device protecting the circuit.

*WALL SPACE (for convenience outlets): All portions of a wall, except that occupied by a fireplace opening. The space occupied by sliding panels in exterior walls is considered wall space. The minimum wall space requiring a convenience outlet is two feet in length at the floor line.

WORK SURFACE: All areas, approximately 36 inches above the floor level, exclusive of appliance or sink surfaces, where used in connection with outlet requirements in kitchen. The minimum frontage of work surface requiring a convenience outlet is one foot.

FLOOR AREA: Where used as the basis for requirements for circuits and service in this standard, area is computed from the outside dimensions of the house and the number of floors, including unfinished spaces which are adaptable to future living use. Open porches and garage may be excluded from the calculation.

VOLTAGES: When mentioned as 115 or 230 volts, voltages shall be understood to be nominal and to include, respectively, voltages of 110 to 125 and 220 to 250. In any location in which the electrical service is furnished at 120/208 volts from a three-phase, four-wire system, the local utility should be consulted regarding necessary changes in the requirements as outlined in this standard.

*Revised to comply with requirements of the 1962 National Electrical Code.

## PORTABLE ELECTRIC TOOLS

Extracted from: *Woodworking Directory and Handbook,* Hitchcock Publishing Co., Wheaton, Illinois.

While portable electric tools are and should be powerful, cost-saving extensions of a worker's hands, they often become costly gadgets for the indifferent. But an understanding of a few general principles which are basic to the industry will help you plan, purchase, provide proper facilities and maintain a profitable variety of these modern labor-expediting devices called portable electric tools.

*The motor:* False economy will lead some buyers to purchase a portable electric tool on a price basis, then overload the nearly-burn-out-proof motor to incur hidden costs far greater than initial savings. The speed and current demand of this universal-type motor depends upon the load. As an overload occurs, the speed tends to slow down, higher torque is developed, the motor demands more current from the line and, as a result, overheating may cause serious trouble.

Because the high-heat resistant insulation materials built into modern motors make them nearly-burn-out-proof, operators often take their lightweight, high-powered abilities for granted. But, since overheating is not likely to burn out the motor, a whole series of other change reactions may develop. The control switch may go pffft-and, perhaps, the operator will, too!.

If the switch remains, it may be the tool cord, the extension cord, the connector plug, the conduit line or fuses and circuit breakers behind that. False economy in the purchase of a poor quality or inadequate tool may be the most costly error made all year. It could cost you a burned-down plant.

Speed control for some motors may be simple rheostats or resistance switches, as with many home appliances, merely to put back power made available to the motor. Other controls may be quite complex with newly developed electronic reactors and other devices.

Therefore, while the typical universal-type motor usually is applicable with ac or dc current, some portable electric tools may employ control systems which require ac only. Damage to the controls will occur if dc is used, although the motor may remain unharmed. You may remove all doubts of such a nature by proper study of the operating manual which accompanies all tools, or by checking with the manufacturer's representative to answer questions.

Whether the current is ac or dc, it is important to see that the motor capacity is adequate for the job to be done and particularly that sufficient power is fed to the motor at every workstation.

*Grounding:* Every electric tool of reputable manufacture for industrial use has provisions for grounding. Every tool should be properly grounded during operation to protect the operator against shock hazards and to protect your plant facility as well. Accepted standards sponsored by the Electric Tool Institute, required by the U.S. National Electric Code, approved by Underwriters' Laboratories and the Canadian Standard Association, make modern tools equipped with a three-wire cord and grounding plug mandatory.

The cord has two power leads, the third wire having no effect on the normal operation of the tool. The ground wire connects with the housing so that the operator will be protected in case the tool should become internally grounded. This wire must be connected to a suitable ground for protection, although the tool will operate just as satisfactorily without it.

Do not permit the ground plug or prong to be damaged. This would incur a safety hazard which no insurance company would tolerate. If the worker must work in or near moisture, the ground wire is even more important. In addition, he should be made to wear protective gear such as rubber gloves and footwear.

If the tool should be disassembled for service or the cord replaced, be sure that the ground wire is connected to the tool housing and not to the switch. A continuity checker will prove out the circuits.

*Extension cords:* For extension of power from a distant outlet to reach a work area, the correct cord must be used to avoid safety hazards and possible damage to the tool. First, the cord should be a three-wire type, the same as the tool cord, so that proper grounding is automatically provided. Second, the wire size must be large enough to carry the necessary current.

All wire conductors have some amount of resistance and are rated on the basis of current-carrying capacity. The larger the wire and the shorter the length, the more current it will carry. Conversely, when the extension must be longer, the wire size must be larger to carry the same amount of current demanded by the tool.

Motor damage may occur should the power supply drop 10% or more below the values shown on the nameplate. ETI standards permit a voltage variation

**Minimum Cord Wire Sizes**
**(Electric Tool Institute Standards)**

| Full-load Ampere Rating of Tool | | Amps 0-2.0 | Amps 2.1-3.4 | Amps 3.5-5.0 | Amps 5.1-7.0 | Amps 7.1-12 | Amps 12.1-16 |
|---|---|---|---|---|---|---|---|
| Length of cord | | | | | | | |
| 115v. | 230 v. | | | | | | |
| 25 ft | 50 ft. | 18 | 18 | 18 | 16 | 14 | 14 |
| 50 ft. | 100 ft. | 18 | 18 | 18 | 16 | 14 | 12 |
| 75 ft. | 150 ft. | 18 | 18 | 16 | 14 | 12 | 10 |
| 100 ft. | 200 ft. | 18 | 16 | 14 | 12 | 10 | 8 |
| 200 ft. | 400 ft. | 16 | 14 | 12 | 10 | 8 | 6 |
| 300 ft. | 600 ft. | 14 | 12 | 10 | 8 | 6 | 4 |
| 400 ft. | 800 ft. | 12 | 10 | 8 | 6 | 4 | 4 |
| 500 ft. | 1000 ft. | 12 | 10 | 8 | 6 | 4 | 2 |
| 600 ft. | 1200 ft. | 10 | 8 | 6 | 4 | 2 | 2 |
| 800 ft. | 1600 ft. | 10 | 8 | 6 | 4 | 2 | 1 |
| 1000 ft. | 2000 ft. | 8 | 6 | 4 | 2 | 1 | 0 |

Note: If voltage is already low at the source (outlet), have voltage increased to standard, or use a larger cord than listed in order to prevent any further loss in voltage.

of plus-or-minus 6% with rated voltages of 115 and 230 as standard for direct and alternating current.

*Drill and driver chucks:* The most common chucks made to accept a wide variety of drill bits and other round shank straight tools are the three-jaw geared key types. These rather expensive, high quality components are precision machines in themselves and demand careful treatment to preserve their quality, accuracy and useful life. A majority of workers, however, give chucks improper treatment and destroy their characteristics almost before a tool has been broken in on the job. The following rules should be considered minimum requirements for a competent worker:

1. Open jaws wide enough to take desired bit. Clean bit shank of all foreign matter. Insert in chuck as far as it will go.
2. Close jaws by hand only, rotating the bit slowly to assure proper alignment and maximum contact between the chuck jaws and bit shank.
3. Insert key in one hole and turn to make snug fit, but not as tight as the chuck jaws may go.
4. Use other holes in sequence, tightening the key in each one as much as possible, remembering that when the key is returned to the first hole, there still may be some slack to take up. All three holes should be used to give maximum tightening pressure, to prevent slippage in operation which may damage the chuck jaws or the bit shank, and to make certain that all jaws have pressure evenly distributed. Otherwise, uneven wear can occur and eventually a bit will not run true. Excessive runout will produce oversize holes in drilling, or other kinds of sloppy and inefficient work.
5. Chuck may be released by using only one hole for the key.
6. Keep chuck clean and free of all dirt or grit.
7. Apply a thin film of oil regularly to prevent rusting and to encourage good operation, but avoid too much oil which will tend to collect dust.
8. Store chucks with jaws open.

*Collet chucks:* Collet chucks, such as are fitted to portable routers, have a major advantage over most other chucks. They are simple in design and hold closer runout tolerance (for dead true running) than any other tool holding device without complex fitting or adjustment.

Their disadvantage is that they come in only one size, therefore all tools for a given collet must have the same shank size within close tolerances. Even greater care must be given the simple looking collet chuck to protect it from damage. A few grains of dust between jaws of another chuck may have no effect, one grain inside a collet may scratch the walls, plug the slots, damage the threads, raise a burr, or gall the bit shank.

It is obvious that greater cleanliness is necessary with a collet chuck than with a geared jaw chuck. This is amplified by the fact that collet chucks, commonly found on routers, usually operate at much higher speeds than any other tool. Inaccuracies in runout or centering of the bit will cause vibration, rough work, and eventual damage to spindle bearings.

*Keyless chucks:* Chucks which tighten merely by hand rotation may appear to be convenient since keys or wrenches are not required, but such chucks are not recommended for industrial applications.

*Special chucks:* A wide variety of sockets, bit holders, adapters and accessories are available for different kinds of drivers and impact wrenches. Positive clutches, adjustable torque, ratcheting and anti-ratcheting, and reversing mechanisms are designed for specific job requirements. Information on their operation, adjustment and maintenance should be obtained from the individual supplier.

*Tool maintenance:* Regular inspection and routine protective measures should be automatic with any portable electric tool to make your investment pay out, to maintain production line efficiency, to obtain quality performance, to provide safety and comfort for workers, and to avoid costly shutdowns.

The universal motor is a delicate instrument. Although its wiring and insulation will withstand high temperature operation, satisfactory running conditions depend upon adequate ventilation engineered into its design. The vent slots, fan blades and armature must be kept clear of an accumulation of dust or dirt to avoid overheating and excessive power demands. Remove such accumulations as frequently as they appear by using a compressed air blower while motor is running.

*Lubrication:* Some tools will have "lifetime" ball or roller bearings which are replaced only after long use, but never lubricated. Others may have oil-soaked porous bronze bearings which require periodic replenishment of the oil. Some units may have a gear train which requires dismantling, cleaning and repacking with a heavy grade of grease, while others may have a gear case which requires a clean bath of oil which is drained, washed with kerosene and refilled like the crankcase of an automobile.

Contary to some misconceptions, proper lubrication of a tool is an engineering science, not a routine maintenance problem. If one drop of oil of a certain viscosity on a felt pad is required, you do not merely grab the nearest oil can and squirt. You may damage expensive parts or ruin a motor. A similar rule applies to a gear train or other parts which call for special greases. Check the maintenance manual or supplier of every electric tool to determine what proper lubrication means. Make sure no tool is purchased or operated without full information.

*Motor brushes:* A high percentage of portable electric tool failures are traced to neglect of motor brushes. Have them checked often and keep them clean. Brushes always should slide freely in the brushholders without sticking. If they should become burned, shipped or worn shorter than about 3/16-in., or if the springs have been twisted or have lost their tension, replace them at once. Good brush check procedures are:

1. Disconnect power cord.
2. Unscrew brush cap, being careful not to release spring pressure too suddenly or tilt so that brush and spring may be lost or damaged by falling.
3. Lift spring and brush without crushing or twisting the spring. Take note of the curve face of the brush where it fits the surface of the commutator. See if the curve is square to the body or offset to one side. Keep this in mind for replacement in exactly the same position to get good commutation of current to the motor, increase brush life, and protect the comutator. Remove and replace one brush at a time.
4. Wipe brush face and sides with clean cloth if there is an accumulation of dusty particles.
5. Blow out the brushholder opening or wipe clean.
6. Replace brush in proper location. Center the spring in the cap. If spring has been compressed, stretch it slightly to maintain good contact pressure. Feel out the threads and screw cap down finger tight.
7. Repeat same steps for other brush.
8. Replace brushes with original factory parts. Brushes are not simply square pieces of carbon. Their formulation is a special process which governs the proper distribution and control of current flow into the commutator by means of a certain frictional characteristic and a balance of conductive and resistive materials. Motors can be ruined with improperly designed or make-shift brushes.
9. Always replace both brushes at the same time with duplicate parts.
10. While inspecting brushes, checking the commutator. If rough or dirty, clean with 3/0 or finer garnet paper or flint paper. Never use emery or other abrasives which may clog, score or short-circuit the contacts. If commutator is grooved deeply (which may be noted by the face appearance of the brushes) repair it promptly. (All portable electric tool information based upon contributions from Skil Corp., Stanley Power Tools, and other members of the Electric Tool Institute.)

## PORTABLE PNEUMATIC TOOLS

Extracted from: *Woodworking Directory and Handbook*, Hitchcock Publishing Co., Wheaton, Ill.

Air-operated tools have certain advantages in convenience, efficiency and overall econmy which make them highly desirable in plants where compressed air supplies are adequate. A major consideration, of course, is whether distribution through airlines, filters, hoses and connectors will build up a cost great enough to offset other economies. However, similar costs are involved in proper distribution of power for electric tools, so the two must be compared on a equitable basis. Some of the advantages of air tools may more than offset power distribution costs even if an airline system should cost more than electric.

Some advantages of air tools of particular interest to large and small plants follow:

1. Air tools can be used for multiple spindle requirements such as multiple drills, mortisers, routers, screwdrivers and nutsetters.
2. Air tools are much lighter in weight for torque or horsepower developed, and feel cool to the operator's hand.
3. Smaller and lighter tools are more readily adapted to areas or positions not suited for other tools of equivalent power.
4. Since there is no commutator sparking and no electric shock hazard, air tools may be used in various operations with wet or dry conditions, as well as with explosive dusts or volatile fumes. This means greater safety in sanding, rubbing, polishing or cleaning.
5. Air tools generally require extremely low maintenance with fewer working parts and less frequent replacements.

Air tools are flexible in meeting torque requirements provided an adequate air supply is available and can be maintained. But most woodworking plants require compressed air for spray finishing and often for air cylinder devices, so a more economical source of common power becomes a potential benefit in considering air driven tools.

Three basic types of air motors are: rotary vane, axial piston and radial piston. The rotary-vane-type develops more horsepower per pound of motor, ranging from 1 to 7 hp at 90 psi air supply. They may be reversible, with or without various choices of gear trains. These units offer a combination of speeds, torques, horsepower, weight, and simple construction, all at low cost.

Radial-piston motors may be had in from 2 to 15 hp, reversible or non-reversible, with or without gearing. High torque is an inherent characteristic, making them especially desirable for applications with heavy starting loads.

Axial-piston motors offer similar piston-type advantages, but in smaller power ratings from 0.6 to 2.7 hp and relatively hight weight with smaller overall dimensions.

*General considerations:* What kind of job is to be done? Is it free running under light load; moderately free running up to a maximum torque when stalling occurs; a prevailing torque application, as in driving a screw, until a clutch is activated at its maximum torque setting; or continuously running under medium load without interruption, as in router operation?

Peak performance in air motors generally occurs at approximately 50% of free speed. Air tool ratings usually are based upon 90 psig (gage pressure) at the tool with an adequate air supply. Performance curves and torque output curves should be available from your supplier to determine operating factors applicable to your job.

Torque requirements vary according to the kind of job. For instance, when there is a "free rundown to a solid makeup," such as in the case of running a nut on a bolt where the nut tightens up firmly against solid work, the momentum of the motor will produce tightening torque above rated torque. On the other hand, in prevailing torque or "soft makeup" conditions, when continuous torque is being applied up to a maximum level, tightening torque never exceeds rated torque and can be even less. Under these conditions, a safety factor of 10 to 20% additional rated torque may be required.

If either cushion or kickout clutches are used, the tool must have sufficient torque to activate the clutch before stalling, otherwise there may be no way to determine how much torque is being applied. A safety factor of 20% is recommended.

*Torque tolerance:* Various methods are used to control torque. Some tools merely stall at a pre-adjusted air flow or pressure. A variation of this method uses a sensing device to shut off the air when a predetermined torque is reached. Cushion clutches are adjustable over a broad range. However, they can be affected by the operator and are subject to rapid wear which will cause inconsistencies. Kick-out or "one-shot" clutches generally produce the most accurate control because they are the least likely to be influenced by the operator.

If a tool operates at, say, 5,000 rpm, it is impossible to stop rotation instantly. There always will be some override from momentum, the product of the mass and velocity of the rotor. In addition to this, some time lag necessarily must occur between the sensing of desired torque level and the stopping of the rotor. The higher the speed and weight of rotor, the greater will be this problem of precise regulation.

Even if the tool is not required to maintain a specified narrow range of torque, the problem of tool or air motor selection may be somewhat complex since speed and torque are interrelated and peak performance occurs around 50% of free running speed. Air-driven routers would be a good example. They operate at extraordinarily high speeds when cutting loads are applied, but is it feasible to purchase a tool merely because its free-running speed is twice as fast? Your supplier's technical consultants should be asked to solve your particular problems.

*Air supply:* Inadequate air supply causes many complaints. Both pressure (90 psig) and volume (cfm) should be within 10% or closer to the tool requirements. If pressure is likely to fall below 90 psig or will fluctuate, the next larger size tool or the next slower speed motor may be necessary. If accurate output is important, especially with a stall type tool, install a pressure regulator just ahead of the tool in the supply line.

*The operator:* Operating position may determine type of handle and valve arrangement. Accessibility, weight and torque arm length required may indicate any one of a variety of controls. Torque reaction may be easy to withstand for one man but not another. It is advisable to suspend the tool from a balancer whenever possible. This protects tool and worker to get more production efficiency from both.

*Production rate:* The time factor allowed may dictate a compromise between tool speed and accuracy of torque range desired. Various sizes of tools may overlap in range of output. If extreme accuracy is not important, the smallest tool in weight and dimension usually is preferred. But the next larger tool in size will do the same job twice as fast.

*Air tool maintenance:* Unless you install a large number of air tools, major repairs or replacements should be done by the factory. If you should have enough air tools to warrant repairs locally, a special mechanic should be sent for factory service training. But, in either case, a well conducted program of preventive maintenance will reduce your major problems to a small percentage. Here is the recommended program:

1. With the purchase of a new tool, order with it suitable suspension equipment such as hooks, eyes, mounted bails; or separate balancer, trolley, beam and other devices. Consider how the tool might be used and plan the installation to prevent abuse.

2. Check the quality of air supply as well as quantity. Clean, dry air is essential. Plan for filters, moisture separators and moisture traps. Install line filters near the tool and replace inferior or worn out hose to avoid tool damage.

3. Proper lubrication protects the vitality of a pneumatic tool. Both type and amount best suited to each tool is determined by engineers and prescribed by the manufacturer. Lubricant recommendations are mentioned in parts lists, data books and maintenance manuals. Light weight, but durable lubricants must be applied continuously to the precision-fitted high speed parts. This comes from line oilers just ahead of the tool hose, but the feed rate should be small enough to avoid "fogging" at the exhaust. When gear trains or transmission parts are located in a chamber separate from the air stream, these parts must be lubricated with light greases. Make certain you know whether the tool needs periodic greasing or is entirely lubricated from the air stream.

4. Efficient maintenance includes "back-up" tools. If production will not allow interruption, duplicate spares or back-up tools will keep things rolling while careful repairs or routine maintenance precautions are taken. The ratio of the number of spares to production tools may be as low as 1:10 for properly maintained tools and, prehaps, as high as 1:2 in plants with careless workers. (Based on material supplied by Gardner-Denver Company, Quincy, Illinois).

## HOW TO ANALYZE YOUR PNEUMATIC NAILING AND STAPLING NEEDS

Extracted from: *Woodworking Directory & Handbook*, Hitchcock Publishing Co., Wheaton, Illinois.

Before you contact your fastening equipment supplier, you can make both of your jobs easier by a simple analysis of your requirements. The following check list will help you determine the extent of your needs and the subsequent information will help your supplier provide you with exactly the right equipment to fill those needs.

In order to solve any pneumatic fastening problem, the fastening equipment manufacturer must know:

1. What materials are to be fastened—wood to wood, wood to metal, other combinations?
2. What is the product?
3. What type of wood is to be used and is it kiln dried, air dried, or green?
4. What are the thicknesses of the parts to be fastened together?
5. Is the fastener to be driven into end grain, cross grain, or a combination of both?
6. What types of stresses are the fastened parts expected to sustain?
7. Is the fastening to be done on an exposed surface where countersinking will be necessary?
8. Should the fastener penetrate both parts and then clinch?
9. Is a special type of point needed on the fastener?
10. How much holding strength is required of the fastener?
11. Are there specifications governing the type of fastener, depth of penetration, other requirements?
12. Will the worker have free clearance to the joint or is it a hard-to-reach spot?
13. What is the rate of production required?
14. Do you have other applications in which the equipment you need can be used?
15. Can your equipment supplier recommend something that will improve quality as well as production and, at the same time, reduce material, production, and labor cost?
16. Is a safety device needed on the fastening machine?
17. Is a coated fastener needed to increase holding power?

If so, specify details in order to determine which type of coating will do the job at a feasible cost.

18. Is a galvanized fastener desirable to inhibit rust or is it mandatory that a fastener made from a nonferrous metal, such as silicon bronze or aluminum, be used?
19. Are your present air supply facilities suitable for pneumatic operations? To answer this question:
    a. Check all compressor electrical curcuits and connections.
    b. Check for proper lubrication of compressor system.
    c. Check air intake for clean filters and intake location.
    d. Check compressor settings so that they are not above standard rate of operating pressures.
    e. Check air lines for proper installation and proper drainage.
    f. Check air filter, regulator and lubricator unit installations.
    g. See that lubrication unit is located as close as possible to the application, preferrably just ahead of hose connection to supply line.
    h. Check for air leaks.
    i. Check diameter of air lines to provide an adequate supply of air in required volume as well as pressure.
    j. Check all air connections—for fit, leaks, foreign particles or dirt.
    k. Determine if present connections are best and/or if they should be located from overhead and/or counterbalanced for the worker.

As a woodworker who needs pneumatic nailers and staplers, there are recognized characteristics you will want to look for in any pneumatic tool you consider buying.

These are:

1. Rapid firing
2. Level of skill required for operation
3. Ability to use as wide a range of staples and nails as possible without making major adjustments
4. Light weight for easy handling and portability
5. Low operating cost
6. Long life with minimum downtime under heavy production
7. Service from a reputable fastening equipment manufacturer.

The cost of pneumatic stapling cannot be expressed by any one factor. It must be considered in relation to a variety of factors: original cost of tool, compressor, and air distribution system; operator skill level; cost of fasteners; production increases; maintenance problems; many more.

For this reason, it is recommended you work as

closely as possible with your supplier and give him full cooperation in his analysis of your needs. To give him the help he will want, allow his sales engineer to look at the fastening problem involved under production line conditions. In this way he will be able to visualize all facets of the problem and what will be needed to solve it.

Listen to what your fastening equipment supplier says with an open mind. If he is a reputable supplier, his recommendations will be reliable. Don't automatically reject ideas which may involve new and, at times, unconventional approaches to the fastening problem.

Try the particular tool and fastener that the supplier suggests. Use them under actual production conditions and let him know at once if they won't do the job. He's just as anxious as you are to see the equipment doing the job you want it to do.

## ACKNOWLEDGMENTS

Banker, Fred W., Manager, Hamilton Plant
Pease Company
Hamilton, Ohio

Bianko, Harvey
ASA Builders Supply
Hazel Park, Michigan

Clemens, Arthur L., Executive President
Components, Inc.
East Chicago, Indiana

Feher, Bud, Manager
P.P.G. Industrial Coatings
DesPlaines, Illinois

Gilchrist, Don L., Director Industry Sales
The Behring Home Division
Fort Lauderdale, Florida 33306

Grasso, Joseph, Vice President
Modular Housing Systems, Inc.
Northumberland, Pennsylvania

Guirlinger, Austin, President
Cardinal Industries, Inc.
Columbus, Ohio

Gurzda, Ed.
Best Homes
Hazelcrest, Illinois

Gustafson, M. O., President
Imperial Homes
Griffin, Georgia

Hendon, Paul
Carpentry Engineering, Inc.
Howell, Michigan

Kirkendorfer, Vice President
Mid-America Homes, Inc.
Crown Point, Indiana

Linsmayer, Robert M., President
Villaume Industries
Saint Paul, Minnesota

LoPresto, Norman J.
Suburban Homes, Inc.
Valparaiso, Indiana

McClary, Tom, Superintendent
Presidential Homes
Pemberton, New Jersey 08068

Olson, Duane
Capp Homes—International Homes
Minneapolis, Minnesota

Pomeranz, Herb, President
Richmond Homes, Inc.
Richmond, Indiana

Puckett, Thomas W., Manager
Art Homes, Inc.
Fairborn, Ohio

Smith, J. Franklin, Vice President
Hallmark Homes
Augusta, Georgia

Starostovic, Ed., Plant Manager & Chief Engineer
Wausau, Wisconsin

Wheeler, J. H., Vice President
Adrian Housing Corp.
Adrian, Georgia

## Equipment Manufacturers

**Following is a list of Equipment Manufacturers and suppliers whose products came to the attention of the author during research for this handbook. The list is not all-inclusive and there may be others who have escaped notice.**

| | Cutting Equipment | Truss Equip. & Plates | Panel Equip. | Nailing Machines | Prehung Door Equipment | Delivery Equipment | Miscellaneous | Remarks |
|---|---|---|---|---|---|---|---|---|
| Addometer Co.<br>14901 Evans St.<br>Dolton, Illinois 60419 | | | | | | | X | Adding device for fractions |
| Advanced Fork Lift Corp.<br>Chestertown, Maryland 21620 | | | | | | X | | |
| Alpine Engineered Products<br>Box 927<br>Pompano Beach, Florida 33061 | | X | | | | | | |
| Aerosmith<br>P.O. Box 3898<br>Visalia, California 93277 | | | | X | | | | |
| Automated Bldg. Components<br>7525 N.W. 37th Ave.<br>Miami, Florida 33147 | | X | X | | | | | |
| Automated Const. Equip., Inc.<br>64 Park St.<br>Troy, Michigan 48084 | X | X | X | X | X | X | X | |
| Auto Crane Company<br>P.O. Box 3808,<br>Utica Sq. Station<br>Tulsa, Oklahoma 74152 | | | | | | X | | |
| Auto Nailer Company<br>5101 Fulton Ind. Blvd. S.W.<br>Atlanta, Georgia 30336 | | | X | X | | | | |
| Barns Lumber & Mfg.<br>P.O. Box 20160<br>Dallas, Texas 75220 | | | | | | X | | Truss Trailers |
| Black & Decker Mfg. Co.<br>Joppa Rd.<br>Towson, Maryland 21204 | X | | | | | | | |
| Bock Industries<br>P.O. Box B 1027<br>Elkhart, Indiana 46514 | | | | | | X | | Trailers for Modules |

| | Cutting Equipment | Truss Equip. & Plates | Panel Equip. | Nailing Machines | Prehung Door Equipment | Delivery Equipment | Miscellaneous | Remarks |
|---|---|---|---|---|---|---|---|---|
| Bostitch<br>East Greenwich, Rhode Island 02818 | | X | | X | | | | |
| Cain Machine & Tool Co.<br>801 Date Street<br>Alhambra, California 91803 | X | | | | | | | Panel Saws |
| Congoleum Industries, Inc.<br>195 Belgrove Dr.<br>Kearney, New Jersey 07032 | | | | | | | X | Equipment to Apply Vinyl Film |
| Carter Products Co., Inc.<br>Grand Rapids, Michigan 49502 | X | | | | | | X | Shadow Lites |
| Delta-Rockwell<br>400 North Lexington Ave.<br>Pittsburgh, Pennsylvania 15208 | X | | | | | | | |
| Distributors Associates<br>P.O. Box 2871<br>Cleveland, Ohio 44116 | X | X | X | X | X | X | X | |
| Douglas Systems, Inc.<br>Box 130<br>Marion, Iowa 52302 | | | X | X | | | | |
| Duo Fast<br>Fastener Corporation<br>3702 River Road<br>Franklin Park, Illinois 60131 | | | | X | | | | |
| Fairfield Eng. & Mfg. Co.<br>Fairfield, Iowa 52556 | X | | | | | | | Swing Saws |
| Foley & Lavish Eng. Co.<br>1235 S. Campbell Ave.<br>Chicago, Illinois 60608 | | X | | | | | | |
| The Galion Iron Works & Mfg. Co.<br>Galion, Ohio 44833 | | | | | | X | | Cranes |

| | Cutting Equipment | Truss Equip. & Plates | Panel Equip. | Nailing Machines | Prehung Door Equipment | Delivery Equipment | Miscellaneous | Remarks |
|---|---|---|---|---|---|---|---|---|
| General Construction & Automation, Inc.<br>P.O. Box 8106<br>Fort Worth, Texas 76112 | X | | X | | X | | | |
| General Trailer Sales Co.<br>Box 52<br>Springfield, Oregon 97477 | | | | | | X | | Trailers for Modules |
| Good-Ko Industries, Inc.<br>352 S. Saginaw St.<br>Flint, Michigan 48502 | X | | X | | | | | |
| Hendrick Mfg. Corporation<br>11 Selman St., Box 63<br>Marblehead, Massachusetts 01945 | X | | | | | | | Panel Saws |
| Hydraulic Materials Handling Div.<br>Omark Industries<br>Zebulon, North Carolina 27597 | | | | | | X | | Prentice Cranes |
| Hydro-Air Eng., Inc.<br>1210 S. Vandeventer Ave.<br>St. Louis, Missouri 63110 | | X | X | X | | | | |
| Hyster Company<br>Box 2902<br>Portland, Oregon 97208 | | | | | | X | | |
| Hyster Company<br>Box 847<br>Danville, Illinois 61832 | | | | | | X | X | Straddle Carriers & Lift Trucks |
| Idaco Eng. & Equip. Co.<br>3233 Peralta St.<br>Oakland, California 94608 | X | X | | | | | | |
| Ideal Industries<br>Sycamore, Illinois 60178 | | | | | | | X | Wire Strippers |
| Klaisler Machine Co.<br>3009 English Ave.<br>Indianapolis, Indiana 46201 | | X | | | | | | |

| | Cutting Equipment | Truss Equip. & Plates | Panel Equip. | Nailing Machines | Prehung Door Equipment | Delivery Equipment | Miscellaneous | Remarks |
|---|---|---|---|---|---|---|---|---|
| Kval Machinery Co.<br>P.O. Drawer A<br>Petaluma, California 94952 | | | | | X | | | |
| Lakeside Mfg. Corp.<br>39 East Main St.<br>Honeoye, New York 14471 | | | | | | X | | Trailers for Modules |
| Robert L. Marczy, Inc.<br>1455 S. Sandbury Terr.<br>Chicago, Illinois 60610 | X | | | | | | | Remote Stop |
| Master Hung Door Equip. Co.<br>P.O.Box 544<br>Pottstown, Pennsylvania 19464 | | | | | X | | | |
| Milwaukee Electric Tool Corp.<br>13135 Lisbon Rd.<br>Brookfield, Wisconsin 53005 | X | | | | X | | | |
| Morgan Drive Away, Inc.<br>2800 West Lexington Ave.<br>Elkhart, Indiana 46514 | | | | | X | | | Common Carrier |
| Morgan Machine Co., Inc.<br>1230 University Ave.<br>Rochester, New York 14607 | | | X | X | | | | |
| Northfield Foundry & Machine Co.<br>400 Water St.<br>Northfield, Minnesota 55057 | X | | | | | | | |
| Northfield Mfg. Co.<br>Box 605<br>Chico, California 95927 | | | | | X | | | |
| Olympic Instruments<br>Vashon, Washington 98070 | | | | | | | X | Wire Length Meter |
| Palesch Machine Co.<br>2203 18th St.<br>Wausau, Wisconsin 54401 | X | | | | | | | |

| | Cutting Equipment | Truss Equip. & Plates | Panel Equip. | Nailing Machines | Prehung Door Equipment | Delivery Equipment | Miscellaneous | Remarks |
|---|---|---|---|---|---|---|---|---|
| Panel-Clip Co.<br>P.O. Box 423<br>Farmington, Michigan 48024 | | X | | | | | X | Jamb Clips |
| The Parks Woodworking Machine Co.<br>Cincinnati, Ohio 45223 | X | | | | | | | |
| Paslode Company<br>8080 McCormick Blvd.<br>Skokie, Illinois 60076 | | | X | X | | | | |
| Pettibone Mulliken Corp.<br>9501 West Devon Ave.<br>Rosemont, Illinois 60018 | | | | | | X | | Cranes |
| Pistorius Machine Co., Inc.<br>3 Bruns Ave.<br>Hicksville, New York 11801 | X | | | | | | | |
| Prefab-Transit Co.<br>Farmer City, Illinois 61842 | | | | | | X | | Common Carrier |
| Proctor Products Co., Inc.<br>210 8th St. S, Box F<br>Kirkland, Washington 98033 | | | X | | | | | |
| Q System, Inc.<br>Drawer Q<br>Big Stone Gap, Virginia 24219 | | | X | | | | | Jigs |
| Quick Stop, Inc.<br>510 W. 6th Street<br>Los Angeles, California 90014 | X | | | | | | | Remote Stop |
| Rockwell Mfg. Co.<br>400 N. Lexington Ave.<br>Pittsburgh, Pennsylvania 15208 | X | | | | | | | |
| Ruvo Automation Corp.<br>200 Aerial Way<br>Syosset, New York 11791 | | | | | X | | | |

| | Cutting Equipment | Truss Equip. & Plates | Panel Equip. | Nailing Machines | Prehung Door Equipment | Delivery Equipment | Miscellaneous | Remarks |
|---|---|---|---|---|---|---|---|---|
| Safety Speed Cut Manufacturing Co., Inc.<br>13460 N. Hwy. 65, Route 4<br>Anoka, Minnesota 55303 | X | | | | | | | Panel Saws |
| Sanford Industries, Inc.<br>Box 1177<br>Pompano Beach, Florida 33061 | | X | | | | | | |
| Senco Products, Inc.<br>8485 Broadwell Rd.<br>Cincinnati, Ohio 45244 | | | X | X | | | | |
| Skil Corporation<br>5033 Elston Avenua<br>Chicago, Illinois 60630 | X | | | | | | | |
| Speed-Cut, Inc.<br>P.O. Box 1125<br>Corvallis, Oregon 97330 | X | | | | | X | | |
| Spot Nails<br>1100 Hicks Road<br>Rolling Meadows, Illinois 60008 | | | X | X | | | | |
| Stanley Hardware<br>New Britain, Connecticut 06052 | | | | | X | | | |
| Structomatic, Inc.<br>230 E. Ohio St.<br>Chicago, Illinois 60611 | | X | | | | | | |
| Tee-Lok Corporation<br>Edenton, North Carolina 27932 | | X | | | | | | |
| Triad Fastener Corp.<br>3706 Lake St.<br>Omaha, Nebraska 68111 | | | X | X | | | | |
| Truswal<br>64 Park Street<br>Troy, Michigan 48084 | X | X | | | X | | X | Jamb Clips |

| | Cutting Equipment | Truss Equip. & Plates | Panel Equip. | Nailing Machines | Prehung Door Equipment | Delivery Equipment | Miscellaneous | Remarks |
|---|---|---|---|---|---|---|---|---|
| Tryco Manufacturing Co., Inc.<br>Box 1277<br>Decatur, Illinois 62525 | | | | | | X | | Trailers for Modules |
| Twin Bay Industries<br>8980 Cairn Hwy., Box 37<br>Elk Rapids, Michigan 49629 | | | | | X | | | |
| United Shoe Machinery Corp.<br>140 Federal St.<br>Boston, Massachusetts 02110 | | | X | X | | | | |
| Westran Corporation<br>1148 West Western Ave.<br>Muskegon, Michigan 49443 | | | | | | | X | Modular Jacks |
| Woodclaw, Inc.<br>10 West Laura Dr.<br>Addison, Illinois 60101 | | X | | | | | | |

# INDEX